Luann 3

LuannsRoom.com

Character bios
Milestones in the strip
Commentary from Greg
So You Want to Become a Cartoonist?
Lots of pages to spend your time on
Lots of stuff to spend your money on

SIXTEEN ISN'T PRETTY
BY GREG EVANS

**Andrews McMeel
Publishing, LLC**

Kansas City

06 07 08 09 10 BBG 10 9 8 7 6 5 4 3 2 1

ISBN-13: 978-0-7407-6193-5
ISBN-10: 0-7407-6193-5

Library of Congress Control Number: 2006925657

www.andrewsmcmeel.com
www.LuannsRoom.com

ATTENTION: SCHOOLS AND BUSINESSES

Andrews McMeel books are available at quantity discounts with bulk purchase for educational, business, or sales promotional use. For information, please write to: Special Sales Department, Andrews McMeel Publishing, LLC, 4520 Main Street, Kansas City, Missouri 64111.

A Poem by Luann DeGroot

My life is a sea of confusion, there's so much i don't understand
Like why do i carefully schedule my day when NOTHING goes how i had planned?

And why does my mouth crave a burger when my head knows an apple is best?
And why should i strive to be tiny and thin but ample and full at my chest?

Why's it ok for guys to smell bad but girls should smell like a rose?
And why must there be a shine on my lips but never a shine on my nose?

The clothing i wear should be sexy but my attitude chaste and sweet
I'm told i should be independent and free—but a boyfriend will make me complete.

We know that the Earth is polluted, yet we hop in our huge SUV's
Drive a few blocks to go to a talk on Earth-friendly strategies.

My school can't afford new computers, yet a bomb costs about 80 grand.
Peace never lasts, war never ends...
There's so much i don't understand.

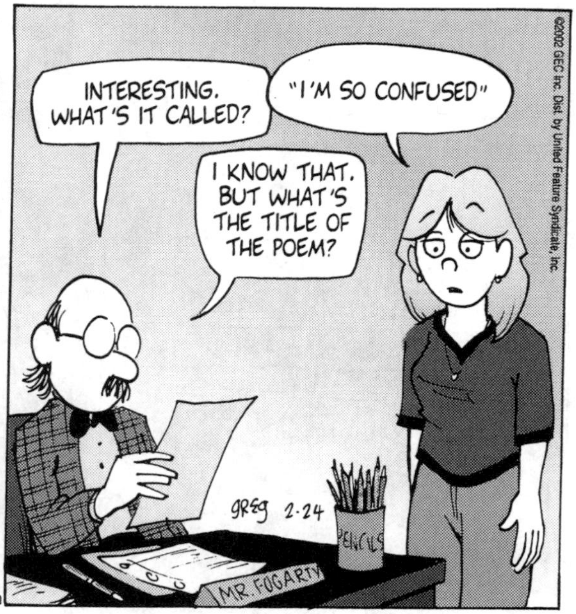

INTERESTING. WHAT'S IT CALLED?
"I'M SO CONFUSED"
I KNOW THAT. BUT WHAT'S THE TITLE OF THE POEM?
GREG 2·24
PENCILS
MR. FOGARTY
©2002 GEC Inc. Dist. by United Feature Syndicate, Inc.

www.LuannsRoom.com

DRAW ME

LUANN! CHECK IT OUT! I DID A COMIC STRIP ABOUT YOUR LIFE!
WHO'D WANNA READ THAT?
LEMME SEE, KNUTE
The PITTS SCHOOL NEWSPAPER
www.LuannsRoom.com
©2002 GEC Inc. Dist. by United Feature Syndicate, Inc.
RIIIIIP!
!
BWANG
AARON!
SWOON... SPLAT
LUANN!!
YEAH, THAT'S HER
WHAT WOULD HAPPEN NEXT? SAME STUFF OVER AND OVER?
THAT'S THE BEAUTY! I ONLY GOTTA DO *ONE*
WHAT ABOUT WHEN LUANN GETS NEW FRIENDS?
GREG 3-3

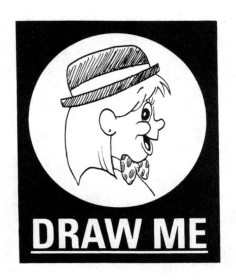

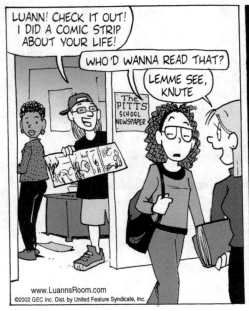

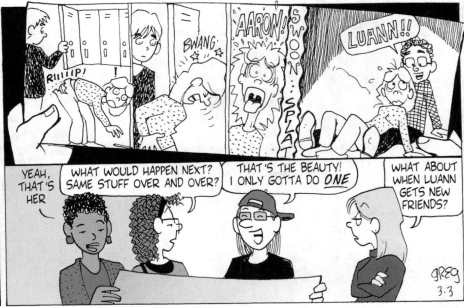

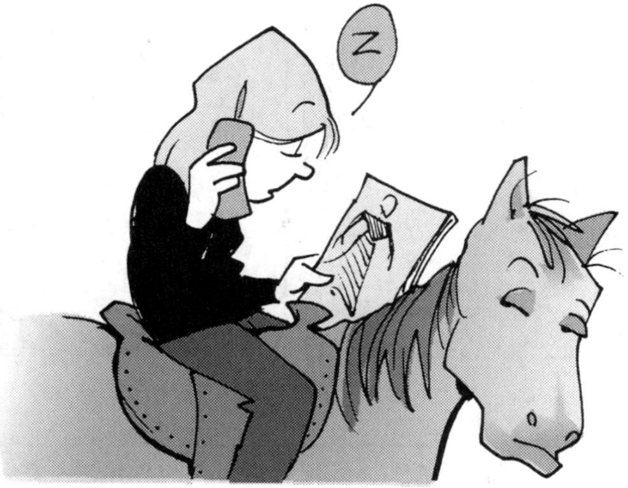

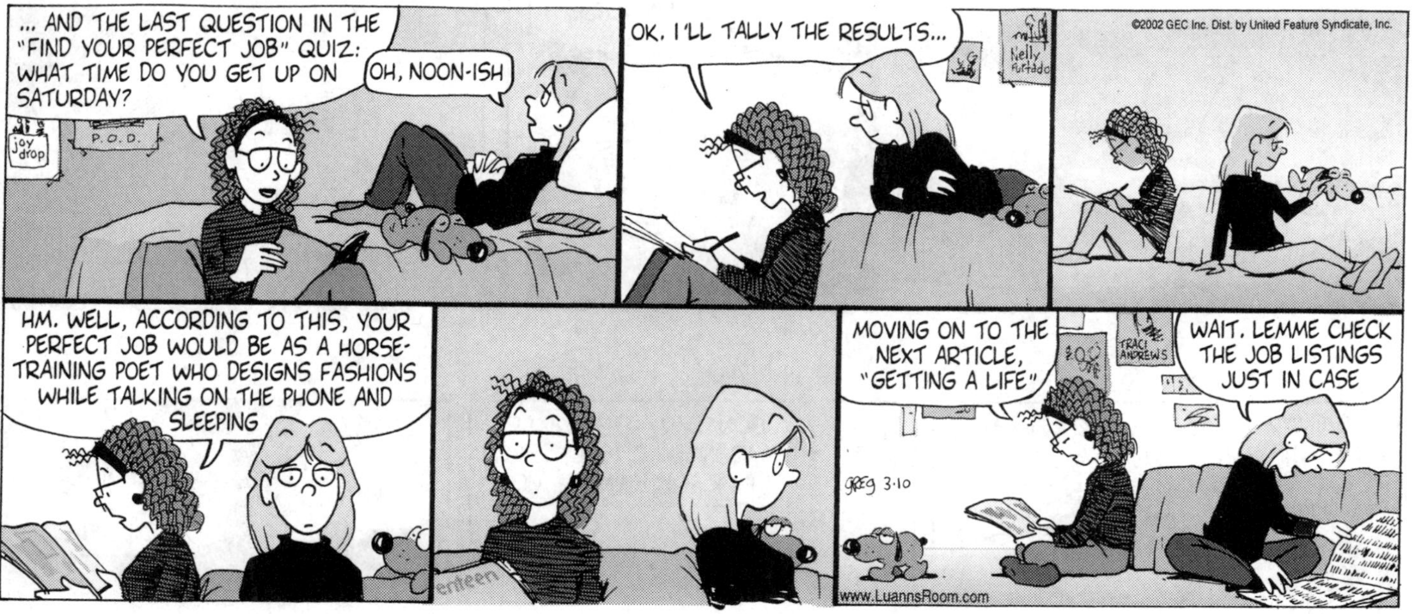
... AND THE LAST QUESTION IN THE "FIND YOUR PERFECT JOB" QUIZ: WHAT TIME DO YOU GET UP ON SATURDAY?
OH, NOON-ISH
joy drop
P.O.D.
OK. I'LL TALLY THE RESULTS...
Nelly Furtado
©2002 GEC Inc. Dist. by United Feature Syndicate, Inc.
HM. WELL, ACCORDING TO THIS, YOUR PERFECT JOB WOULD BE AS A HORSE-TRAINING POET WHO DESIGNS FASHIONS WHILE TALKING ON THE PHONE AND SLEEPING
MOVING ON TO THE NEXT ARTICLE, "GETTING A LIFE"
TRACI ANDREWS
WAIT. LEMME CHECK THE JOB LISTINGS JUST IN CASE
GREG 3-10
www.LuannsRoom.com

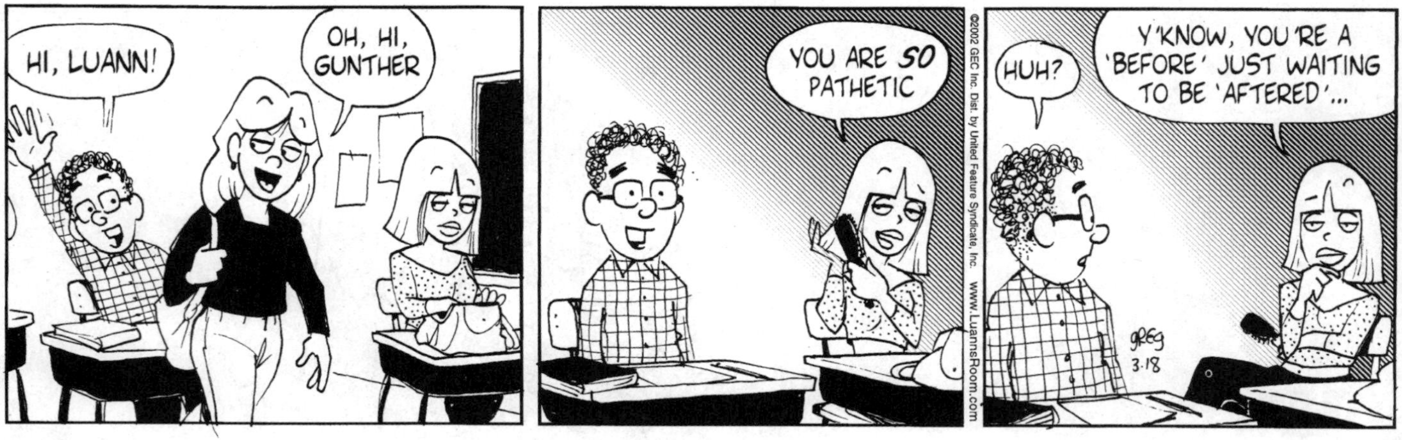
HI, LUANN!
OH, HI, GUNTHER
YOU ARE SO PATHETIC
HUH?
Y'KNOW, YOU'RE A 'BEFORE' JUST WAITING TO BE 'AFTERED'...
GREG 3.18
©2002 GEC Inc. Dist. by United Feature Syndicate, Inc. www.LuannsRoom.com

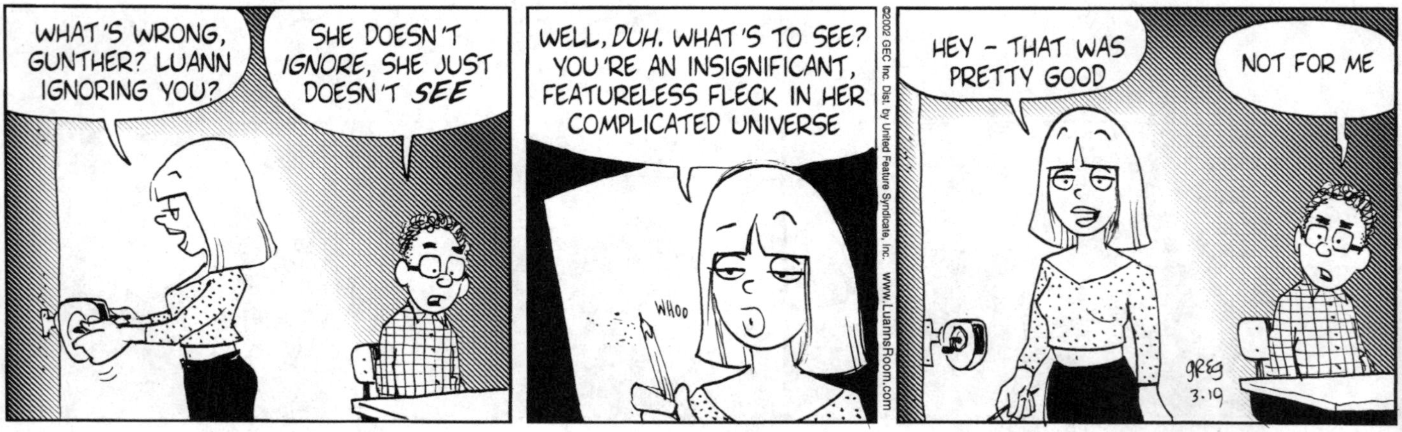
WHAT'S WRONG, GUNTHER? LUANN IGNORING YOU?
SHE DOESN'T IGNORE, SHE JUST DOESN'T SEE
WELL, DUH. WHAT'S TO SEE? YOU'RE AN INSIGNIFICANT, FEATURELESS FLECK IN HER COMPLICATED UNIVERSE
WHOO
HEY - THAT WAS PRETTY GOOD
NOT FOR ME
GREG 3.19
©2002 GEC Inc. Dist. by United Feature Syndicate, Inc. www.LuannsRoom.com

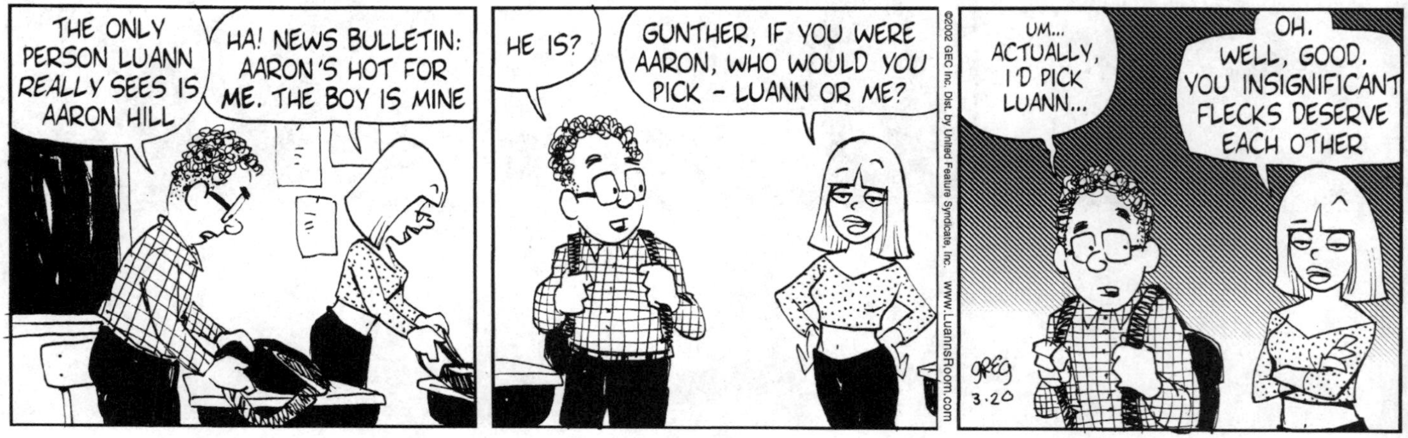
THE ONLY PERSON LUANN REALLY SEES IS AARON HILL
HA! NEWS BULLETIN: AARON'S HOT FOR ME. THE BOY IS MINE
HE IS?
GUNTHER, IF YOU WERE AARON, WHO WOULD YOU PICK - LUANN OR ME?
UM... ACTUALLY, I'D PICK LUANN...
OH. WELL, GOOD. YOU INSIGNIFICANT FLECKS DESERVE EACH OTHER
GREG 3.20
©2002 GEC Inc. Dist. by United Feature Syndicate, Inc. www.LuannsRoom.com

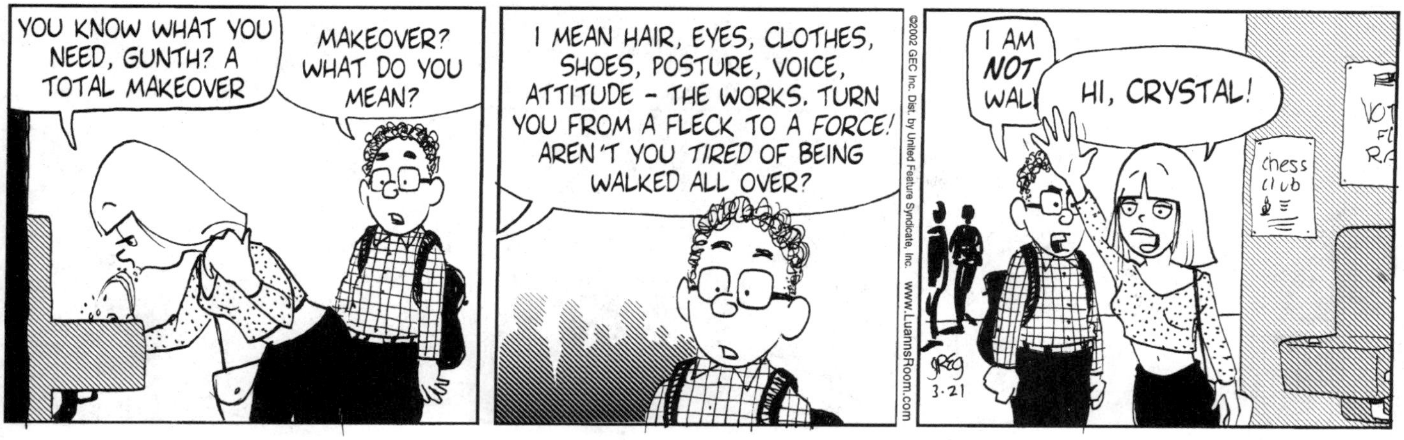
YOU KNOW WHAT YOU NEED, GUNTH? A TOTAL MAKEOVER
MAKEOVER? WHAT DO YOU MEAN?
I MEAN HAIR, EYES, CLOTHES, SHOES, POSTURE, VOICE, ATTITUDE – THE WORKS. TURN YOU FROM A FLECK TO A *FORCE*! AREN'T YOU *TIRED* OF BEING WALKED ALL OVER?
©2002 GEC Inc. Dist. by United Feature Syndicate, Inc. www.LuannsRoom.com
I AM **NOT** WAL
HI, CRYSTAL!
chess club
GREG 3-21

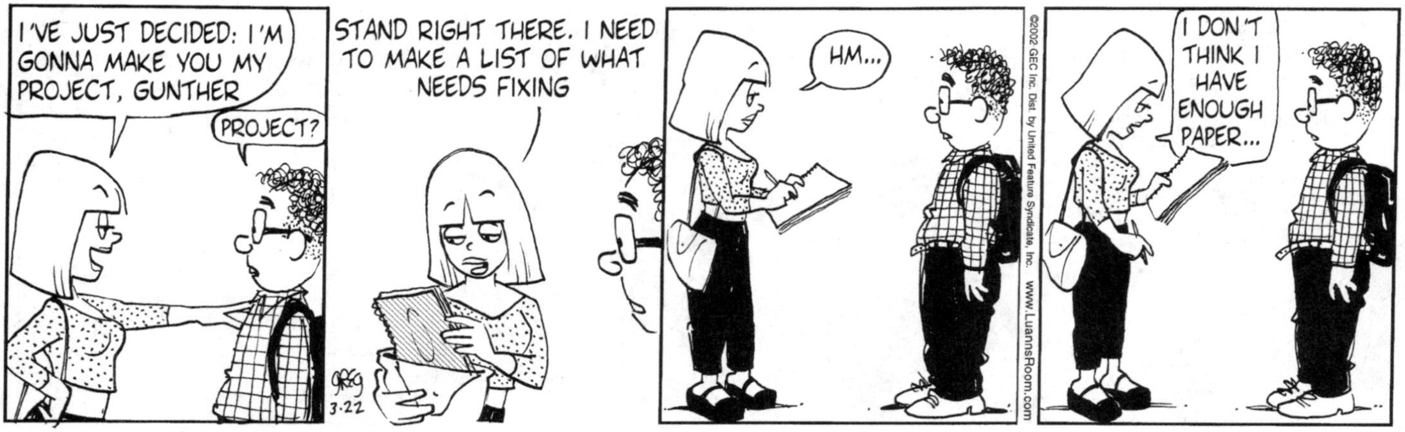
I'VE JUST DECIDED: I'M GONNA MAKE YOU MY PROJECT, GUNTHER
PROJECT?
STAND RIGHT THERE. I NEED TO MAKE A LIST OF WHAT NEEDS FIXING
GREG 3-22
HM...
©2002 GEC Inc. Dist. by United Feature Syndicate, Inc. www.LuannsRoom.com
I DON'T THINK I HAVE ENOUGH PAPER...

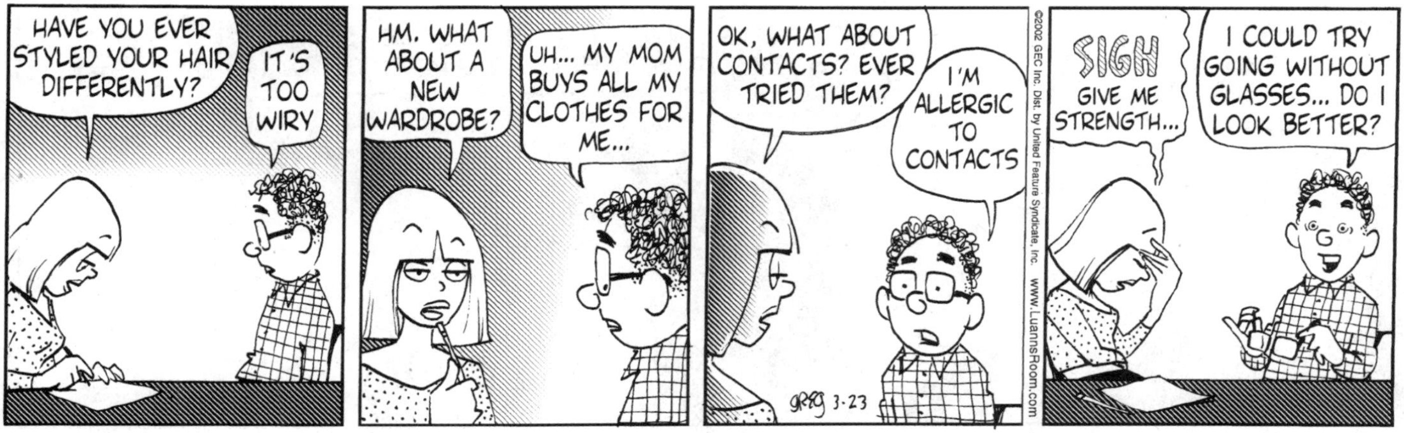
HAVE YOU EVER STYLED YOUR HAIR DIFFERENTLY?
IT'S TOO WIRY
HM. WHAT ABOUT A NEW WARDROBE?
UH... MY MOM BUYS ALL MY CLOTHES FOR ME...
OK, WHAT ABOUT CONTACTS? EVER TRIED THEM?
I'M ALLERGIC TO CONTACTS
GREG 3-23
©2002 GEC Inc. Dist. by United Feature Syndicate, Inc. www.LuannsRoom.com
SIGH
GIVE ME STRENGTH...
I COULD TRY GOING WITHOUT GLASSES... DO I LOOK BETTER?

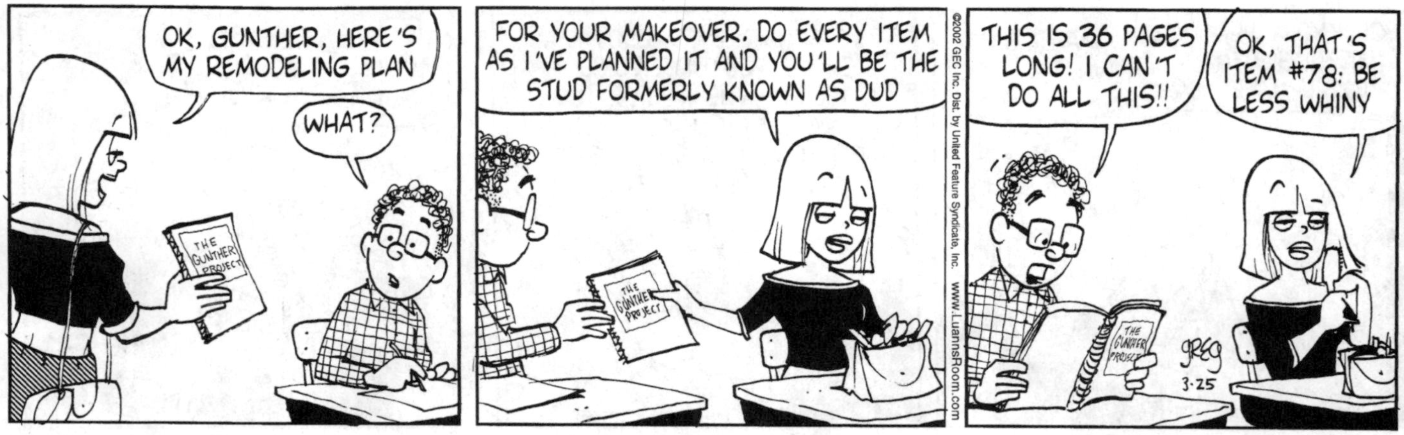
OK, GUNTHER, HERE'S MY REMODELING PLAN
WHAT?
THE GUNTHER PROJECT
FOR YOUR MAKEOVER. DO EVERY ITEM AS I'VE PLANNED IT AND YOU'LL BE THE STUD FORMERLY KNOWN AS DUD
©2002 GEC Inc. Dist. by United Feature Syndicate, Inc. www.LuannsRoom.com
THIS IS 36 PAGES LONG! I CAN'T DO ALL THIS!!
OK, THAT'S ITEM #78: BE LESS WHINY
GREG 3-25

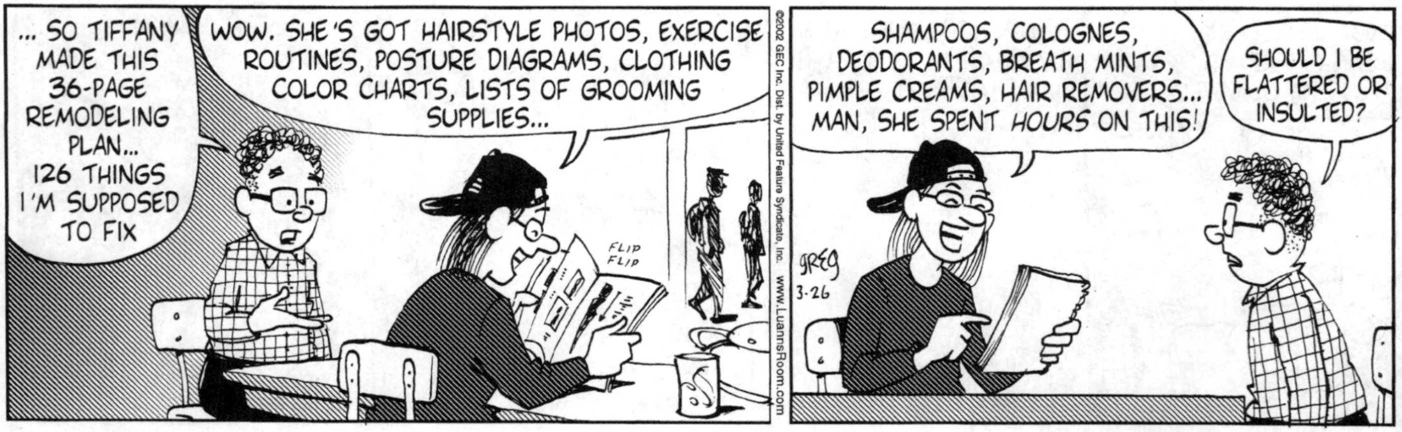
... SO TIFFANY MADE THIS 36-PAGE REMODELING PLAN... 126 THINGS I'M SUPPOSED TO FIX
WOW. SHE'S GOT HAIRSTYLE PHOTOS, EXERCISE ROUTINES, POSTURE DIAGRAMS, CLOTHING COLOR CHARTS, LISTS OF GROOMING SUPPLIES...
FLIP FLIP
©2002 GEC Inc. Dist. by United Feature Syndicate, Inc. www.LuannsRoom.com
SHAMPOOS, COLOGNES, DEODORANTS, BREATH MINTS, PIMPLE CREAMS, HAIR REMOVERS... MAN, SHE SPENT *HOURS* ON THIS!
SHOULD I BE FLATTERED OR INSULTED?
GREG 3-26

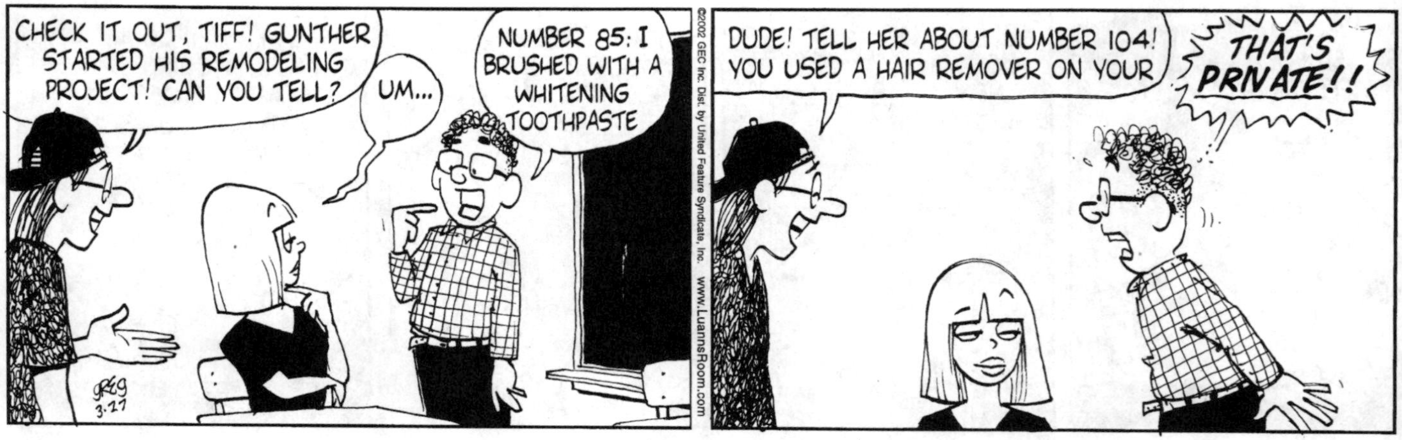
CHECK IT OUT, TIFF! GUNTHER STARTED HIS REMODELING PROJECT! CAN YOU TELL?
UM...
NUMBER 85: I BRUSHED WITH A WHITENING TOOTHPASTE
GREG 3-27
©2002 GEC Inc. Dist. by United Feature Syndicate, Inc. www.LuannsRoom.com
DUDE! TELL HER ABOUT NUMBER 104! YOU USED A HAIR REMOVER ON YOUR
THAT'S PRIVATE!!

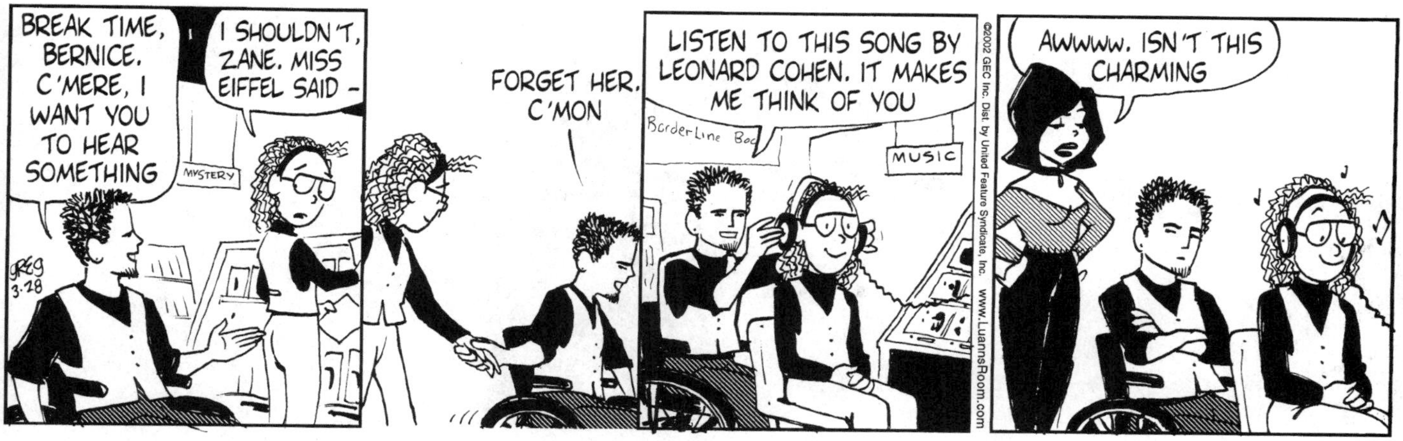
BREAK TIME, BERNICE. C'MERE, I WANT YOU TO HEAR SOMETHING
I SHOULDN'T, ZANE. MISS EIFFEL SAID -
MYSTERY
GREG 3·28
FORGET HER. C'MON
LISTEN TO THIS SONG BY LEONARD COHEN. IT MAKES ME THINK OF YOU
BorderLine Boo
MUSIC
©2002 GEC Inc. Dist. by United Feature Syndicate, Inc. www.LuannsRoom.com
AWWWW. ISN'T THIS CHARMING

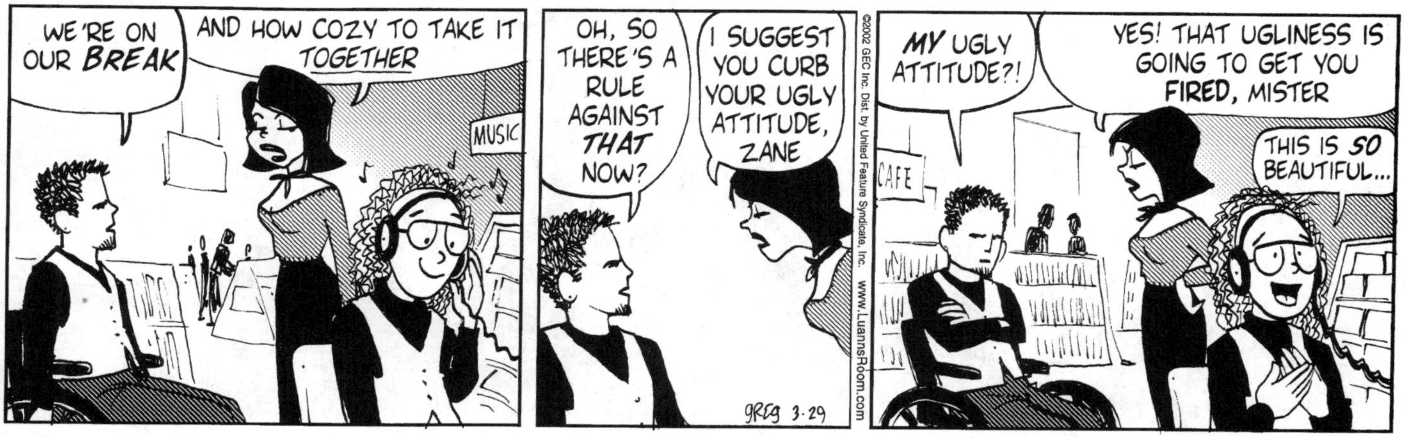
WE'RE ON OUR **BREAK**
AND HOW COZY TO TAKE IT *TOGETHER*
MUSIC
OH, SO THERE'S A RULE AGAINST ***THAT*** NOW?
I SUGGEST YOU CURB YOUR UGLY ATTITUDE, ZANE
GREG 3·29
©2002 GEC Inc. Dist. by United Feature Syndicate, Inc. www.LuannsRoom.com
MY UGLY ATTITUDE?!
YES! THAT UGLINESS IS GOING TO GET YOU **FIRED**, MISTER
CAFE
THIS IS *SO* BEAUTIFUL...

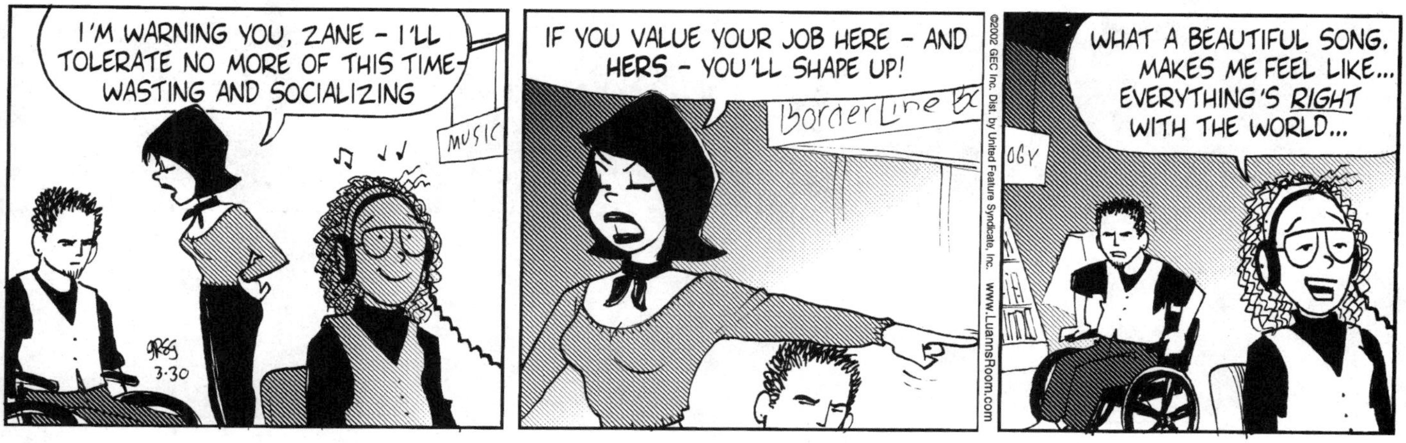
I'M WARNING YOU, ZANE - I'LL TOLERATE NO MORE OF THIS TIME-WASTING AND SOCIALIZING
MUSIC
GREG 3·30
IF YOU VALUE YOUR JOB HERE - AND **HERS** - YOU'LL SHAPE UP!
BorderLine Bo
©2002 GEC Inc. Dist. by United Feature Syndicate, Inc. www.LuannsRoom.com
WHAT A BEAUTIFUL SONG. MAKES ME FEEL LIKE... EVERYTHING'S *RIGHT* WITH THE WORLD...
OGY

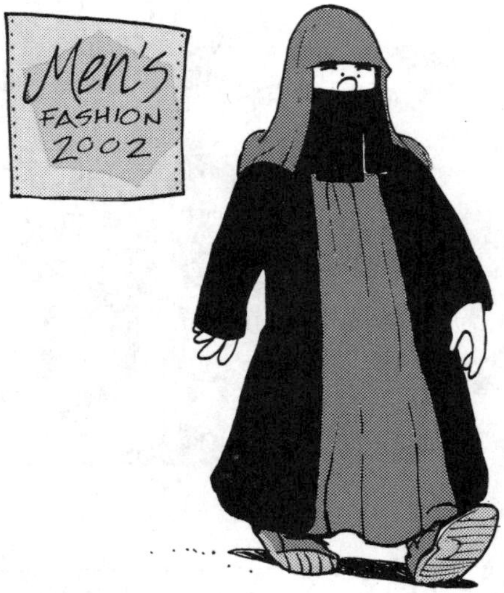
Men's
FASHION
2002

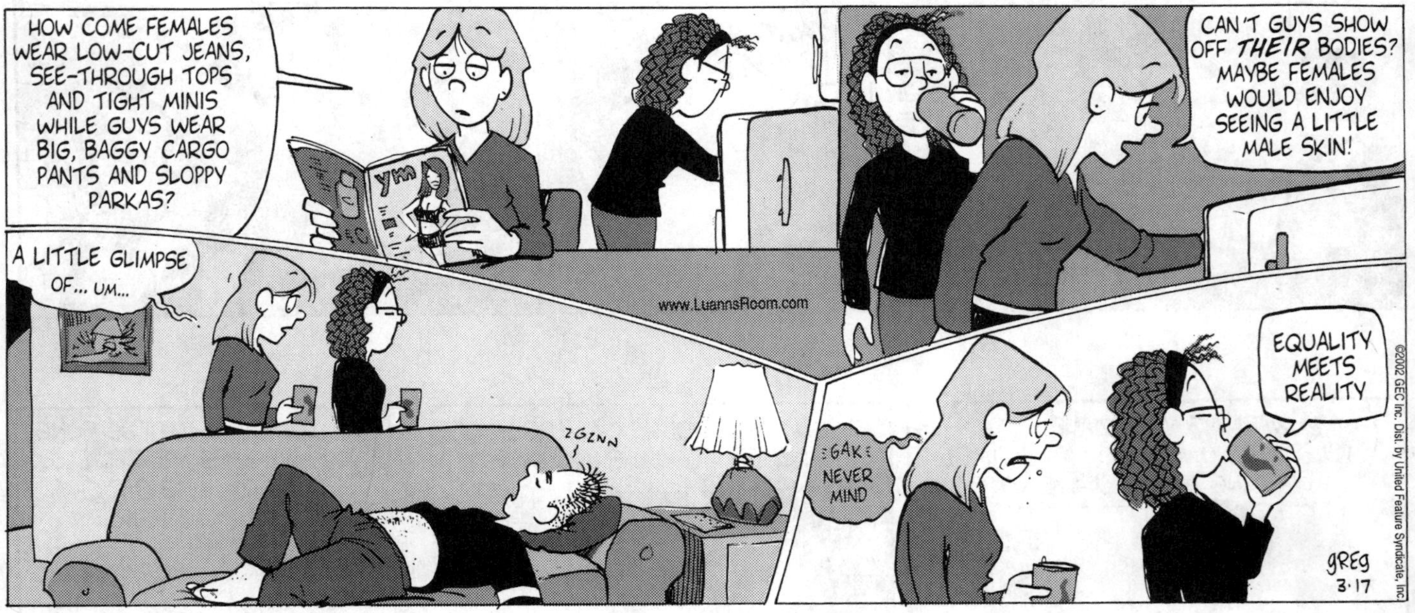
HOW COME FEMALES WEAR LOW-CUT JEANS, SEE-THROUGH TOPS AND TIGHT MINIS WHILE GUYS WEAR BIG, BAGGY CARGO PANTS AND SLOPPY PARKAS?
CAN'T GUYS SHOW OFF *THEIR* BODIES? MAYBE FEMALES WOULD ENJOY SEEING A LITTLE MALE SKIN!
A LITTLE GLIMPSE OF... UM...
www.LuannsRoom.com
ZGZNN
GAK NEVER MIND
EQUALITY MEETS REALITY
©2002 GEC Inc. Dist. by United Feature Syndicate, Inc.
GREG 3·17

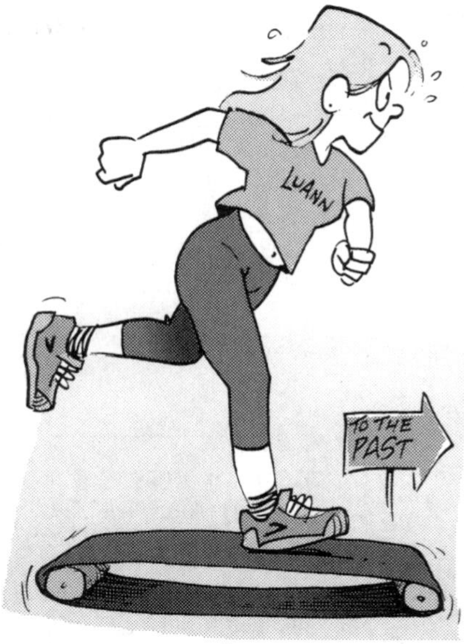
LUANN
TO THE PAST

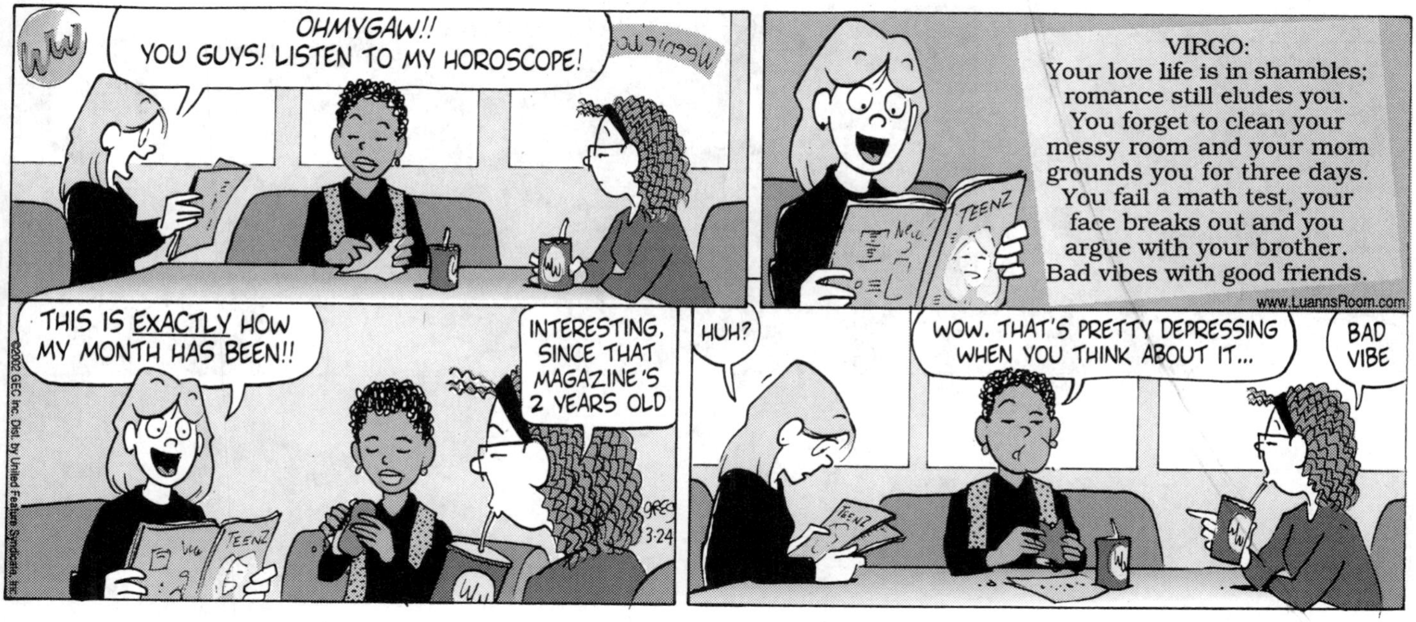
OHMYGAW!!
YOU GUYS! LISTEN TO MY HOROSCOPE!
VIRGO:
Your love life is in shambles; romance still eludes you. You forget to clean your messy room and your mom grounds you for three days. You fail a math test, your face breaks out and you argue with your brother. Bad vibes with good friends.
www.LuannsRoom.com
TEENZ
THIS IS EXACTLY HOW MY MONTH HAS BEEN!!
INTERESTING, SINCE THAT MAGAZINE'S 2 YEARS OLD
HUH?
WOW. THAT'S PRETTY DEPRESSING WHEN YOU THINK ABOUT IT...
BAD VIBE
GREG 3-24
©2002 GEC Inc. Dist. by United Feature Syndicate, Inc.

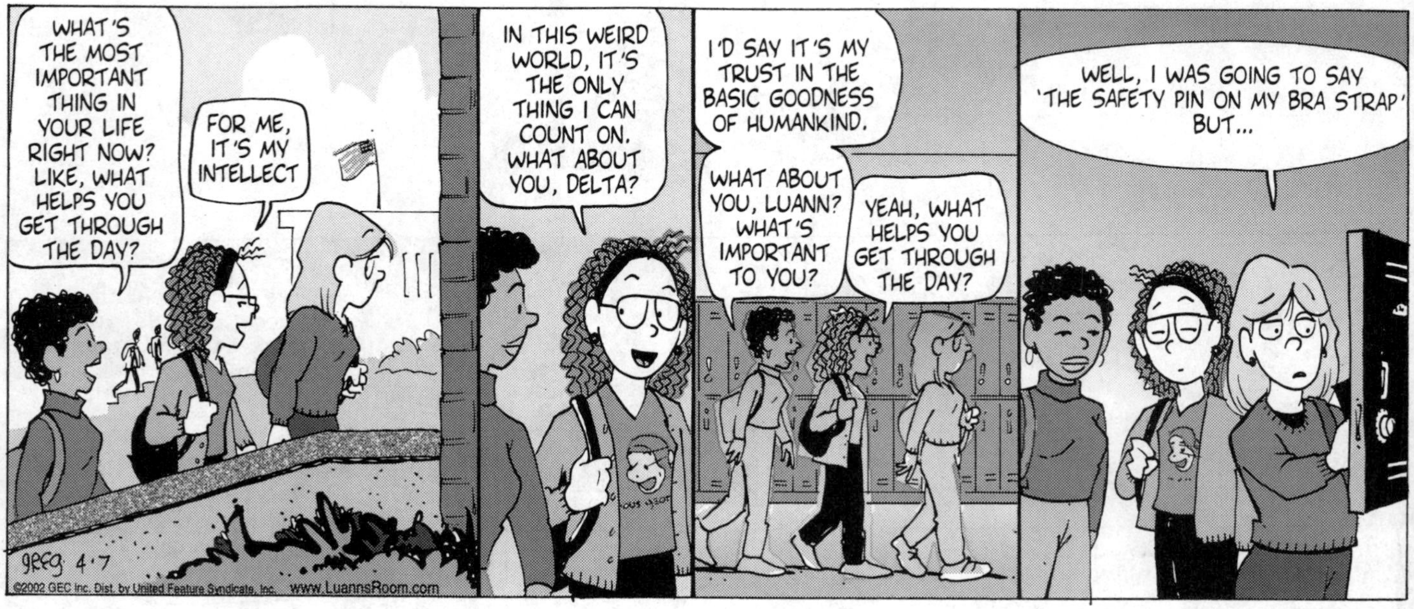
WHAT'S THE MOST IMPORTANT THING IN YOUR LIFE RIGHT NOW? LIKE, WHAT HELPS YOU GET THROUGH THE DAY?
FOR ME, IT'S MY INTELLECT
GREG 4·7
©2002 GEC Inc. Dist. by United Feature Syndicate, Inc. www.LuannsRoom.com
IN THIS WEIRD WORLD, IT'S THE ONLY THING I CAN COUNT ON. WHAT ABOUT YOU, DELTA?
I'D SAY IT'S MY TRUST IN THE BASIC GOODNESS OF HUMANKIND.
WHAT ABOUT YOU, LUANN? WHAT'S IMPORTANT TO YOU?
YEAH, WHAT HELPS YOU GET THROUGH THE DAY?
WELL, I WAS GOING TO SAY 'THE SAFETY PIN ON MY BRA STRAP' BUT...

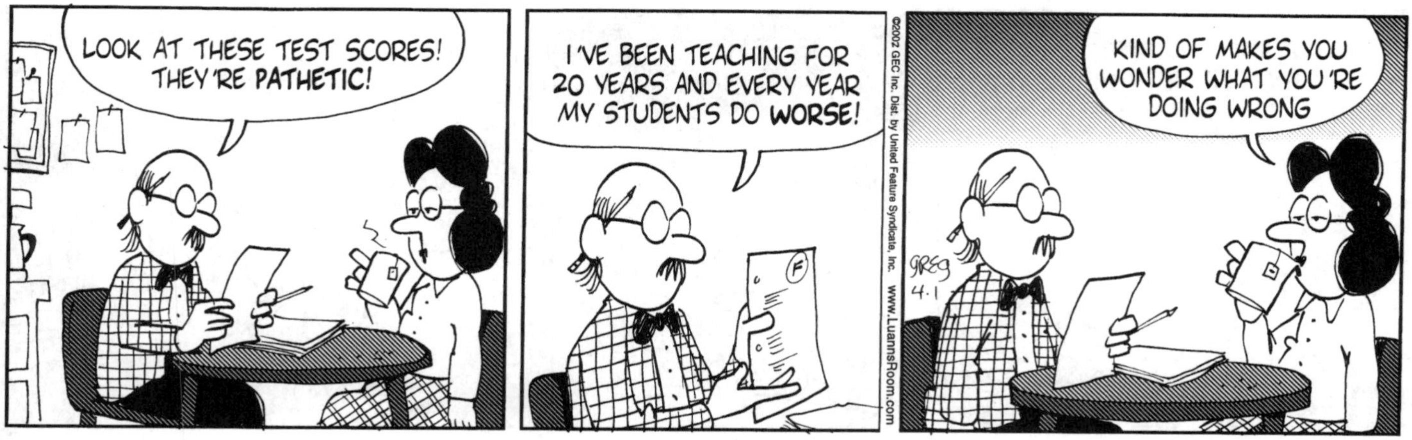
LOOK AT THESE TEST SCORES! THEY'RE PATHETIC!
I'VE BEEN TEACHING FOR 20 YEARS AND EVERY YEAR MY STUDENTS DO WORSE!
©2002 GEC Inc. Dist. by United Feature Syndicate, Inc. www.LuannsRoom.com
KIND OF MAKES YOU WONDER WHAT YOU'RE DOING WRONG
GREG 4.1

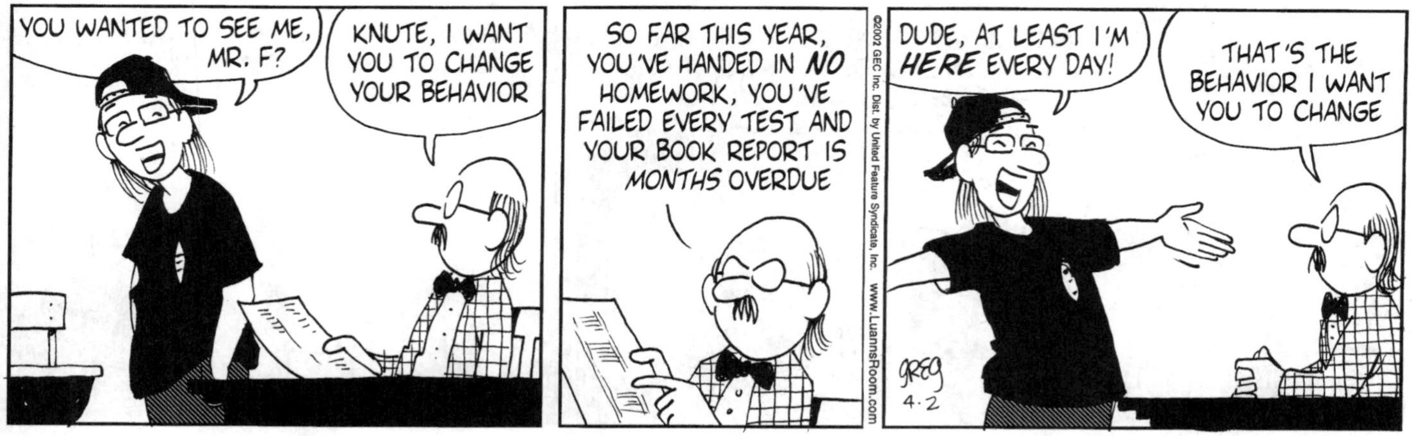
YOU WANTED TO SEE ME, MR. F?
KNUTE, I WANT YOU TO CHANGE YOUR BEHAVIOR
SO FAR THIS YEAR, YOU'VE HANDED IN NO HOMEWORK, YOU'VE FAILED EVERY TEST AND YOUR BOOK REPORT IS MONTHS OVERDUE
©2002 GEC Inc. Dist. by United Feature Syndicate, Inc. www.LuannsRoom.com
DUDE, AT LEAST I'M HERE EVERY DAY!
THAT'S THE BEHAVIOR I WANT YOU TO CHANGE
GREG 4.2

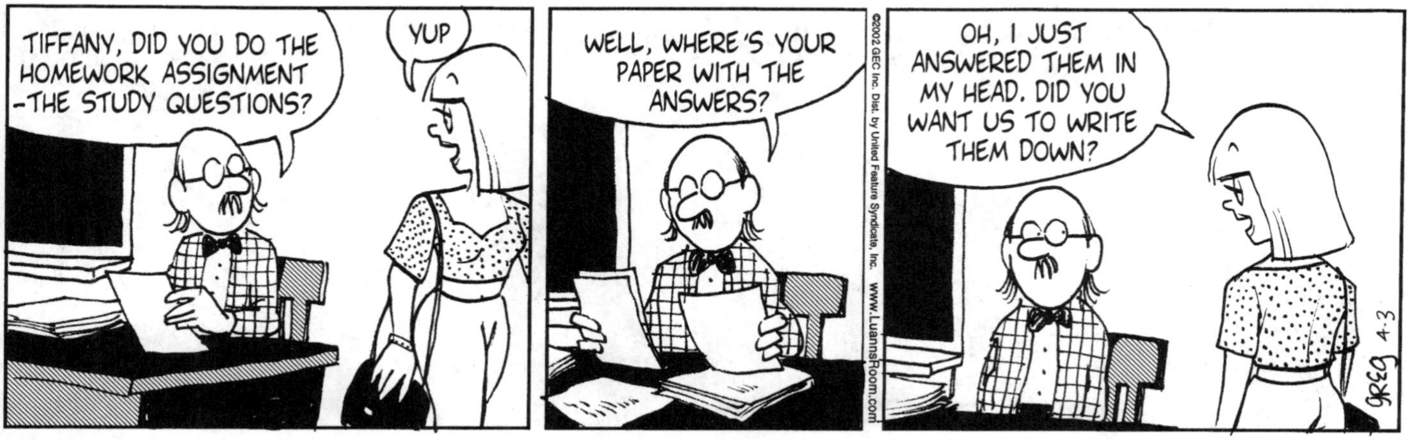
TIFFANY, DID YOU DO THE HOMEWORK ASSIGNMENT -THE STUDY QUESTIONS?
YUP
WELL, WHERE'S YOUR PAPER WITH THE ANSWERS?
©2002 GEC Inc. Dist. by United Feature Syndicate, Inc. www.LuannsRoom.com
OH, I JUST ANSWERED THEM IN MY HEAD. DID YOU WANT US TO WRITE THEM DOWN?
GREG 4.3

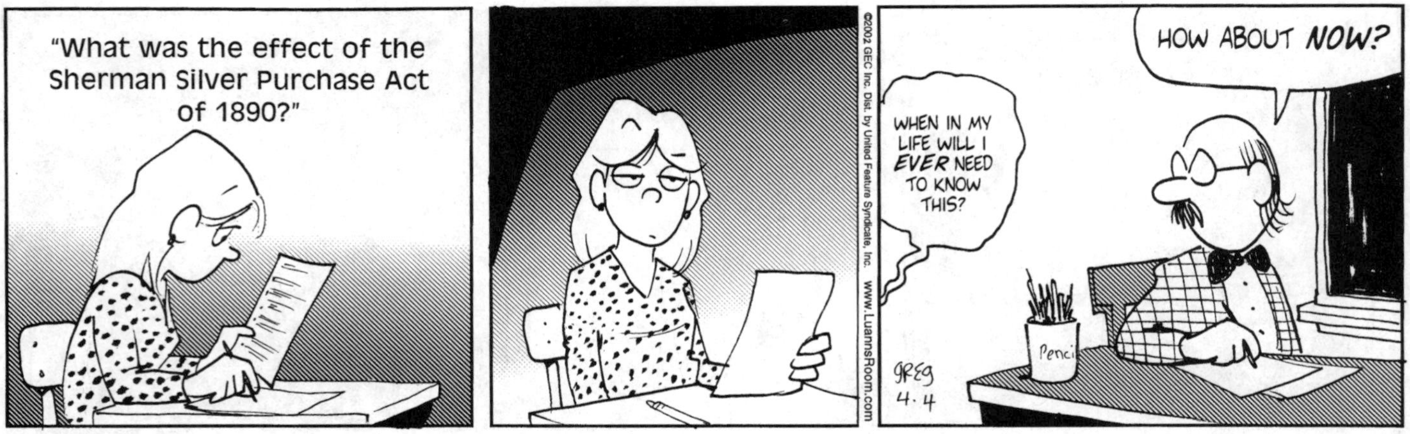
"What was the effect of the Sherman Silver Purchase Act of 1890?"
©2002 GEC Inc. Dist. by United Feature Syndicate, Inc. www.LuannsRoom.com
WHEN IN MY LIFE WILL I EVER NEED TO KNOW THIS?
HOW ABOUT NOW?
Penci
GREG 4.4

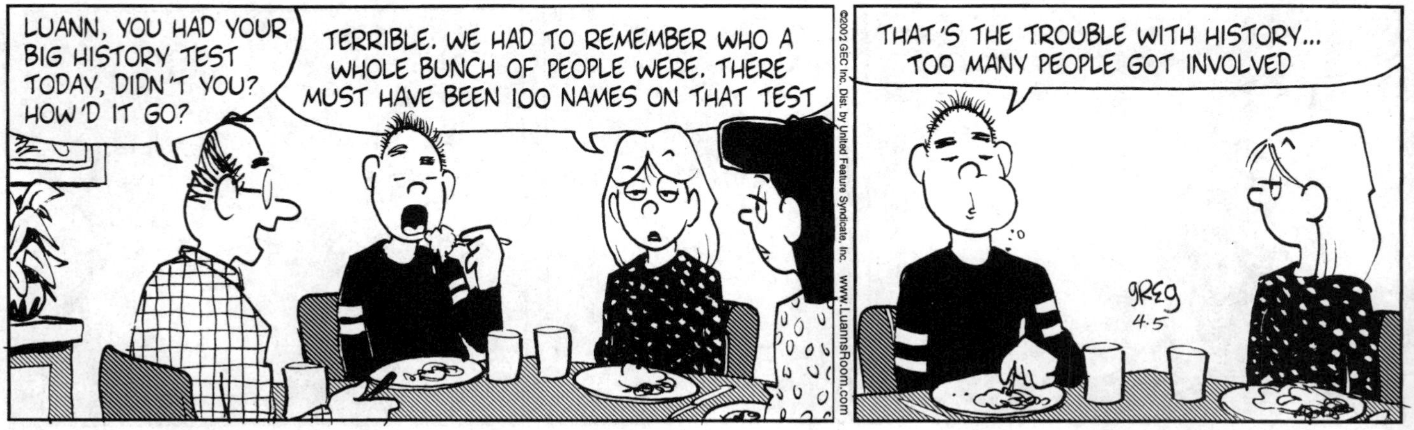
LUANN, YOU HAD YOUR BIG HISTORY TEST TODAY, DIDN'T YOU? HOW'D IT GO?
TERRIBLE. WE HAD TO REMEMBER WHO A WHOLE BUNCH OF PEOPLE WERE. THERE MUST HAVE BEEN 100 NAMES ON THAT TEST
©2002 GEC Inc. Dist. by United Feature Syndicate, Inc. www.LuannsRoom.com
THAT'S THE TROUBLE WITH HISTORY... TOO MANY PEOPLE GOT INVOLVED
GREG 4.5

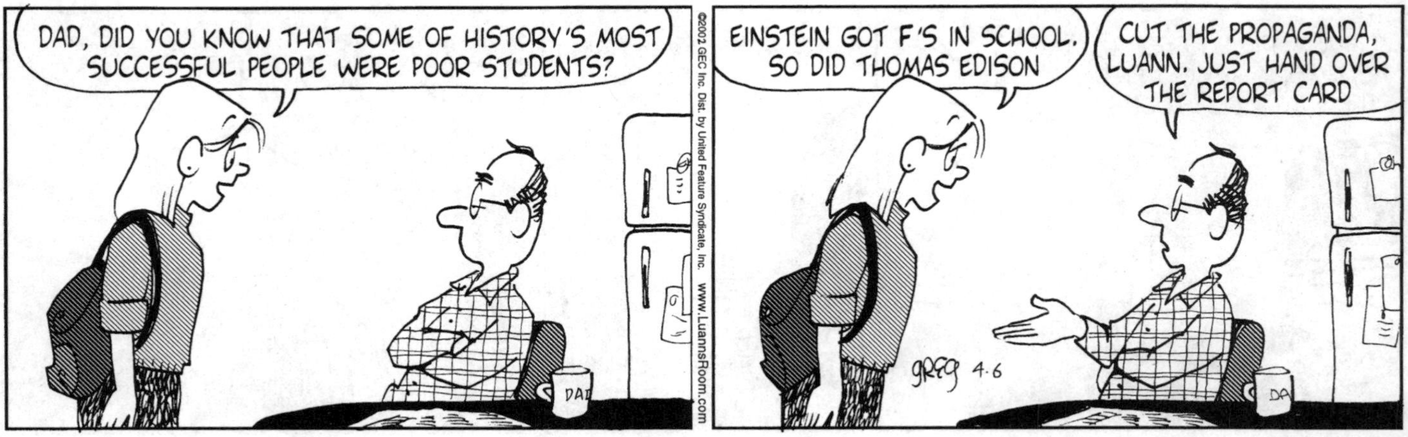
DAD, DID YOU KNOW THAT SOME OF HISTORY'S MOST SUCCESSFUL PEOPLE WERE POOR STUDENTS?
©2002 GEC Inc. Dist. by United Feature Syndicate, Inc. www.LuannsRoom.com
EINSTEIN GOT F'S IN SCHOOL. SO DID THOMAS EDISON
CUT THE PROPAGANDA, LUANN. JUST HAND OVER THE REPORT CARD
GREG 4.6

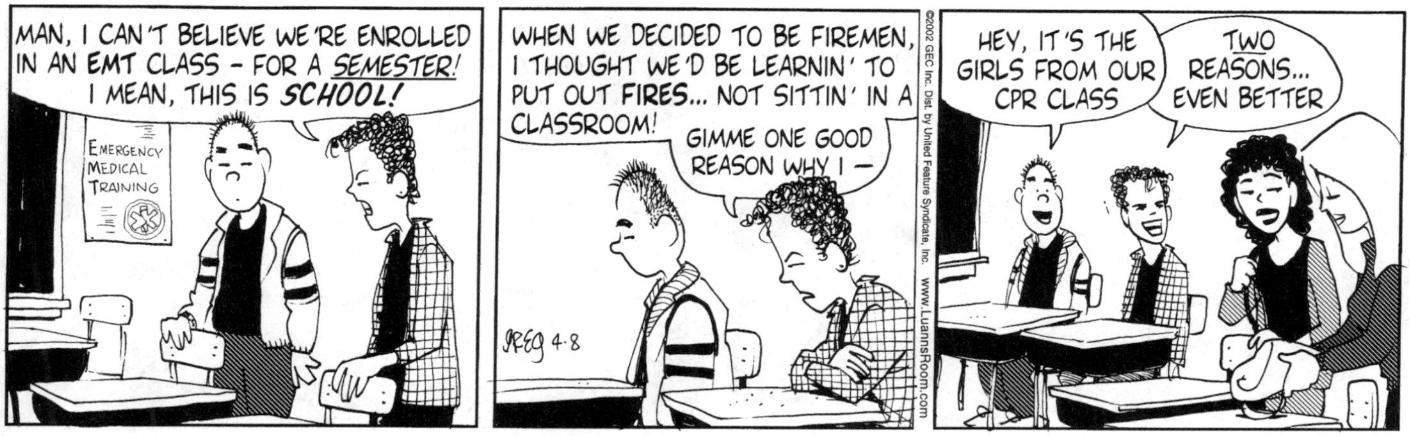

MAN, I CAN'T BELIEVE WE'RE ENROLLED IN AN EMT CLASS – FOR A SEMESTER! I MEAN, THIS IS SCHOOL!
EMERGENCY MEDICAL TRAINING
WHEN WE DECIDED TO BE FIREMEN, I THOUGHT WE'D BE LEARNIN' TO PUT OUT FIRES... NOT SITTIN' IN A CLASSROOM!
GIMME ONE GOOD REASON WHY I —
GREG 4·8
©2002 GEC Inc. Dist. by United Feature Syndicate, Inc. www.LuannsRoom.com
HEY, IT'S THE GIRLS FROM OUR CPR CLASS
TWO REASONS... EVEN BETTER

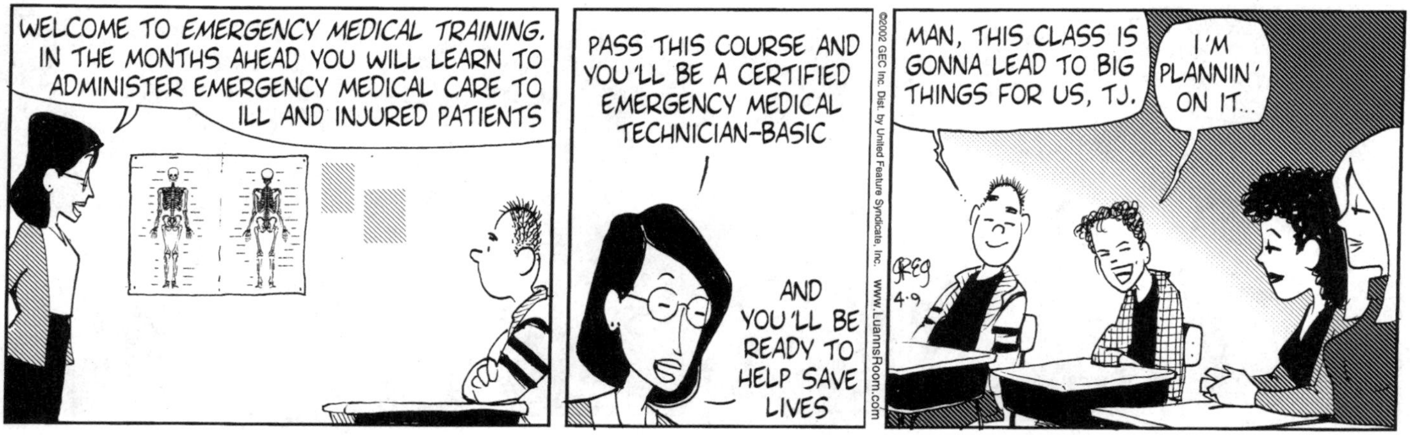

WELCOME TO EMERGENCY MEDICAL TRAINING. IN THE MONTHS AHEAD YOU WILL LEARN TO ADMINISTER EMERGENCY MEDICAL CARE TO ILL AND INJURED PATIENTS
PASS THIS COURSE AND YOU'LL BE A CERTIFIED EMERGENCY MEDICAL TECHNICIAN-BASIC
AND YOU'LL BE READY TO HELP SAVE LIVES
©2002 GEC Inc. Dist. by United Feature Syndicate, Inc. www.LuannsRoom.com
MAN, THIS CLASS IS GONNA LEAD TO BIG THINGS FOR US, TJ.
I'M PLANNIN' ON IT...
GREG 4·9

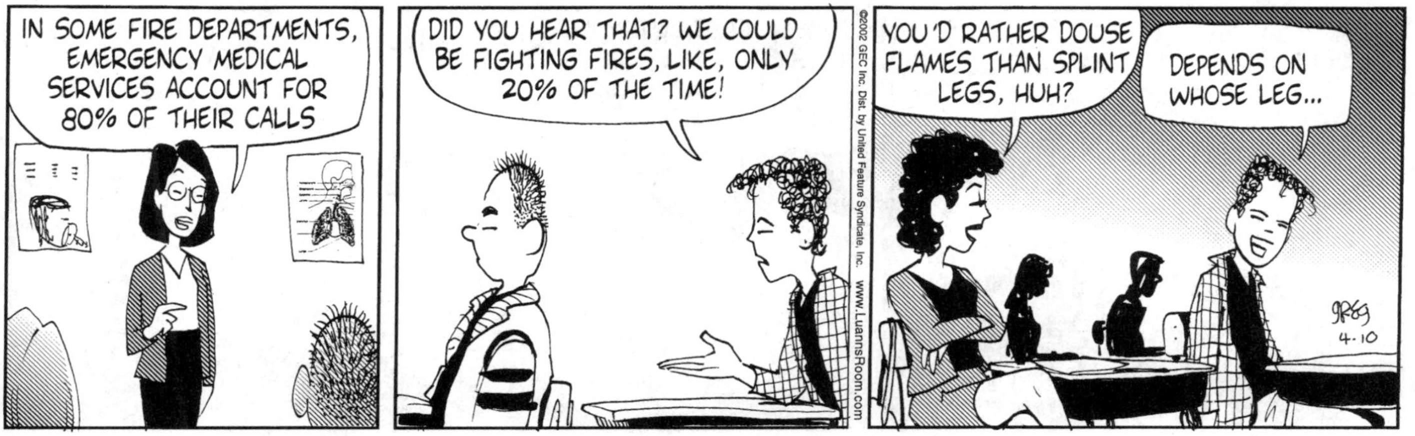

IN SOME FIRE DEPARTMENTS, EMERGENCY MEDICAL SERVICES ACCOUNT FOR 80% OF THEIR CALLS
DID YOU HEAR THAT? WE COULD BE FIGHTING FIRES, LIKE, ONLY 20% OF THE TIME!
©2002 GEC Inc. Dist. by United Feature Syndicate, Inc. www.LuannsRoom.com
YOU'D RATHER DOUSE FLAMES THAN SPLINT LEGS, HUH?
DEPENDS ON WHOSE LEG...
GREG 4·10

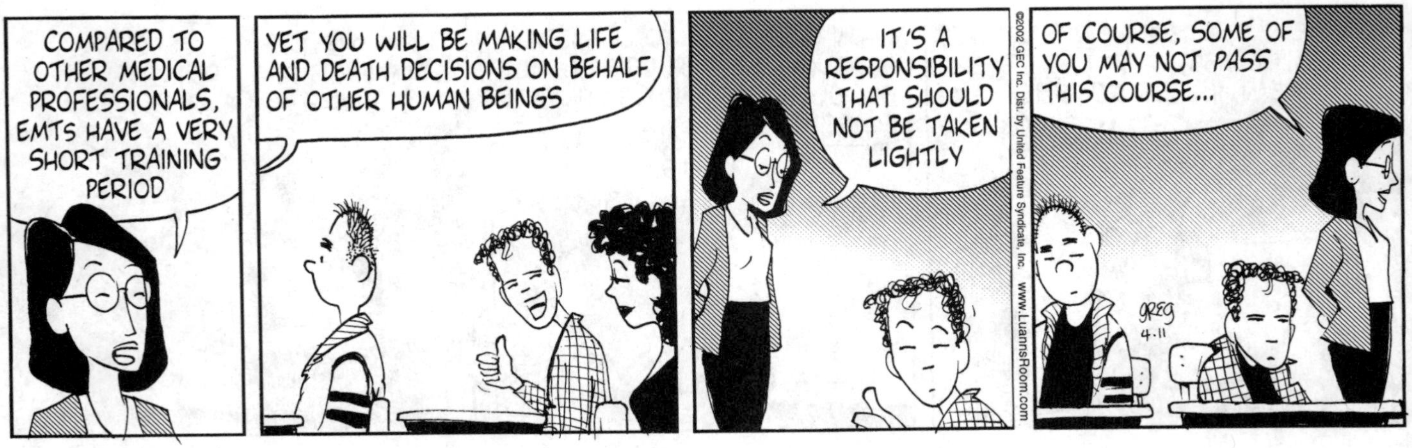
COMPARED TO OTHER MEDICAL PROFESSIONALS, EMTS HAVE A VERY SHORT TRAINING PERIOD
YET YOU WILL BE MAKING LIFE AND DEATH DECISIONS ON BEHALF OF OTHER HUMAN BEINGS
IT'S A RESPONSIBILITY THAT SHOULD NOT BE TAKEN LIGHTLY
©2002 GEC Inc. Dist. by United Feature Syndicate, Inc. www.LuannsRoom.com
OF COURSE, SOME OF YOU MAY NOT *PASS* THIS COURSE...
GREG 4·11

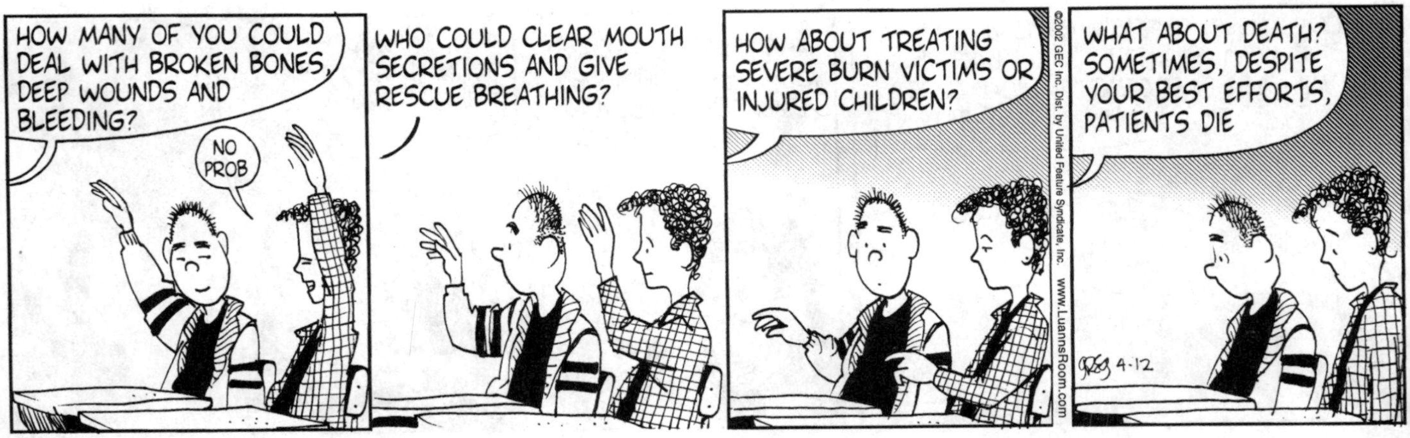
HOW MANY OF YOU COULD DEAL WITH BROKEN BONES, DEEP WOUNDS AND BLEEDING?
NO PROB
WHO COULD CLEAR MOUTH SECRETIONS AND GIVE RESCUE BREATHING?
HOW ABOUT TREATING SEVERE BURN VICTIMS OR INJURED CHILDREN?
©2002 GEC Inc. Dist. by United Feature Syndicate, Inc. www.LuannsRoom.com
WHAT ABOUT DEATH? SOMETIMES, DESPITE YOUR BEST EFFORTS, PATIENTS DIE
GREG 4·12

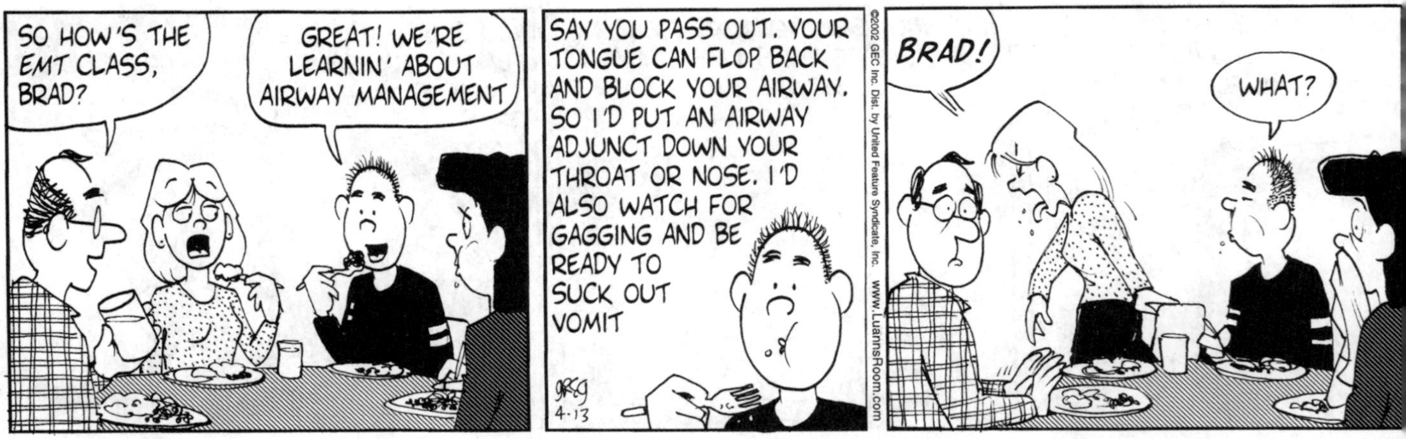
SO HOW'S THE EMT CLASS, BRAD?
GREAT! WE'RE LEARNIN' ABOUT AIRWAY MANAGEMENT
SAY YOU PASS OUT. YOUR TONGUE CAN FLOP BACK AND BLOCK YOUR AIRWAY. SO I'D PUT AN AIRWAY ADJUNCT DOWN YOUR THROAT OR NOSE. I'D ALSO WATCH FOR GAGGING AND BE READY TO SUCK OUT VOMIT
GREG 4·13
©2002 GEC Inc. Dist. by United Feature Syndicate, Inc. www.LuannsRoom.com
BRAD!
WHAT?

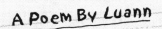

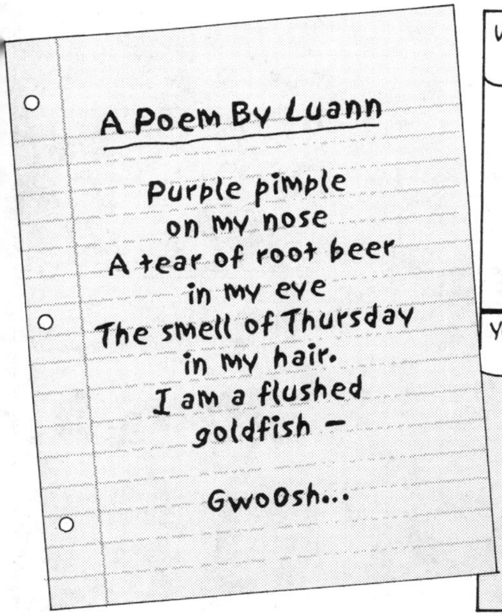

A Poem By Luann
Purple pimple
on my nose
A tear of root beer
in my eye
The smell of Thursday
in my hair.
I am a flushed
goldfish —
GwoOsh...

WELL? THINK I COULD BE A RICH POET?
ABSOLUTELY! JUST LIKE... LIKE...
OH, WHATZIZ FACE... THAT WEALTHY POET...
SNAP SNAP
www.LuannsRoom.com
©2002 GEC Inc. Dist. by United Feature Syndicate, Inc.
YOU KNOW! THAT REALLY RICH POET...
ACH!
OH WAIT. THERE ARE NO REALLY RICH POETS...
ONLY REALLY ANGRY ONES
GREG 4.14

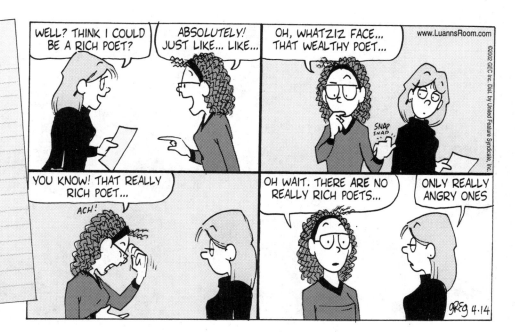

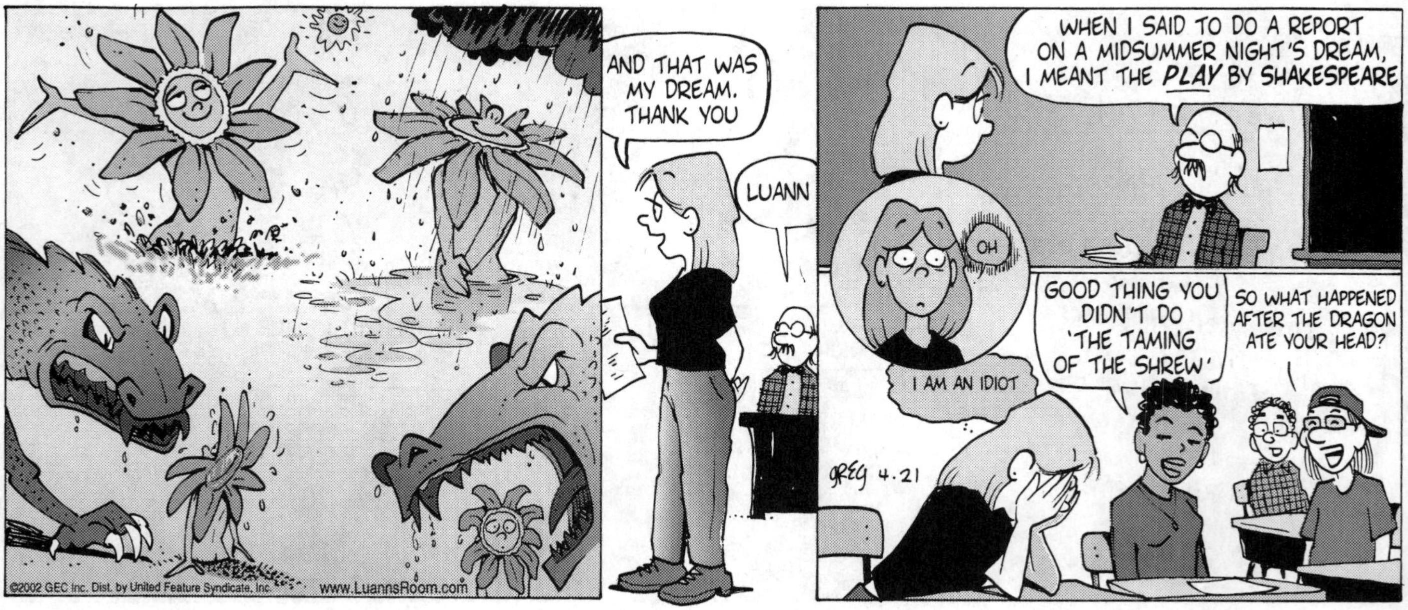
AND THAT WAS MY DREAM. THANK YOU
LUANN
WHEN I SAID TO DO A REPORT ON A MIDSUMMER NIGHT'S DREAM, I MEANT THE PLAY BY SHAKESPEARE
OH
I AM AN IDIOT
GOOD THING YOU DIDN'T DO 'THE TAMING OF THE SHREW'
SO WHAT HAPPENED AFTER THE DRAGON ATE YOUR HEAD?
GREG 4.21
©2002 GEC Inc. Dist. by United Feature Syndicate, Inc.
www.LuannsRoom.com

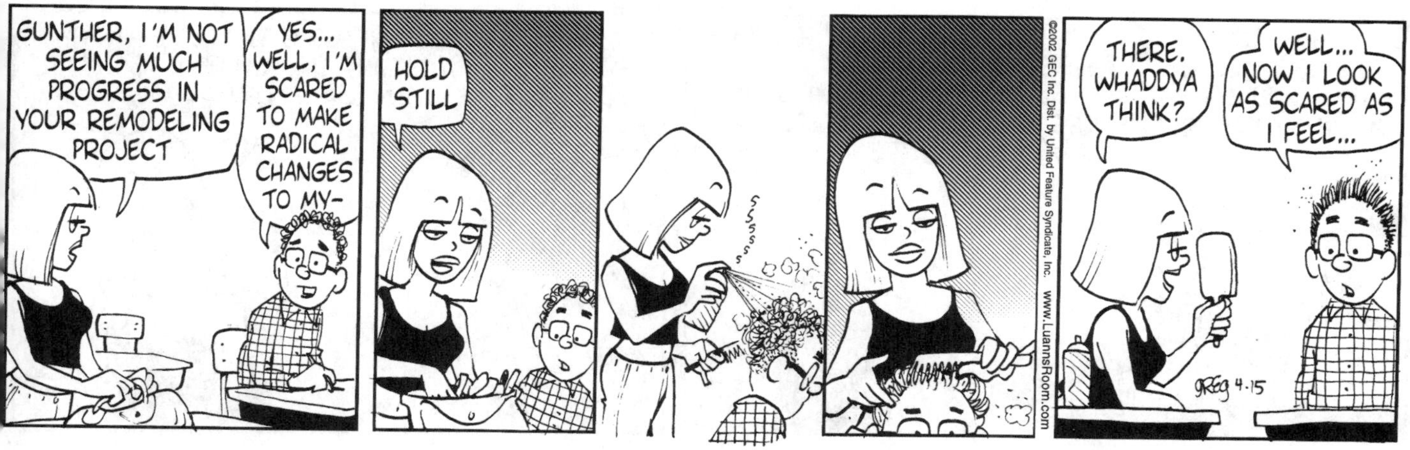
GUNTHER, I'M NOT SEEING MUCH PROGRESS IN YOUR REMODELING PROJECT
YES... WELL, I'M SCARED TO MAKE RADICAL CHANGES TO MY-
HOLD STILL
©2002 GEC Inc. Dist. by United Feature Syndicate, Inc. www.LuannsRoom.com
THERE. WHADDYA THINK?
WELL... NOW I LOOK AS SCARED AS I FEEL...
GREG 4·15

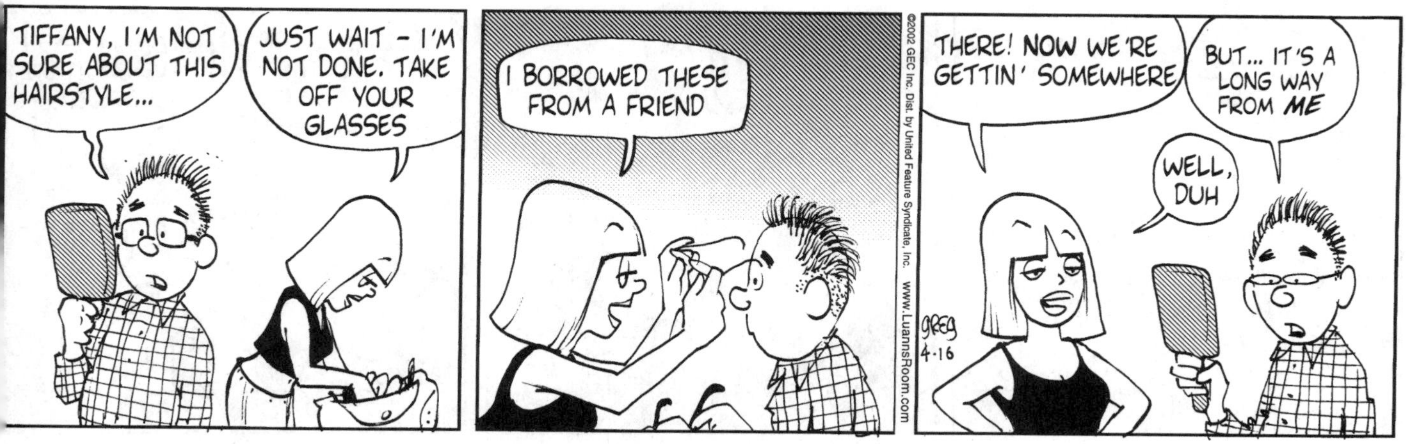
TIFFANY, I'M NOT SURE ABOUT THIS HAIRSTYLE...
JUST WAIT - I'M NOT DONE. TAKE OFF YOUR GLASSES
I BORROWED THESE FROM A FRIEND
©2002 GEC Inc. Dist. by United Feature Syndicate, Inc. www.LuannsRoom.com
THERE! NOW WE'RE GETTIN' SOMEWHERE
BUT... IT'S A LONG WAY FROM *ME*
WELL, DUH
GREG 4·16

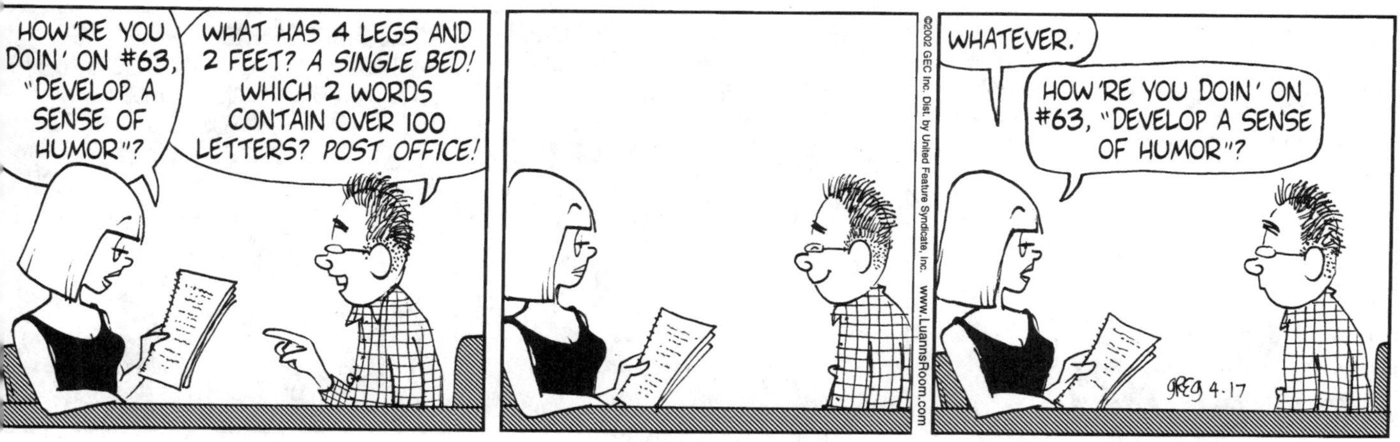
HOW'RE YOU DOIN' ON #63, "DEVELOP A SENSE OF HUMOR"?
WHAT HAS 4 LEGS AND 2 FEET? *A SINGLE BED!* WHICH 2 WORDS CONTAIN OVER 100 LETTERS? *POST OFFICE!*
©2002 GEC Inc. Dist. by United Feature Syndicate, Inc. www.LuannsRoom.com
WHATEVER.
HOW'RE YOU DOIN' ON #63, "DEVELOP A SENSE OF HUMOR"?
GREG 4·17

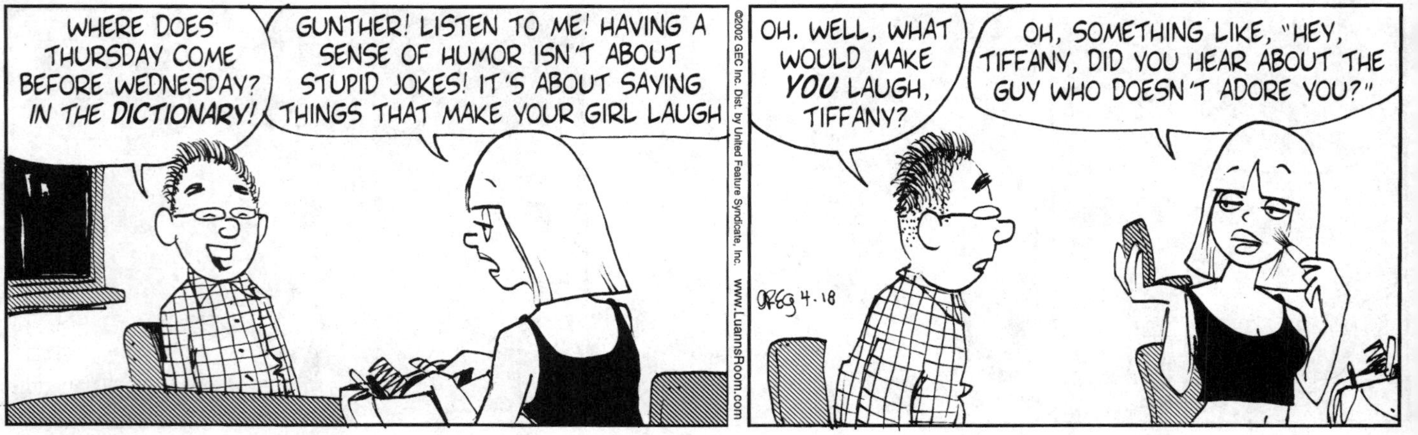
WHERE DOES THURSDAY COME BEFORE WEDNESDAY? IN THE DICTIONARY!
GUNTHER! LISTEN TO ME! HAVING A SENSE OF HUMOR ISN'T ABOUT STUPID JOKES! IT'S ABOUT SAYING THINGS THAT MAKE YOUR GIRL LAUGH
©2002 GEC Inc. Dist. by United Feature Syndicate, Inc. www.LuannsRoom.com
OH. WELL, WHAT WOULD MAKE YOU LAUGH, TIFFANY?
OH, SOMETHING LIKE, "HEY, TIFFANY, DID YOU HEAR ABOUT THE GUY WHO DOESN'T ADORE YOU?"
GREG 4.18

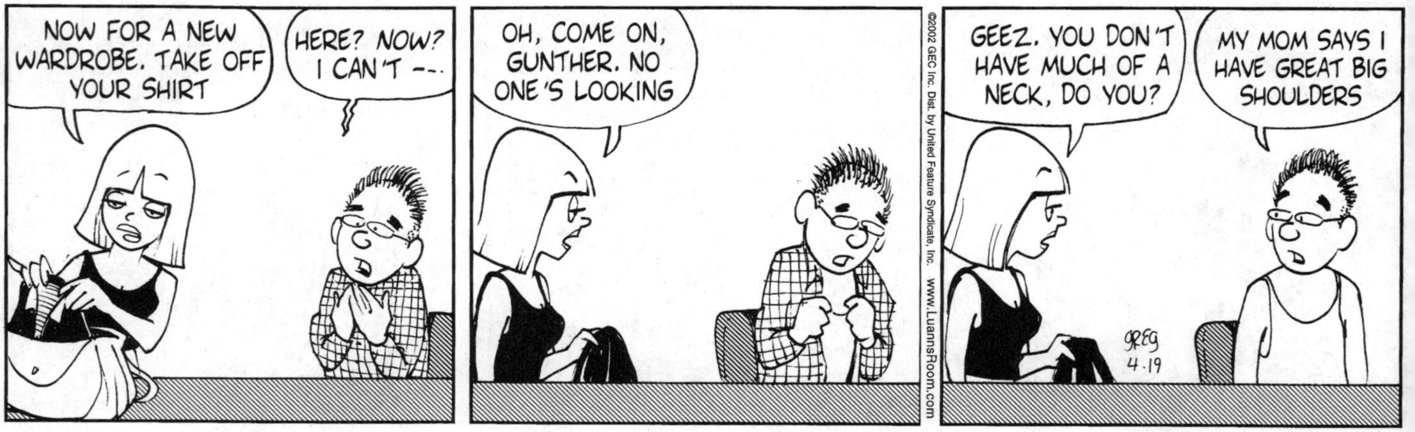
NOW FOR A NEW WARDROBE. TAKE OFF YOUR SHIRT
HERE? NOW? I CAN'T --.
OH, COME ON, GUNTHER. NO ONE'S LOOKING
©2002 GEC Inc. Dist. by United Feature Syndicate, Inc. www.LuannsRoom.com
GEEZ. YOU DON'T HAVE MUCH OF A NECK, DO YOU?
MY MOM SAYS I HAVE GREAT BIG SHOULDERS
GREG 4.19

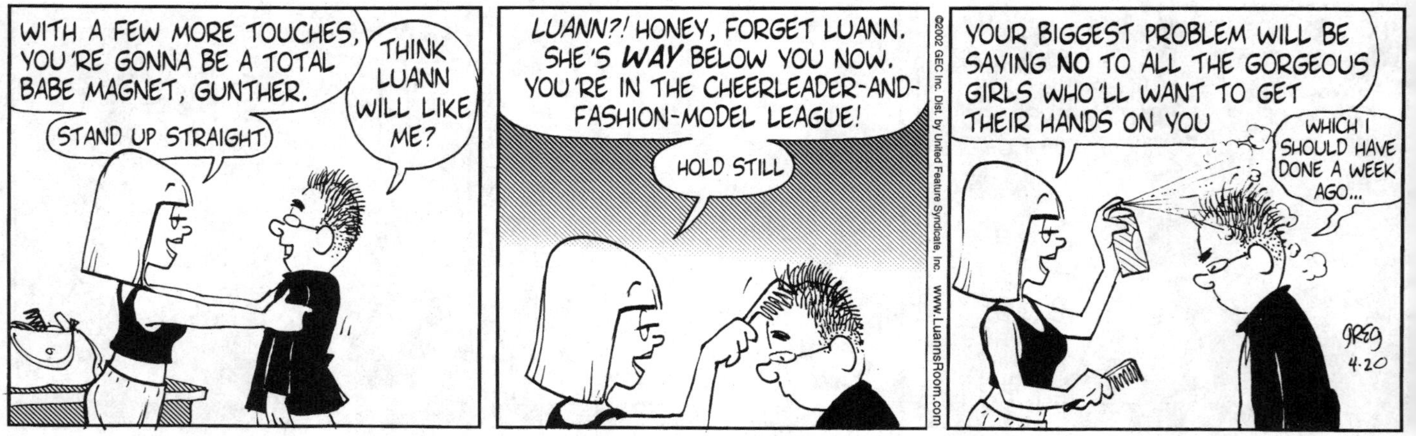
WITH A FEW MORE TOUCHES, YOU'RE GONNA BE A TOTAL BABE MAGNET, GUNTHER.
STAND UP STRAIGHT
THINK LUANN WILL LIKE ME?
LUANN?! HONEY, FORGET LUANN. SHE'S WAY BELOW YOU NOW. YOU'RE IN THE CHEERLEADER-AND-FASHION-MODEL LEAGUE!
HOLD STILL
©2002 GEC Inc. Dist. by United Feature Syndicate, Inc. www.LuannsRoom.com
YOUR BIGGEST PROBLEM WILL BE SAYING NO TO ALL THE GORGEOUS GIRLS WHO'LL WANT TO GET THEIR HANDS ON YOU
WHICH I SHOULD HAVE DONE A WEEK AGO...
GREG 4.20

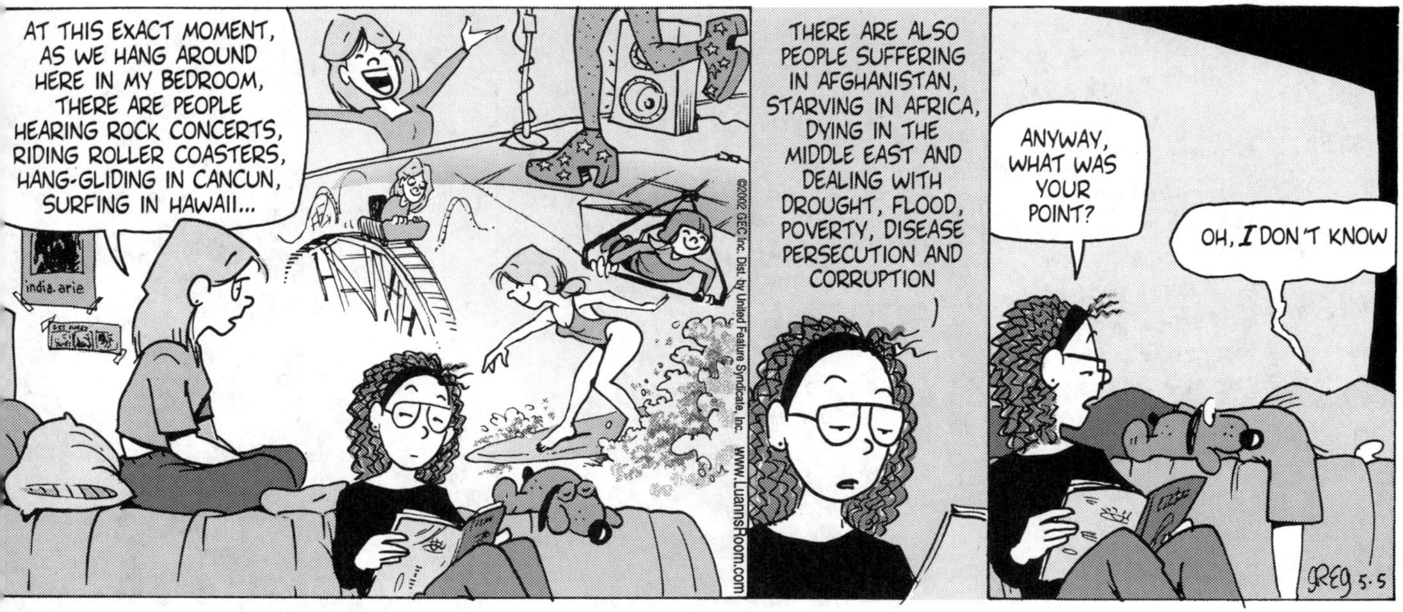

AT THIS EXACT MOMENT, AS WE HANG AROUND HERE IN MY BEDROOM, THERE ARE PEOPLE HEARING ROCK CONCERTS, RIDING ROLLER COASTERS, HANG-GLIDING IN CANCUN, SURFING IN HAWAII...
india.arie
©2002 GEC Inc. Dist. by United Feature Syndicate, Inc.
www.LuannsRoom.com
THERE ARE ALSO PEOPLE SUFFERING IN AFGHANISTAN, STARVING IN AFRICA, DYING IN THE MIDDLE EAST AND DEALING WITH DROUGHT, FLOOD, POVERTY, DISEASE PERSECUTION AND CORRUPTION
ANYWAY, WHAT WAS YOUR POINT?
OH, *I* DON'T KNOW
GREG 5-5

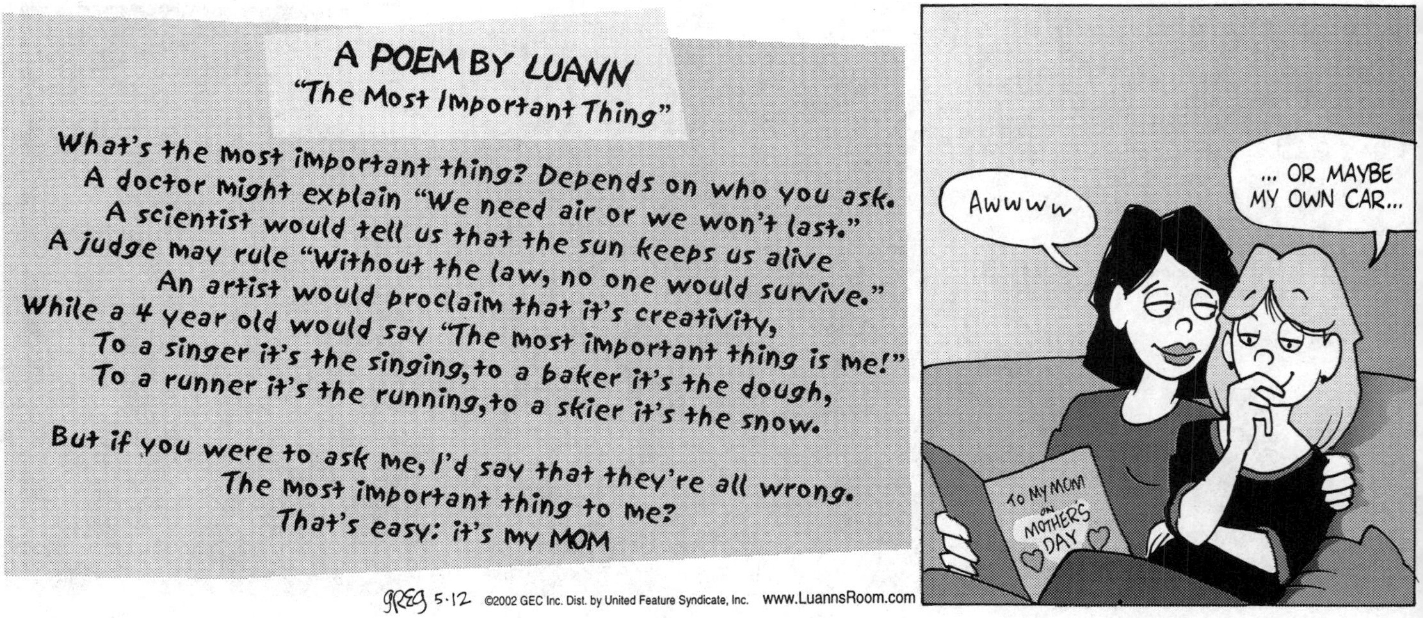
A POEM BY LUANN
"The Most Important Thing"
What's the most important thing? Depends on who you ask.
A doctor might explain "We need air or we won't last."
A scientist would tell us that the sun keeps us alive
A judge may rule "Without the law, no one would survive."
An artist would proclaim that it's creativity,
While a 4 year old would say "The most important thing is me!"
To a singer it's the singing, to a baker it's the dough,
To a runner it's the running, to a skier it's the snow.
But if you were to ask me, I'd say that they're all wrong.
The most important thing to me?
That's easy: it's my MOM
GREG 5·12
©2002 GEC Inc. Dist. by United Feature Syndicate, Inc.
www.LuannsRoom.com
AWWWW
... OR MAYBE MY OWN CAR...
TO MY MOM ON MOTHER'S DAY

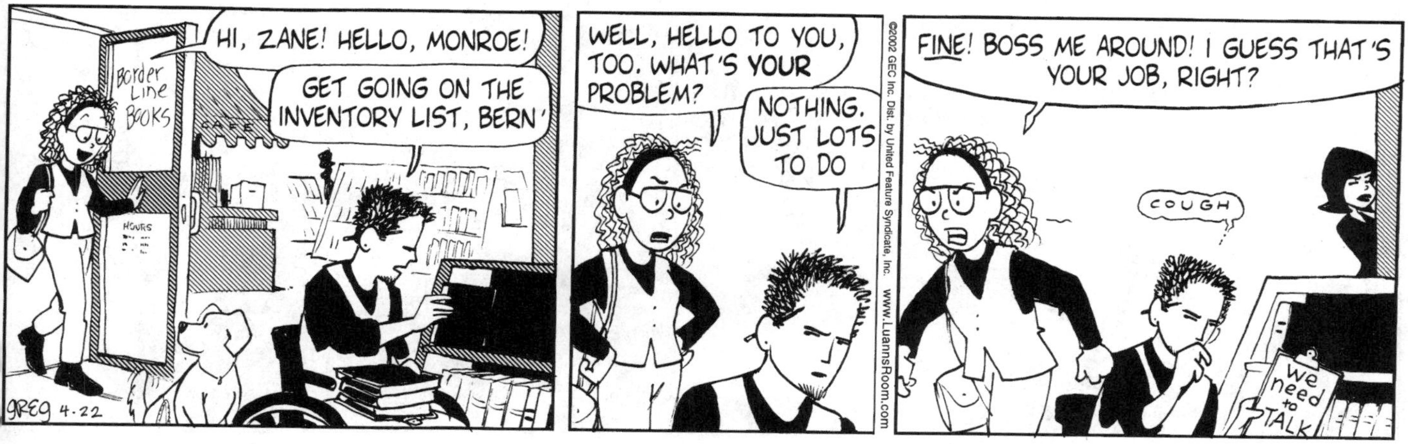
HI, ZANE! HELLO, MONROE!
GET GOING ON THE INVENTORY LIST, BERN'
Border Line Books
HOURS
WELL, HELLO TO YOU, TOO. WHAT'S **YOUR** PROBLEM?
NOTHING. JUST LOTS TO DO
FINE! BOSS ME AROUND! I GUESS THAT'S YOUR JOB, RIGHT?
COUGH
we need to TALK
GREG 4·22
©2002 GEC Inc. Dist. by United Feature Syndicate, Inc. www.LuannsRoom.com

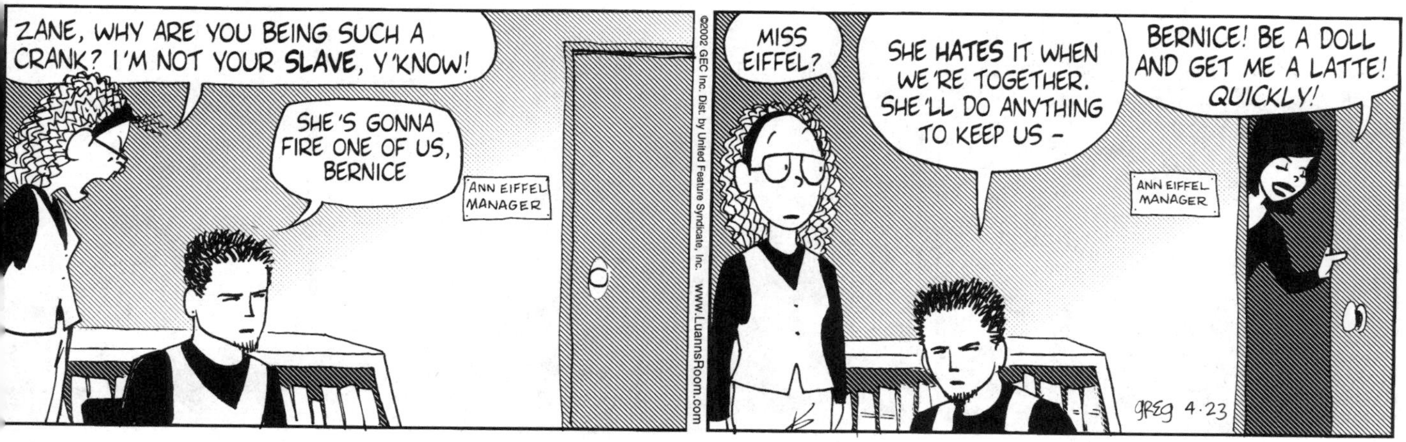
ZANE, WHY ARE YOU BEING SUCH A CRANK? I'M NOT YOUR **SLAVE**, Y'KNOW!
SHE'S GONNA FIRE ONE OF US, BERNICE
ANN EIFFEL MANAGER
MISS EIFFEL?
SHE **HATES** IT WHEN WE'RE TOGETHER. SHE'LL DO ANYTHING TO KEEP US –
BERNICE! BE A DOLL AND GET ME A LATTE! *QUICKLY!*
ANN EIFFEL MANAGER
GREG 4·23
©2002 GEC Inc. Dist. by United Feature Syndicate, Inc. www.LuannsRoom.com

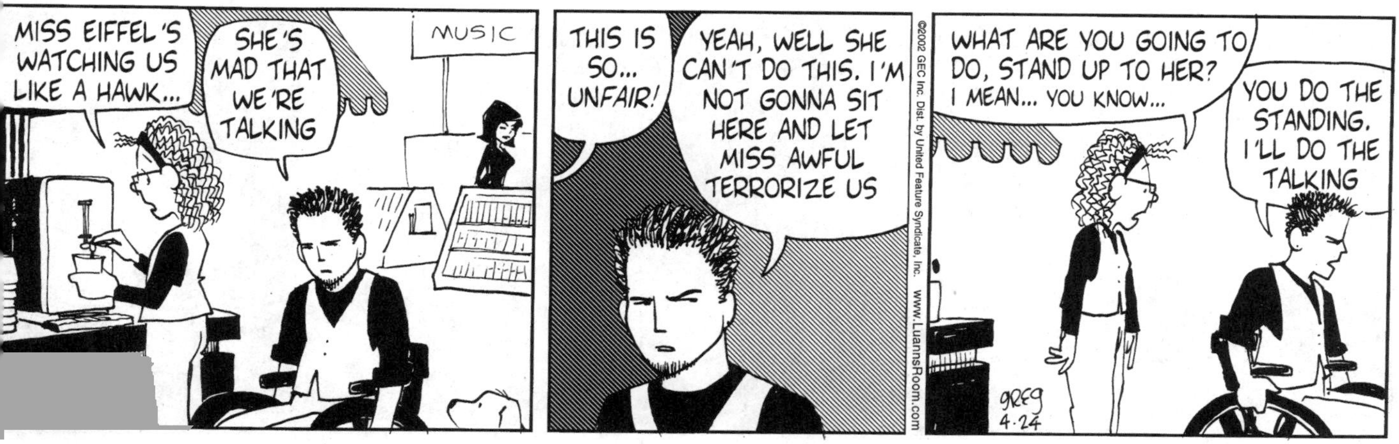
MISS EIFFEL'S WATCHING US LIKE A HAWK...
SHE'S MAD THAT WE'RE TALKING
MUSIC
THIS IS SO... UN*FAIR*!
YEAH, WELL SHE CAN'T DO THIS. I'M NOT GONNA SIT HERE AND LET MISS AWFUL TERRORIZE US
WHAT ARE YOU GOING TO DO, STAND UP TO HER? I MEAN... YOU KNOW...
YOU DO THE STANDING. I'LL DO THE TALKING
GREG 4·24
©2002 GEC Inc. Dist. by United Feature Syndicate, Inc. www.LuannsRoom.com

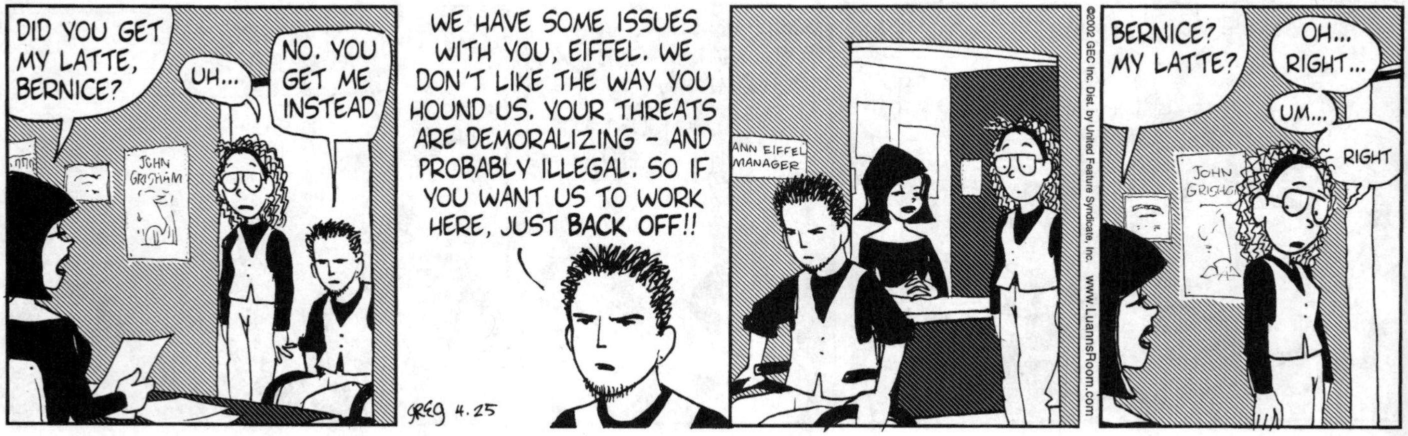
DID YOU GET MY LATTE, BERNICE?
UH...
NO. YOU GET ME INSTEAD
JOHN GRISHAM
GREG 4.25
WE HAVE SOME ISSUES WITH YOU, EIFFEL. WE DON'T LIKE THE WAY YOU HOUND US. YOUR THREATS ARE DEMORALIZING – AND PROBABLY ILLEGAL. SO IF YOU WANT US TO WORK HERE, JUST BACK OFF!!
ANN EIFFEL MANAGER
©2002 GEC Inc. Dist. by United Feature Syndicate, Inc. www.LuannsRoom.com
BERNICE? MY LATTE?
OH... RIGHT...
UM...
RIGHT

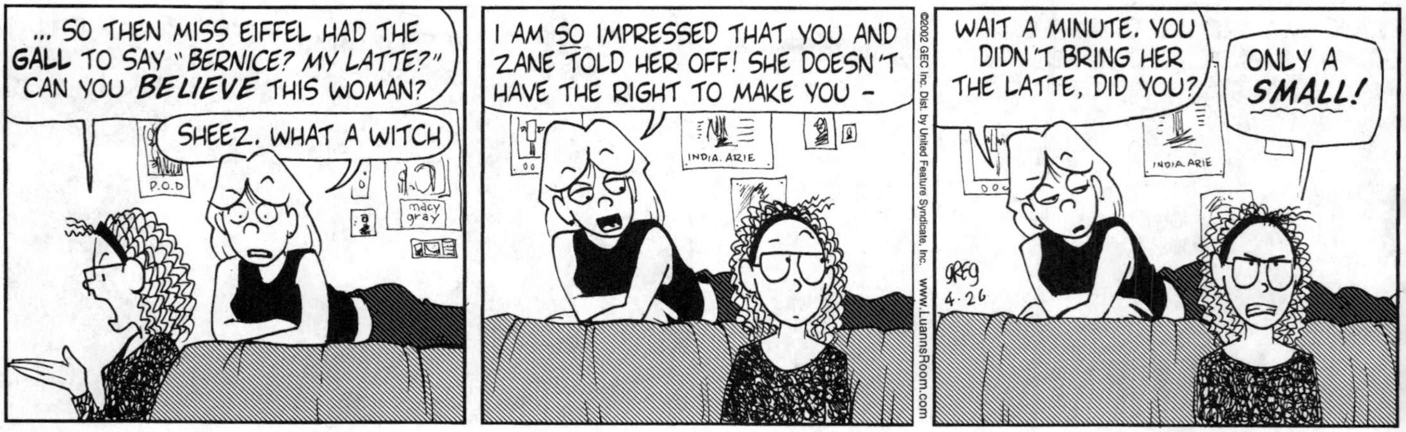
... SO THEN MISS EIFFEL HAD THE GALL TO SAY "BERNICE? MY LATTE?" CAN YOU BELIEVE THIS WOMAN?
SHEEZ. WHAT A WITCH
P.O.D
macy gray
I AM SO IMPRESSED THAT YOU AND ZANE TOLD HER OFF! SHE DOESN'T HAVE THE RIGHT TO MAKE YOU –
INDIA. ARIE
©2002 GEC Inc. Dist. by United Feature Syndicate, Inc. www.LuannsRoom.com
WAIT A MINUTE. YOU DIDN'T BRING HER THE LATTE, DID YOU?
ONLY A SMALL!
INDIA ARIE
GREG 4.26

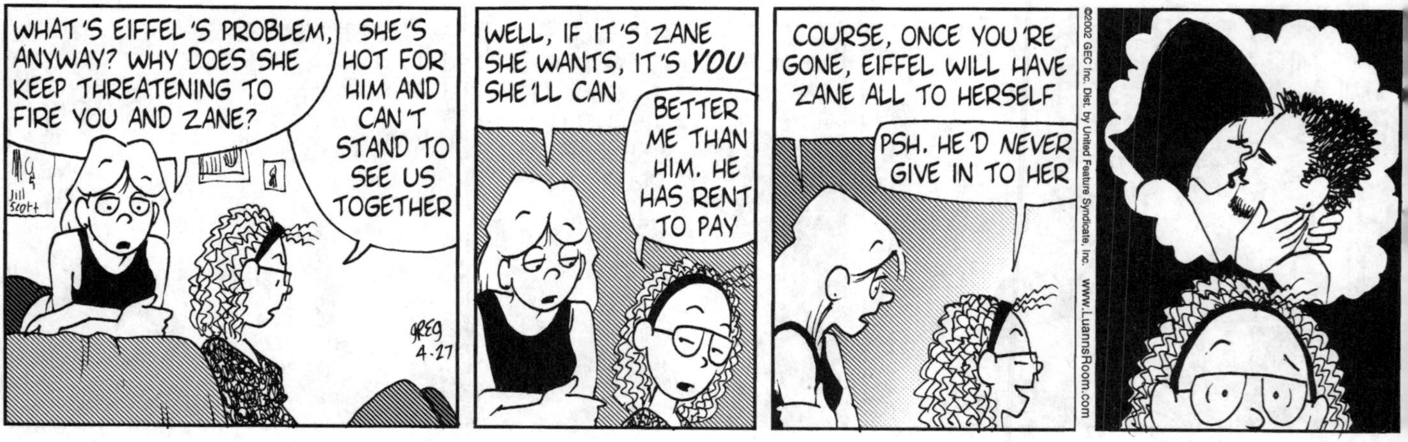
WHAT'S EIFFEL'S PROBLEM, ANYWAY? WHY DOES SHE KEEP THREATENING TO FIRE YOU AND ZANE?
SHE'S HOT FOR HIM AND CAN'T STAND TO SEE US TOGETHER
Jill Scott
GREG 4.27
WELL, IF IT'S ZANE SHE WANTS, IT'S YOU SHE'LL CAN
BETTER ME THAN HIM. HE HAS RENT TO PAY
COURSE, ONCE YOU'RE GONE, EIFFEL WILL HAVE ZANE ALL TO HERSELF
PSH. HE'D NEVER GIVE IN TO HER
©2002 GEC Inc. Dist. by United Feature Syndicate, Inc. www.LuannsRoom.com

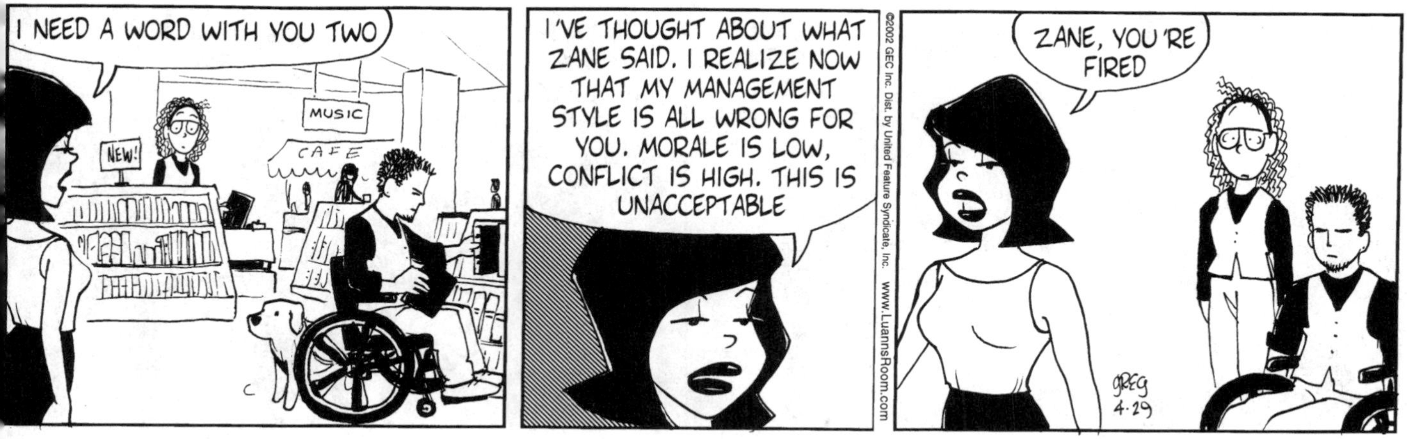

I NEED A WORD WITH YOU TWO
NEW!
MUSIC
CAFE
I'VE THOUGHT ABOUT WHAT ZANE SAID. I REALIZE NOW THAT MY MANAGEMENT STYLE IS ALL WRONG FOR YOU. MORALE IS LOW, CONFLICT IS HIGH. THIS IS UNACCEPTABLE
©2002 GEC Inc. Dist. by United Feature Syndicate, Inc. www.LuannsRoom.com
ZANE, YOU'RE FIRED
GREG 4·29

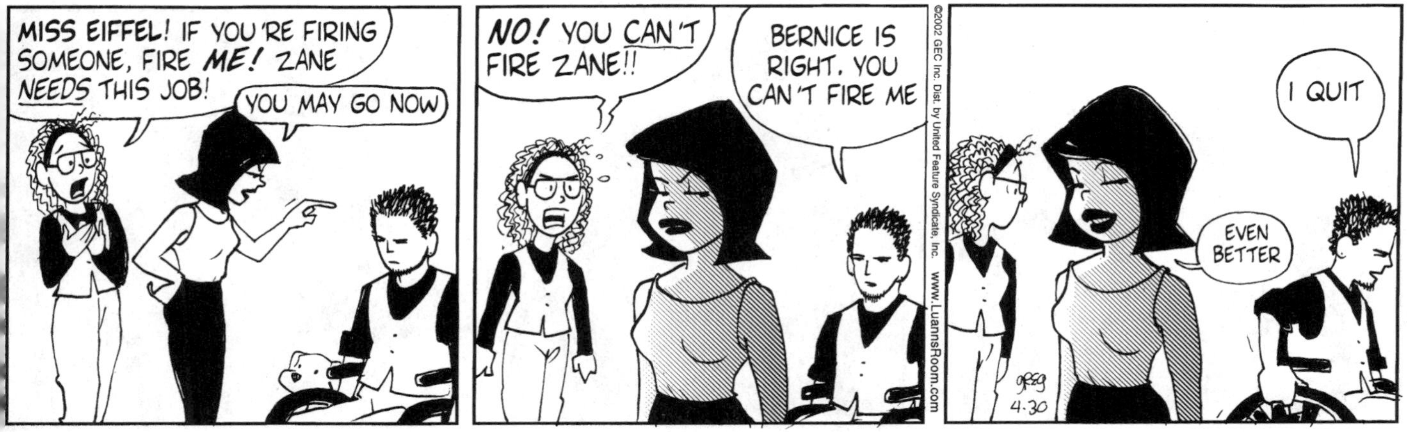

MISS EIFFEL! IF YOU'RE FIRING SOMEONE, FIRE ME! ZANE NEEDS THIS JOB!
YOU MAY GO NOW
NO! YOU CAN'T FIRE ZANE!!
BERNICE IS RIGHT. YOU CAN'T FIRE ME
©2002 GEC Inc. Dist. by United Feature Syndicate, Inc. www.LuannsRoom.com
I QUIT
EVEN BETTER
GREG 4·30

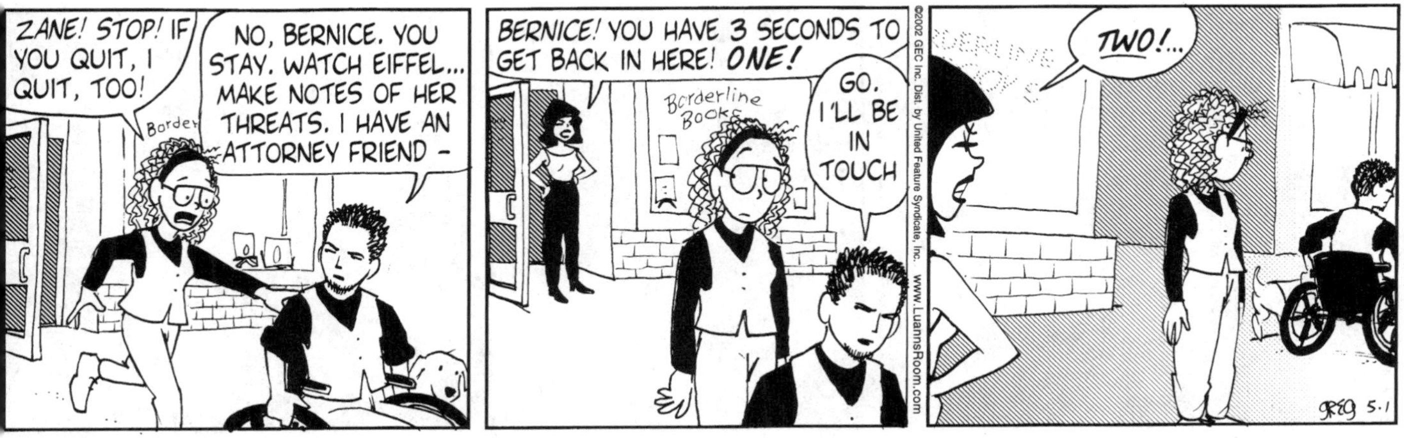

ZANE! STOP! IF YOU QUIT, I QUIT, TOO!
NO, BERNICE. YOU STAY. WATCH EIFFEL... MAKE NOTES OF HER THREATS. I HAVE AN ATTORNEY FRIEND –
Border
BERNICE! YOU HAVE 3 SECONDS TO GET BACK IN HERE! ONE!
GO. I'LL BE IN TOUCH
Borderline Books
©2002 GEC Inc. Dist. by United Feature Syndicate, Inc. www.LuannsRoom.com
TWO!...
GREG 5·1

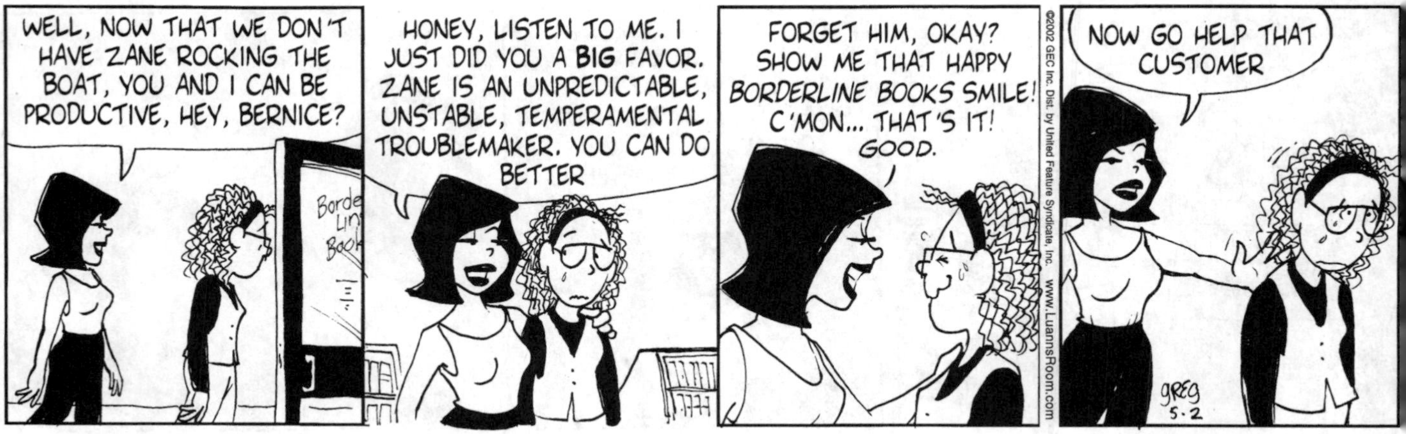
WELL, NOW THAT WE DON'T HAVE ZANE ROCKING THE BOAT, YOU AND I CAN BE PRODUCTIVE, HEY, BERNICE?
HONEY, LISTEN TO ME. I JUST DID YOU A **BIG** FAVOR. ZANE IS AN UNPREDICTABLE, UNSTABLE, TEMPERAMENTAL TROUBLEMAKER. YOU CAN DO BETTER
FORGET HIM, OKAY? SHOW ME THAT HAPPY *BORDERLINE BOOKS* SMILE! C'MON... THAT'S IT! *GOOD.*
©2002 GEC Inc. Dist. by United Feature Syndicate, Inc. www.LuannsRoom.com
NOW GO HELP THAT CUSTOMER
GREG 5·2

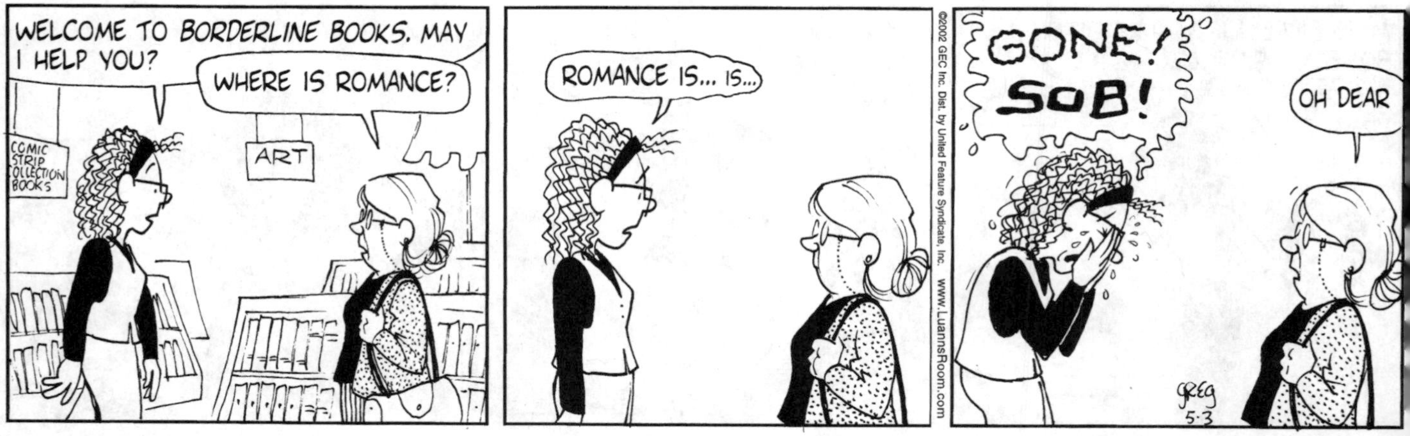
WELCOME TO *BORDERLINE BOOKS.* MAY I HELP YOU?
WHERE IS ROMANCE?
COMIC STRIP COLLECTION BOOKS
ART
ROMANCE IS... IS...
©2002 GEC Inc. Dist. by United Feature Syndicate, Inc. www.LuannsRoom.com
GONE! SOB!
OH DEAR
GREG 5·3

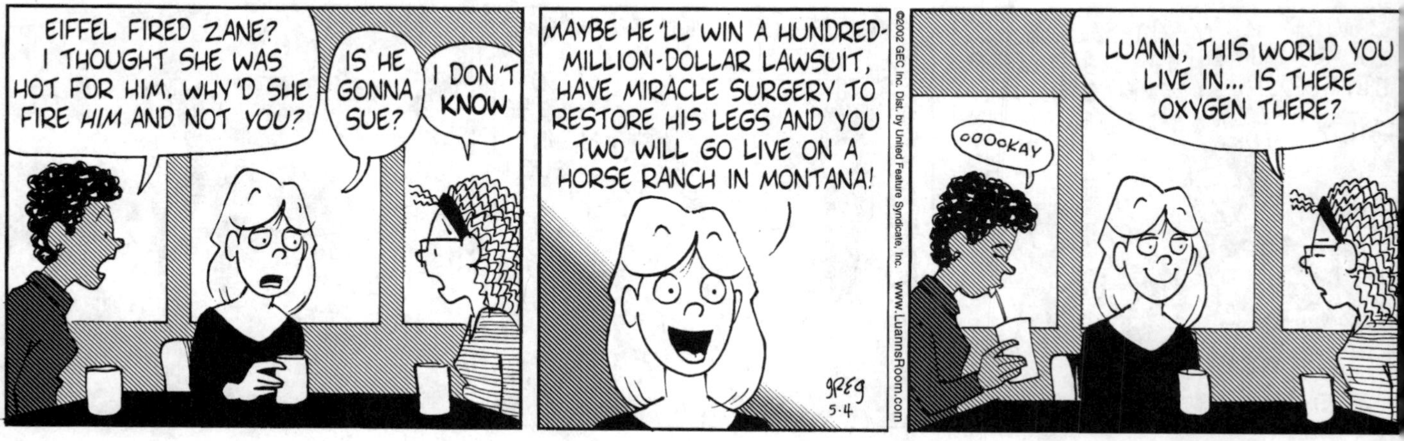
EIFFEL FIRED ZANE? I THOUGHT SHE WAS HOT FOR HIM. WHY'D SHE FIRE *HIM* AND NOT *YOU?*
IS HE GONNA SUE?
I DON'T **KNOW**
MAYBE HE'LL WIN A HUNDRED-MILLION-DOLLAR LAWSUIT, HAVE MIRACLE SURGERY TO RESTORE HIS LEGS AND YOU TWO WILL GO LIVE ON A HORSE RANCH IN MONTANA!
GREG 5·4
©2002 GEC Inc. Dist. by United Feature Syndicate, Inc. www.LuannsRoom.com
OOOOKAY
LUANN, THIS WORLD YOU LIVE IN... IS THERE OXYGEN THERE?

YOU KNOW WHAT THE BEST WORD IN THE ENGLISH LANGUAGE IS?
"RINNNNG"?
"SUMMER." IT MEANS NO MORE SCHOOL, NO MORE TESTS, NO MORE ALARM CLOCKS, SCHEDULES, OR STINKY GYM CLOTHES... JUST LONG, LAZY, DO-NOTHING DAYS. EVEN THE WORD "SUMMER" SOUNDS SOFT AND WARM, LIKE A ROMANTIC BEACH...
GREG 5·19
www.LuannsRoom.com
©2002 GEC Inc. Dist. by United Feature Syndicate, Inc.
CAN YOU THINK OF A WORD THAT CONJURES UP A MORE SENSUOUS, EXCITING FEELING?
"THONG"

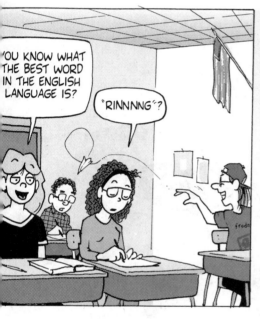

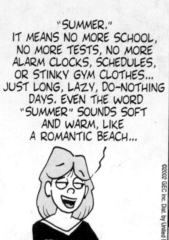

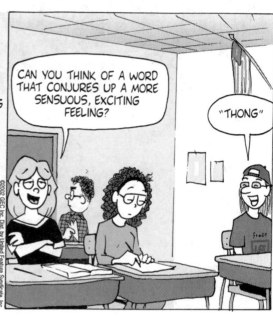

DAD, I'VE DECIDED I DON'T NEED A CAR RIGHT AWAY
OH?
©2002 GEC Inc. Dist. by United Feature Syndicate, Inc. www.LuannsRoom.com
GREG 5·26
I NEED A TRUCK
OH...

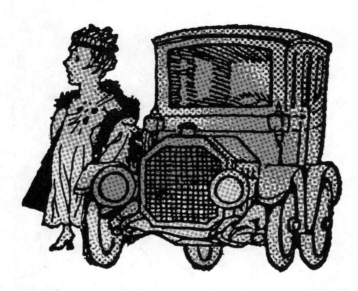

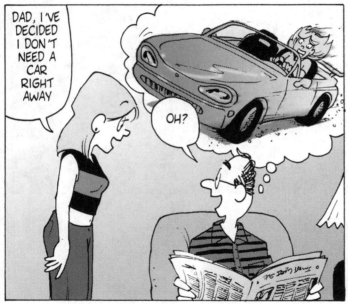

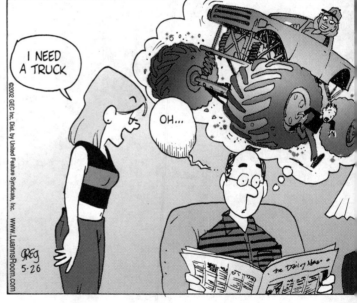

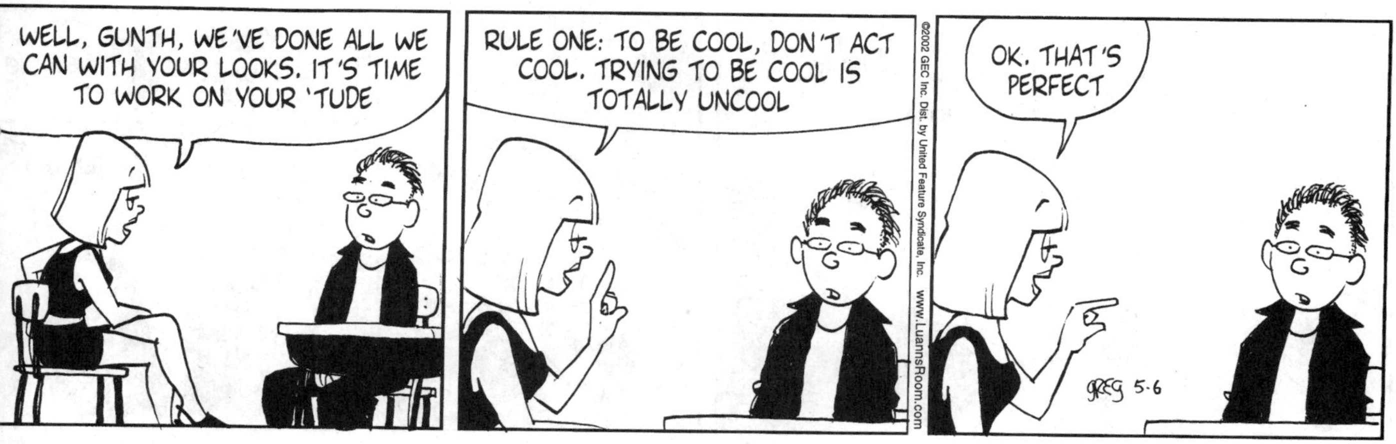
WELL, GUNTH, WE'VE DONE ALL WE CAN WITH YOUR LOOKS. IT'S TIME TO WORK ON YOUR 'TUDE
RULE ONE: TO BE COOL, DON'T ACT COOL. TRYING TO BE COOL IS TOTALLY UNCOOL
OK. THAT'S PERFECT
GREG 5·6
©2002 GEC Inc. Dist. by United Feature Syndicate, Inc. www.LuannsRoom.com

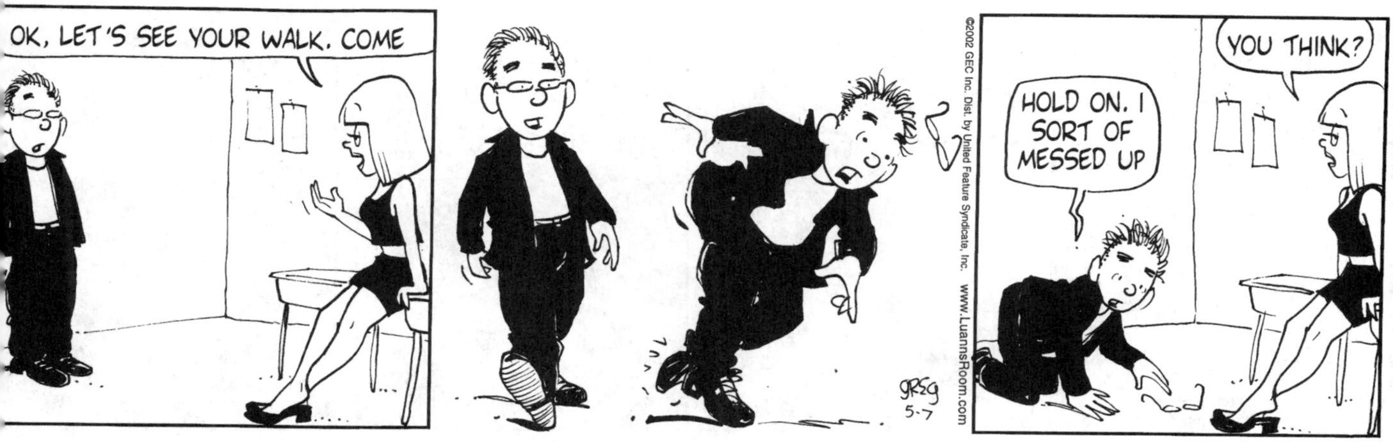
OK, LET'S SEE YOUR WALK. COME
HOLD ON. I SORT OF MESSED UP
YOU THINK?
GREG 5·7
©2002 GEC Inc. Dist. by United Feature Syndicate, Inc. www.LuannsRoom.com

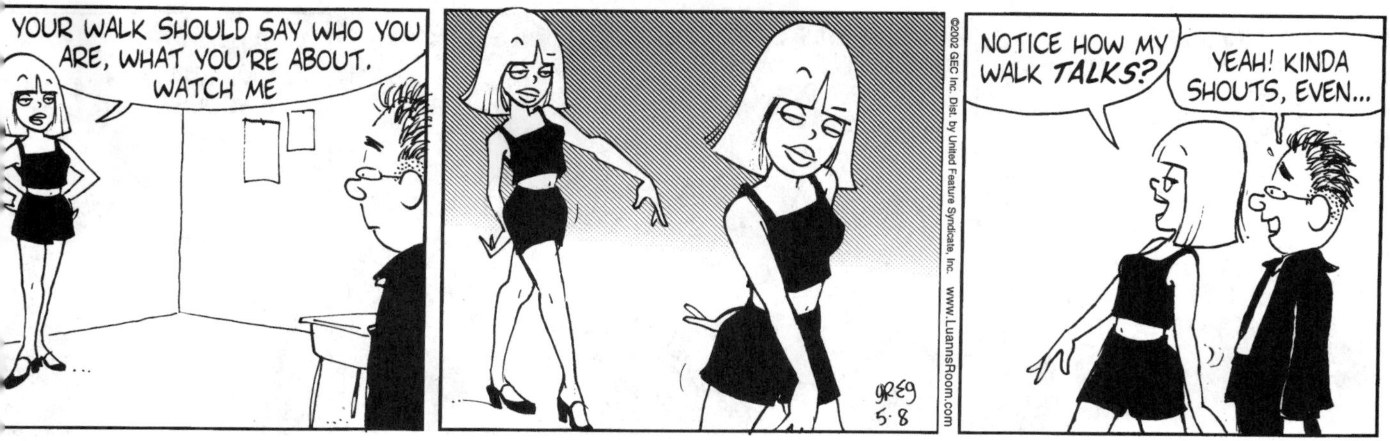
YOUR WALK SHOULD SAY WHO YOU ARE, WHAT YOU'RE ABOUT. WATCH ME
NOTICE HOW MY WALK ***TALKS?***
YEAH! KINDA SHOUTS, EVEN...
GREG 5·8
©2002 GEC Inc. Dist. by United Feature Syndicate, Inc. www.LuannsRoom.com

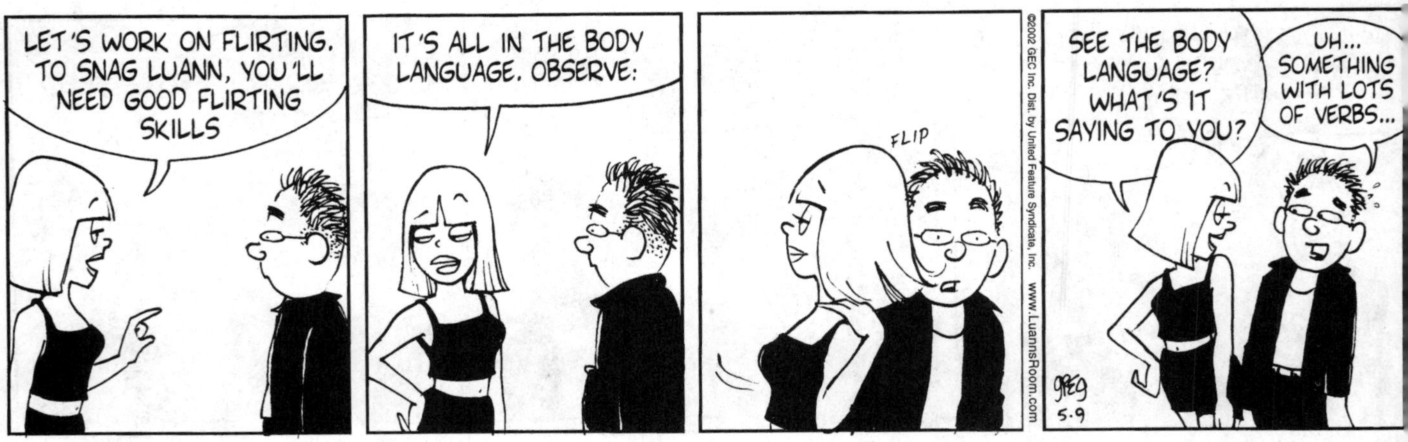
LET'S WORK ON FLIRTING. TO SNAG LUANN, YOU'LL NEED GOOD FLIRTING SKILLS
IT'S ALL IN THE BODY LANGUAGE. OBSERVE:
FLIP
©2002 GEC Inc. Dist. by United Feature Syndicate, Inc. www.LuannsRoom.com
SEE THE BODY LANGUAGE? WHAT'S IT SAYING TO YOU?
UH... SOMETHING WITH LOTS OF VERBS...
GREG 5-9

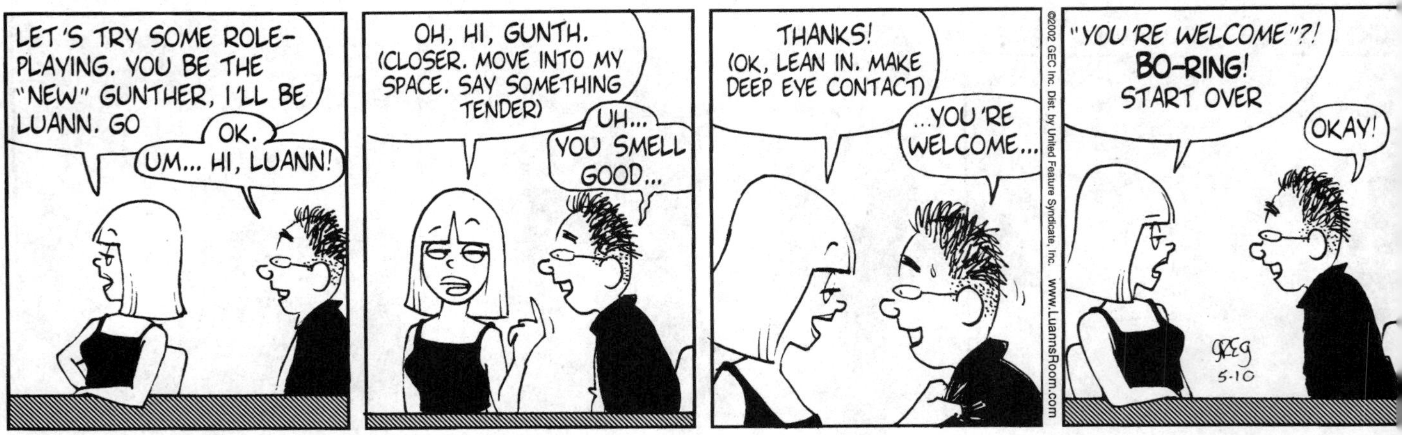
LET'S TRY SOME ROLE-PLAYING. YOU BE THE "NEW" GUNTHER, I'LL BE LUANN. GO
OK.
UM... HI, LUANN!
OH, HI, GUNTH. (CLOSER. MOVE INTO MY SPACE. SAY SOMETHING TENDER)
UH... YOU SMELL GOOD...
THANKS! (OK, LEAN IN. MAKE DEEP EYE CONTACT)
...YOU'RE WELCOME...
©2002 GEC Inc. Dist. by United Feature Syndicate, Inc. www.LuannsRoom.com
"YOU'RE WELCOME"?! BO-RING! START OVER
OKAY!
GREG 5-10

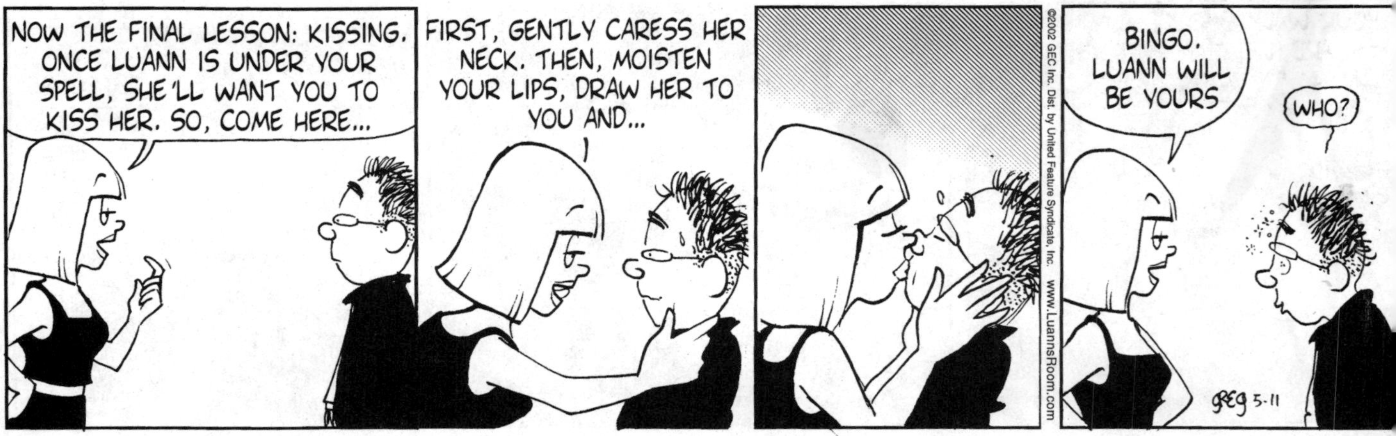
NOW THE FINAL LESSON: KISSING. ONCE LUANN IS UNDER YOUR SPELL, SHE'LL WANT YOU TO KISS HER. SO, COME HERE...
FIRST, GENTLY CARESS HER NECK. THEN, MOISTEN YOUR LIPS, DRAW HER TO YOU AND...
©2002 GEC Inc. Dist. by United Feature Syndicate, Inc. www.LuannsRoom.com
BINGO. LUANN WILL BE YOURS
WHO?
GREG 5-11

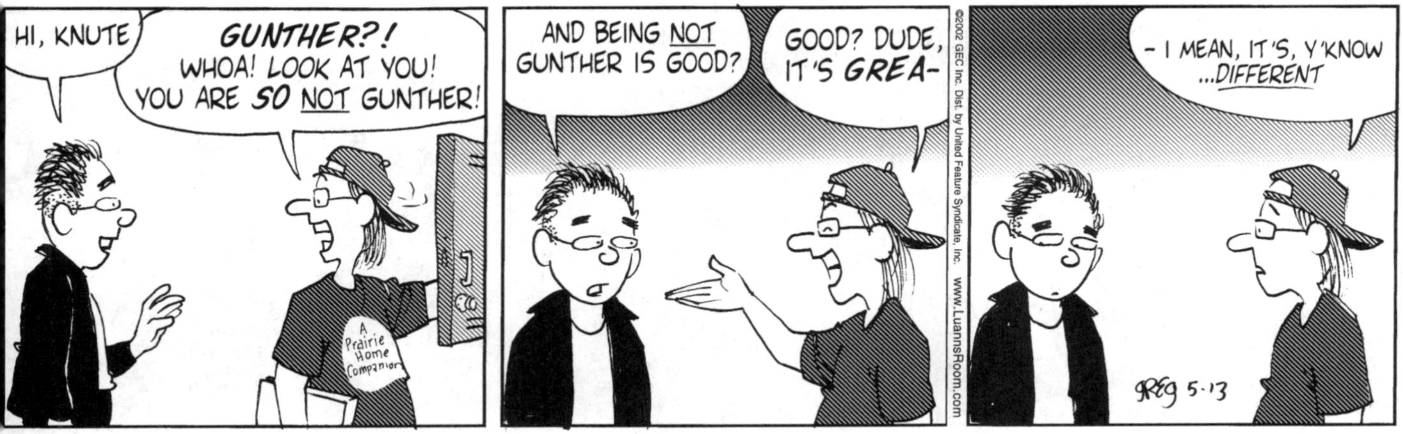
HI, KNUTE
GUNTHER?! WHOA! LOOK AT YOU! YOU ARE SO NOT GUNTHER!
A Prairie Home Companion
AND BEING NOT GUNTHER IS GOOD?
GOOD? DUDE, IT'S GREA-
©2002 GEC Inc. Dist. by United Feature Syndicate, Inc. www.LuannsRoom.com
– I MEAN, IT'S, Y'KNOW ...DIFFERENT
GREG 5-13

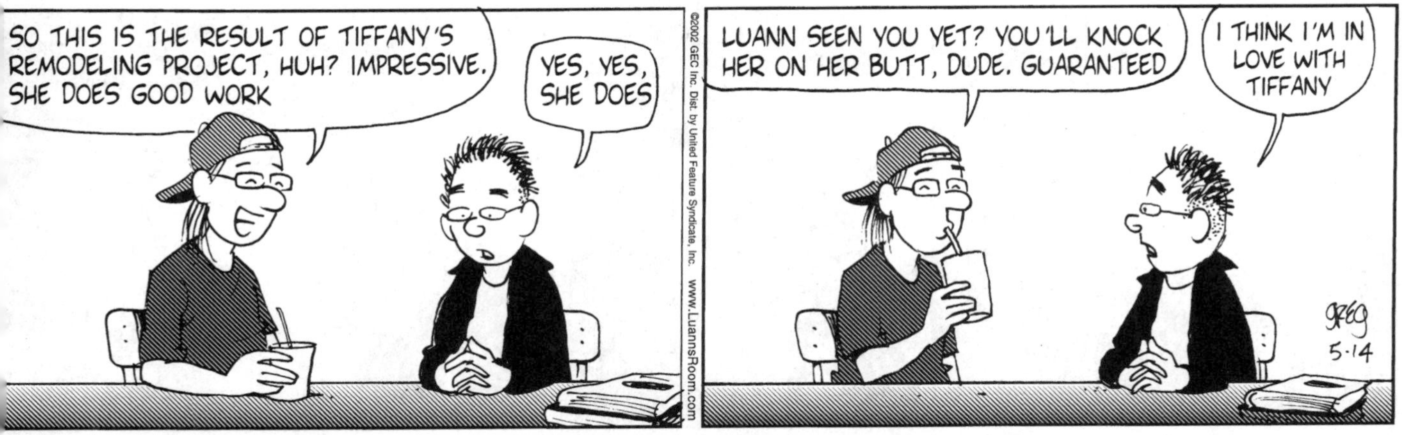
SO THIS IS THE RESULT OF TIFFANY'S REMODELING PROJECT, HUH? IMPRESSIVE. SHE DOES GOOD WORK
YES, YES, SHE DOES
©2002 GEC Inc. Dist. by United Feature Syndicate, Inc. www.LuannsRoom.com
LUANN SEEN YOU YET? YOU'LL KNOCK HER ON HER BUTT, DUDE. GUARANTEED
I THINK I'M IN LOVE WITH TIFFANY
GREG 5-14

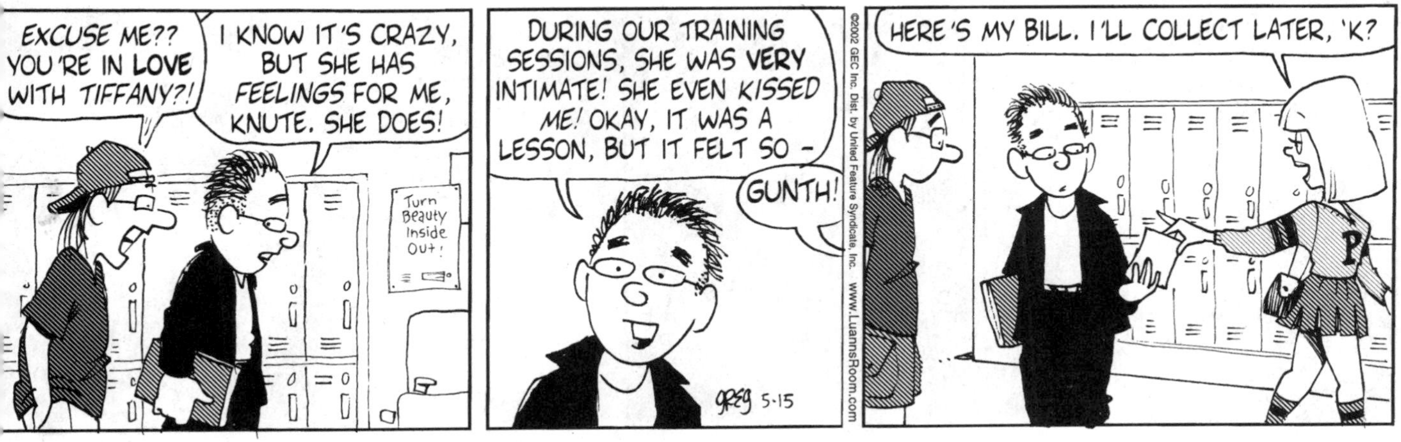
EXCUSE ME?? YOU'RE IN LOVE WITH TIFFANY?!
I KNOW IT'S CRAZY, BUT SHE HAS FEELINGS FOR ME, KNUTE. SHE DOES!
Turn Beauty Inside Out!
DURING OUR TRAINING SESSIONS, SHE WAS VERY INTIMATE! SHE EVEN KISSED ME! OKAY, IT WAS A LESSON, BUT IT FELT SO –
GUNTH!
GREG 5-15
©2002 GEC Inc. Dist. by United Feature Syndicate, Inc. www.LuannsRoom.com
HERE'S MY BILL. I'LL COLLECT LATER, 'K?

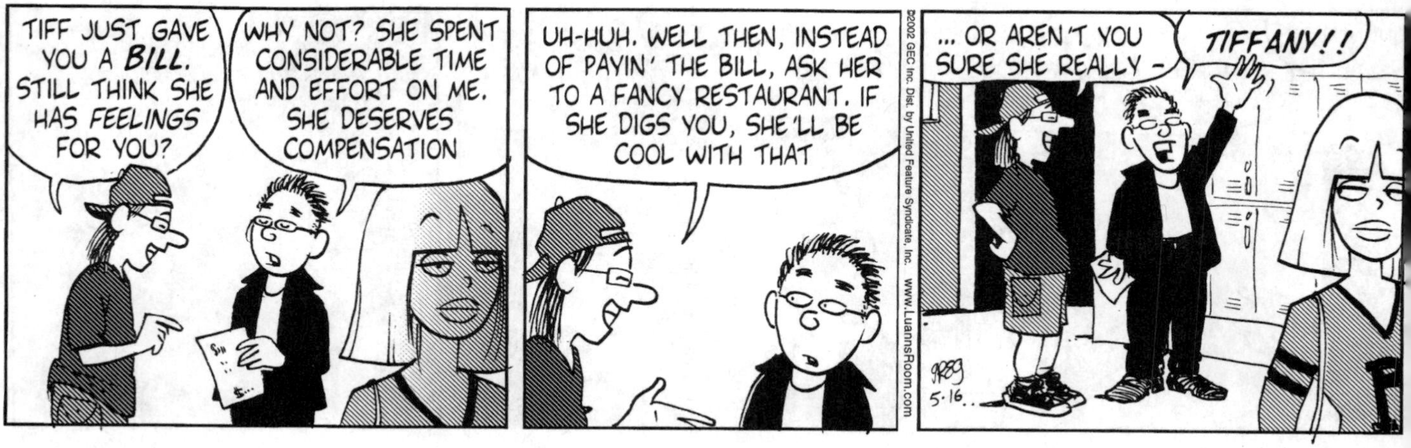
TIFF JUST GAVE YOU A BILL. STILL THINK SHE HAS FEELINGS FOR YOU?
WHY NOT? SHE SPENT CONSIDERABLE TIME AND EFFORT ON ME. SHE DESERVES COMPENSATION
UH-HUH. WELL THEN, INSTEAD OF PAYIN' THE BILL, ASK HER TO A FANCY RESTAURANT. IF SHE DIGS YOU, SHE'LL BE COOL WITH THAT
©2002 GEC Inc. Dist. by United Feature Syndicate, Inc. www.LuannsRoom.com
... OR AREN'T YOU SURE SHE REALLY –
TIFFANY!!
GREG 5·16

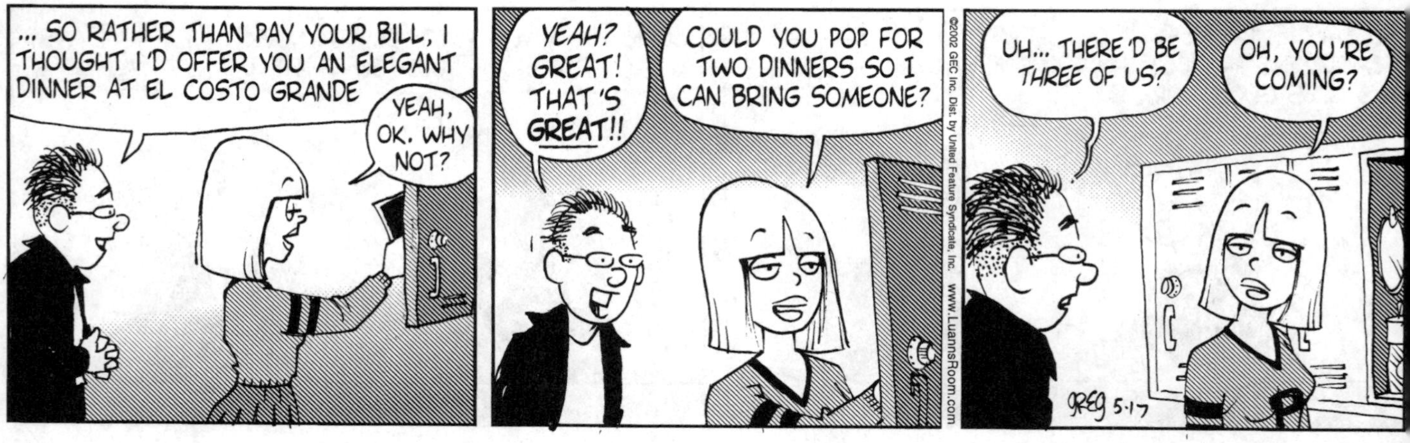
... SO RATHER THAN PAY YOUR BILL, I THOUGHT I'D OFFER YOU AN ELEGANT DINNER AT EL COSTO GRANDE
YEAH, OK. WHY NOT?
YEAH? GREAT! THAT'S GREAT!!
COULD YOU POP FOR TWO DINNERS SO I CAN BRING SOMEONE?
©2002 GEC Inc. Dist. by United Feature Syndicate, Inc. www.LuannsRoom.com
UH... THERE'D BE THREE OF US?
OH, YOU'RE COMING?
GREG 5·17

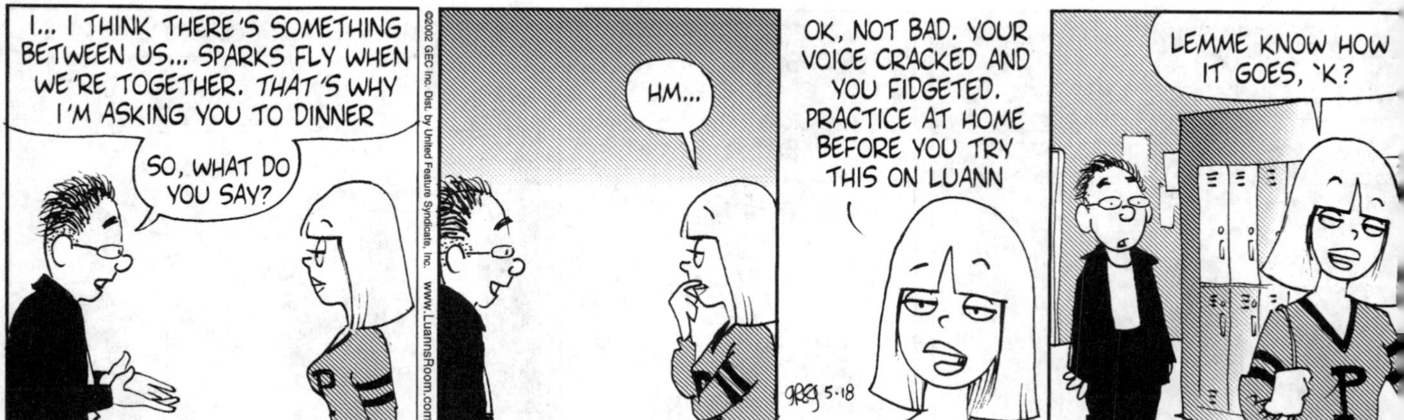
I... I THINK THERE'S SOMETHING BETWEEN US... SPARKS FLY WHEN WE'RE TOGETHER. THAT'S WHY I'M ASKING YOU TO DINNER
SO, WHAT DO YOU SAY?
©2002 GEC Inc. Dist. by United Feature Syndicate, Inc. www.LuannsRoom.com
HM...
OK, NOT BAD. YOUR VOICE CRACKED AND YOU FIDGETED. PRACTICE AT HOME BEFORE YOU TRY THIS ON LUANN
GREG 5·18
LEMME KNOW HOW IT GOES, 'K?

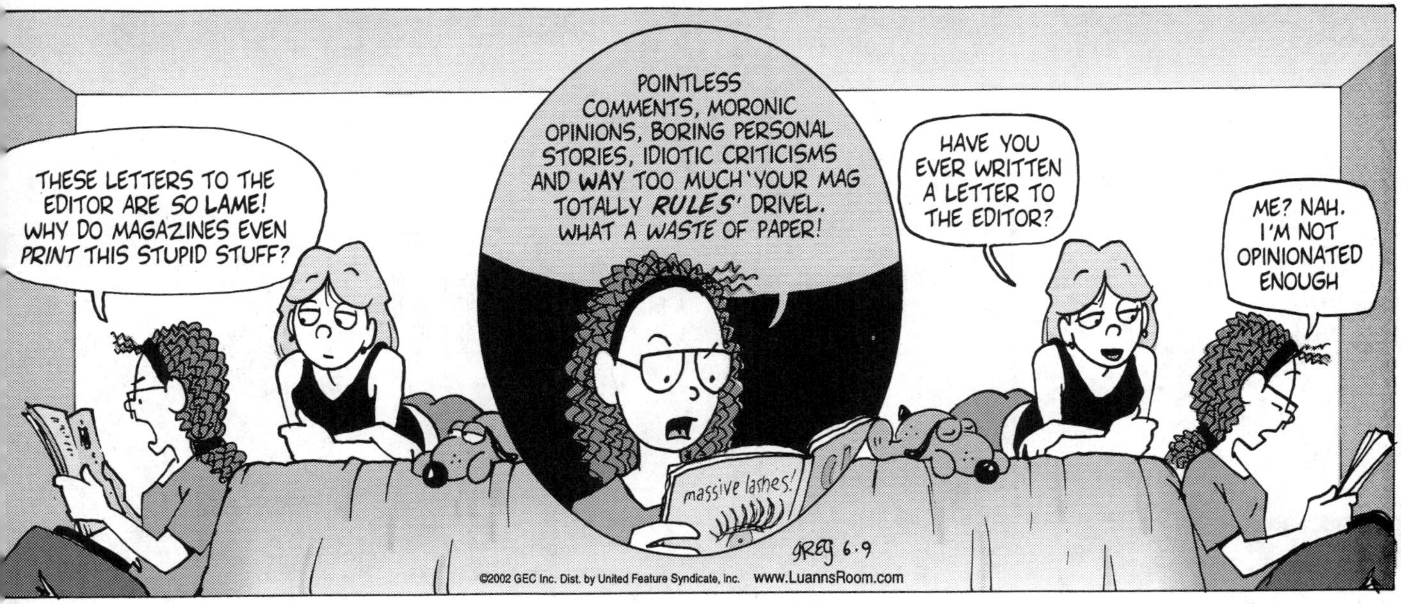
THESE LETTERS TO THE EDITOR ARE SO LAME! WHY DO MAGAZINES EVEN PRINT THIS STUPID STUFF?
POINTLESS COMMENTS, MORONIC OPINIONS, BORING PERSONAL STORIES, IDIOTIC CRITICISMS AND WAY TOO MUCH 'YOUR MAG TOTALLY RULES' DRIVEL. WHAT A WASTE OF PAPER!
massive lashes!
HAVE YOU EVER WRITTEN A LETTER TO THE EDITOR?
ME? NAH. I'M NOT OPINIONATED ENOUGH
GREG 6.9
©2002 GEC Inc. Dist. by United Feature Syndicate, Inc. www.LuannsRoom.com

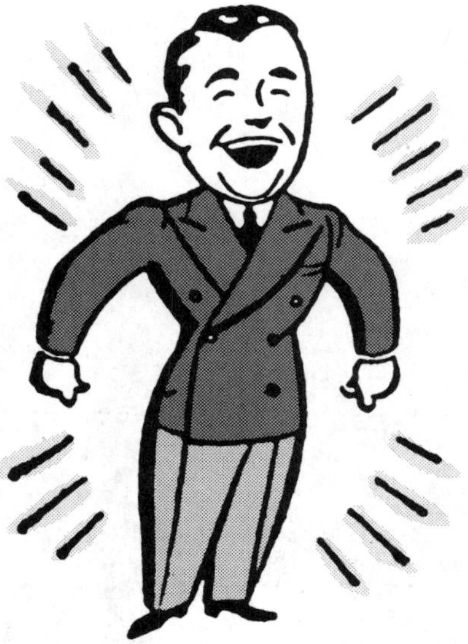

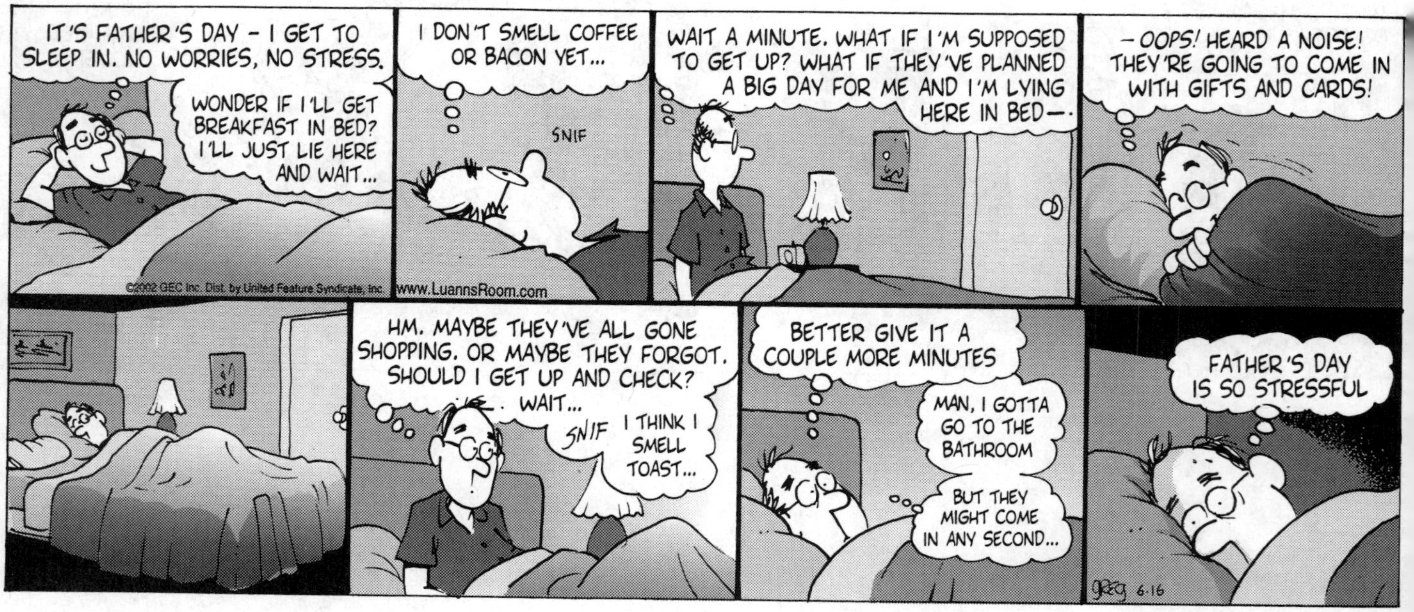

IT'S FATHER'S DAY - I GET TO SLEEP IN. NO WORRIES, NO STRESS.
WONDER IF I'LL GET BREAKFAST IN BED? I'LL JUST LIE HERE AND WAIT...
I DON'T SMELL COFFEE OR BACON YET...
SNIF
WAIT A MINUTE. WHAT IF I'M SUPPOSED TO GET UP? WHAT IF THEY'VE PLANNED A BIG DAY FOR ME AND I'M LYING HERE IN BED—.
—OOPS! HEARD A NOISE! THEY'RE GOING TO COME IN WITH GIFTS AND CARDS!
©2002 GEC Inc. Dist. by United Feature Syndicate, Inc.
www.LuannsRoom.com
HM. MAYBE THEY'VE ALL GONE SHOPPING. OR MAYBE THEY FORGOT. SHOULD I GET UP AND CHECK? WAIT...
SNIF
I THINK I SMELL TOAST...
BETTER GIVE IT A COUPLE MORE MINUTES
MAN, I GOTTA GO TO THE BATHROOM
BUT THEY MIGHT COME IN ANY SECOND...
FATHER'S DAY IS SO STRESSFUL
greg 6-16

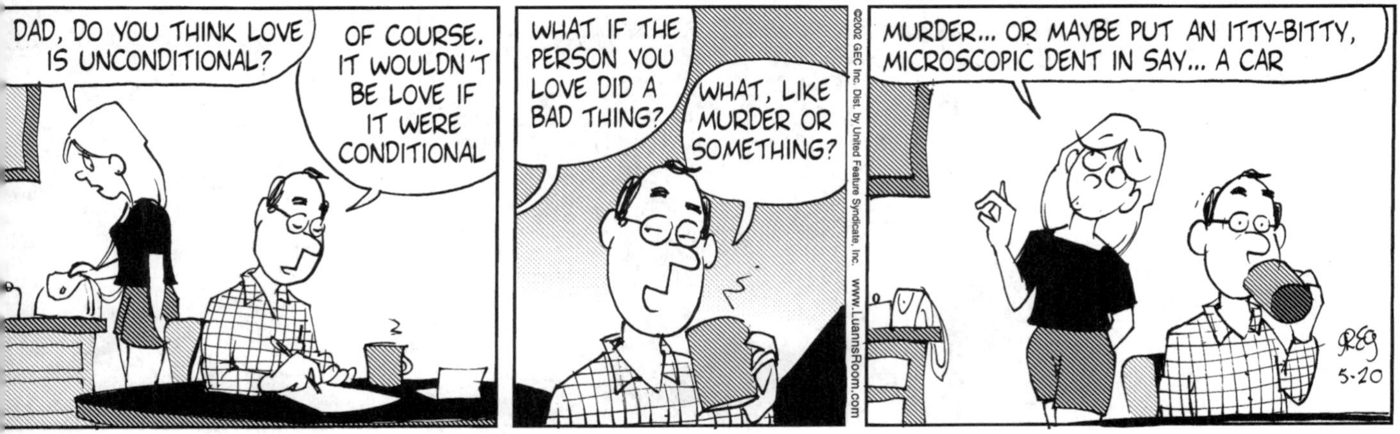
DAD, DO YOU THINK LOVE IS UNCONDITIONAL?
OF COURSE. IT WOULDN'T BE LOVE IF IT WERE CONDITIONAL
WHAT IF THE PERSON YOU LOVE DID A BAD THING?
WHAT, LIKE MURDER OR SOMETHING?
©2002 GEC Inc. Dist. by United Feature Syndicate, Inc. www.LuannsRoom.com
MURDER... OR MAYBE PUT AN ITTY-BITTY, MICROSCOPIC DENT IN SAY... A CAR
GREG 5-20

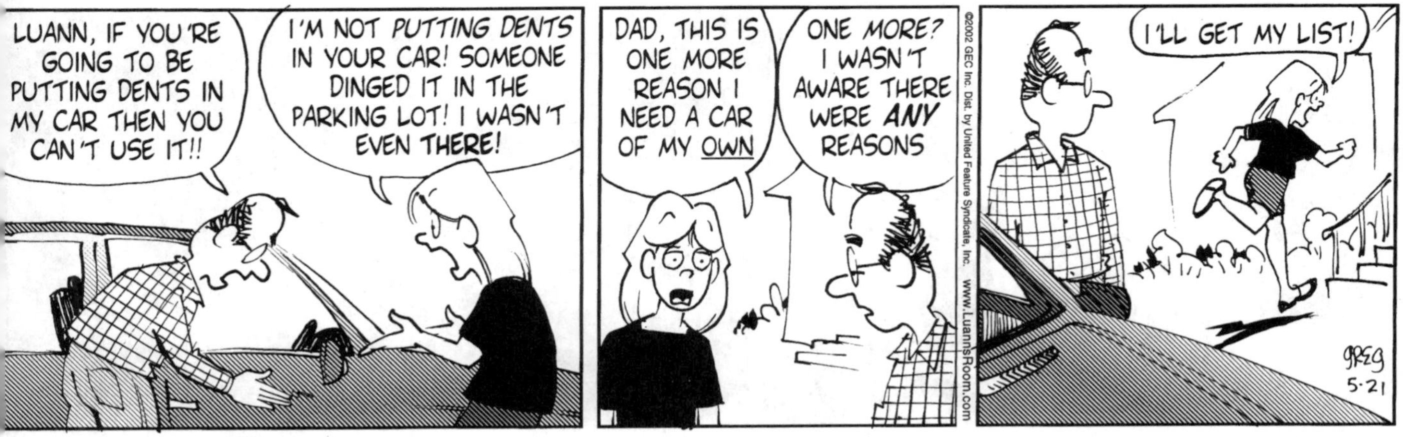
LUANN, IF YOU'RE GOING TO BE PUTTING DENTS IN MY CAR THEN YOU CAN'T USE IT!!
I'M NOT *PUTTING DENTS* IN YOUR CAR! SOMEONE DINGED IT IN THE PARKING LOT! I WASN'T EVEN **THERE!**
DAD, THIS IS ONE MORE REASON I NEED A CAR OF MY OWN
ONE *MORE?* I WASN'T AWARE THERE WERE ***ANY*** REASONS
©2002 GEC Inc. Dist. by United Feature Syndicate, Inc. www.LuannsRoom.com
I'LL GET MY LIST!
GREG 5-21

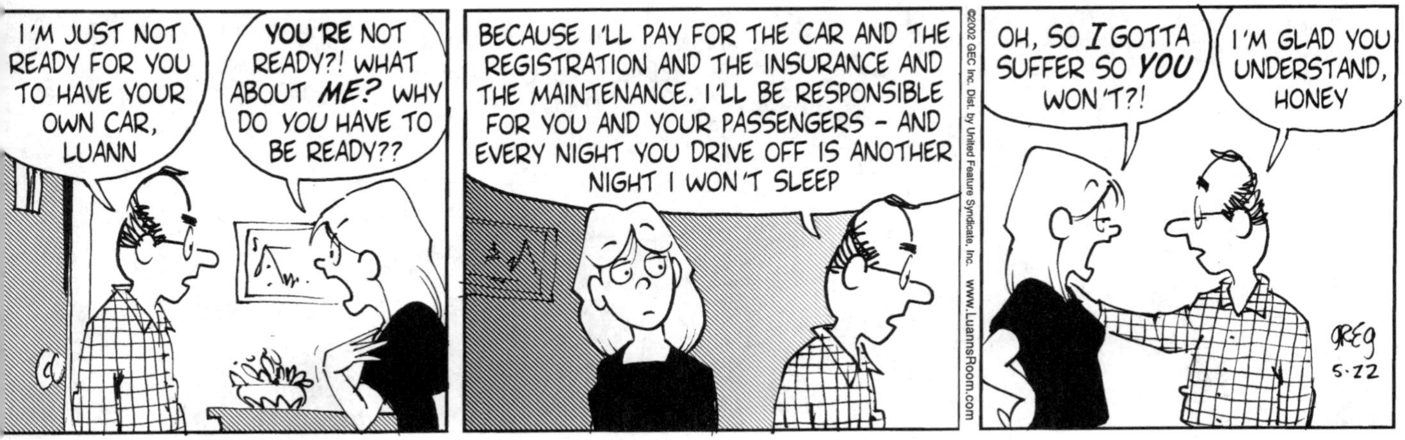
I'M JUST NOT READY FOR YOU TO HAVE YOUR OWN CAR, LUANN
YOU'RE NOT READY?! WHAT ABOUT ***ME?*** WHY DO *YOU* HAVE TO BE READY??
BECAUSE I'LL PAY FOR THE CAR AND THE REGISTRATION AND THE INSURANCE AND THE MAINTENANCE. I'LL BE RESPONSIBLE FOR YOU AND YOUR PASSENGERS – AND EVERY NIGHT YOU DRIVE OFF IS ANOTHER NIGHT I WON'T SLEEP
©2002 GEC Inc. Dist. by United Feature Syndicate, Inc. www.LuannsRoom.com
OH, SO ***I*** GOTTA SUFFER SO ***YOU*** WON'T?!
I'M GLAD YOU UNDERSTAND, HONEY
GREG 5-22

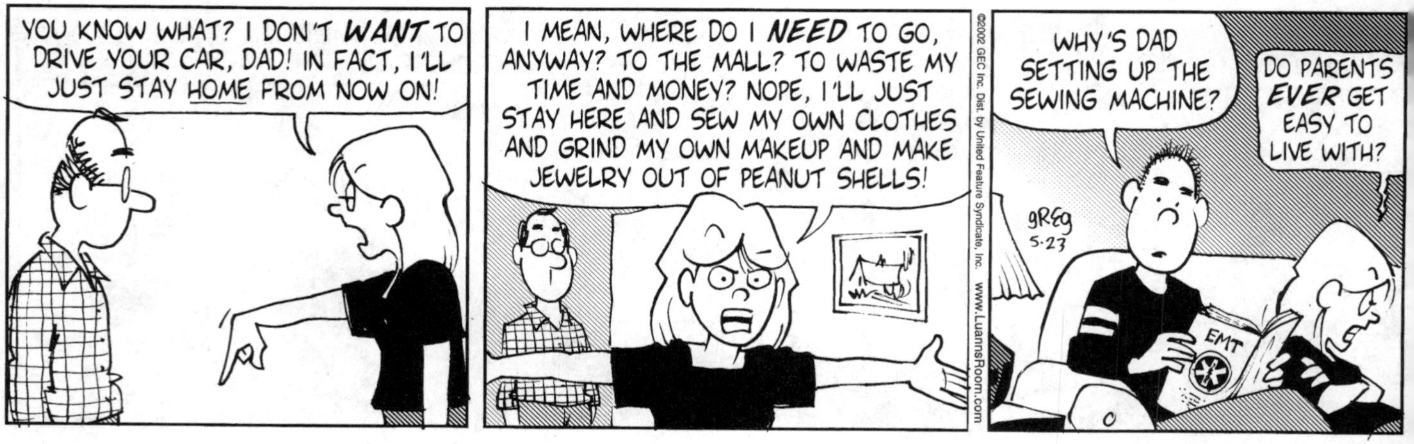
YOU KNOW WHAT? I DON'T *WANT* TO DRIVE YOUR CAR, DAD! IN FACT, I'LL JUST STAY HOME FROM NOW ON!
I MEAN, WHERE DO I *NEED* TO GO, ANYWAY? TO THE MALL? TO WASTE MY TIME AND MONEY? NOPE, I'LL JUST STAY HERE AND SEW MY OWN CLOTHES AND GRIND MY OWN MAKEUP AND MAKE JEWELRY OUT OF PEANUT SHELLS!
©2002 GEC Inc. Dist. by United Feature Syndicate, Inc. www.LuannsRoom.com
WHY'S DAD SETTING UP THE SEWING MACHINE?
DO PARENTS *EVER* GET EASY TO LIVE WITH?
EMT
GREG 5·23

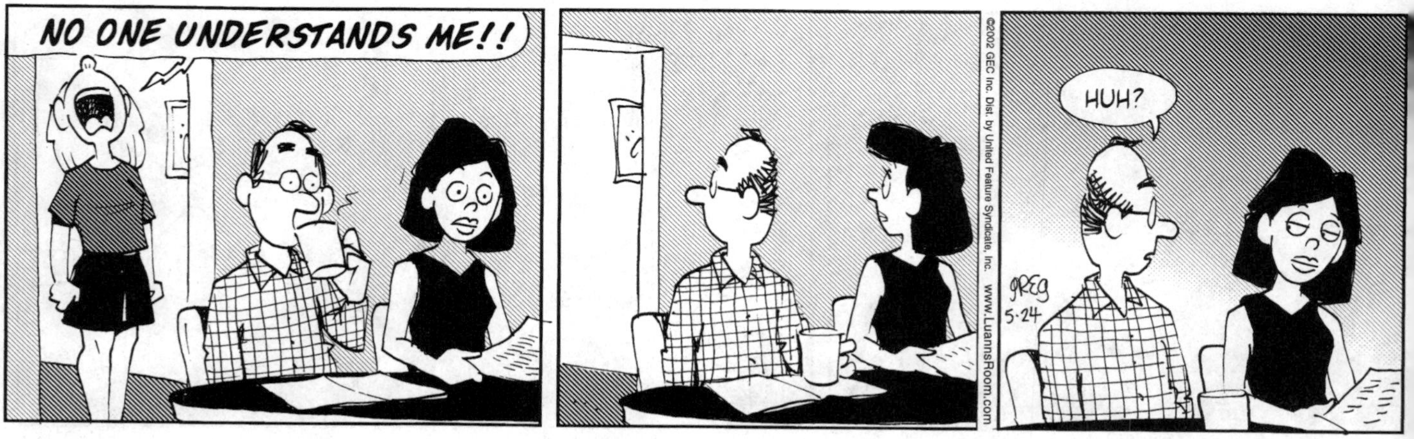
NO ONE UNDERSTANDS ME!!
©2002 GEC Inc. Dist. by United Feature Syndicate, Inc. www.LuannsRoom.com
HUH?
GREG 5·24

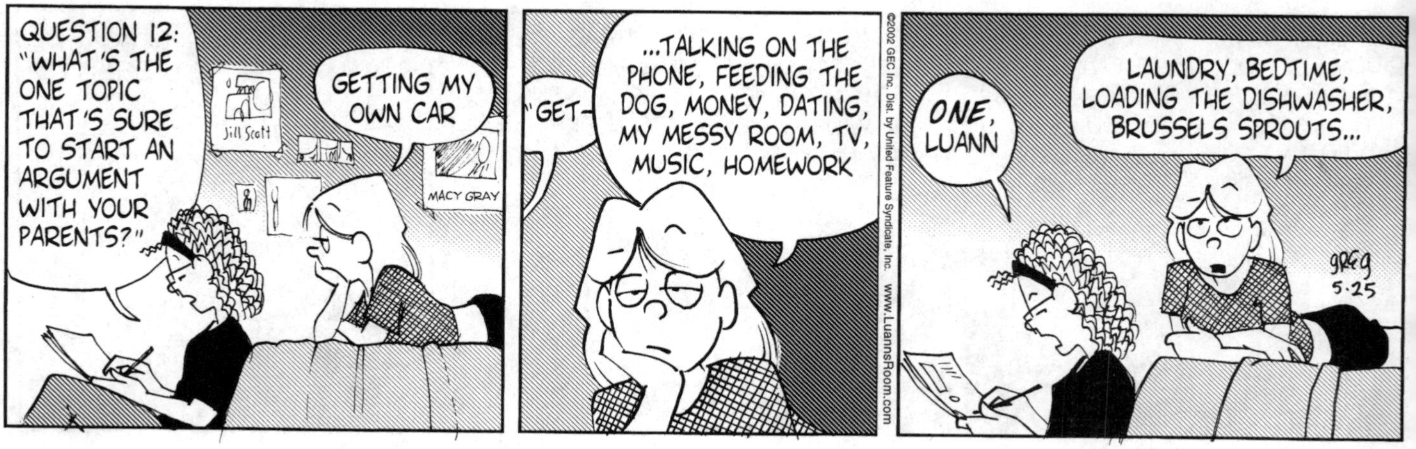
QUESTION 12: "WHAT'S THE ONE TOPIC THAT'S SURE TO START AN ARGUMENT WITH YOUR PARENTS?"
GETTING MY OWN CAR
Jill Scott
MACY GRAY
"GET-
...TALKING ON THE PHONE, FEEDING THE DOG, MONEY, DATING, MY MESSY ROOM, TV, MUSIC, HOMEWORK
©2002 GEC Inc. Dist. by United Feature Syndicate, Inc. www.LuannsRoom.com
ONE, LUANN
LAUNDRY, BEDTIME, LOADING THE DISHWASHER, BRUSSELS SPROUTS...
GREG 5·25

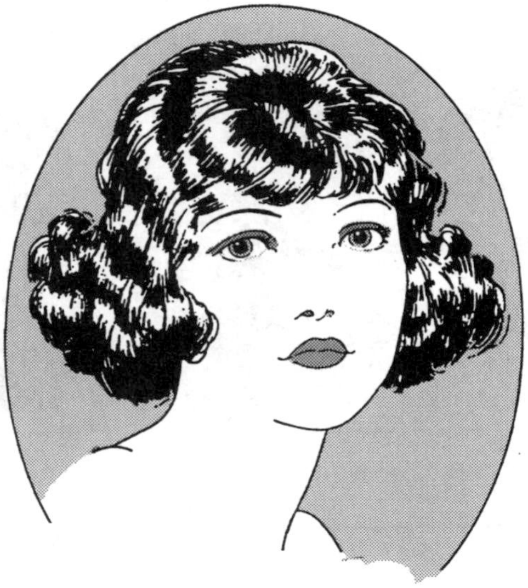

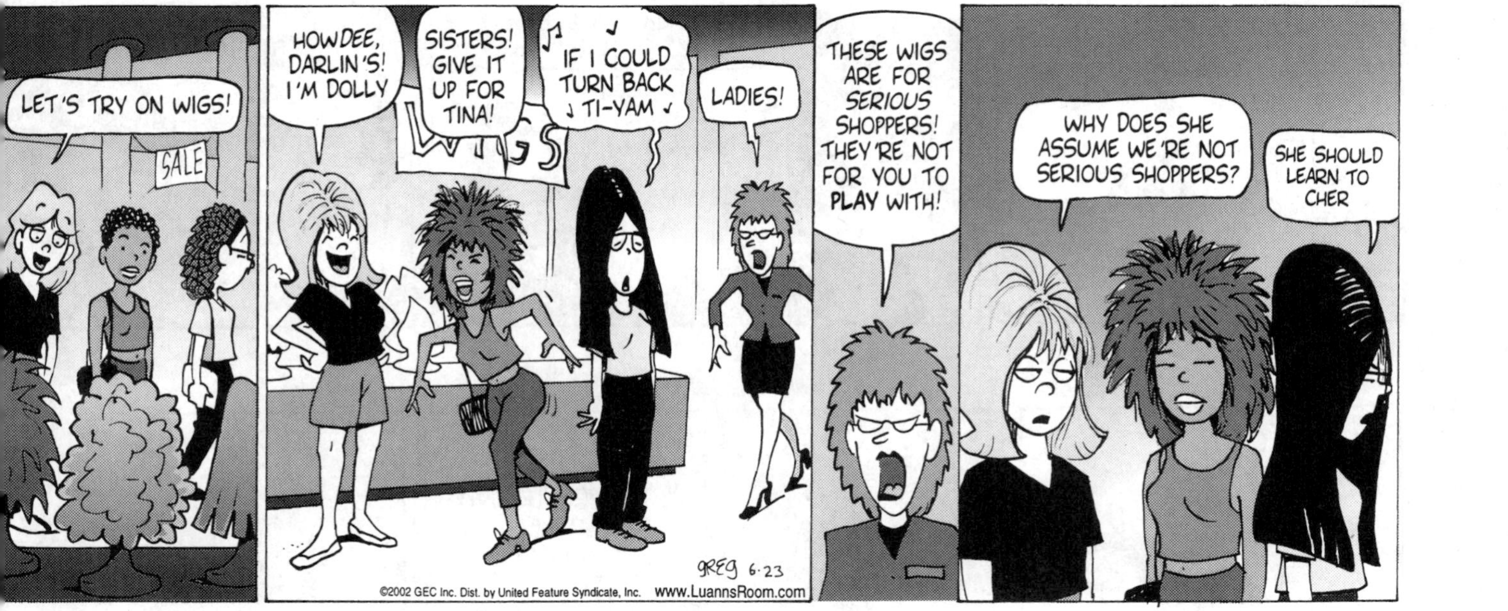
LET'S TRY ON WIGS!
SALE
HOWDEE, DARLIN'S! I'M DOLLY
SISTERS! GIVE IT UP FOR TINA!
IF I COULD TURN BACK TI-YAM
WIGS
LADIES!
GREG 6·23
©2002 GEC Inc. Dist. by United Feature Syndicate, Inc.
www.LuannsRoom.com
THESE WIGS ARE FOR SERIOUS SHOPPERS! THEY'RE NOT FOR YOU TO PLAY WITH!
WHY DOES SHE ASSUME WE'RE NOT SERIOUS SHOPPERS?
SHE SHOULD LEARN TO CHER

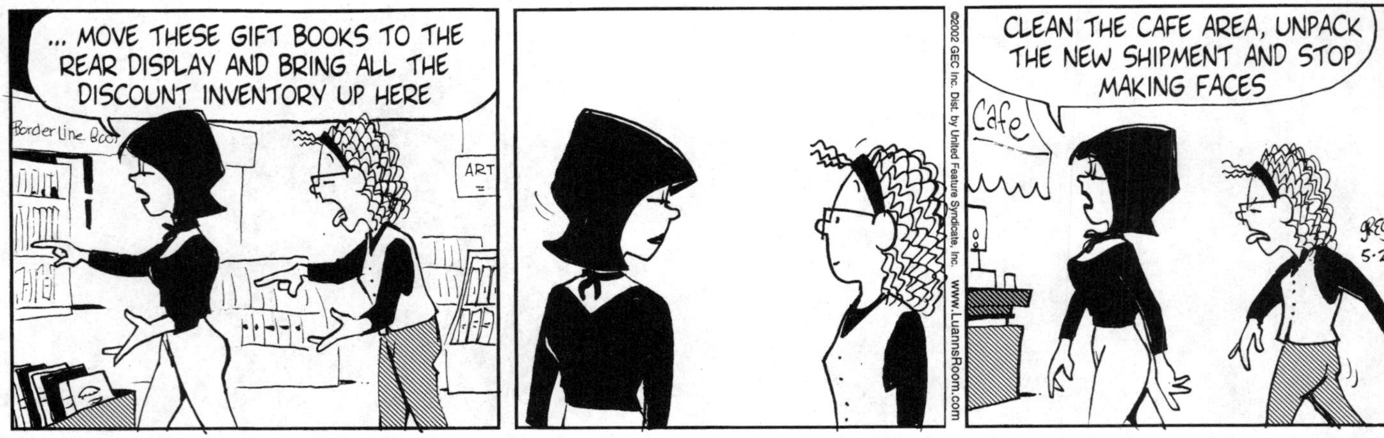
... MOVE THESE GIFT BOOKS TO THE REAR DISPLAY AND BRING ALL THE DISCOUNT INVENTORY UP HERE
ART
©2002 GEC Inc. Dist. by United Feature Syndicate, Inc. www.LuannsRoom.com
CLEAN THE CAFE AREA, UNPACK THE NEW SHIPMENT AND STOP MAKING FACES
Cafe
GREG 5-27

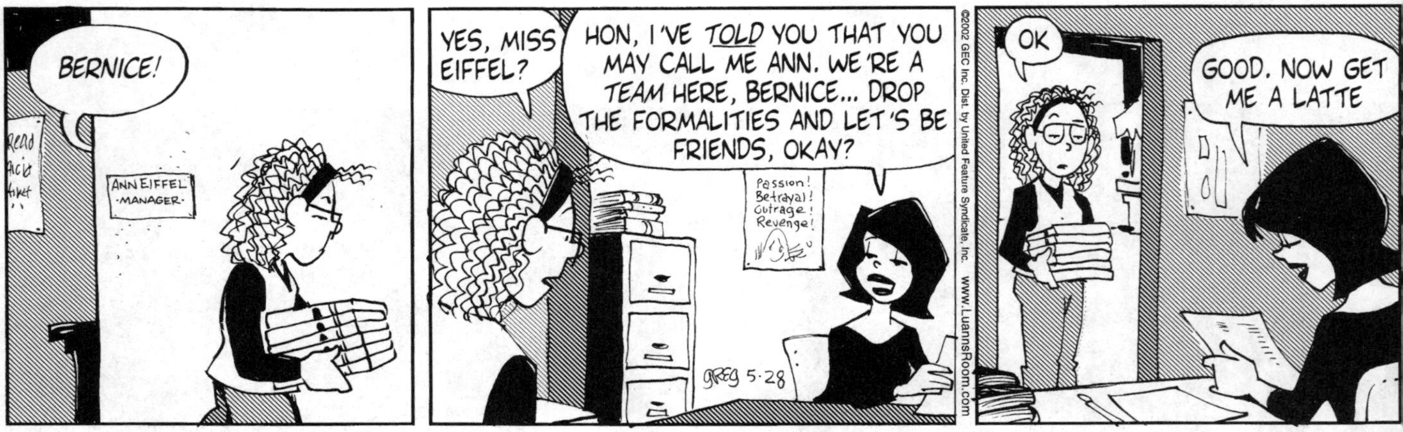
BERNICE!
ANN EIFFEL ·MANAGER·
YES, MISS EIFFEL?
HON, I'VE *TOLD* YOU THAT YOU MAY CALL ME ANN. WE'RE A *TEAM* HERE, BERNICE... DROP THE FORMALITIES AND LET'S BE FRIENDS, OKAY?
Passion! Betrayal! Outrage! Revenge!
GREG 5-28
©2002 GEC Inc. Dist. by United Feature Syndicate, Inc. www.LuannsRoom.com
OK
GOOD. NOW GET ME A LATTE

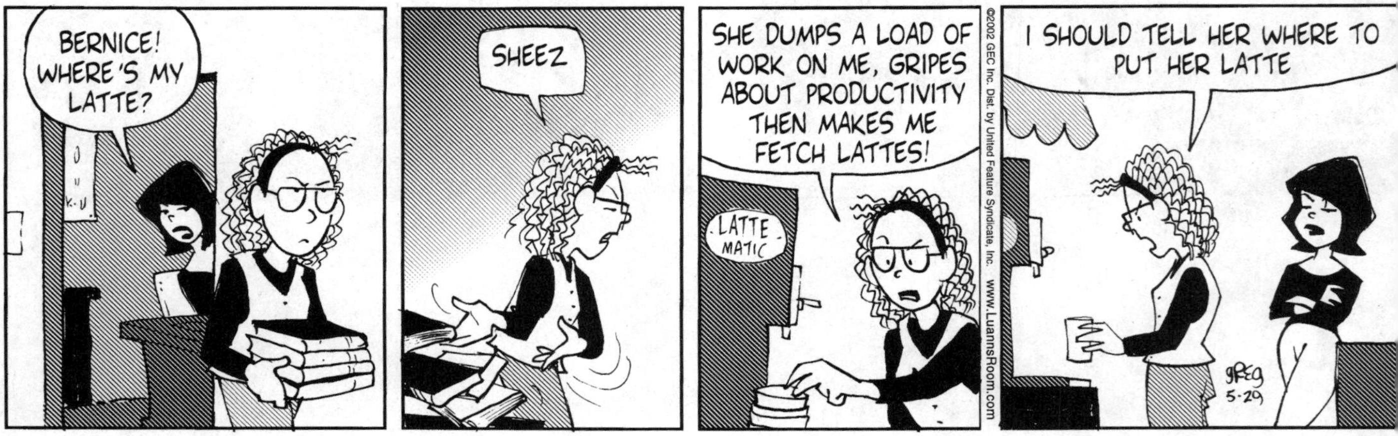
BERNICE! WHERE'S MY LATTE?
SHEEZ
SHE DUMPS A LOAD OF WORK ON ME, GRIPES ABOUT PRODUCTIVITY THEN MAKES ME FETCH LATTES!
LATTE MATIC
©2002 GEC Inc. Dist. by United Feature Syndicate, Inc. www.LuannsRoom.com
I SHOULD TELL HER WHERE TO PUT HER LATTE
GREG 5-29

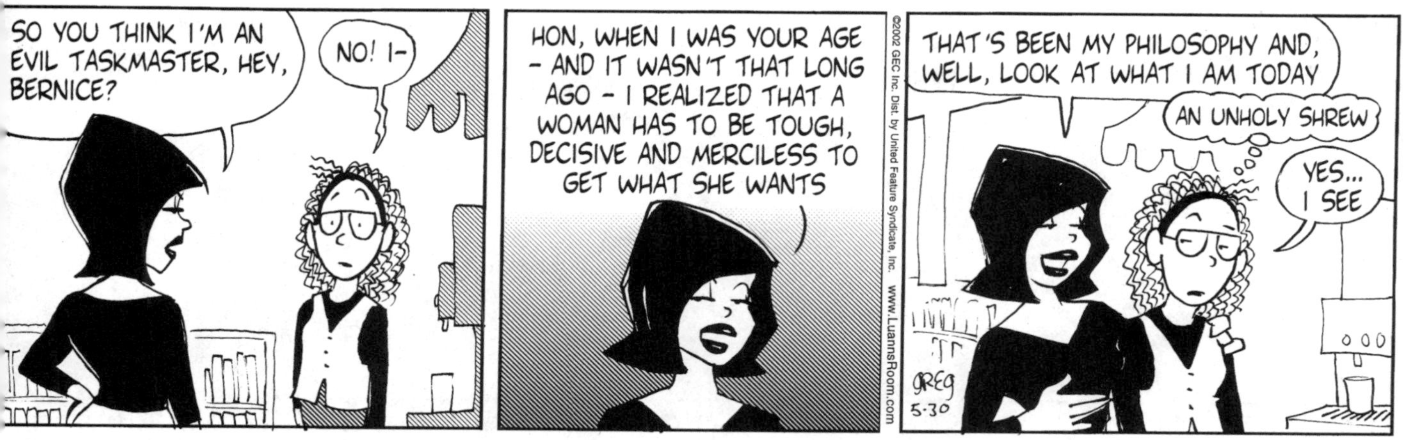
SO YOU THINK I'M AN EVIL TASKMASTER, HEY, BERNICE?
NO! I-
HON, WHEN I WAS YOUR AGE - AND IT WASN'T THAT LONG AGO - I REALIZED THAT A WOMAN HAS TO BE TOUGH, DECISIVE AND MERCILESS TO GET WHAT SHE WANTS
©2002 GEC Inc. Dist. by United Feature Syndicate, Inc. www.LuannsRoom.com
THAT'S BEEN MY PHILOSOPHY AND, WELL, LOOK AT WHAT I AM TODAY
AN UNHOLY SHREW
YES... I SEE
GREG 5-30

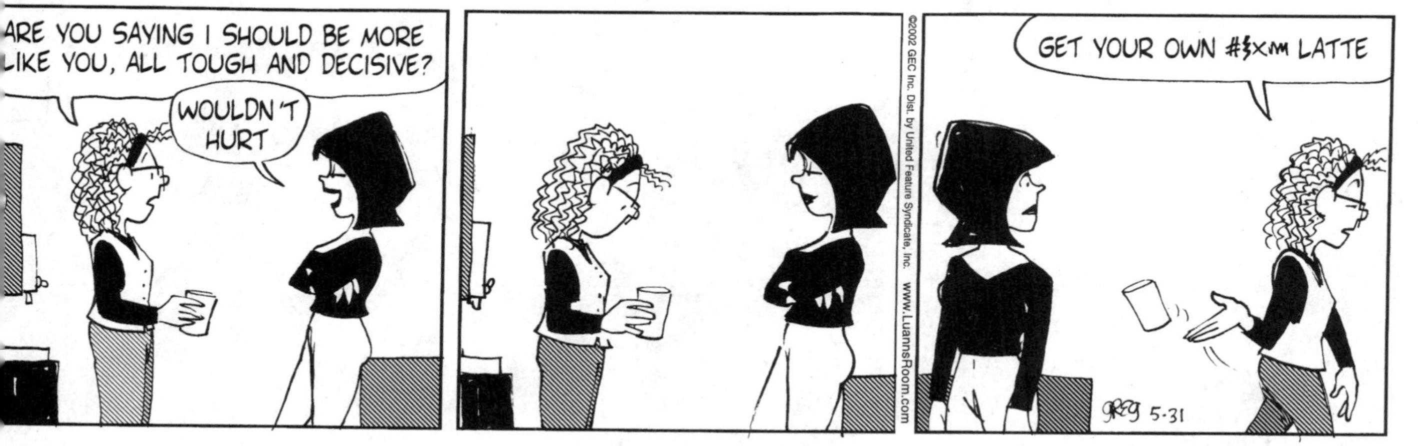
ARE YOU SAYING I SHOULD BE MORE LIKE YOU, ALL TOUGH AND DECISIVE?
WOULDN'T HURT
©2002 GEC Inc. Dist. by United Feature Syndicate, Inc. www.LuannsRoom.com
GET YOUR OWN #$×m LATTE
GREG 5-31

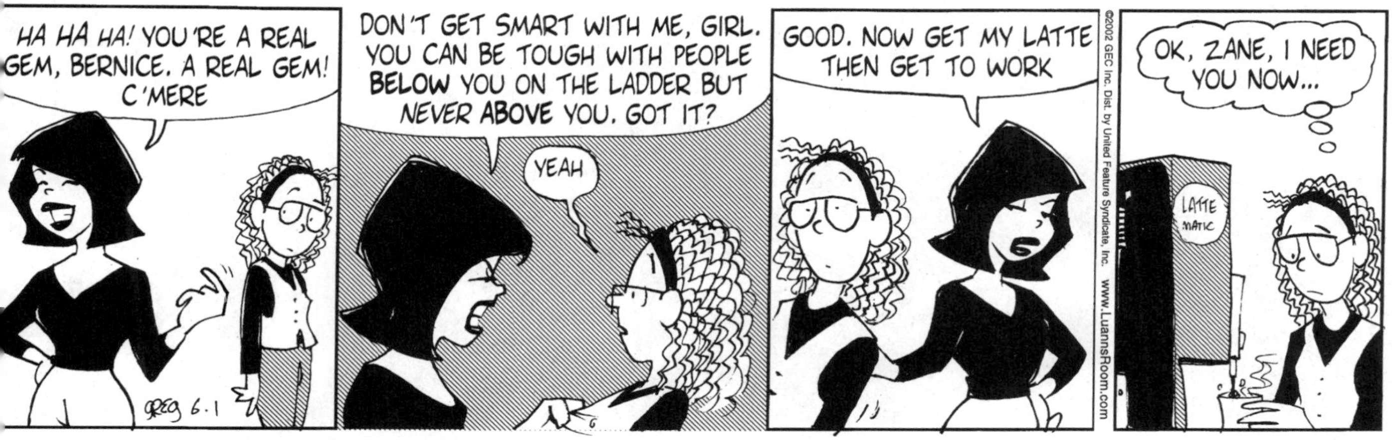
HA HA HA! YOU'RE A REAL GEM, BERNICE. A REAL GEM! C'MERE
GREG 6-1
DON'T GET SMART WITH ME, GIRL. YOU CAN BE TOUGH WITH PEOPLE **BELOW** YOU ON THE LADDER BUT *NEVER* **ABOVE** YOU. GOT IT?
YEAH
GOOD. NOW GET MY LATTE THEN GET TO WORK
©2002 GEC Inc. Dist. by United Feature Syndicate, Inc. www.LuannsRoom.com
OK, ZANE, I NEED YOU NOW...
LATTE MATIC

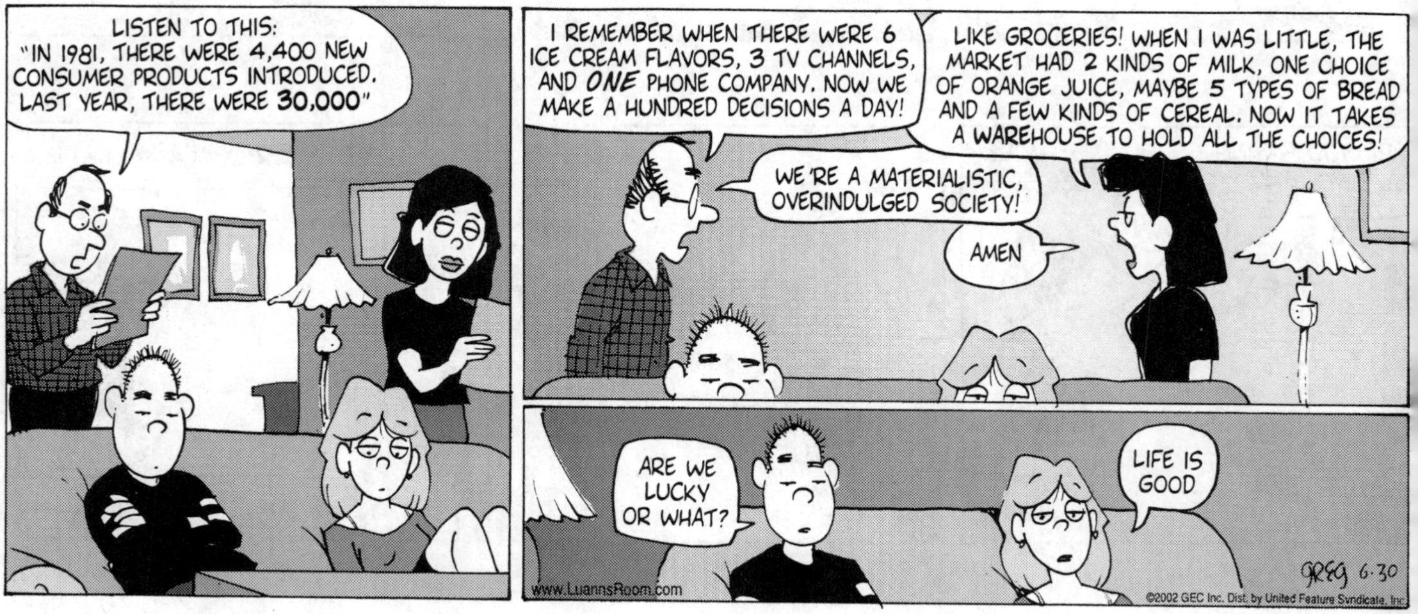
LISTEN TO THIS: "IN 1981, THERE WERE 4,400 NEW CONSUMER PRODUCTS INTRODUCED. LAST YEAR, THERE WERE 30,000"
I REMEMBER WHEN THERE WERE 6 ICE CREAM FLAVORS, 3 TV CHANNELS, AND ONE PHONE COMPANY. NOW WE MAKE A HUNDRED DECISIONS A DAY!
LIKE GROCERIES! WHEN I WAS LITTLE, THE MARKET HAD 2 KINDS OF MILK, ONE CHOICE OF ORANGE JUICE, MAYBE 5 TYPES OF BREAD AND A FEW KINDS OF CEREAL. NOW IT TAKES A WAREHOUSE TO HOLD ALL THE CHOICES!
WE'RE A MATERIALISTIC, OVERINDULGED SOCIETY!
AMEN
ARE WE LUCKY OR WHAT?
LIFE IS GOOD
GREG 6·30
www.LuannsRoom.com
©2002 GEC Inc. Dist. by United Feature Syndicate, Inc.

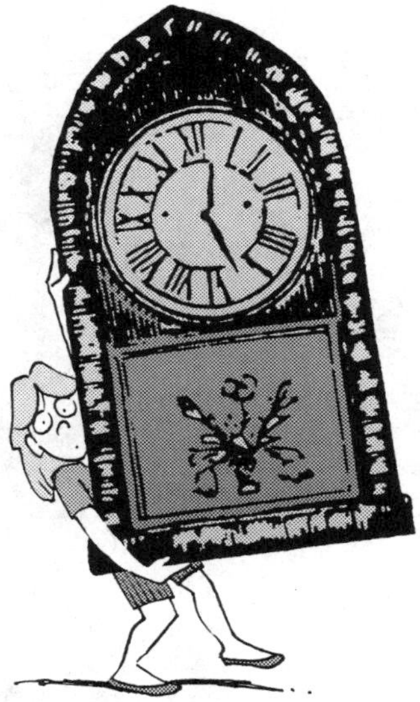

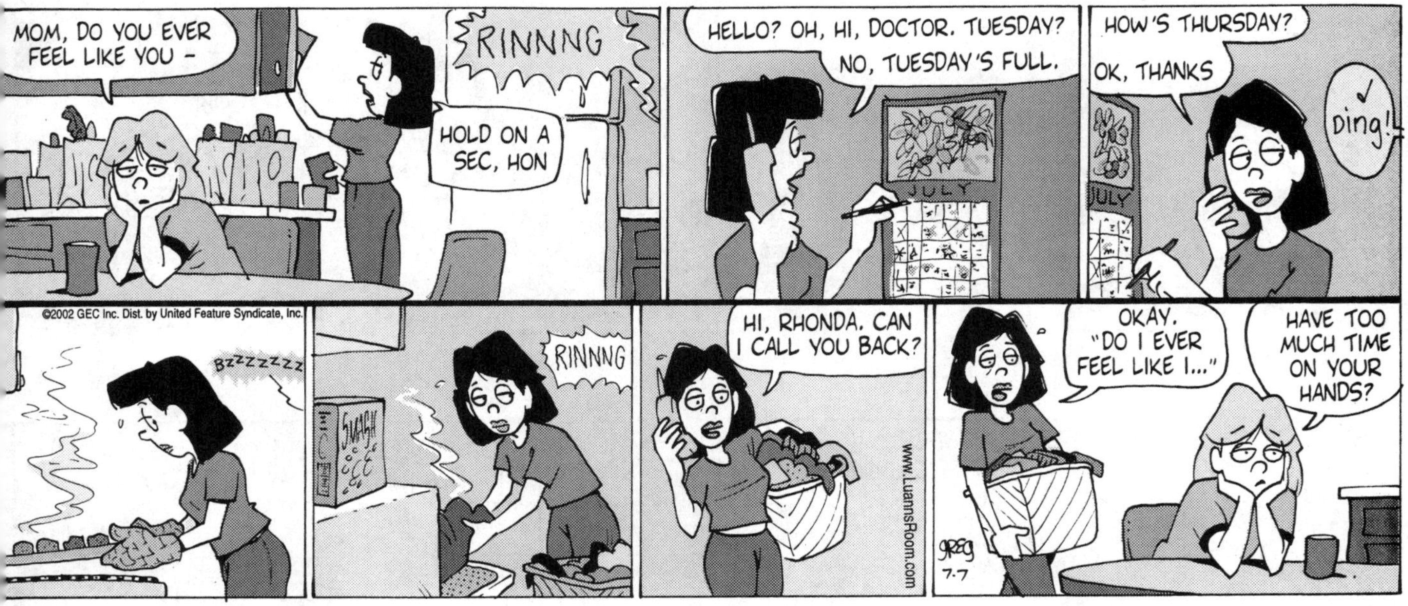
MOM, DO YOU EVER FEEL LIKE YOU –
RINNNG
HOLD ON A SEC, HON
HELLO? OH, HI, DOCTOR. TUESDAY?
NO, TUESDAY'S FULL.
JULY
HOW'S THURSDAY?
OK, THANKS
Ding!
JULY
©2002 GEC Inc. Dist. by United Feature Syndicate, Inc.
BZZZZZZZ
RINNNG
HI, RHONDA. CAN I CALL YOU BACK?
www.LuannsRoom.com
OKAY. "DO I EVER FEEL LIKE I..."
HAVE TOO MUCH TIME ON YOUR HANDS?
GREG 7-7

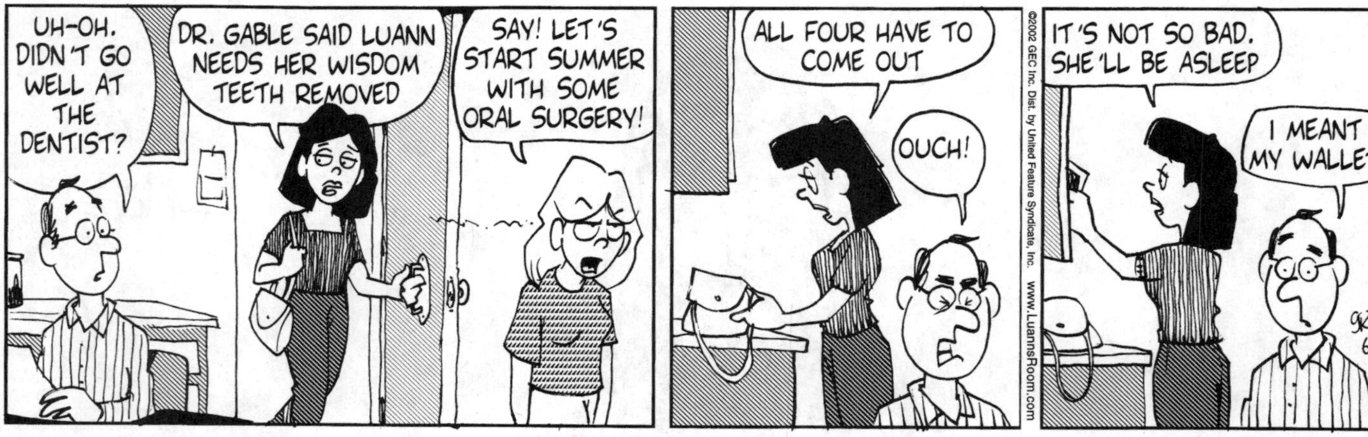
UH-OH. DIDN'T GO WELL AT THE DENTIST?
DR. GABLE SAID LUANN NEEDS HER WISDOM TEETH REMOVED
SAY! LET'S START SUMMER WITH SOME ORAL SURGERY!
ALL FOUR HAVE TO COME OUT
OUCH!
©2002 GEC Inc. Dist. by United Feature Syndicate, Inc. www.LuannsRoom.com
IT'S NOT SO BAD. SHE'LL BE ASLEEP
I MEANT MY WALLET
GREG 6·3

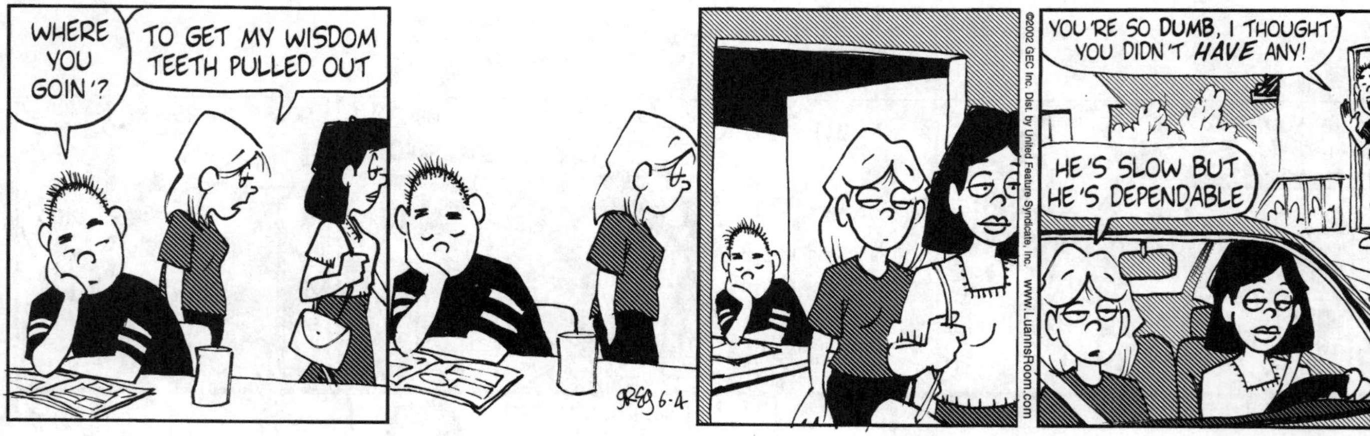
WHERE YOU GOIN'?
TO GET MY WISDOM TEETH PULLED OUT
GREG 6·4
©2002 GEC Inc. Dist. by United Feature Syndicate, Inc. www.LuannsRoom.com
YOU'RE SO DUMB, I THOUGHT YOU DIDN'T HAVE ANY!
HE'S SLOW BUT HE'S DEPENDABLE

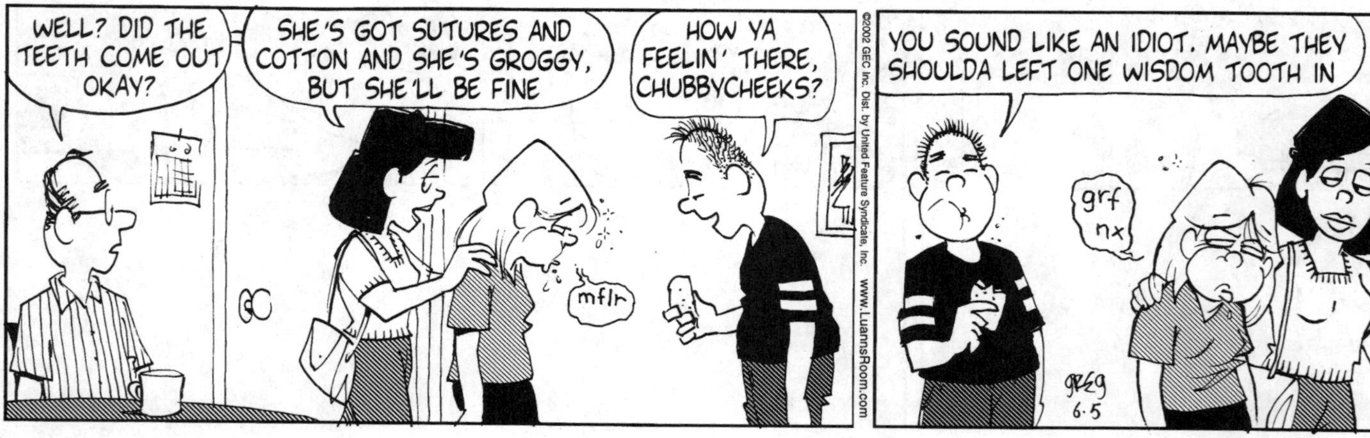
WELL? DID THE TEETH COME OUT OKAY?
SHE'S GOT SUTURES AND COTTON AND SHE'S GROGGY, BUT SHE'LL BE FINE
mflr
HOW YA FEELIN' THERE, CHUBBYCHEEKS?
©2002 GEC Inc. Dist. by United Feature Syndicate, Inc. www.LuannsRoom.com
YOU SOUND LIKE AN IDIOT. MAYBE THEY SHOULDA LEFT ONE WISDOM TOOTH IN
grf nx
GREG 6·5

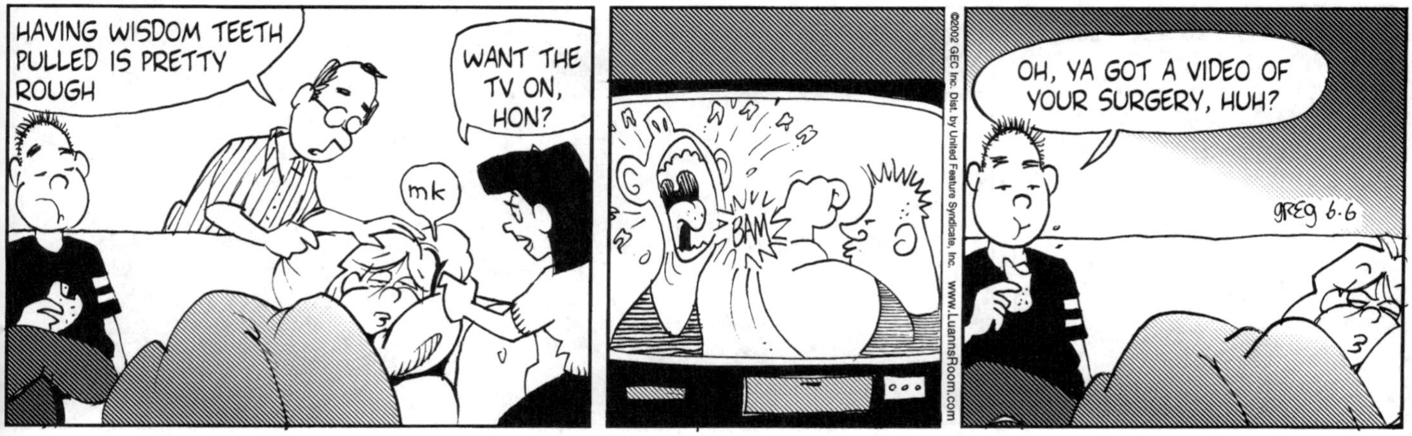
HAVING WISDOM TEETH PULLED IS PRETTY ROUGH
WANT THE TV ON, HON?
mk
BAM
OH, YA GOT A VIDEO OF YOUR SURGERY, HUH?
GREG 6.6
©2002 GEC Inc. Dist. by United Feature Syndicate, Inc.
www.LuannsRoom.com

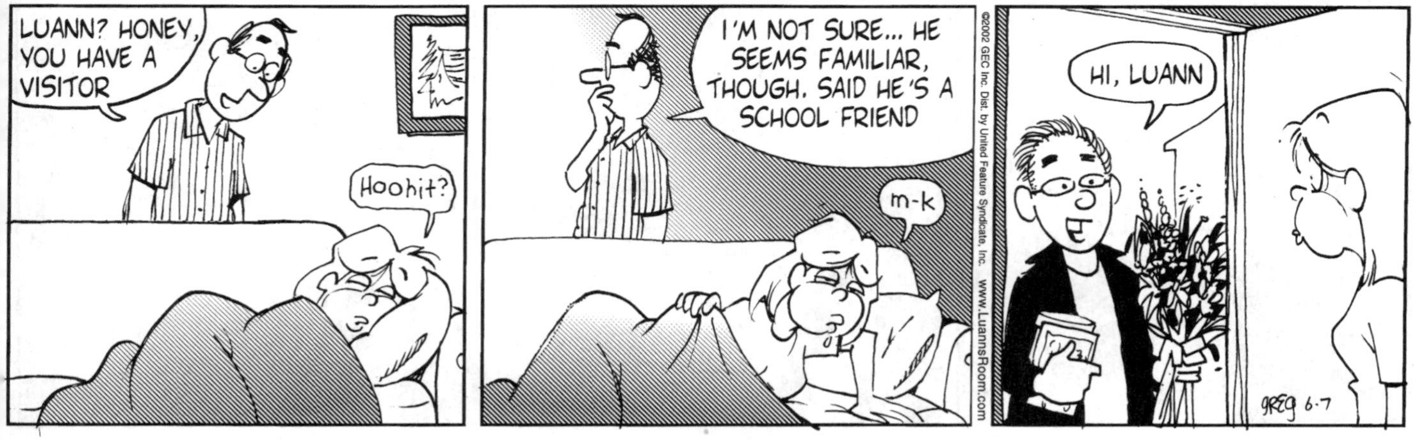
LUANN? HONEY, YOU HAVE A VISITOR
Hoohit?
I'M NOT SURE... HE SEEMS FAMILIAR, THOUGH. SAID HE'S A SCHOOL FRIEND
m-k
HI, LUANN
GREG 6-7
©2002 GEC Inc. Dist. by United Feature Syndicate, Inc.
www.LuannsRoom.com

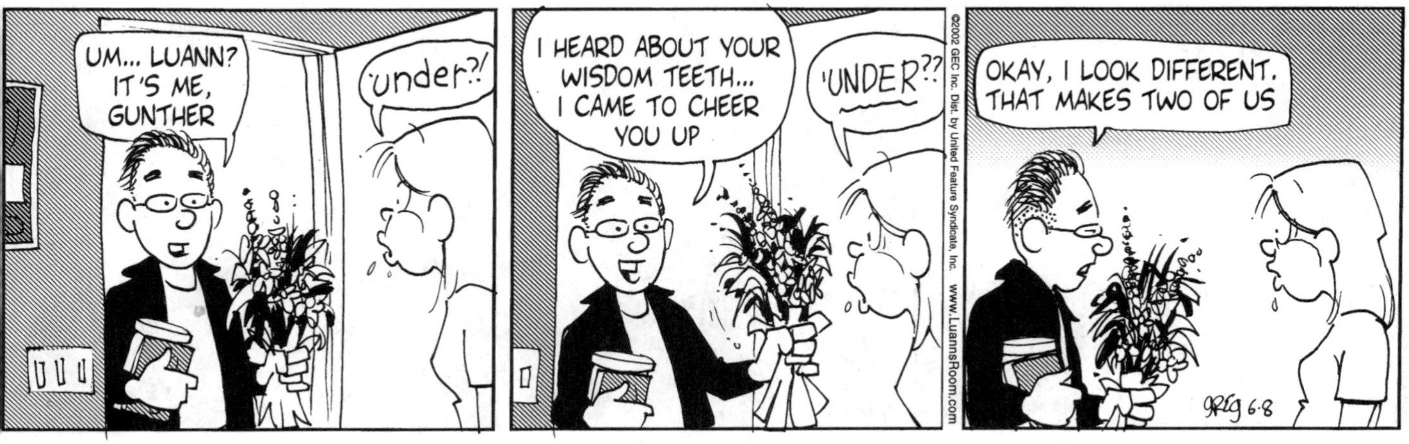
UM... LUANN? IT'S ME, GUNTHER
'under?!
I HEARD ABOUT YOUR WISDOM TEETH... I CAME TO CHEER YOU UP
'UNDER??
OKAY, I LOOK DIFFERENT. THAT MAKES TWO OF US
GREG 6-8
©2002 GEC Inc. Dist. by United Feature Syndicate, Inc.
www.LuannsRoom.com

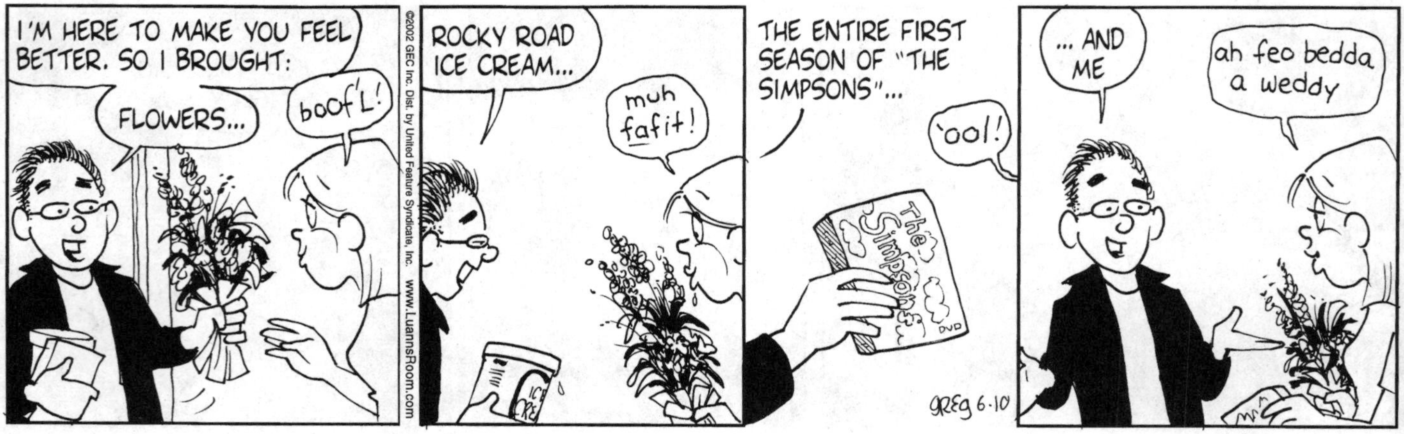
I'M HERE TO MAKE YOU FEEL BETTER. SO I BROUGHT:
FLOWERS...
boof'L!
©2002 GEC Inc. Dist. by United Feature Syndicate, Inc. www.LuannsRoom.com
ROCKY ROAD ICE CREAM...
muh fafit!
ICE CRE
THE ENTIRE FIRST SEASON OF "THE SIMPSONS"...
`ool!
The Simpsons
DVD
GREG 6·10
... AND ME
ah feo bedda a weddy

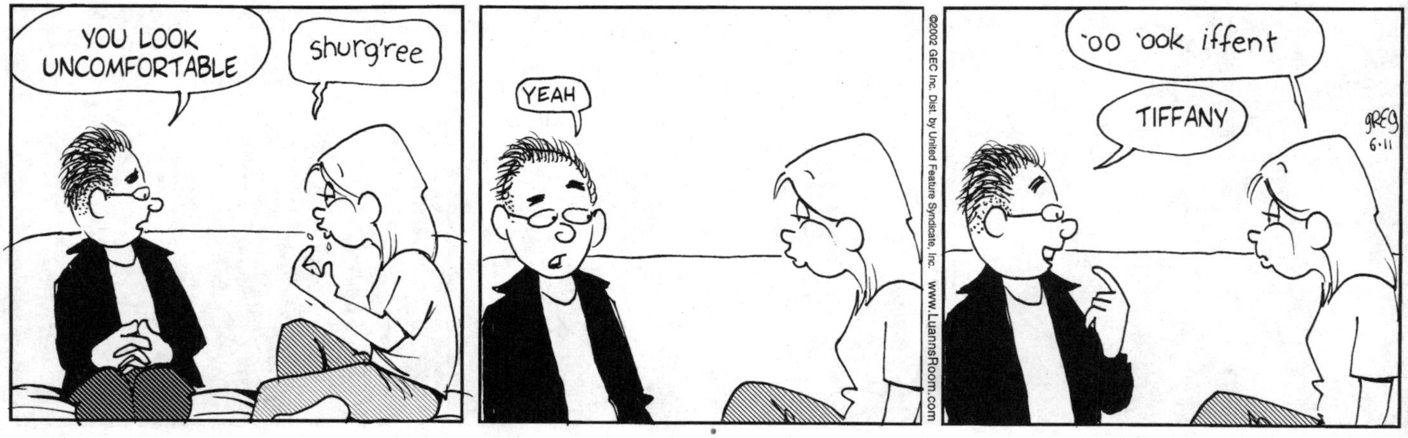
YOU LOOK UNCOMFORTABLE
shurg'ree
YEAH
©2002 GEC Inc. Dist. by United Feature Syndicate, Inc. www.LuannsRoom.com
`oo `ook iffent
TIFFANY
GREG 6·11

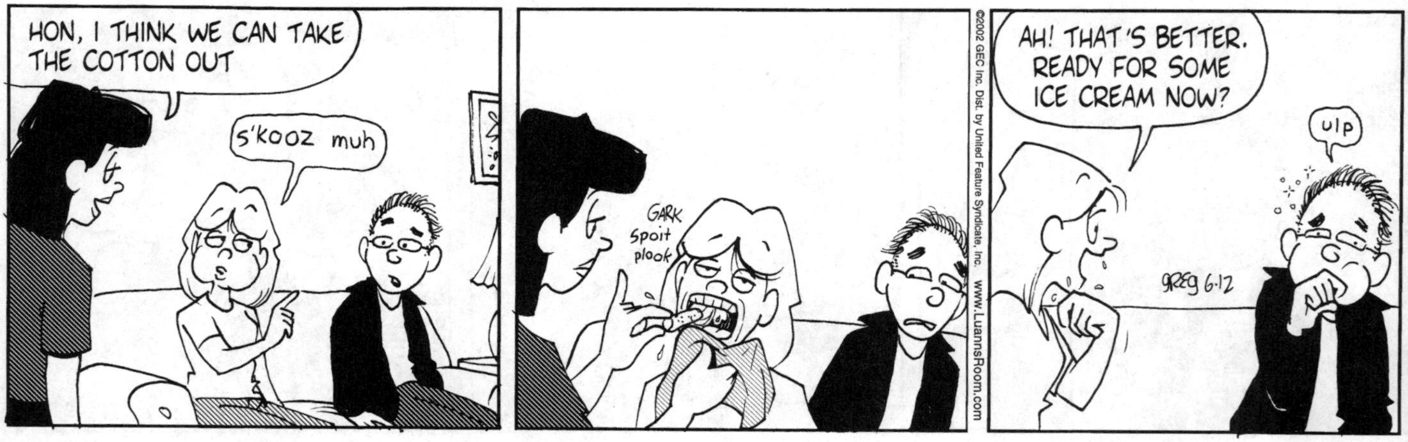
HON, I THINK WE CAN TAKE THE COTTON OUT
s'kooz muh
GARK
Spoit
plook
©2002 GEC Inc. Dist. by United Feature Syndicate, Inc. www.LuannsRoom.com
AH! THAT'S BETTER. READY FOR SOME ICE CREAM NOW?
ulp
GREG 6·12

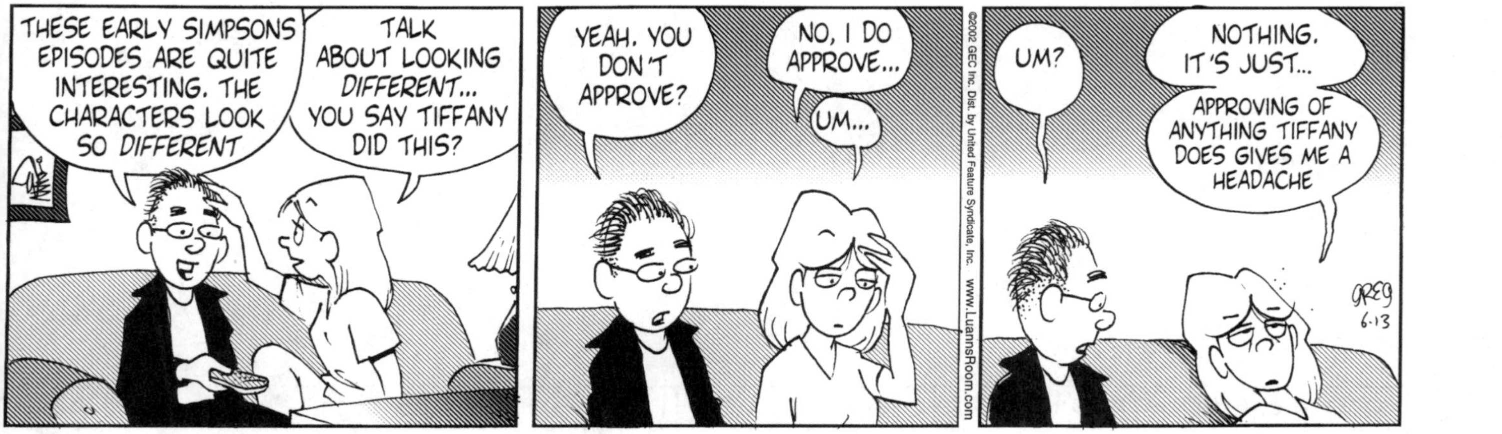
THESE EARLY SIMPSONS EPISODES ARE QUITE INTERESTING. THE CHARACTERS LOOK SO *DIFFERENT*
TALK ABOUT LOOKING *DIFFERENT*... YOU SAY TIFFANY DID THIS?
YEAH. YOU DON'T APPROVE?
NO, I DO APPROVE...
UM...
©2002 GEC Inc. Dist. by United Feature Syndicate, Inc. www.LuannsRoom.com
UM?
NOTHING. IT'S JUST...
APPROVING OF ANYTHING TIFFANY DOES GIVES ME A HEADACHE
GREG 6-13

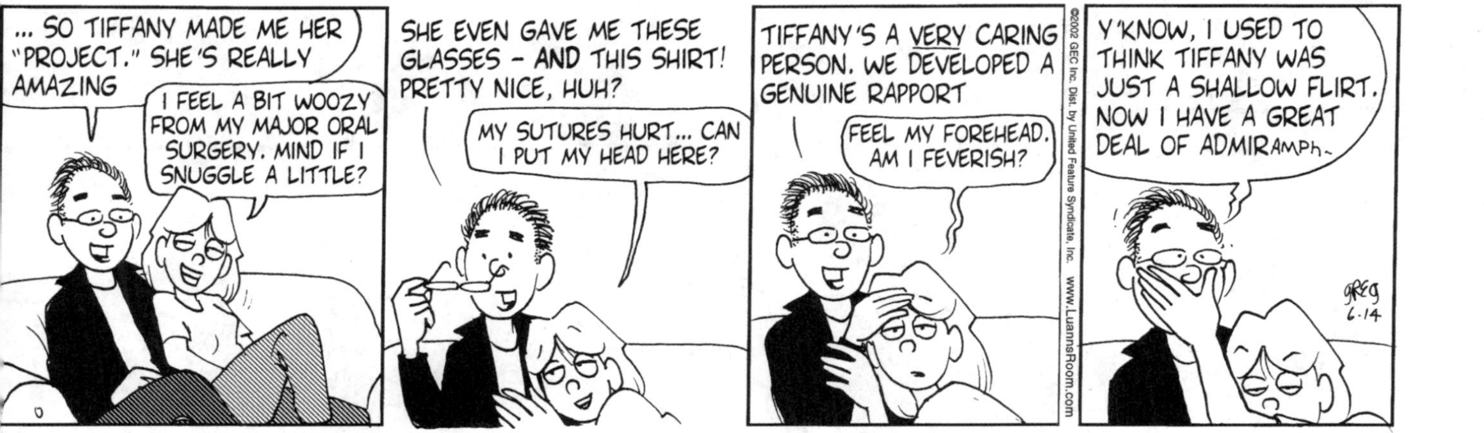
... SO TIFFANY MADE ME HER "PROJECT." SHE'S REALLY AMAZING
I FEEL A BIT WOOZY FROM MY MAJOR ORAL SURGERY. MIND IF I SNUGGLE A LITTLE?
SHE EVEN GAVE ME THESE GLASSES – **AND** THIS SHIRT! PRETTY NICE, HUH?
MY SUTURES HURT... CAN I PUT MY HEAD HERE?
TIFFANY'S A VERY CARING PERSON. WE DEVELOPED A GENUINE RAPPORT
FEEL MY FOREHEAD. AM I FEVERISH?
©2002 GEC Inc. Dist. by United Feature Syndicate, Inc. www.LuannsRoom.com
Y'KNOW, I USED TO THINK TIFFANY WAS JUST A SHALLOW FLIRT. NOW I HAVE A GREAT DEAL OF ADMIRAMPH
GREG 6-14

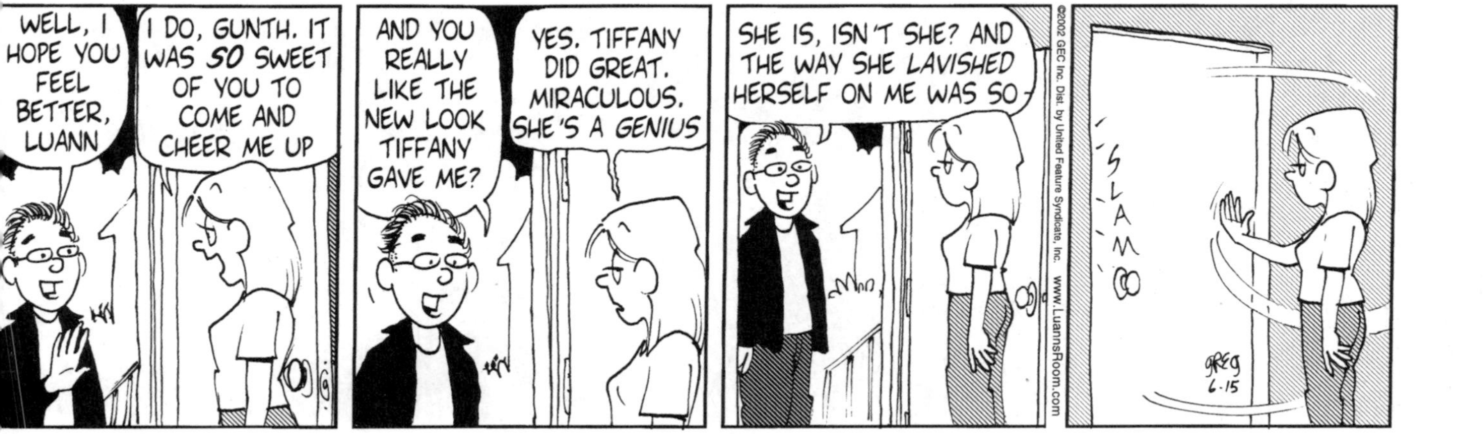
WELL, I HOPE YOU FEEL BETTER, LUANN
I DO, GUNTH. IT WAS ***SO*** SWEET OF YOU TO COME AND CHEER ME UP
AND YOU REALLY LIKE THE NEW LOOK TIFFANY GAVE ME?
YES. TIFFANY DID GREAT. MIRACULOUS. SHE'S A *GENIUS*
SHE IS, ISN'T SHE? AND THE WAY SHE *LAVISHED* HERSELF ON ME WAS SO–
©2002 GEC Inc. Dist. by United Feature Syndicate, Inc. www.LuannsRoom.com
SLAM
GREG 6-15

CHECK IT OUT, BERN! I USED A STRAWBERRY TO COLOR MY LIPS, HONEY FOR GLOSS, GRAPE JUICE FOR EYE SHADOW AND POWDERED SPAGHETTI SAUCE MIX FOR BLUSH!
PLUS, I USED A TOUCH OF CHEETOS DUST TO HIGHLIGHT MY HAIR AND A SPRITZ OF NONSTICK PAN SPRAY FOR SHEEN!
©2002 GEC Inc. Dist. by United Feature Syndicate, Inc.
I CAN PUT ON MAKEUP AND EAT *AT THE SAME TIME!*
OHMYGAW! YOU'VE BEAT THE SYSTEM!
AND I'M QUITE ATTRACTIVE, IF I DO SAY SO MYSELF
IF YOU LIKE FLIES...
GREG 7.14
www.LuannsRoom.com

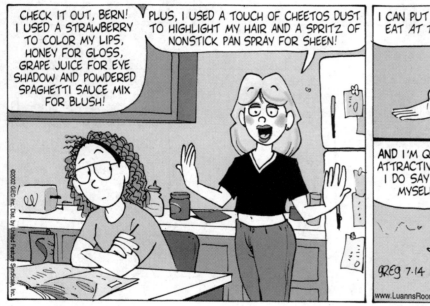

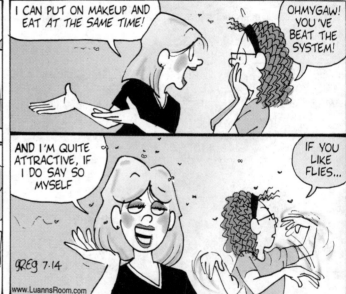

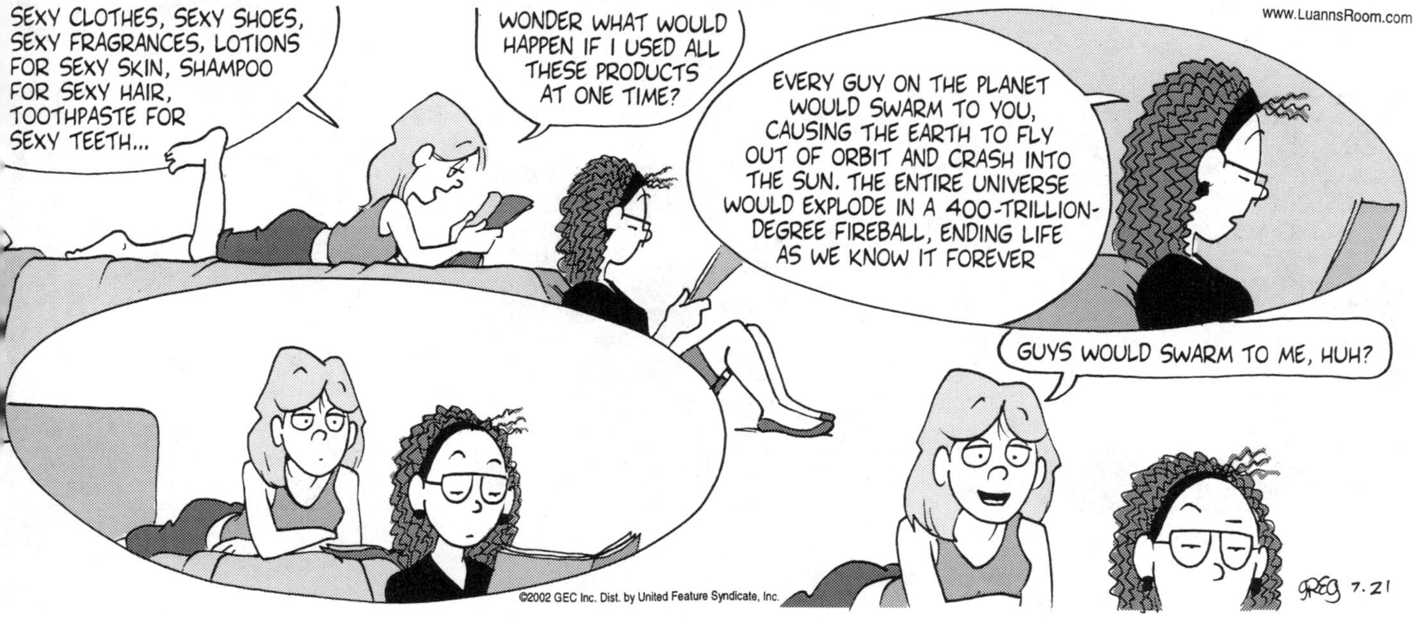
www.LuannsRoom.com
SEXY CLOTHES, SEXY SHOES, SEXY FRAGRANCES, LOTIONS FOR SEXY SKIN, SHAMPOO FOR SEXY HAIR, TOOTHPASTE FOR SEXY TEETH...
WONDER WHAT WOULD HAPPEN IF I USED ALL THESE PRODUCTS AT ONE TIME?
EVERY GUY ON THE PLANET WOULD SWARM TO YOU, CAUSING THE EARTH TO FLY OUT OF ORBIT AND CRASH INTO THE SUN. THE ENTIRE UNIVERSE WOULD EXPLODE IN A 400-TRILLION-DEGREE FIREBALL, ENDING LIFE AS WE KNOW IT FOREVER
GUYS WOULD SWARM TO ME, HUH?
GREG 7.21
©2002 GEC Inc. Dist. by United Feature Syndicate, Inc.

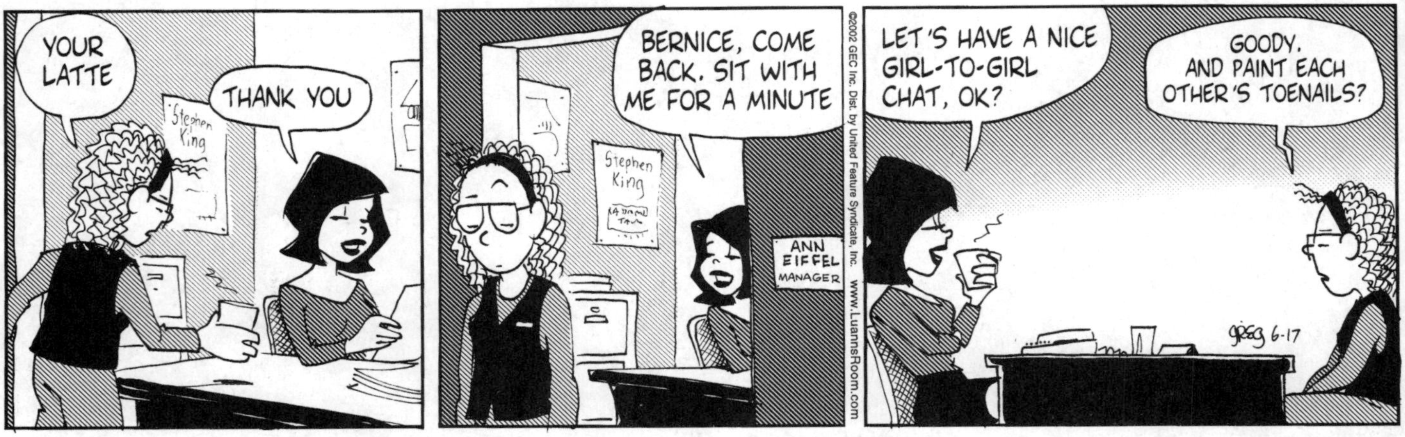
YOUR LATTE
THANK YOU
Stephen King
BERNICE, COME BACK. SIT WITH ME FOR A MINUTE
Stephen King
ANN EIFFEL MANAGER
©2002 GEC Inc. Dist. by United Feature Syndicate, Inc. www.LuannsRoom.com
LET'S HAVE A NICE GIRL-TO-GIRL CHAT, OK?
GOODY. AND PAINT EACH OTHER'S TOENAILS?
GREG 6-17

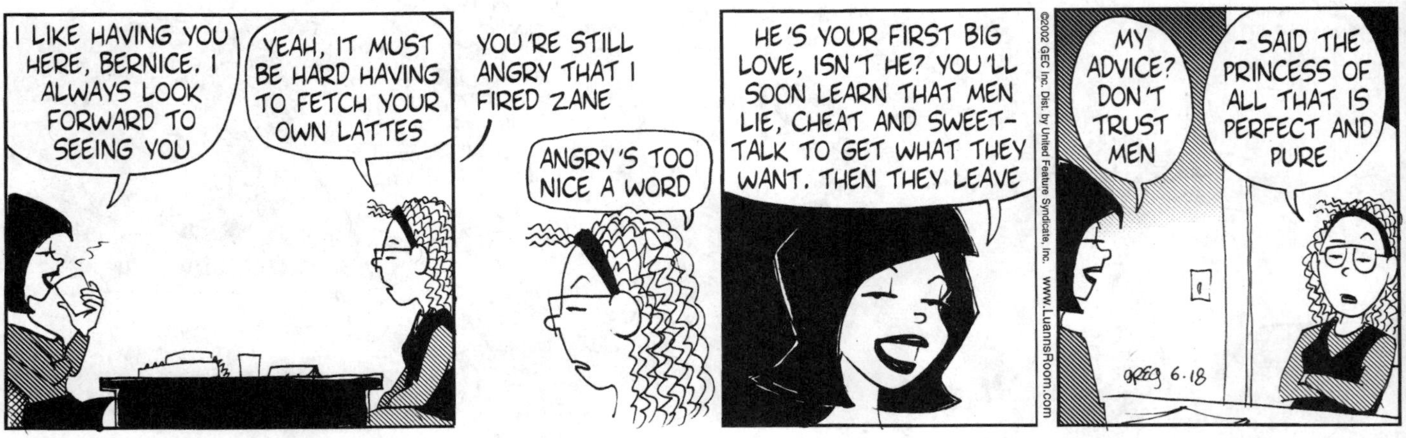
I LIKE HAVING YOU HERE, BERNICE. I ALWAYS LOOK FORWARD TO SEEING YOU
YEAH, IT MUST BE HARD HAVING TO FETCH YOUR OWN LATTES
YOU'RE STILL ANGRY THAT I FIRED ZANE
ANGRY'S TOO NICE A WORD
HE'S YOUR FIRST BIG LOVE, ISN'T HE? YOU'LL SOON LEARN THAT MEN LIE, CHEAT AND SWEET-TALK TO GET WHAT THEY WANT. THEN THEY LEAVE
©2002 GEC Inc. Dist. by United Feature Syndicate, Inc. www.LuannsRoom.com
MY ADVICE? DON'T TRUST MEN
- SAID THE PRINCESS OF ALL THAT IS PERFECT AND PURE
GREG 6-18

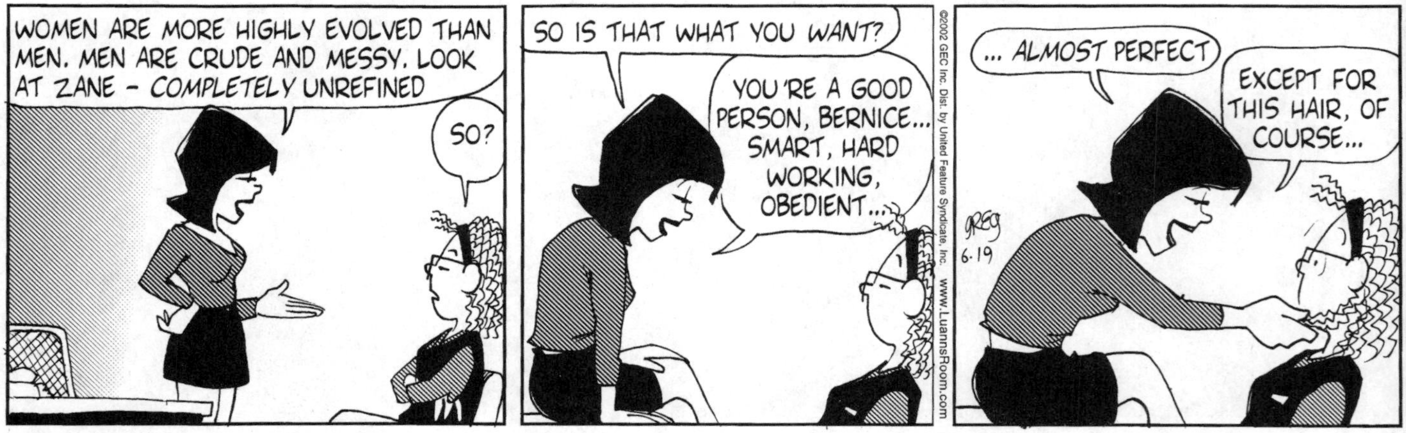
WOMEN ARE MORE HIGHLY EVOLVED THAN MEN. MEN ARE CRUDE AND MESSY. LOOK AT ZANE - *COMPLETELY* UNREFINED
SO?
SO IS THAT WHAT YOU *WANT*?
YOU'RE A GOOD PERSON, BERNICE... SMART, HARD WORKING, OBEDIENT...
©2002 GEC Inc. Dist. by United Feature Syndicate, Inc. www.LuannsRoom.com
GREG 6-19
... *ALMOST* PERFECT
EXCEPT FOR THIS HAIR, OF COURSE...

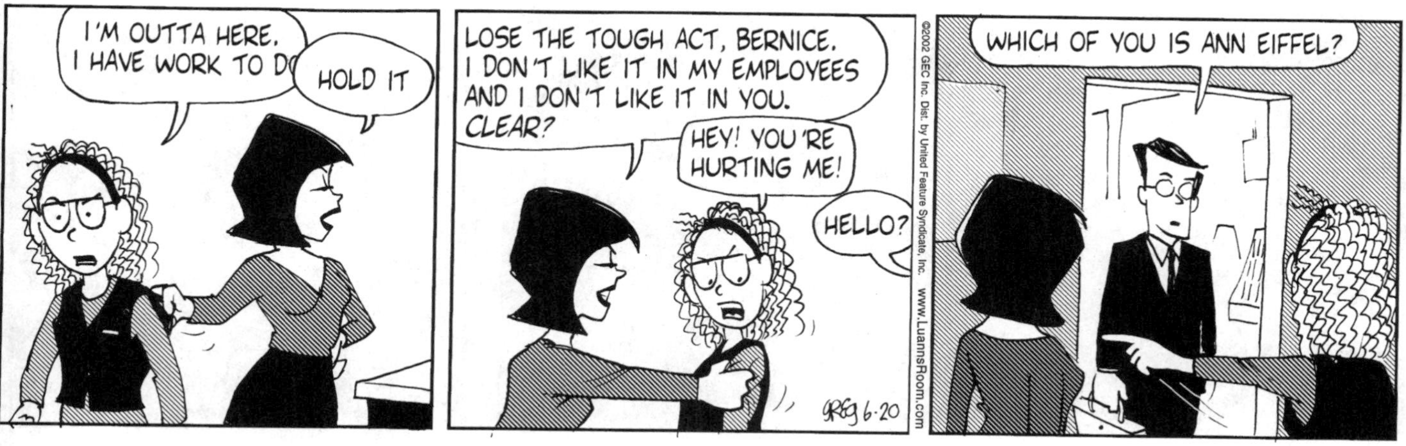
I'M OUTTA HERE. I HAVE WORK TO D
HOLD IT
LOSE THE TOUGH ACT, BERNICE. I DON'T LIKE IT IN MY EMPLOYEES AND I DON'T LIKE IT IN YOU. CLEAR?
HEY! YOU'RE HURTING ME!
HELLO?
GREG 6·20
©2002 GEC Inc. Dist. by United Feature Syndicate, Inc. www.LuannsRoom.com
WHICH OF YOU IS ANN EIFFEL?

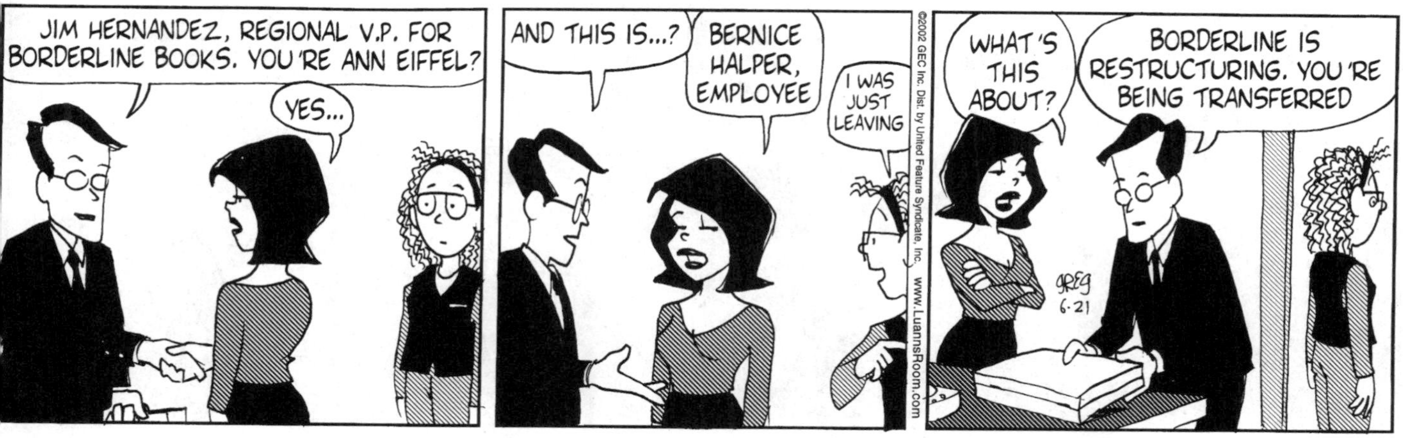
JIM HERNANDEZ, REGIONAL V.P. FOR BORDERLINE BOOKS. YOU'RE ANN EIFFEL?
YES...
AND THIS IS...?
BERNICE HALPER, EMPLOYEE
I WAS JUST LEAVING
©2002 GEC Inc. Dist. by United Feature Syndicate, Inc. www.LuannsRoom.com
WHAT'S THIS ABOUT?
BORDERLINE IS RESTRUCTURING. YOU'RE BEING TRANSFERRED
GREG 6·21

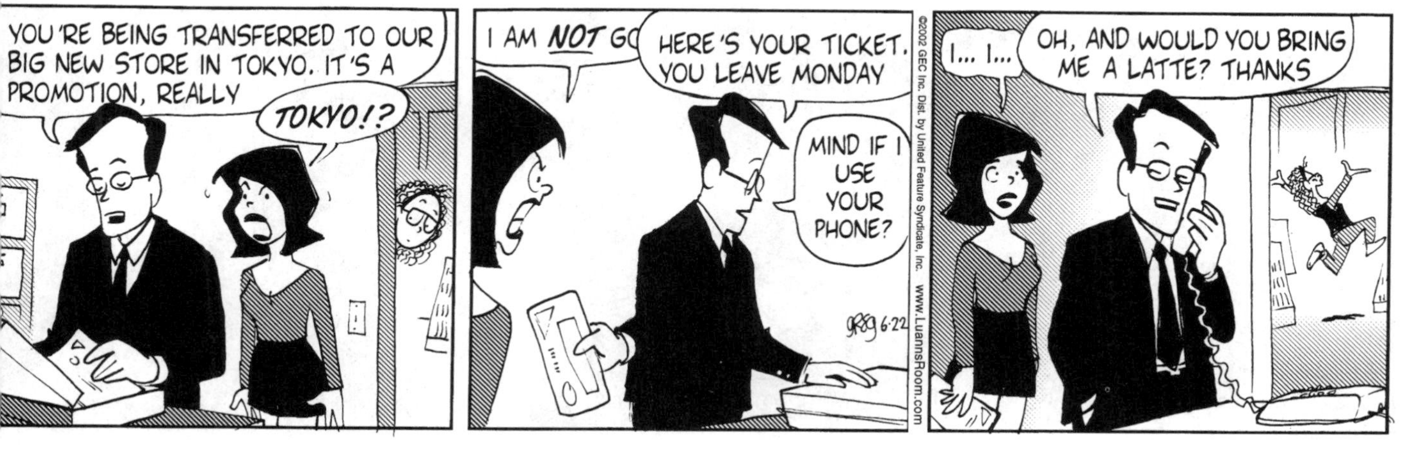
YOU'RE BEING TRANSFERRED TO OUR BIG NEW STORE IN TOKYO. IT'S A PROMOTION, REALLY
TOKYO!?
I AM NOT G
HERE'S YOUR TICKET. YOU LEAVE MONDAY
MIND IF I USE YOUR PHONE?
GREG 6·22
©2002 GEC Inc. Dist. by United Feature Syndicate, Inc. www.LuannsRoom.com
I... I...
OH, AND WOULD YOU BRING ME A LATTE? THANKS

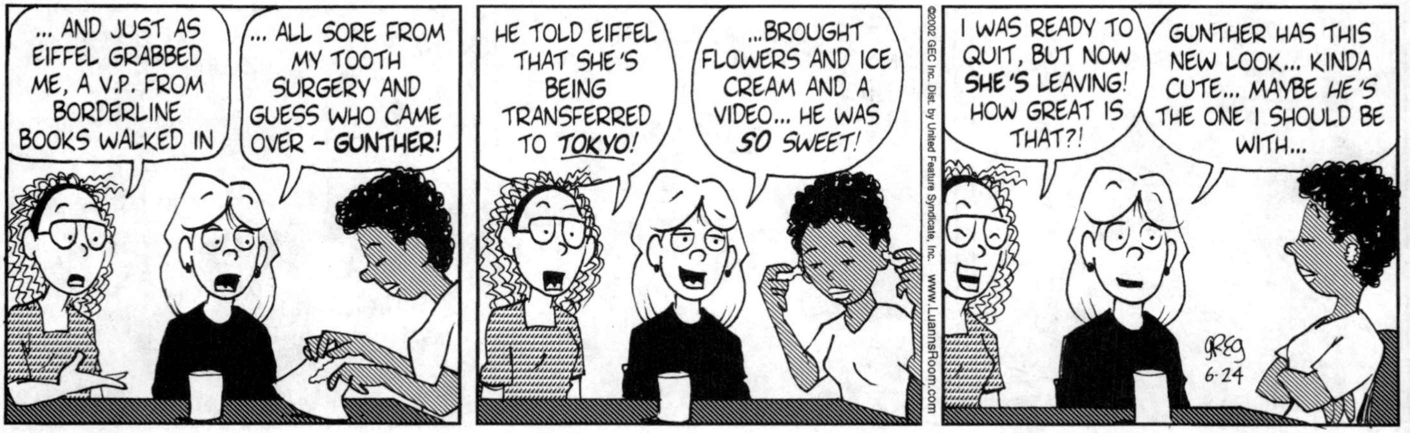
... AND JUST AS EIFFEL GRABBED ME, A V.P. FROM BORDERLINE BOOKS WALKED IN
... ALL SORE FROM MY TOOTH SURGERY AND GUESS WHO CAME OVER – **GUNTHER**!
HE TOLD EIFFEL THAT SHE'S BEING TRANSFERRED TO ***TOKYO***!
...BROUGHT FLOWERS AND ICE CREAM AND A VIDEO... HE WAS ***SO*** *SWEET*!
©2002 GEC Inc. Dist. by United Feature Syndicate, Inc. www.LuannsRoom.com
I WAS READY TO QUIT, BUT NOW **SHE'S** LEAVING! HOW GREAT IS THAT?!
GUNTHER HAS THIS NEW LOOK... KINDA CUTE... MAYBE *HE'S* THE ONE I SHOULD BE WITH...
GREG 6·24

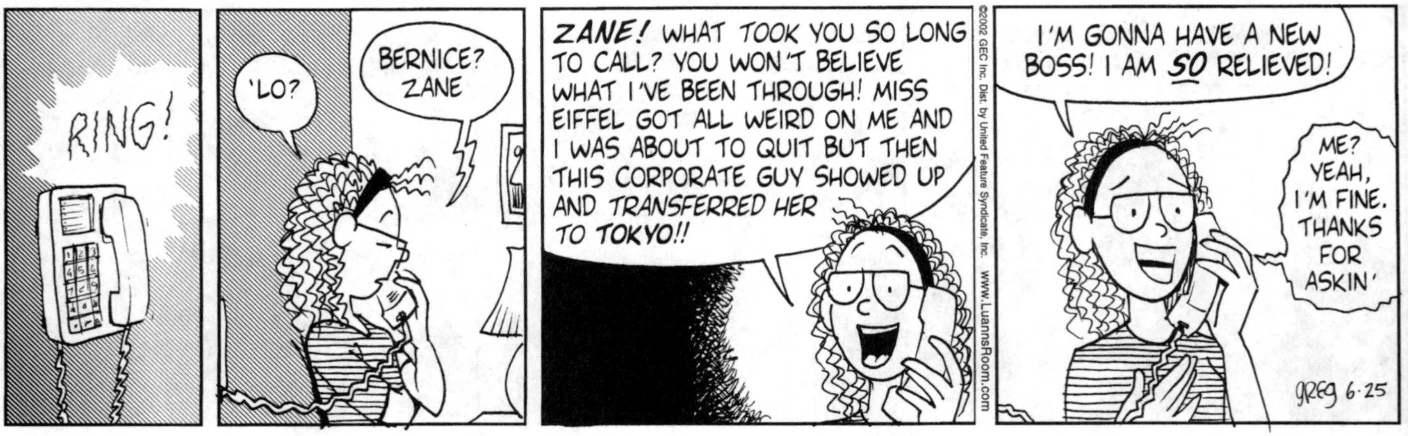
RING!
'LO?
BERNICE? ZANE
ZANE! WHAT *TOOK* YOU SO LONG TO CALL? YOU WON'T BELIEVE WHAT I'VE BEEN THROUGH! MISS EIFFEL GOT ALL WEIRD ON ME AND I WAS ABOUT TO QUIT BUT THEN THIS CORPORATE GUY SHOWED UP AND *TRANSFERRED* HER TO ***TOKYO***!!
©2002 GEC Inc. Dist. by United Feature Syndicate, Inc. www.LuannsRoom.com
I'M GONNA HAVE A NEW BOSS! I AM ***SO*** RELIEVED!
ME? YEAH, I'M FINE. THANKS FOR ASKIN'
GREG 6·25

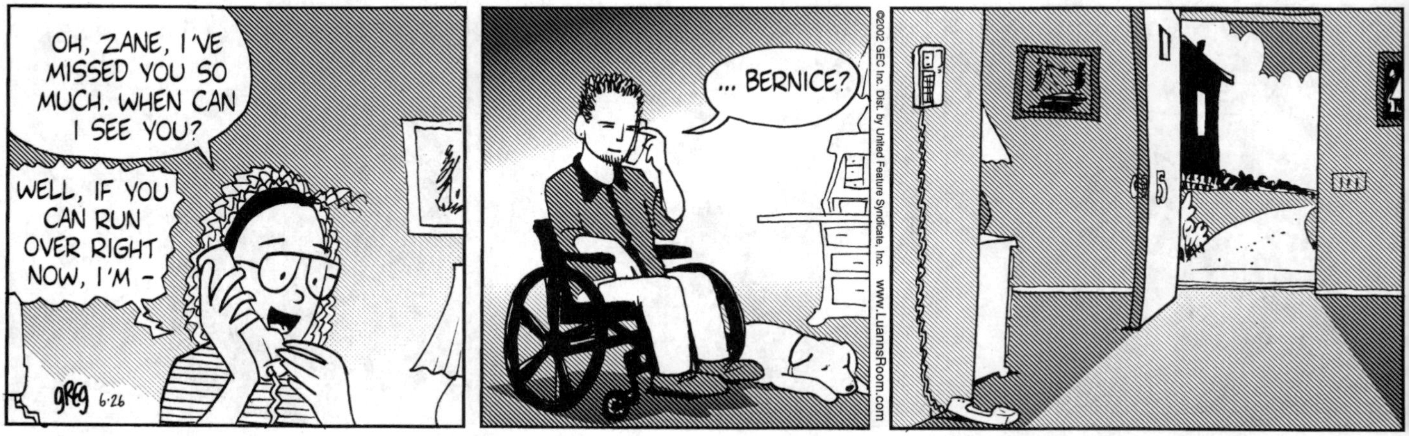
OH, ZANE, I'VE MISSED YOU SO MUCH. WHEN CAN I SEE YOU?
WELL, IF YOU CAN RUN OVER RIGHT NOW, I'M –
GREG 6·26
©2002 GEC Inc. Dist. by United Feature Syndicate, Inc. www.LuannsRoom.com
... BERNICE?

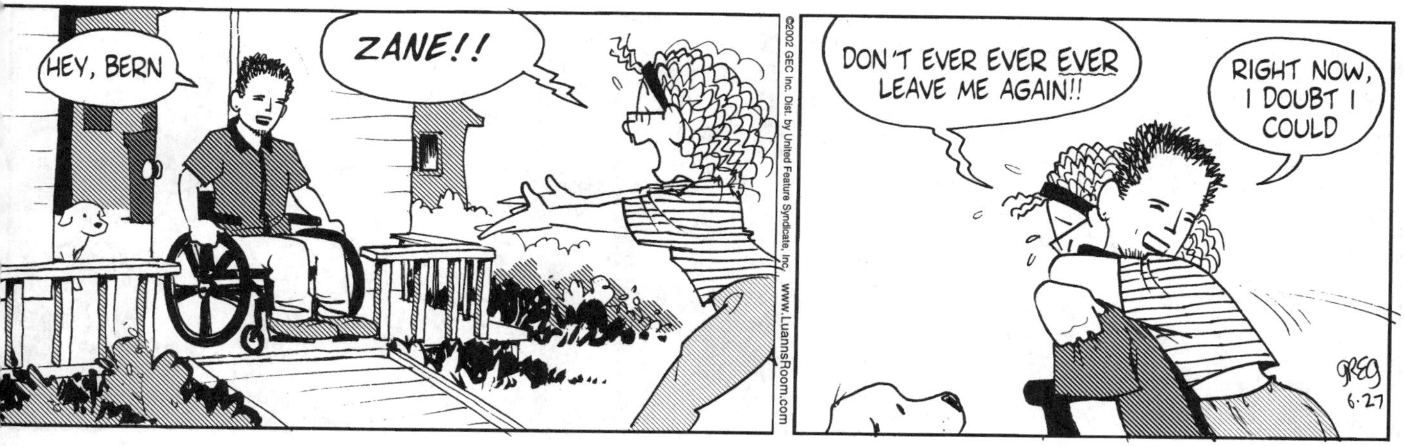
HEY, BERN
ZANE!!
©2002 GEC Inc. Dist. by United Feature Syndicate, Inc. www.LuannsRoom.com
DON'T EVER EVER EVER LEAVE ME AGAIN!!
RIGHT NOW, I DOUBT I COULD
GREG 6·27

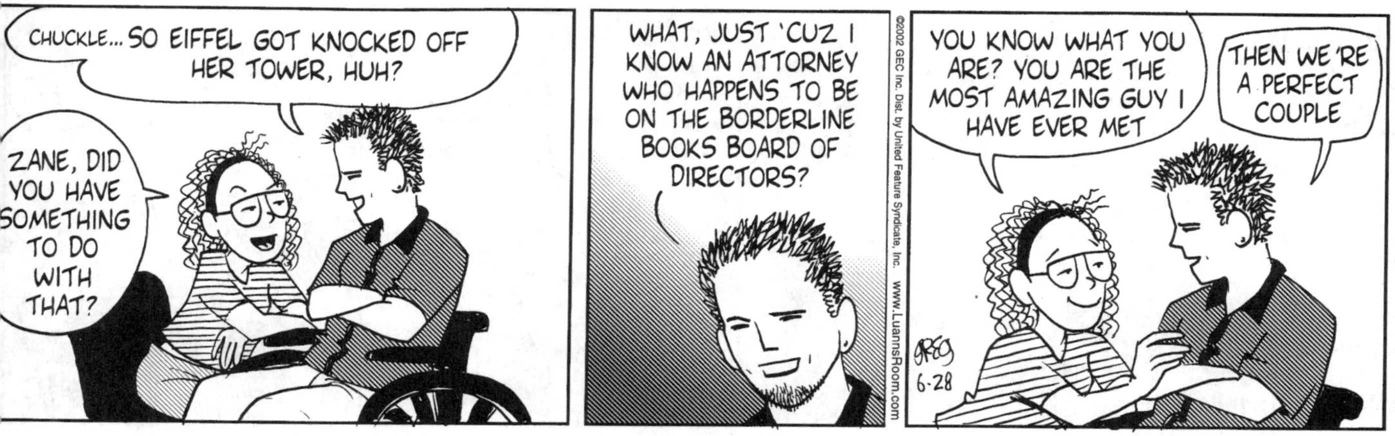
CHUCKLE... SO EIFFEL GOT KNOCKED OFF HER TOWER, HUH?
ZANE, DID YOU HAVE SOMETHING TO DO WITH THAT?
WHAT, JUST 'CUZ I KNOW AN ATTORNEY WHO HAPPENS TO BE ON THE BORDERLINE BOOKS BOARD OF DIRECTORS?
©2002 GEC Inc. Dist. by United Feature Syndicate, Inc. www.LuannsRoom.com
YOU KNOW WHAT YOU ARE? YOU ARE THE MOST AMAZING GUY I HAVE EVER MET
THEN WE'RE A PERFECT COUPLE
GREG 6·28

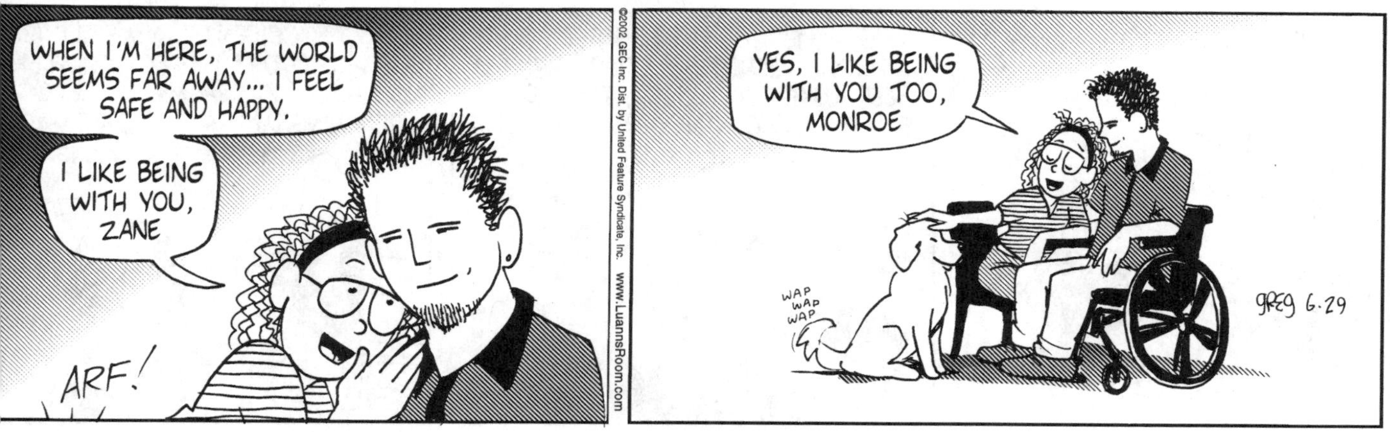
WHEN I'M HERE, THE WORLD SEEMS FAR AWAY... I FEEL SAFE AND HAPPY.
I LIKE BEING WITH YOU, ZANE
ARF!
©2002 GEC Inc. Dist. by United Feature Syndicate, Inc. www.LuannsRoom.com
YES, I LIKE BEING WITH YOU TOO, MONROE
WAP WAP WAP
GREG 6·29

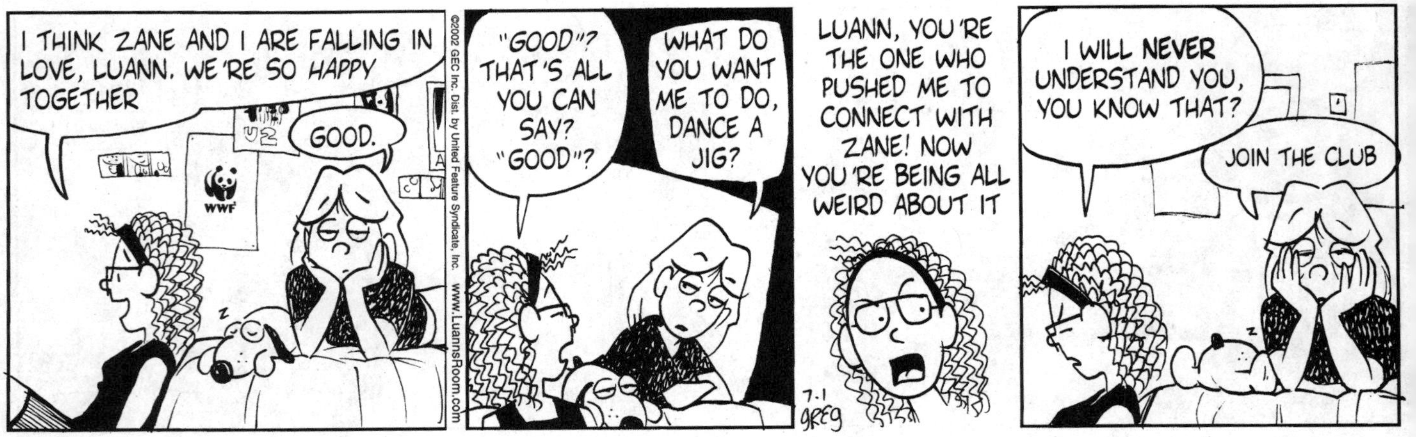
I THINK ZANE AND I ARE FALLING IN LOVE, LUANN. WE'RE SO *HAPPY* TOGETHER
GOOD.
"*GOOD*"? THAT'S ALL YOU CAN SAY? "GOOD"?
WHAT DO YOU WANT ME TO DO, DANCE A JIG?
LUANN, YOU'RE THE ONE WHO PUSHED ME TO CONNECT WITH ZANE! NOW YOU'RE BEING ALL WEIRD ABOUT IT
I WILL **NEVER** UNDERSTAND YOU, YOU KNOW THAT?
JOIN THE CLUB
©2002 GEC Inc. Dist. by United Feature Syndicate, Inc. www.LuannsRoom.com
7·1 GREG

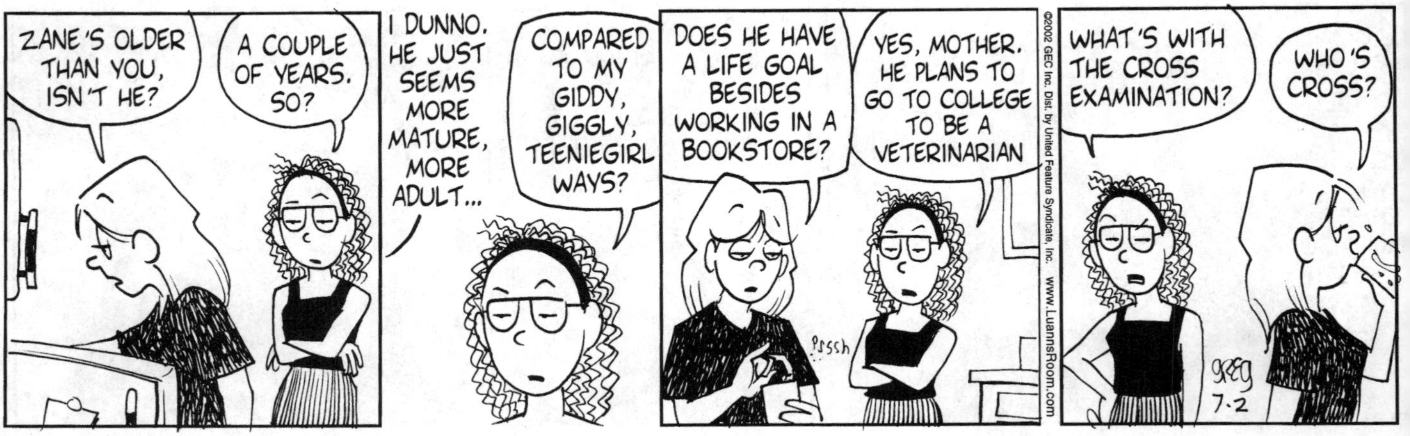
ZANE'S OLDER THAN YOU, ISN'T HE?
A COUPLE OF YEARS. SO?
I DUNNO. HE JUST SEEMS MORE MATURE, MORE ADULT...
COMPARED TO MY GIDDY, GIGGLY, TEENIEGIRL WAYS?
DOES HE HAVE A LIFE GOAL BESIDES WORKING IN A BOOKSTORE?
YES, MOTHER. HE PLANS TO GO TO COLLEGE TO BE A VETERINARIAN
PSSSH
WHAT'S WITH THE CROSS EXAMINATION?
WHO'S CROSS?
©2002 GEC Inc. Dist. by United Feature Syndicate, Inc. www.LuannsRoom.com
GREG 7·2

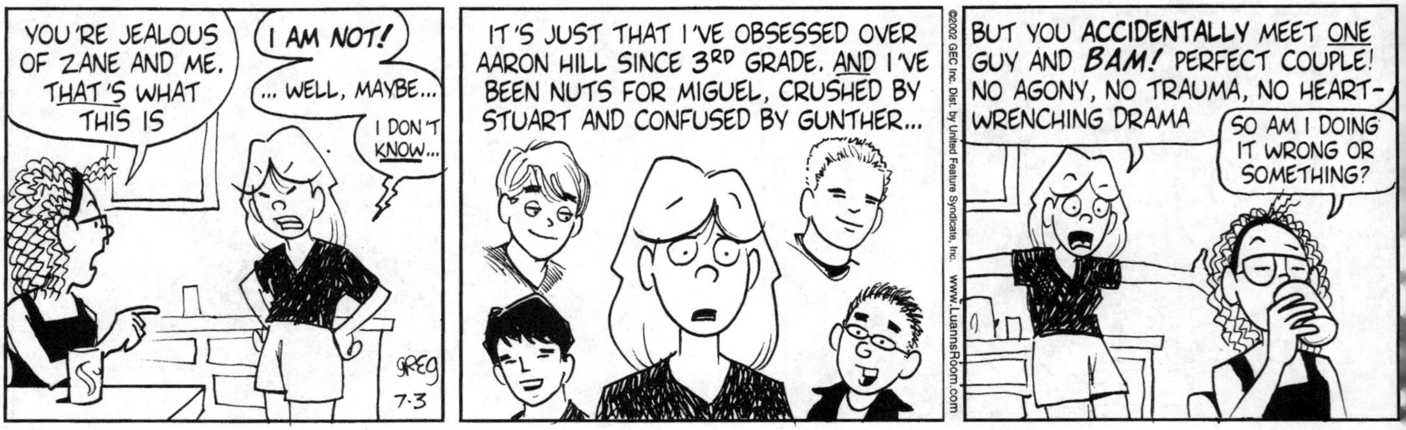
YOU'RE JEALOUS OF ZANE AND ME. THAT'S WHAT THIS IS
I AM *NOT*!
... WELL, MAYBE...
I DON'T KNOW...
IT'S JUST THAT I'VE OBSESSED OVER AARON HILL SINCE 3RD GRADE. AND I'VE BEEN NUTS FOR MIGUEL, CRUSHED BY STUART AND CONFUSED BY GUNTHER...
BUT YOU **ACCIDENTALLY** MEET ONE GUY AND ***BAM!*** PERFECT COUPLE! NO AGONY, NO TRAUMA, NO HEART-WRENCHING DRAMA
SO AM I DOING IT WRONG OR SOMETHING?
©2002 GEC Inc. Dist. by United Feature Syndicate, Inc. www.LuannsRoom.com
GREG 7·3

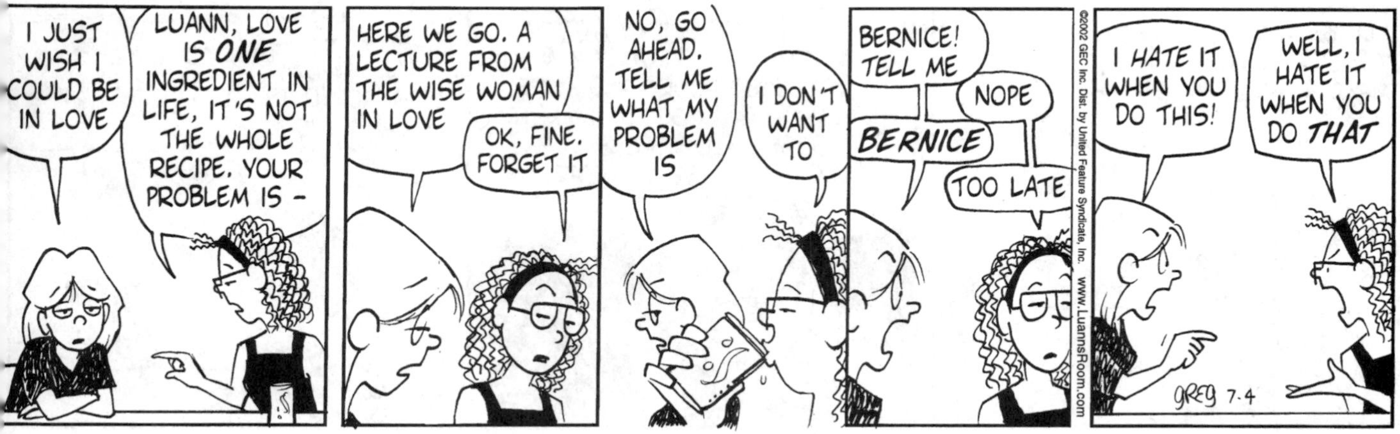
I JUST WISH I COULD BE IN LOVE
LUANN, LOVE IS *ONE* INGREDIENT IN LIFE, IT'S NOT THE WHOLE RECIPE. YOUR PROBLEM IS –
HERE WE GO. A LECTURE FROM THE WISE WOMAN IN LOVE
OK, FINE. FORGET IT
NO, GO AHEAD. TELL ME WHAT MY PROBLEM IS
I DON'T WANT TO
BERNICE! TELL ME
NOPE
BERNICE
TOO LATE
©2002 GEC Inc. Dist. by United Feature Syndicate, Inc. www.LuannsRoom.com
I *HATE* IT WHEN YOU DO THIS!
WELL, I HATE IT WHEN YOU DO ***THAT***
GREG 7·4

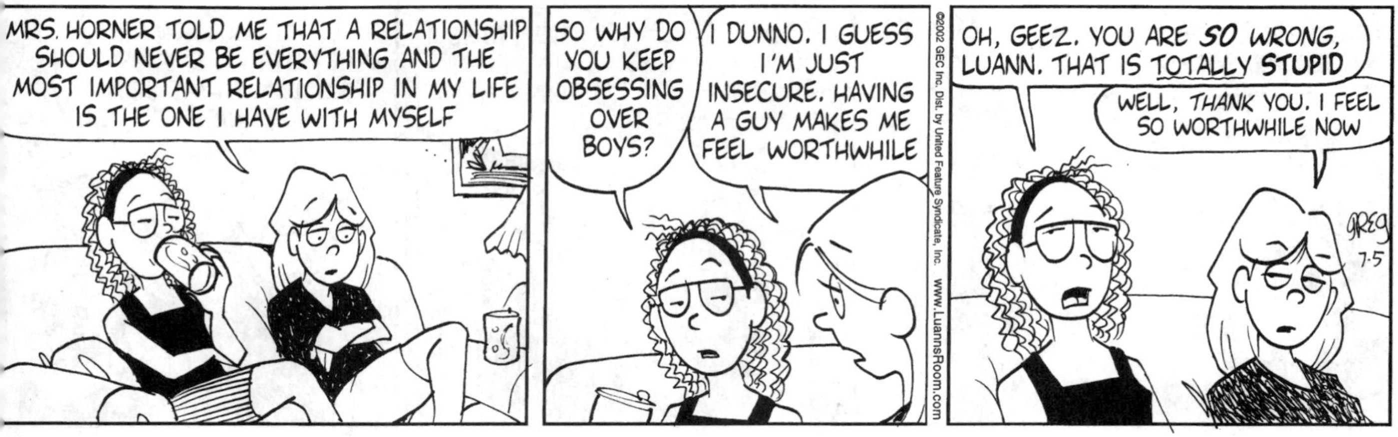
MRS. HORNER TOLD ME THAT A RELATIONSHIP SHOULD NEVER BE EVERYTHING AND THE MOST IMPORTANT RELATIONSHIP IN MY LIFE IS THE ONE I HAVE WITH MYSELF
SO WHY DO YOU KEEP OBSESSING OVER BOYS?
I DUNNO. I GUESS I'M JUST INSECURE. HAVING A GUY MAKES ME FEEL WORTHWHILE
©2002 GEC Inc. Dist. by United Feature Syndicate, Inc. www.LuannsRoom.com
OH, GEEZ. YOU ARE ***SO WRONG***, LUANN. THAT IS TOTALLY **STUPID**
WELL, *THANK* YOU. I FEEL SO WORTHWHILE NOW
GREG 7·5

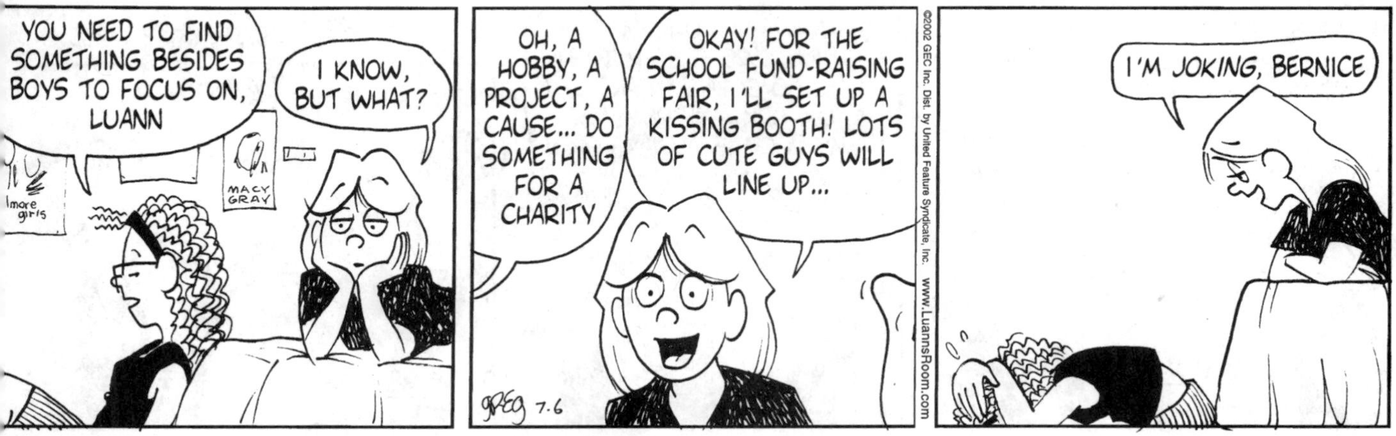
YOU NEED TO FIND SOMETHING BESIDES BOYS TO FOCUS ON, LUANN
I KNOW, BUT WHAT?
MACY GRAY
I more girls
OH, A HOBBY, A PROJECT, A CAUSE... DO SOMETHING FOR A CHARITY
OKAY! FOR THE SCHOOL FUND-RAISING FAIR, I'LL SET UP A KISSING BOOTH! LOTS OF CUTE GUYS WILL LINE UP...
GREG 7·6
©2002 GEC Inc. Dist. by United Feature Syndicate, Inc. www.LuannsRoom.com
I'M *JOKING*, BERNICE

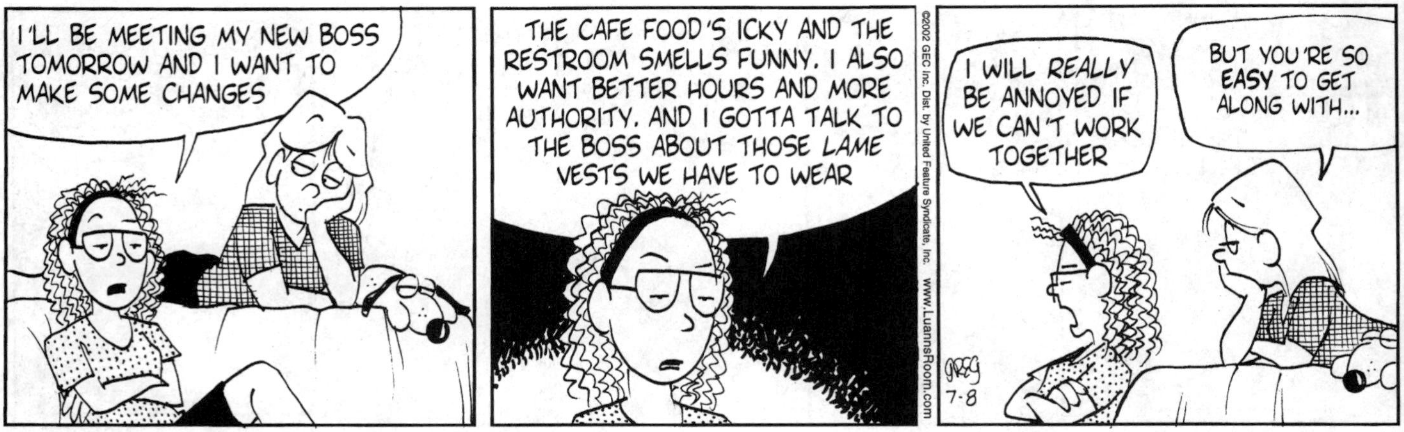
I'LL BE MEETING MY NEW BOSS TOMORROW AND I WANT TO MAKE SOME CHANGES
THE CAFE FOOD'S ICKY AND THE RESTROOM SMELLS FUNNY. I ALSO WANT BETTER HOURS AND MORE AUTHORITY. AND I GOTTA TALK TO THE BOSS ABOUT THOSE *LAME* VESTS WE HAVE TO WEAR
©2002 GEC Inc. Dist. by United Feature Syndicate, Inc. www.LuannsRoom.com
I WILL *REALLY* BE ANNOYED IF WE CAN'T WORK TOGETHER
BUT YOU'RE SO **EASY** TO GET ALONG WITH...
GREG 7-8

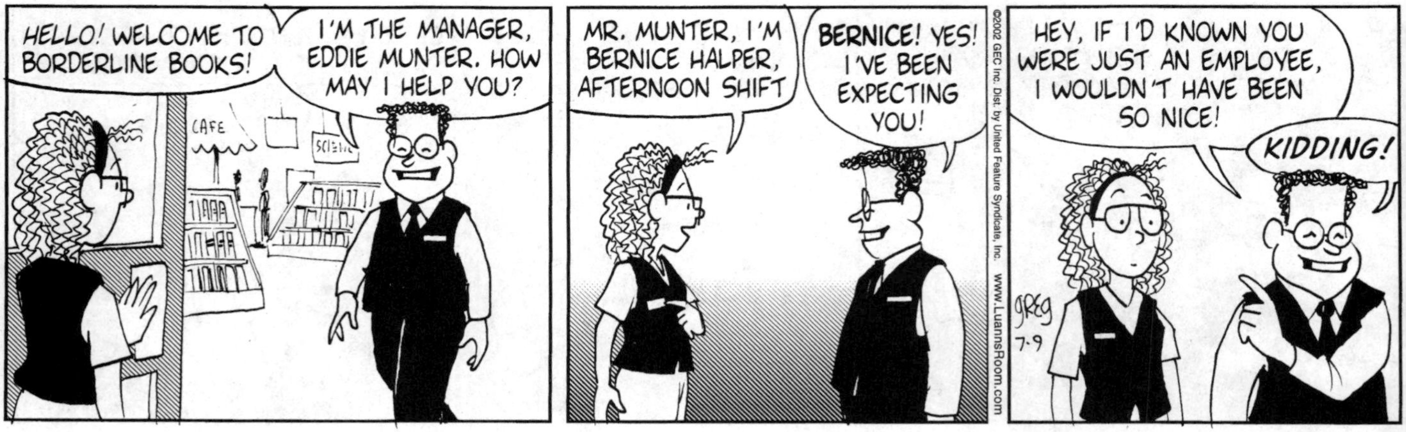
HELLO! WELCOME TO BORDERLINE BOOKS!
I'M THE MANAGER, EDDIE MUNTER. HOW MAY I HELP YOU?
CAFE
MR. MUNTER, I'M BERNICE HALPER, AFTERNOON SHIFT
BERNICE! YES! I'VE BEEN EXPECTING YOU!
©2002 GEC Inc. Dist. by United Feature Syndicate, Inc. www.LuannsRoom.com
HEY, IF I'D KNOWN YOU WERE JUST AN EMPLOYEE, I WOULDN'T HAVE BEEN SO NICE!
KIDDING!
GREG 7-9

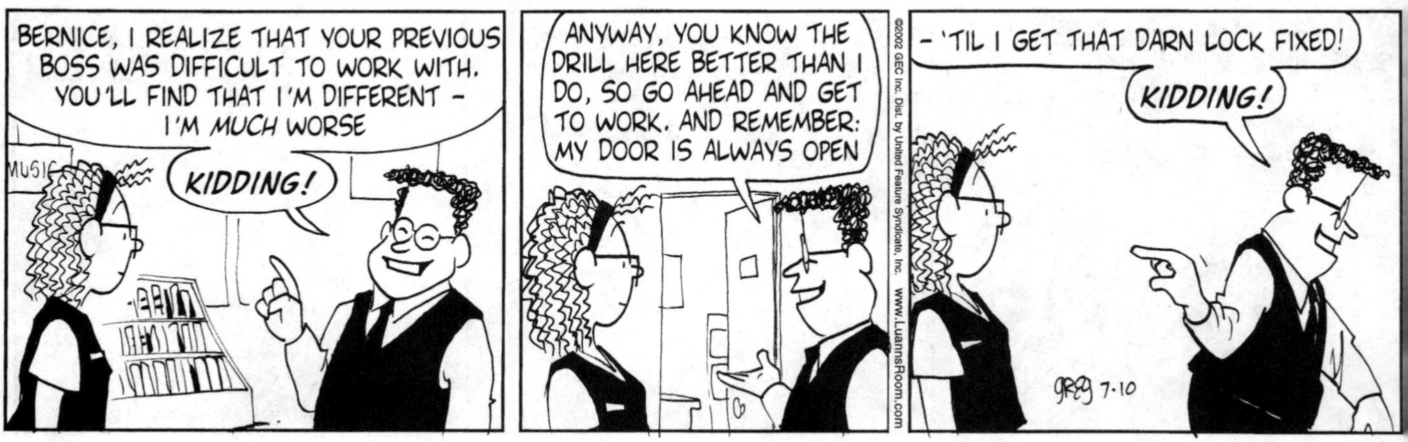
BERNICE, I REALIZE THAT YOUR PREVIOUS BOSS WAS DIFFICULT TO WORK WITH. YOU'LL FIND THAT I'M DIFFERENT – I'M *MUCH* WORSE
MUSIC
KIDDING!
ANYWAY, YOU KNOW THE DRILL HERE BETTER THAN I DO, SO GO AHEAD AND GET TO WORK. AND REMEMBER: MY DOOR IS ALWAYS OPEN
©2002 GEC Inc. Dist. by United Feature Syndicate, Inc. www.LuannsRoom.com
– 'TIL I GET THAT DARN LOCK FIXED!
KIDDING!
GREG 7-10

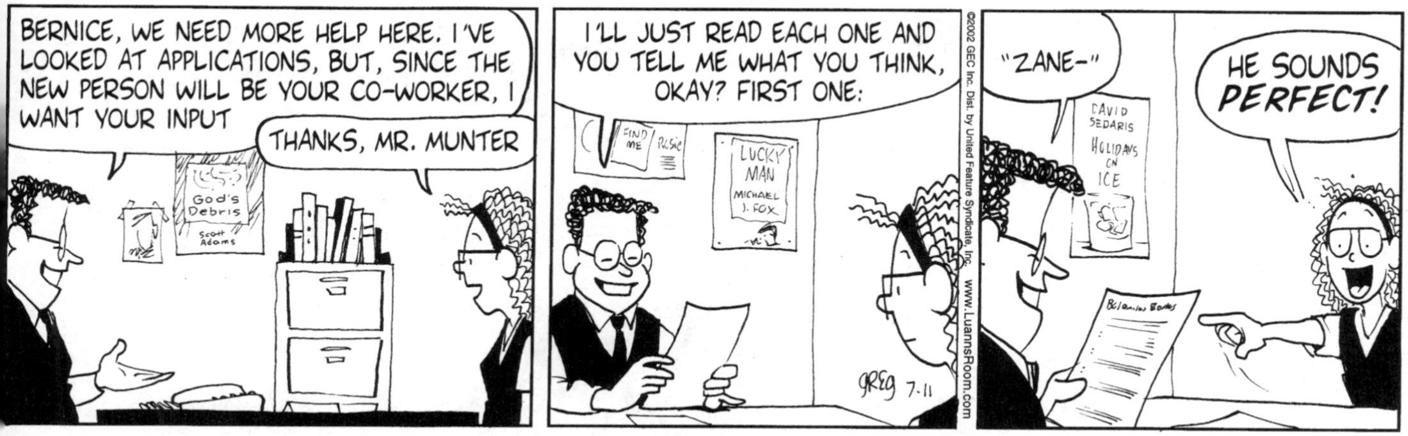
BERNICE, WE NEED MORE HELP HERE. I'VE LOOKED AT APPLICATIONS, BUT, SINCE THE NEW PERSON WILL BE YOUR CO-WORKER, I WANT YOUR INPUT
THANKS, MR. MUNTER
God's Debris
Scott Adams
I'LL JUST READ EACH ONE AND YOU TELL ME WHAT YOU THINK, OKAY? FIRST ONE:
FIND ME
LUCKY MAN
MICHAEL J. FOX
GREG 7-11
©2002 GEC Inc. Dist. by United Feature Syndicate, Inc. www.LuannsRoom.com
"ZANE-"
DAVID SEDARIS
HOLIDAYS ON ICE
HE SOUNDS PERFECT!

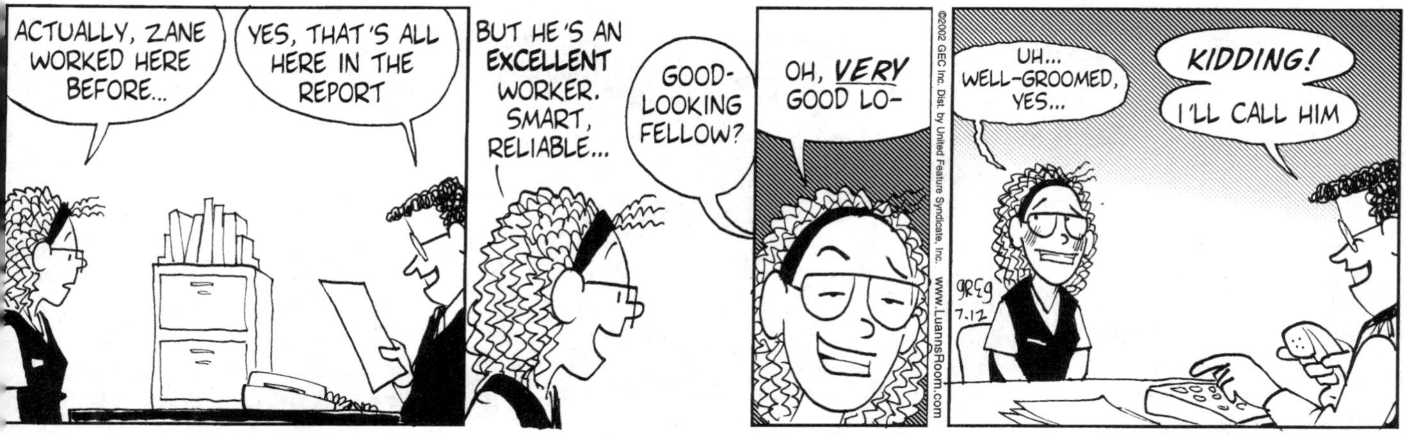
ACTUALLY, ZANE WORKED HERE BEFORE...
YES, THAT'S ALL HERE IN THE REPORT
BUT HE'S AN EXCELLENT WORKER. SMART, RELIABLE...
GOOD-LOOKING FELLOW?
OH, VERY GOOD LO-
©2002 GEC Inc. Dist. by United Feature Syndicate, Inc. www.LuannsRoom.com
UH... WELL-GROOMED, YES...
GREG 7-12
KIDDING!
I'LL CALL HIM

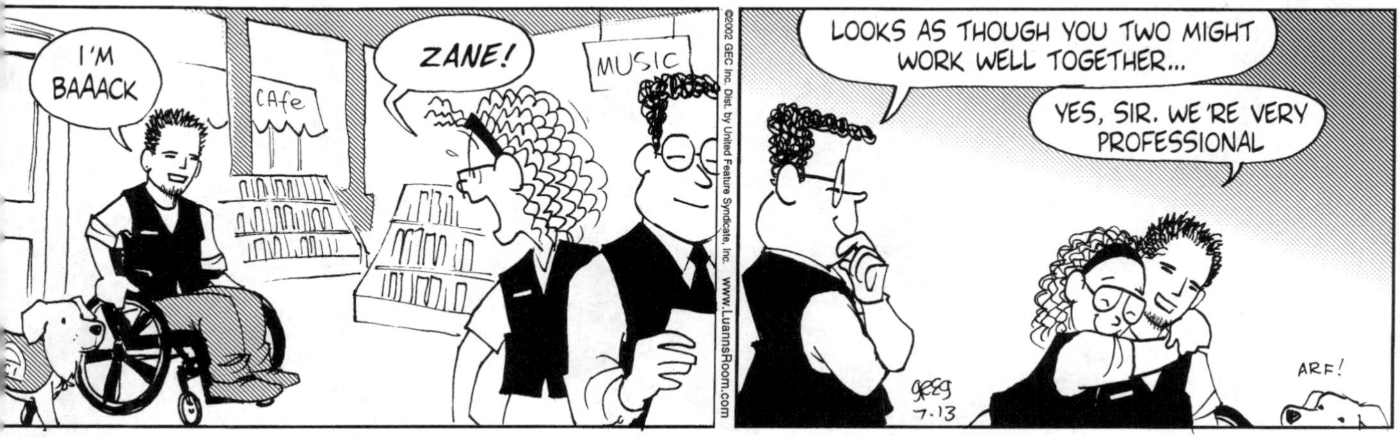
I'M BAAACK
CAfe
ZANE!
MUSIC
©2002 GEC Inc. Dist. by United Feature Syndicate, Inc. www.LuannsRoom.com
LOOKS AS THOUGH YOU TWO MIGHT WORK WELL TOGETHER...
YES, SIR. WE'RE VERY PROFESSIONAL
GREG 7-13
ARF!

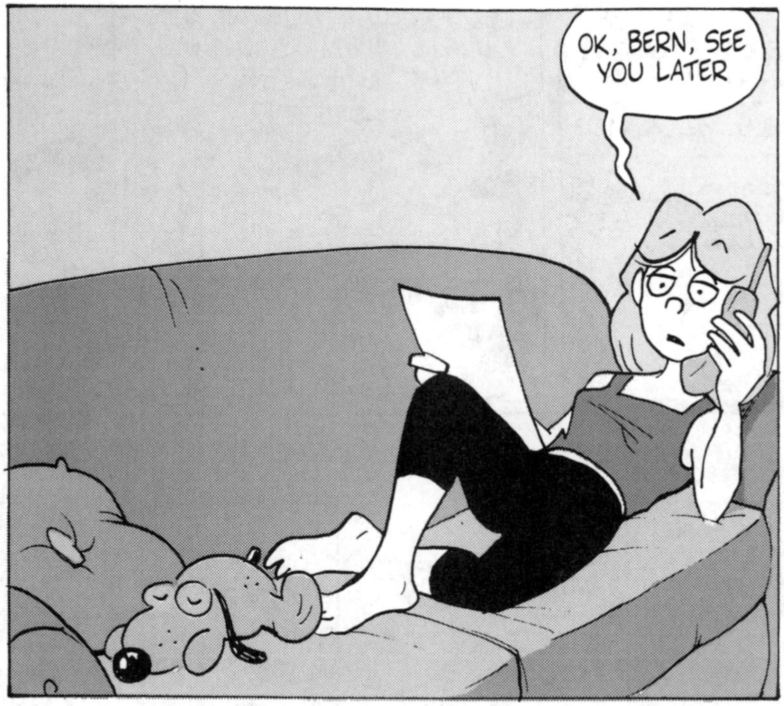
OK, BERN, SEE YOU LATER

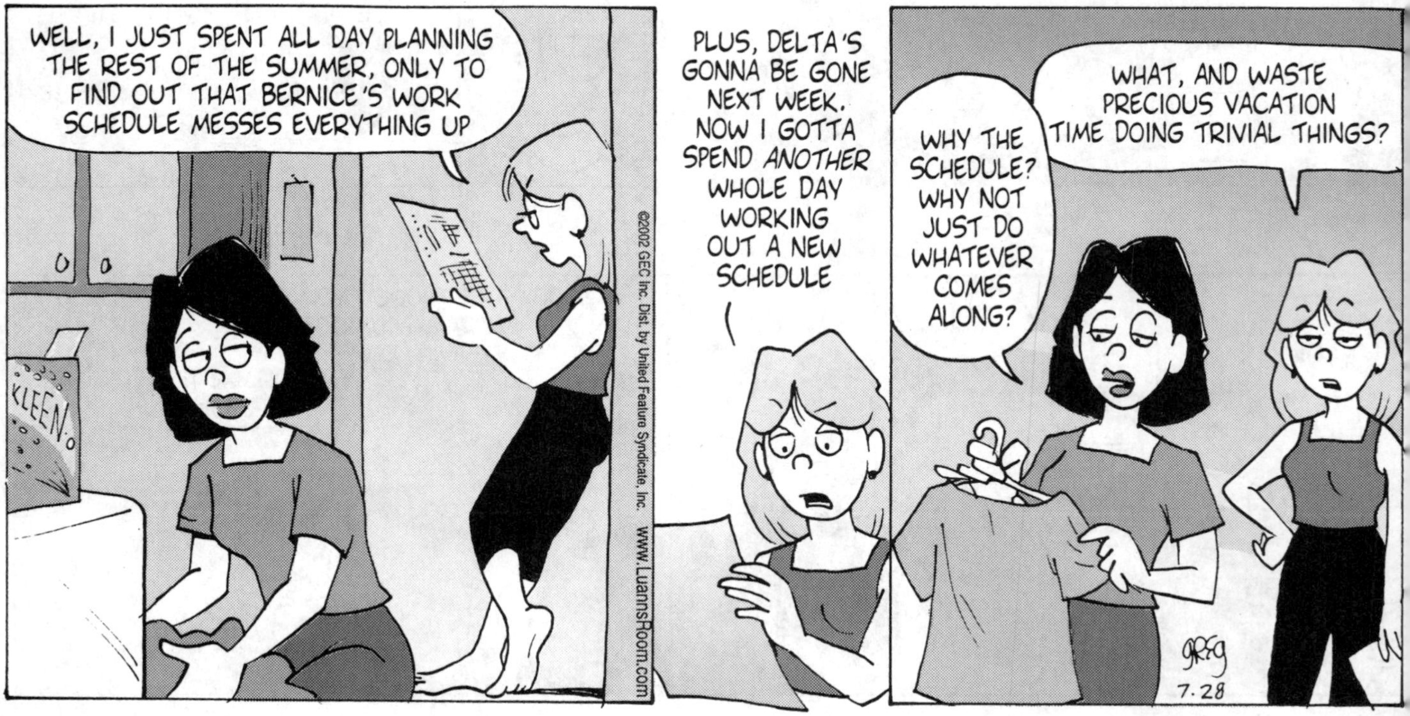
WELL, I JUST SPENT ALL DAY PLANNING THE REST OF THE SUMMER, ONLY TO FIND OUT THAT BERNICE'S WORK SCHEDULE MESSES EVERYTHING UP
KLEEN
©2002 GEC Inc. Dist. by United Feature Syndicate, Inc.
www.LuannsRoom.com
PLUS, DELTA'S GONNA BE GONE NEXT WEEK. NOW I GOTTA SPEND *ANOTHER* WHOLE DAY WORKING OUT A NEW SCHEDULE
WHY THE SCHEDULE? WHY NOT JUST DO WHATEVER COMES ALONG?
WHAT, AND WASTE PRECIOUS VACATION TIME DOING TRIVIAL THINGS?
GREG
7·28

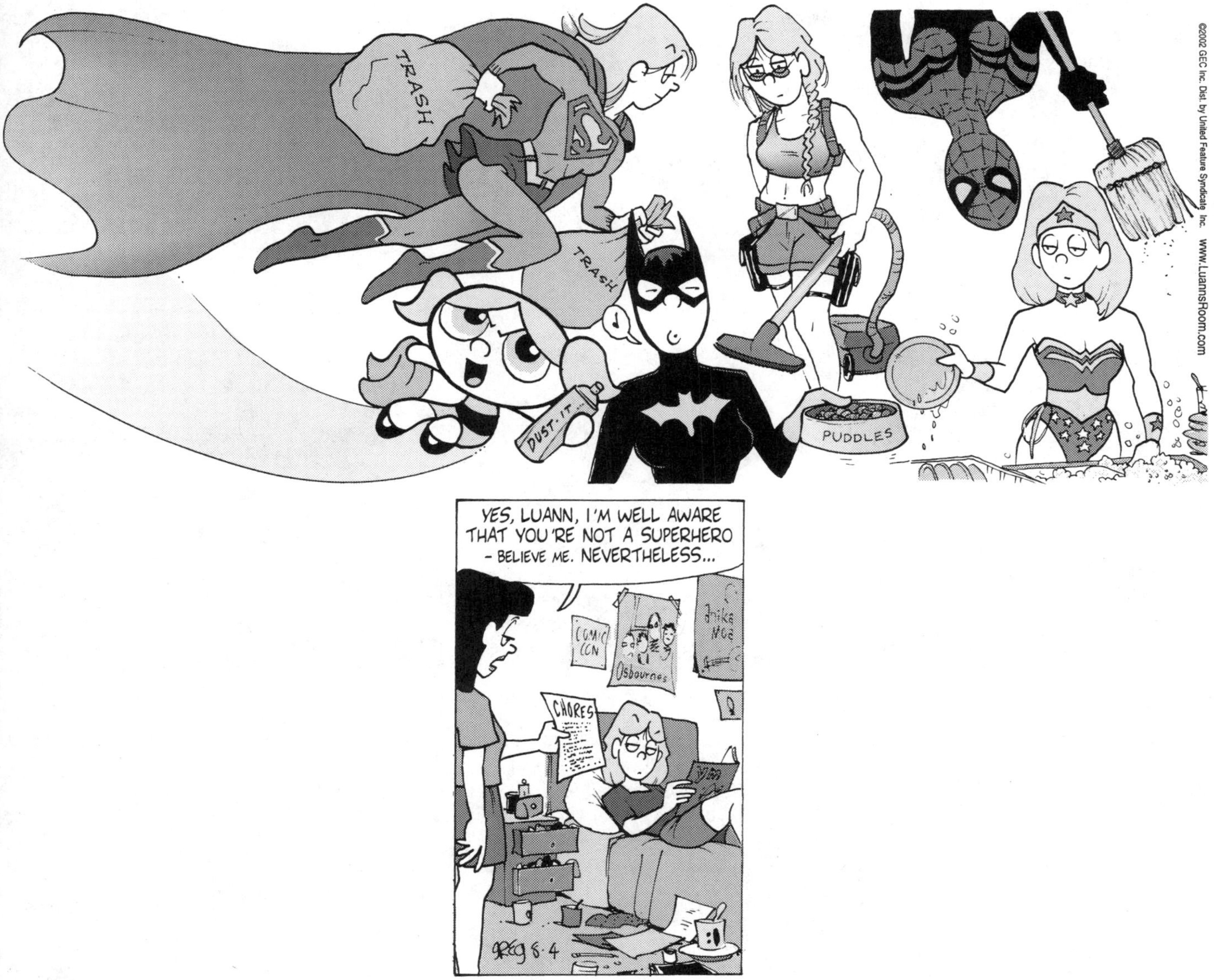
TRASH
TRASH
DUST-IT...
PUDDLES
©2002 GEC Inc. Dist. by United Feature Syndicate Inc. www.LuannsRoom.com
YES, LUANN, I'M WELL AWARE THAT YOU'RE NOT A SUPERHERO - BELIEVE ME. NEVERTHELESS...
COMIC CON
Osbournes
CHORES
greg 8-4

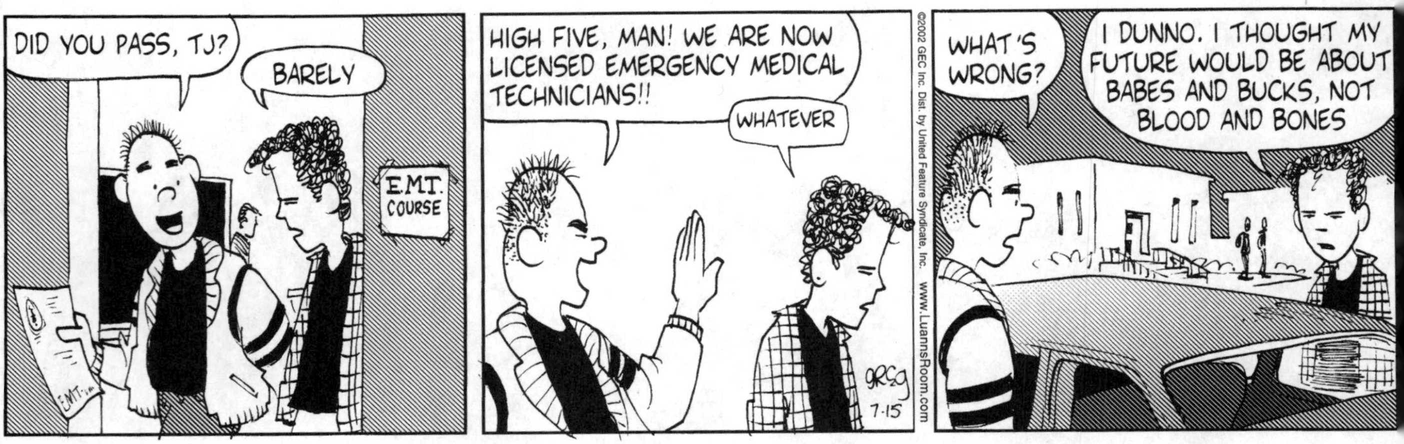
DID YOU PASS, TJ?
BARELY
E.M.T. COURSE
HIGH FIVE, MAN! WE ARE NOW LICENSED EMERGENCY MEDICAL TECHNICIANS!!
WHATEVER
GREG 7·15
©2002 GEC Inc. Dist. by United Feature Syndicate, Inc. www.LuannsRoom.com
WHAT'S WRONG?
I DUNNO. I THOUGHT MY FUTURE WOULD BE ABOUT BABES AND BUCKS, NOT BLOOD AND BONES

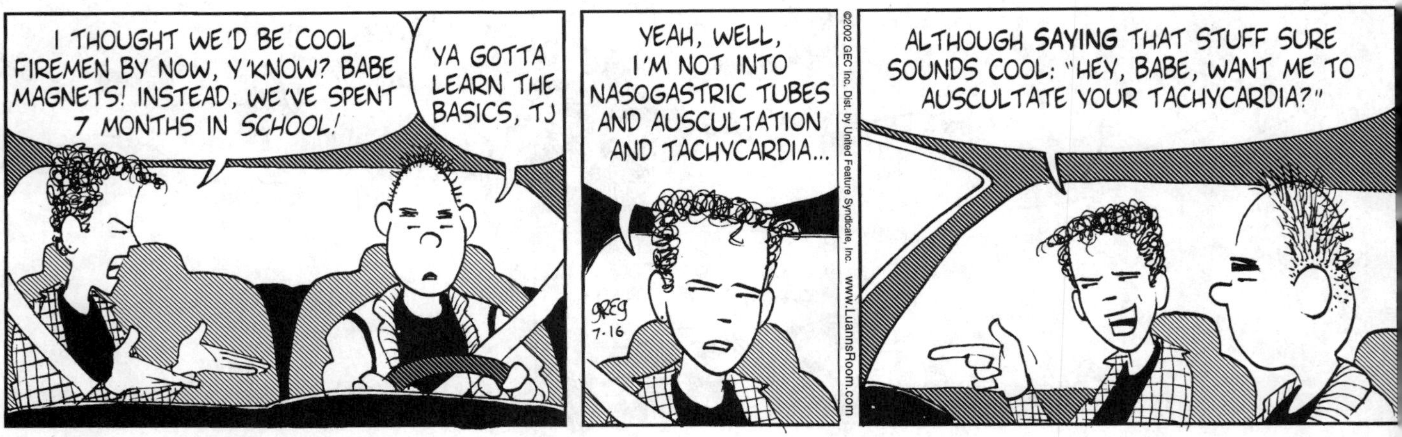
I THOUGHT WE'D BE COOL FIREMEN BY NOW, Y'KNOW? BABE MAGNETS! INSTEAD, WE'VE SPENT 7 MONTHS IN *SCHOOL*!
YA GOTTA LEARN THE BASICS, TJ
YEAH, WELL, I'M NOT INTO NASOGASTRIC TUBES AND AUSCULTATION AND TACHYCARDIA...
GREG 7·16
©2002 GEC Inc. Dist. by United Feature Syndicate, Inc. www.LuannsRoom.com
ALTHOUGH **SAYING** THAT STUFF SURE SOUNDS COOL: "HEY, BABE, WANT ME TO AUSCULTATE YOUR TACHYCARDIA?"

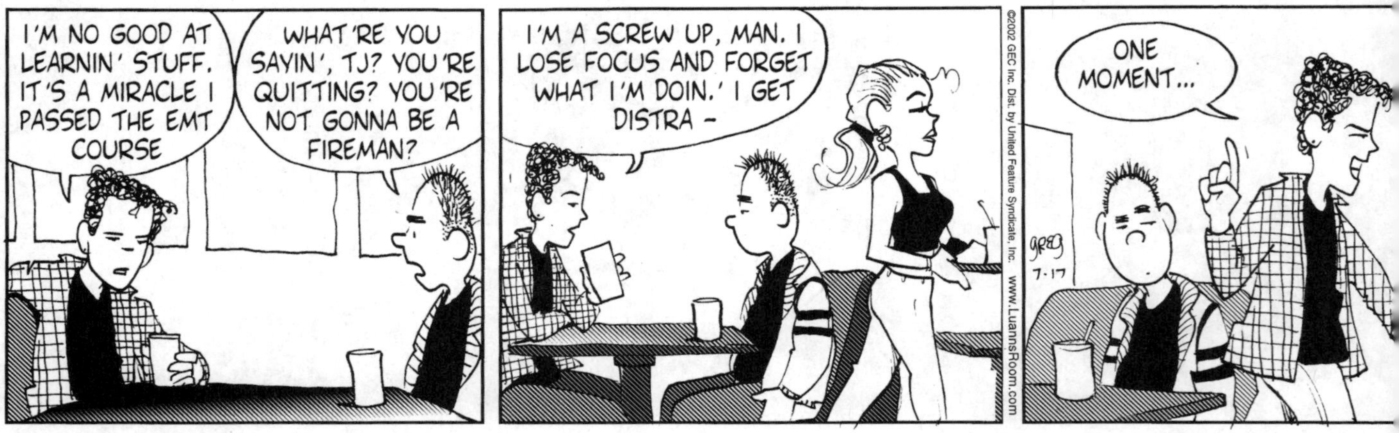
I'M NO GOOD AT LEARNIN' STUFF. IT'S A MIRACLE I PASSED THE EMT COURSE
WHAT'RE YOU SAYIN', TJ? YOU'RE QUITTING? YOU'RE NOT GONNA BE A FIREMAN?
I'M A SCREW UP, MAN. I LOSE FOCUS AND FORGET WHAT I'M DOIN.' I GET DISTRA –
©2002 GEC Inc. Dist. by United Feature Syndicate, Inc. www.LuannsRoom.com
GREG 7·17
ONE MOMENT...

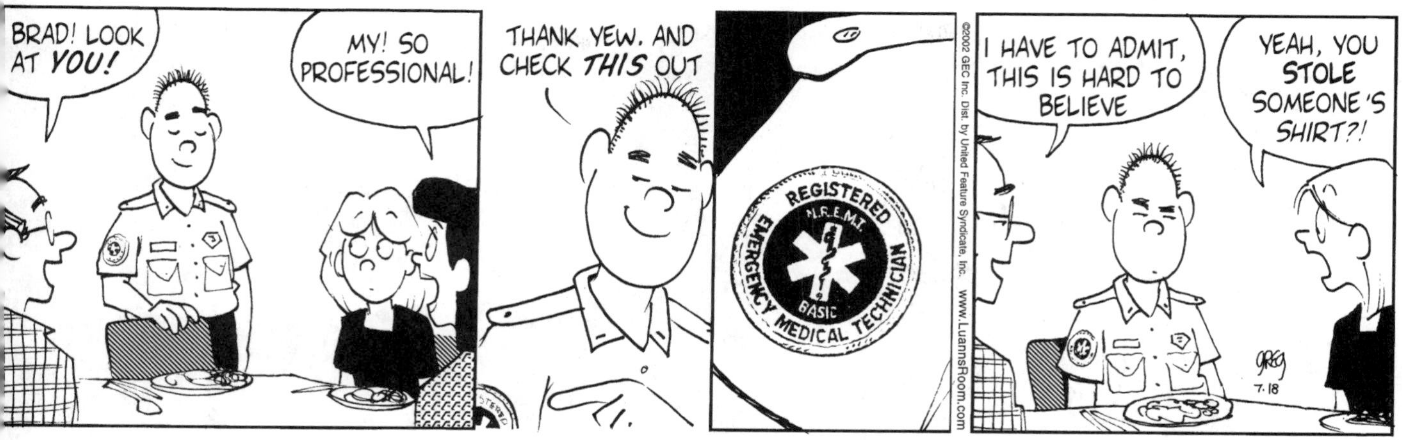
BRAD! LOOK AT YOU!
MY! SO PROFESSIONAL!
THANK YEW. AND CHECK THIS OUT
REGISTERED EMERGENCY MEDICAL TECHNICIAN
N.R.E.M.T.
BASIC
©2002 GEC Inc. Dist. by United Feature Syndicate, Inc. www.LuannsRoom.com
I HAVE TO ADMIT, THIS IS HARD TO BELIEVE
YEAH, YOU STOLE SOMEONE'S SHIRT?!
GREG 7.18

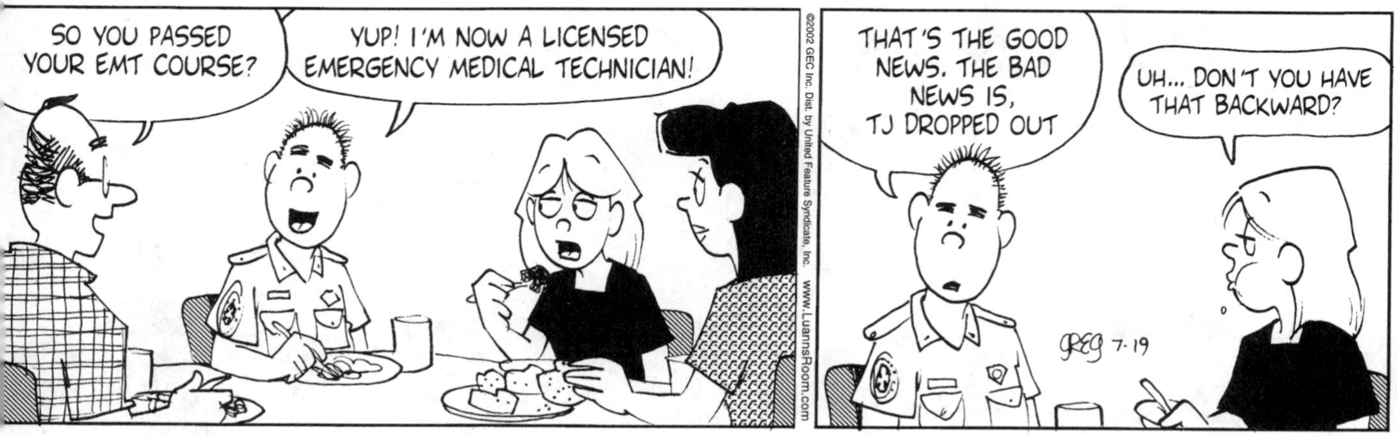
SO YOU PASSED YOUR EMT COURSE?
YUP! I'M NOW A LICENSED EMERGENCY MEDICAL TECHNICIAN!
©2002 GEC Inc. Dist. by United Feature Syndicate, Inc. www.LuannsRoom.com
THAT'S THE GOOD NEWS. THE BAD NEWS IS, TJ DROPPED OUT
UH... DON'T YOU HAVE THAT BACKWARD?
GREG 7.19

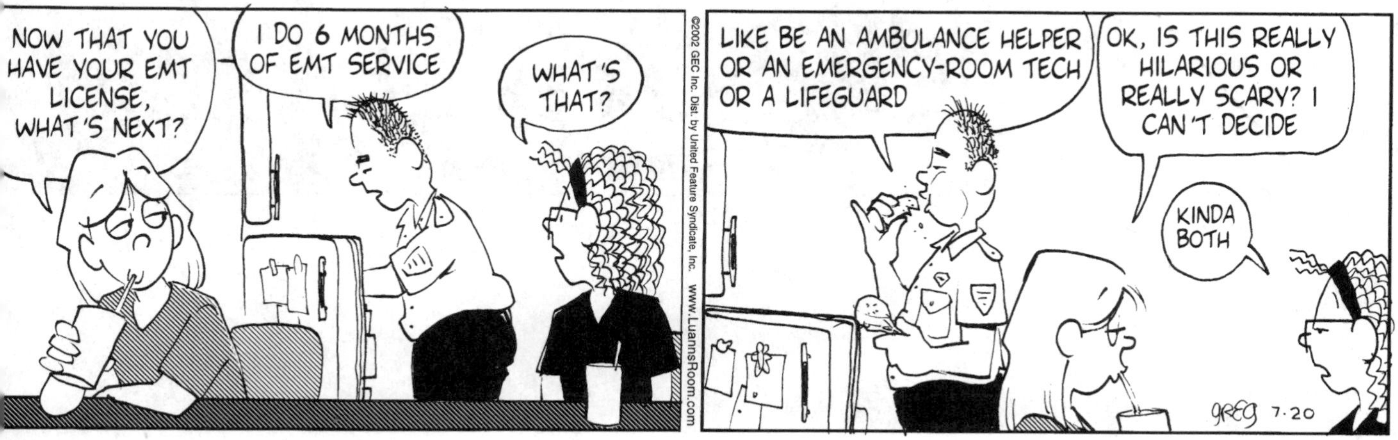
NOW THAT YOU HAVE YOUR EMT LICENSE, WHAT'S NEXT?
I DO 6 MONTHS OF EMT SERVICE
WHAT'S THAT?
©2002 GEC Inc. Dist. by United Feature Syndicate, Inc. www.LuannsRoom.com
LIKE BE AN AMBULANCE HELPER OR AN EMERGENCY-ROOM TECH OR A LIFEGUARD
OK, IS THIS REALLY HILARIOUS OR REALLY SCARY? I CAN'T DECIDE
KINDA BOTH
GREG 7.20

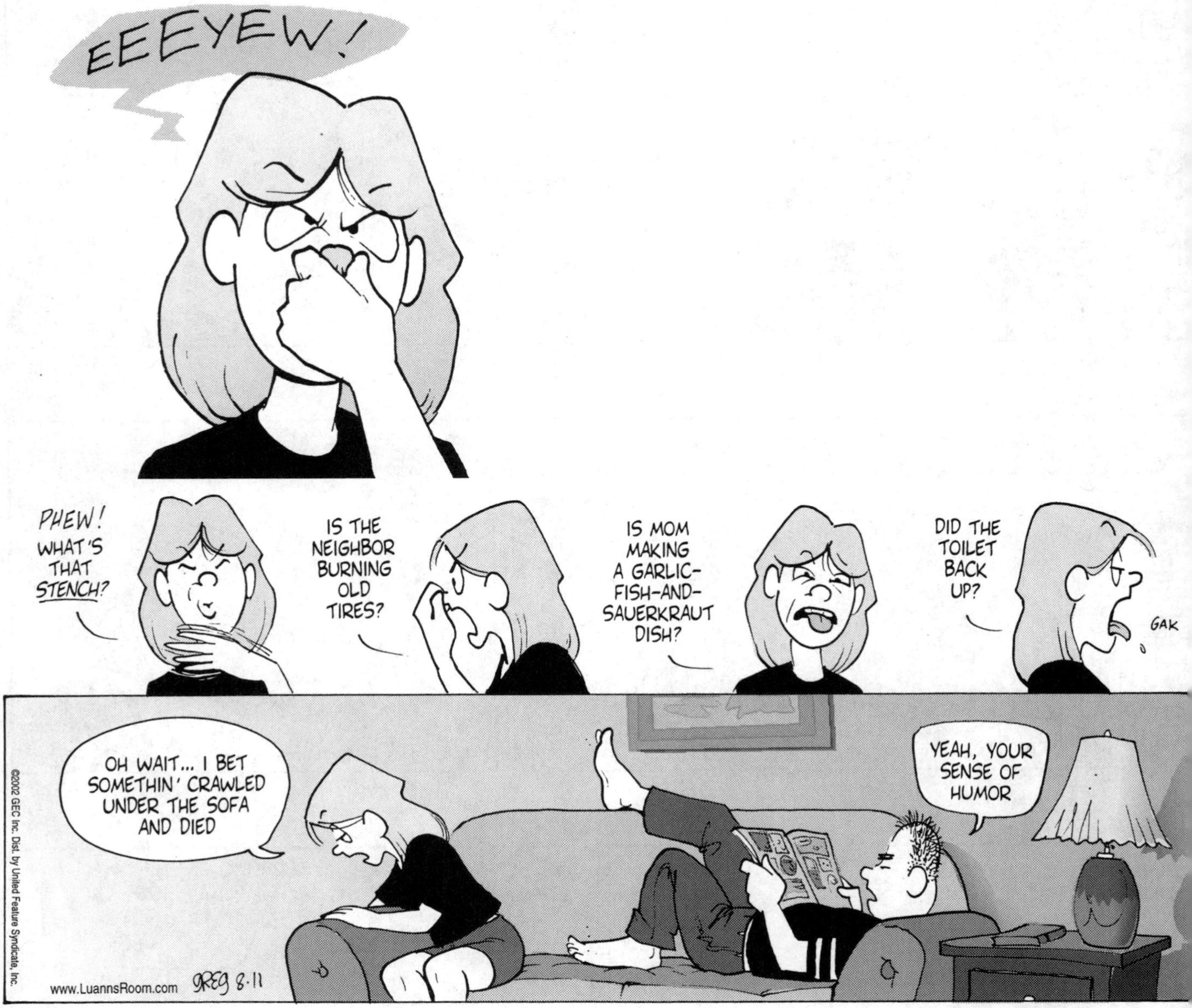
EEEYEW!
PHEW! WHAT'S THAT STENCH?
IS THE NEIGHBOR BURNING OLD TIRES?
IS MOM MAKING A GARLIC-FISH-AND-SAUERKRAUT DISH?
DID THE TOILET BACK UP?
GAK
OH WAIT... I BET SOMETHIN' CRAWLED UNDER THE SOFA AND DIED
YEAH, YOUR SENSE OF HUMOR
©2002 GEC Inc. Dist. by United Feature Syndicate, Inc.
www.LuannsRoom.com
GREG 8-11

OK, HERE'S THE NEW OUTFIT I BOUGHT, AND DON'T EVEN SAY YOU DON'T LIKE IT 'CUZ I'M NOT TAKING IT BACK!
WIPE OUT
©2002 GEC Inc. Dist. by United Feature Syndicate, Inc. www.LuannsRoom.com
I NEED TO EXPRESS MYSELF, MOM. I WANT TO DRESS HOW MY GENERATION DRESSES. THIS OUTFIT IS ME
PHOTOS 1970'S
'BYE
GOT YOUR RECEIPT?
GREG 8.18

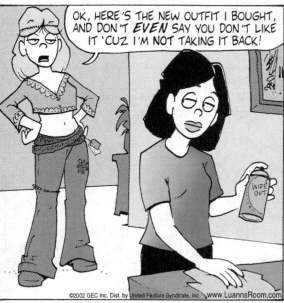

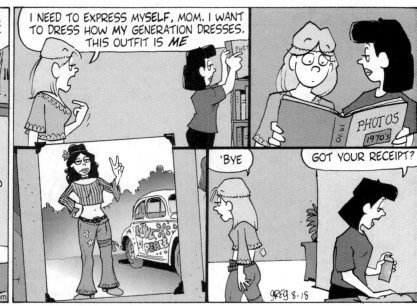

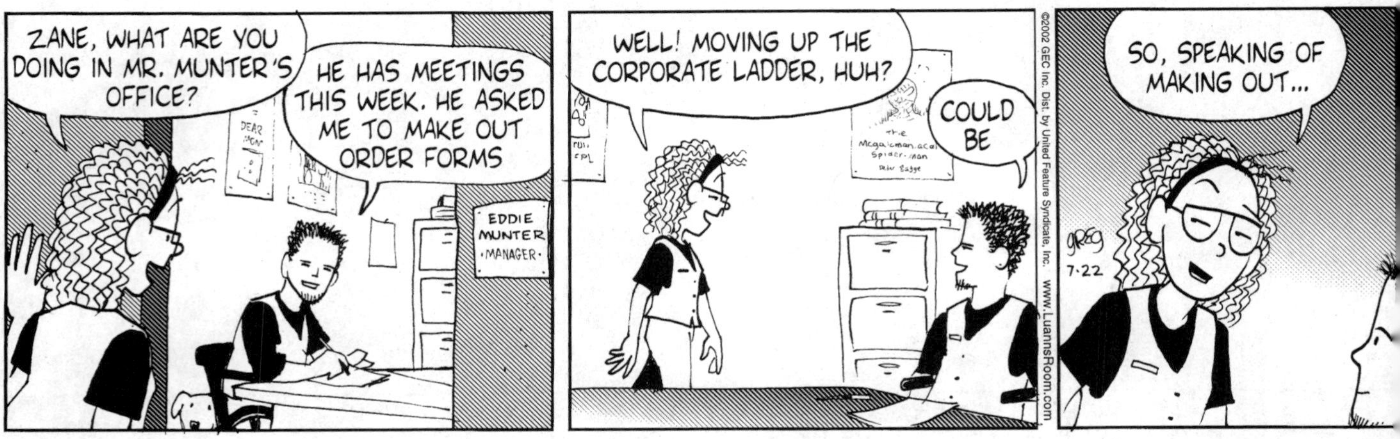
ZANE, WHAT ARE YOU DOING IN MR. MUNTER'S OFFICE?
HE HAS MEETINGS THIS WEEK. HE ASKED ME TO MAKE OUT ORDER FORMS
EDDIE MUNTER ·MANAGER·
WELL! MOVING UP THE CORPORATE LADDER, HUH?
COULD BE
©2002 GEC Inc. Dist. by United Feature Syndicate, Inc. www.LuannsRoom.com
SO, SPEAKING OF MAKING OUT...
GREG 7·22

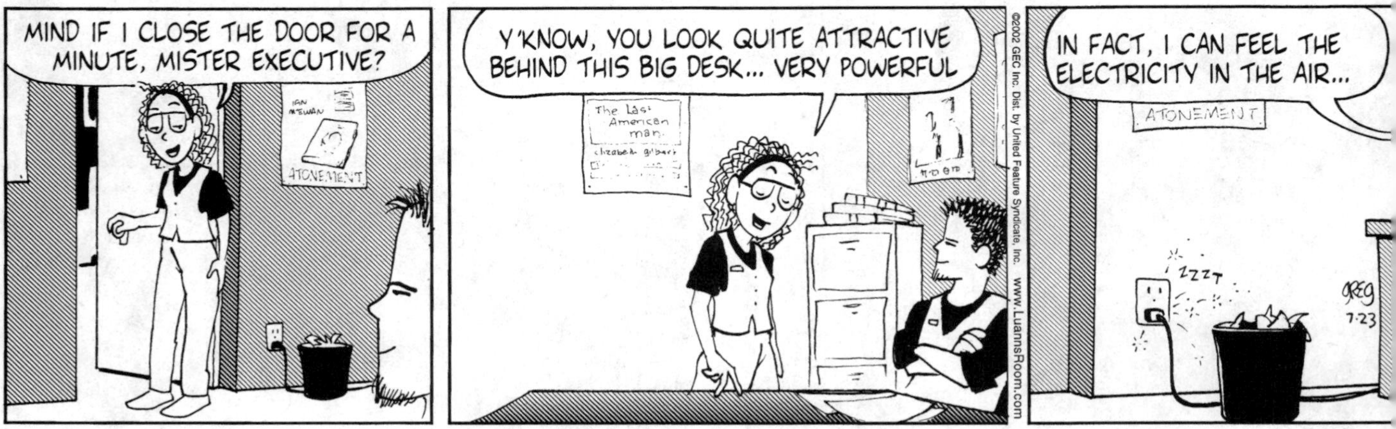
MIND IF I CLOSE THE DOOR FOR A MINUTE, MISTER EXECUTIVE?
IAN McEWAN
ATONEMENT
Y'KNOW, YOU LOOK QUITE ATTRACTIVE BEHIND THIS BIG DESK... VERY POWERFUL
The Last American man
elizabeth gilbert
©2002 GEC Inc. Dist. by United Feature Syndicate, Inc. www.LuannsRoom.com
IN FACT, I CAN FEEL THE ELECTRICITY IN THE AIR...
ATONEMENT
ZZZT
GREG 7·23

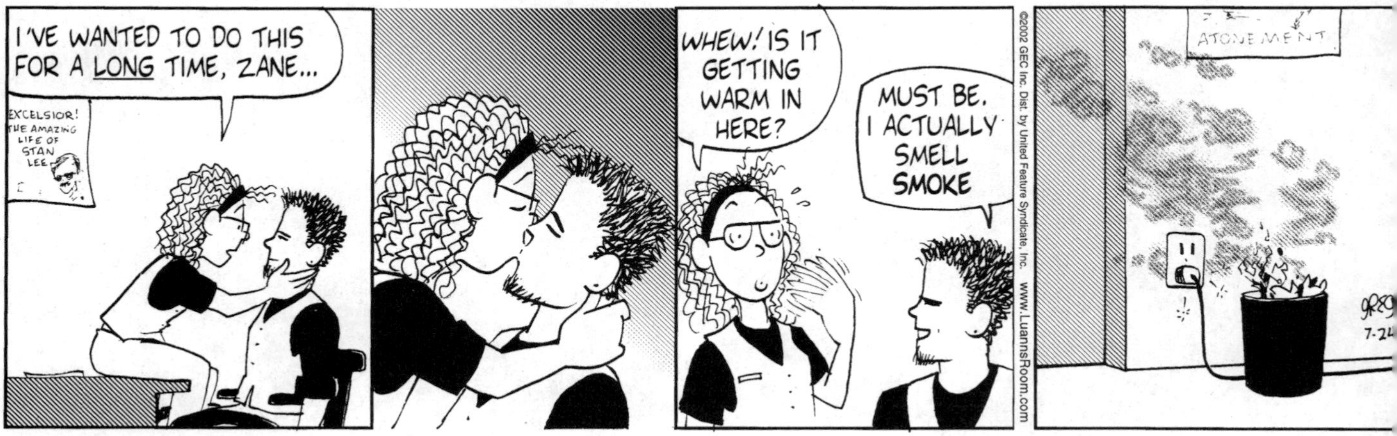
I'VE WANTED TO DO THIS FOR A LONG TIME, ZANE...
EXCELSIOR! THE AMAZING LIFE OF STAN LEE
WHEW! IS IT GETTING WARM IN HERE?
MUST BE. I ACTUALLY SMELL SMOKE
©2002 GEC Inc. Dist. by United Feature Syndicate, Inc. www.LuannsRoom.com
ATONEMENT
GREG 7·24

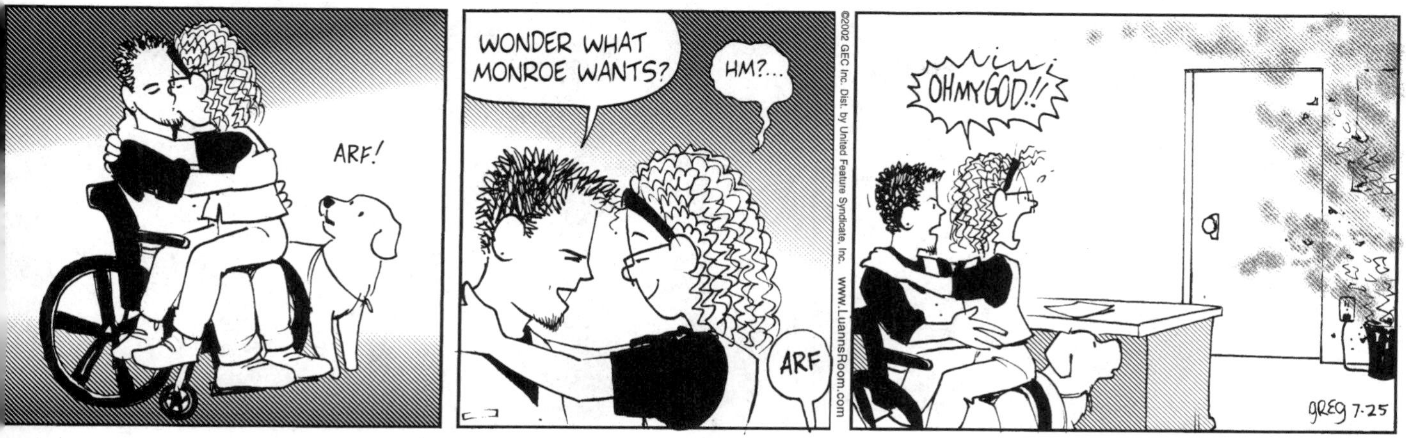
ARF!
WONDER WHAT MONROE WANTS?
HM?...
ARF
OHMYGOD!!
©2002 GEC Inc. Dist. by United Feature Syndicate, Inc.
www.LuannsRoom.com
GREG 7·25

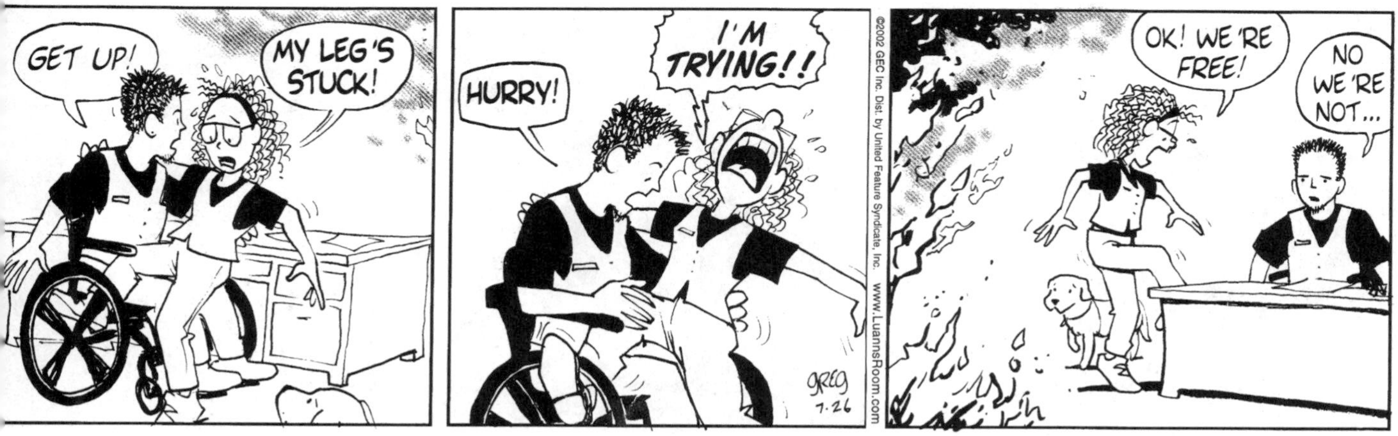
GET UP!
MY LEG'S STUCK!
HURRY!
I'M TRYING!!
OK! WE'RE FREE!
NO WE'RE NOT...
©2002 GEC Inc. Dist. by United Feature Syndicate, Inc.
www.LuannsRoom.com
GREG 7·26

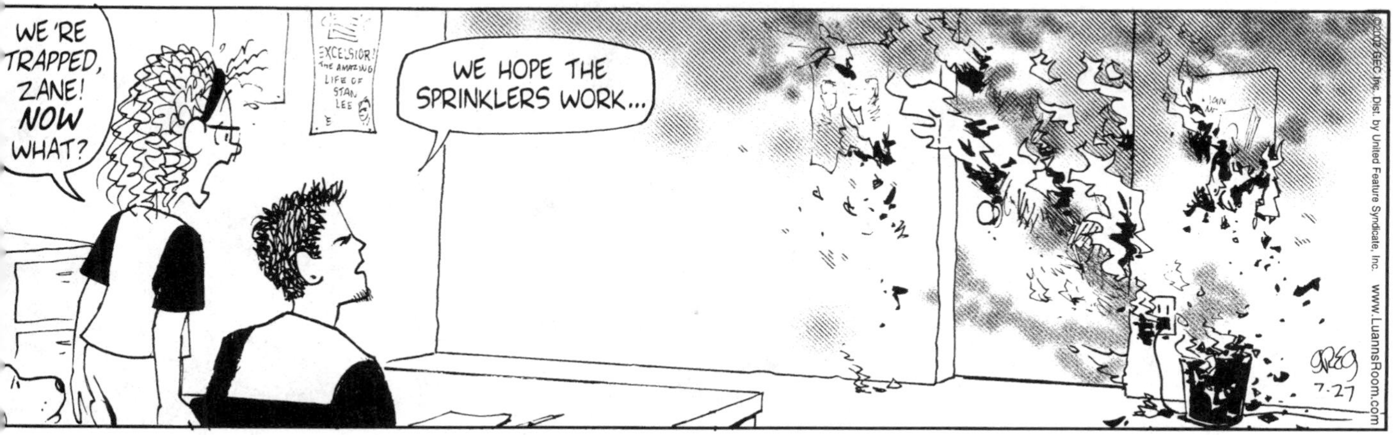
WE'RE TRAPPED, ZANE! NOW WHAT?
EXCELSIOR! THE AMAZING LIFE OF STAN LEE
WE HOPE THE SPRINKLERS WORK...
©2002 GEC Inc. Dist. by United Feature Syndicate, Inc.
www.LuannsRoom.com
GREG 7·27

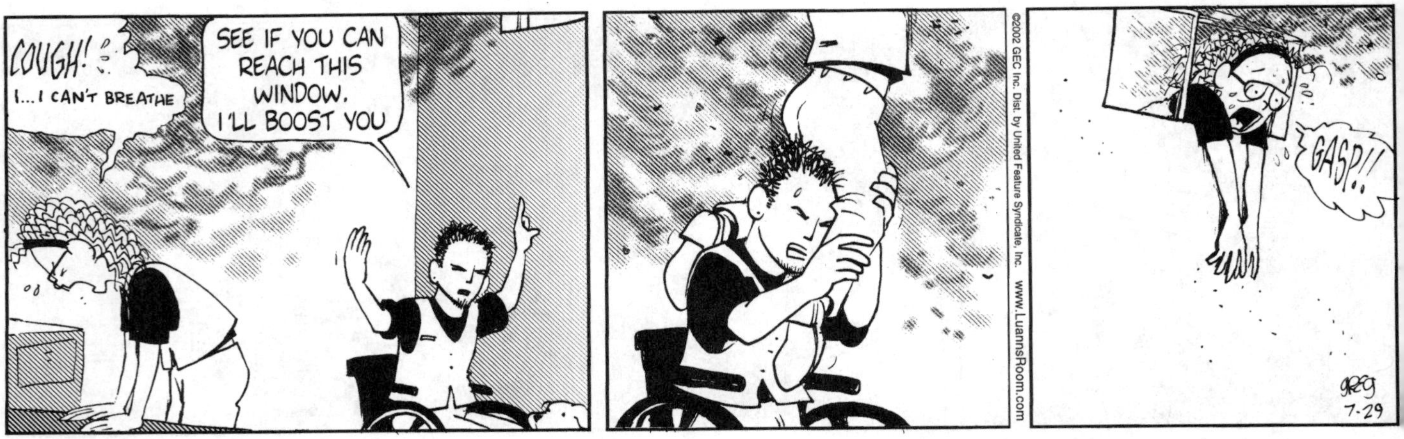
COUGH!
I... I CAN'T BREATHE
SEE IF YOU CAN REACH THIS WINDOW. I'LL BOOST YOU
©2002 GEC Inc. Dist. by United Feature Syndicate, Inc. www.LuannsRoom.com
GASP!!
GREG 7-29

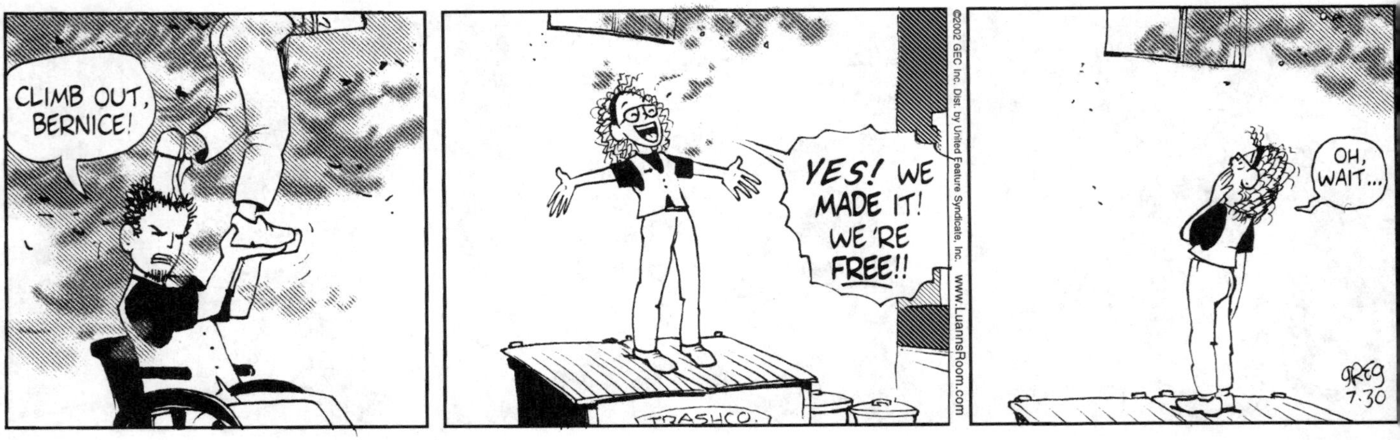
CLIMB OUT, BERNICE!
YES! WE MADE IT! WE'RE FREE!!
TRASHCO.
©2002 GEC Inc. Dist. by United Feature Syndicate, Inc. www.LuannsRoom.com
OH, WAIT...
GREG 7-30

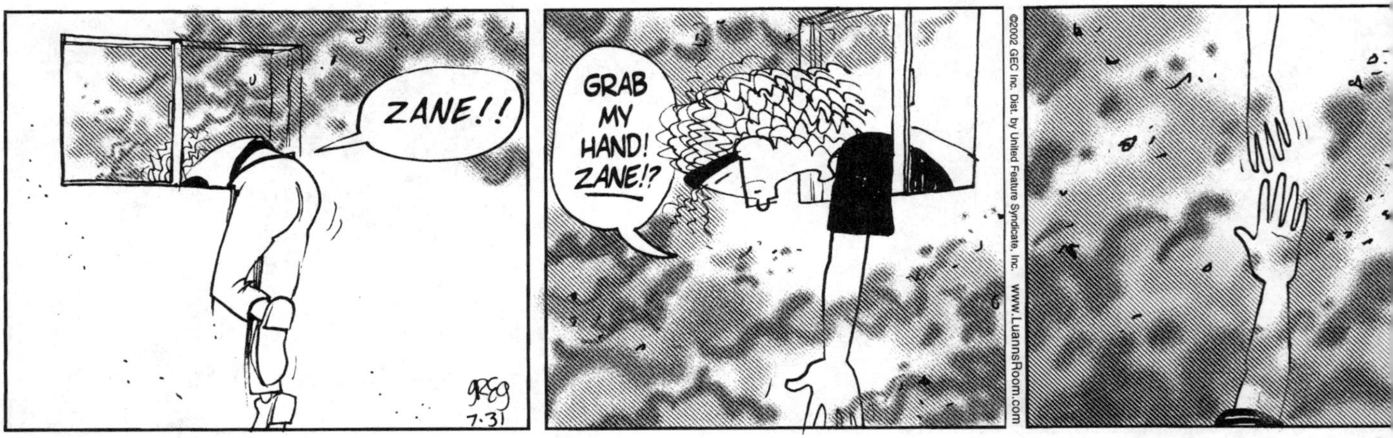
ZANE!!
GREG 7-31
GRAB MY HAND! ZANE!?
©2002 GEC Inc. Dist. by United Feature Syndicate, Inc. www.LuannsRoom.com

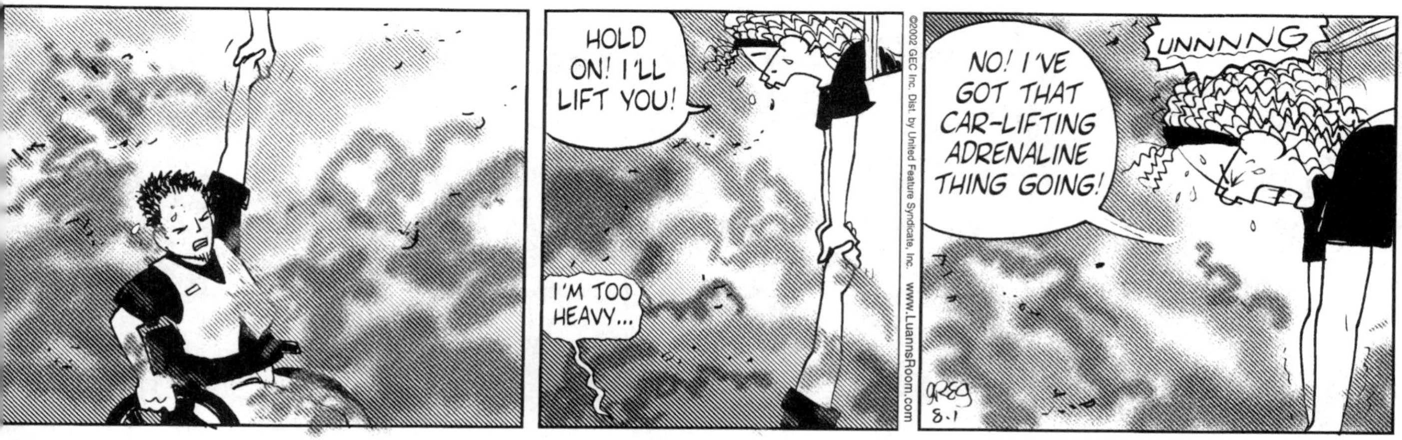
HOLD ON! I'LL LIFT YOU!
I'M TOO HEAVY...
UNNNNG
NO! I'VE GOT THAT CAR-LIFTING ADRENALINE THING GOING!
©2002 GEC Inc. Dist. by United Feature Syndicate, Inc. www.LuannsRoom.com
GREG 8·1

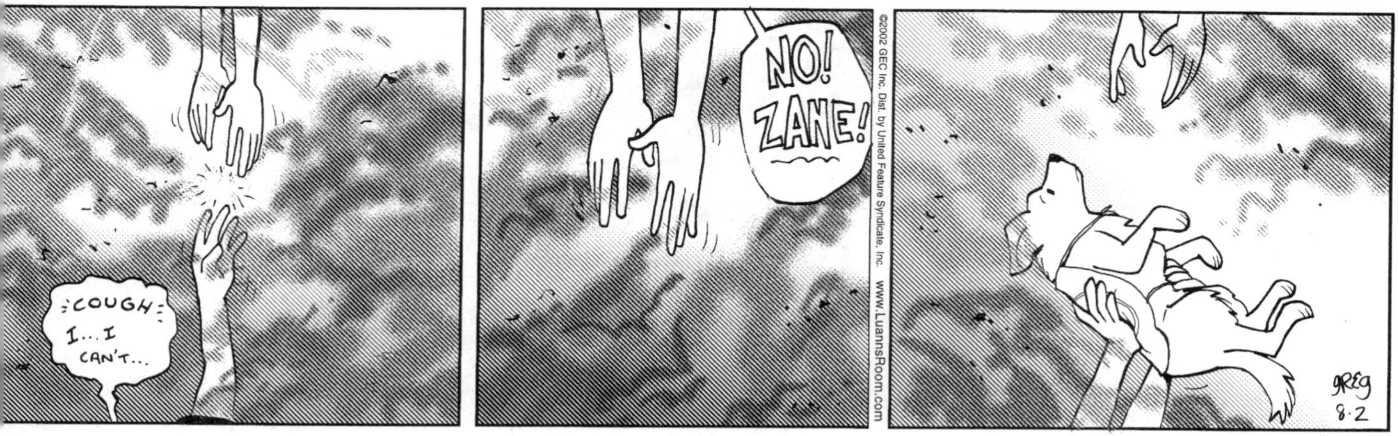
COUGH
I... I CAN'T...
NO! ZANE!
©2002 GEC Inc. Dist. by United Feature Syndicate, Inc. www.LuannsRoom.com
GREG 8·2

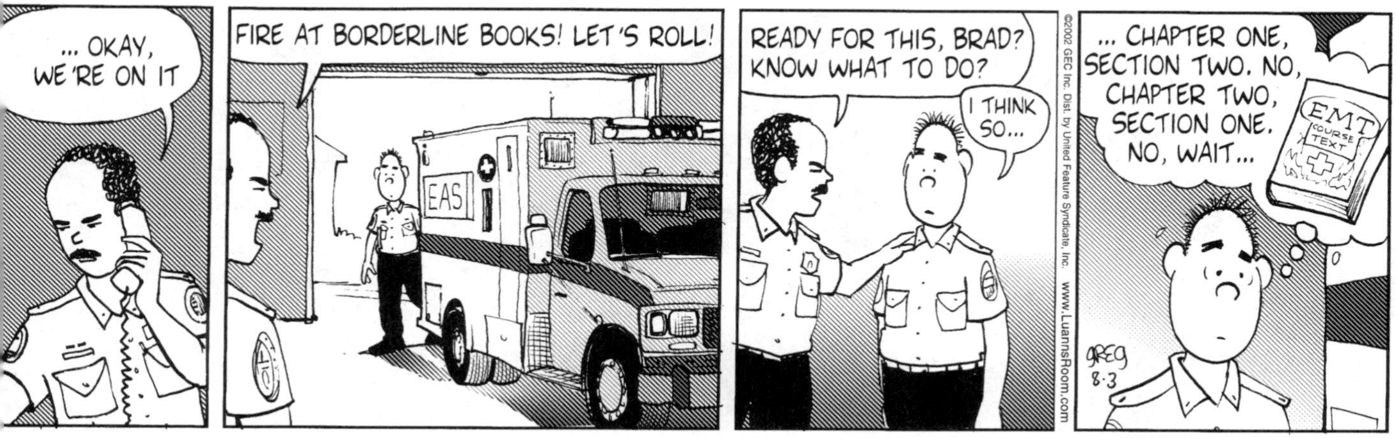
... OKAY, WE'RE ON IT
FIRE AT BORDERLINE BOOKS! LET'S ROLL!
EAS
READY FOR THIS, BRAD? KNOW WHAT TO DO?
I THINK SO...
©2002 GEC Inc. Dist. by United Feature Syndicate, Inc. www.LuannsRoom.com
... CHAPTER ONE, SECTION TWO. NO, CHAPTER TWO, SECTION ONE. NO, WAIT...
EMT COURSE TEXT
GREG 8·3

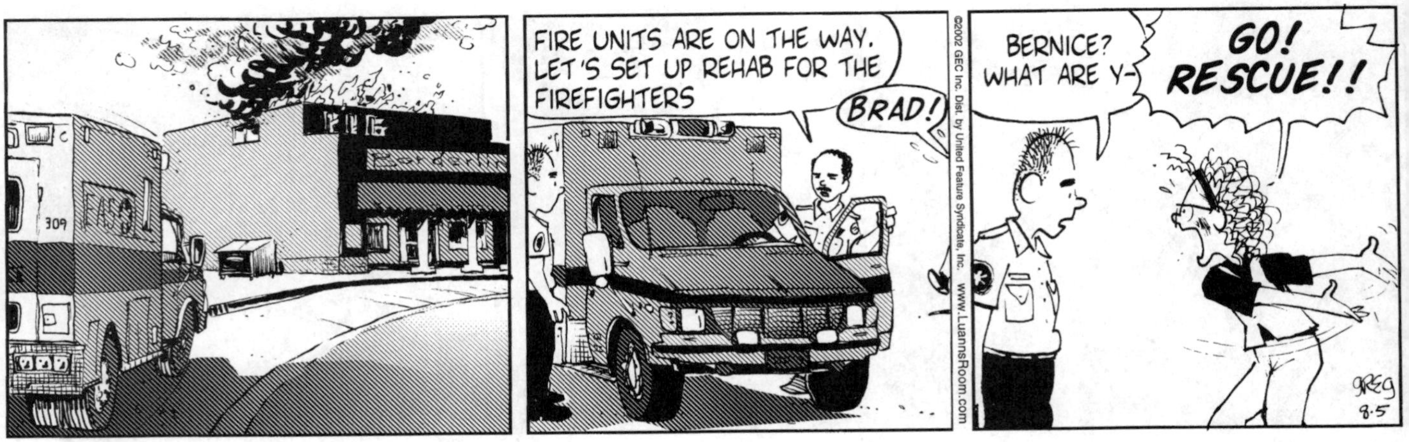
FIRE UNITS ARE ON THE WAY. LET'S SET UP REHAB FOR THE FIREFIGHTERS
BRAD!
©2002 GEC Inc. Dist. by United Feature Syndicate, Inc. www.LuannsRoom.com
BERNICE? WHAT ARE Y-
GO! RESCUE!!
GREG 8·5

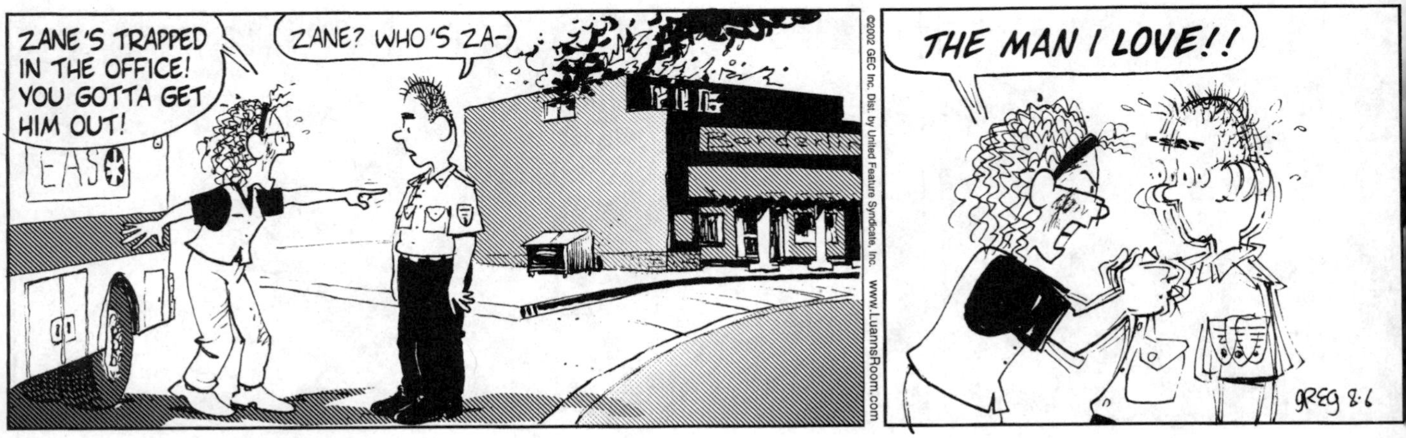
ZANE'S TRAPPED IN THE OFFICE! YOU GOTTA GET HIM OUT!
ZANE? WHO'S ZA-
©2002 GEC Inc. Dist. by United Feature Syndicate, Inc. www.LuannsRoom.com
THE MAN I LOVE!!
GREG 8·6

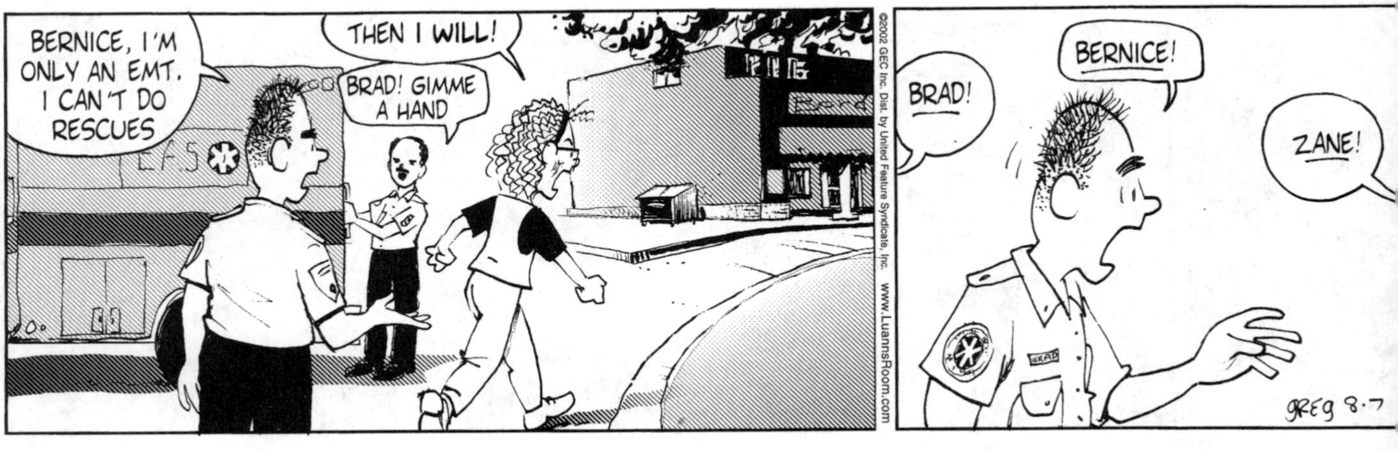
BERNICE, I'M ONLY AN EMT. I CAN'T DO RESCUES
THEN I WILL!
BRAD! GIMME A HAND
©2002 GEC Inc. Dist. by United Feature Syndicate, Inc. www.LuannsRoom.com
BRAD!
BERNICE!
ZANE!
GREG 8·7

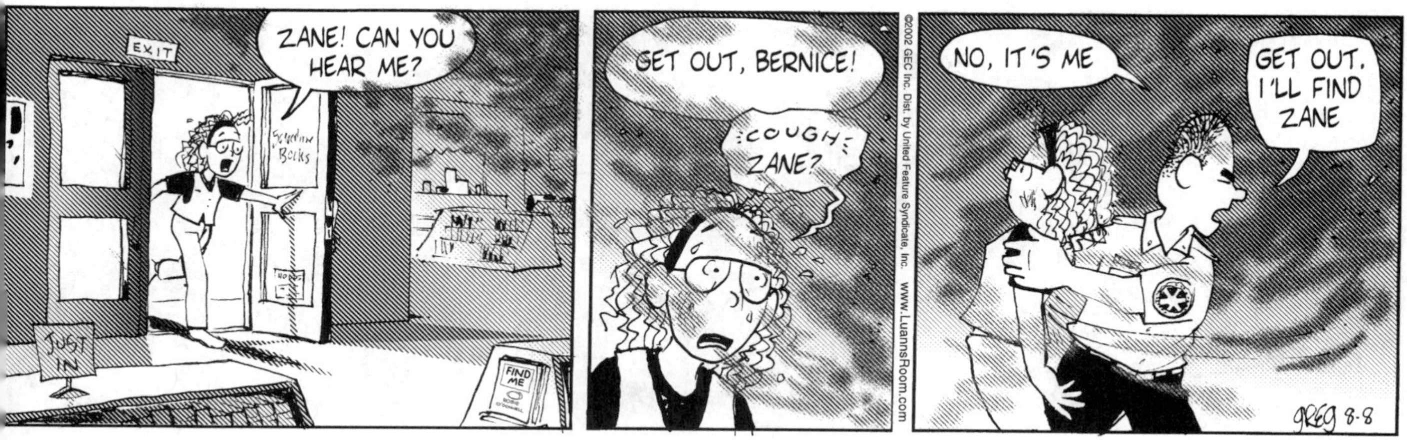
EXIT
ZANE! CAN YOU HEAR ME?
JUST IN
FIND ME
GET OUT, BERNICE!
COUGH
ZANE?
©2002 GEC Inc. Dist. by United Feature Syndicate, Inc. www.LuannsRoom.com
NO, IT'S ME
GET OUT. I'LL FIND ZANE
GREG 8-8

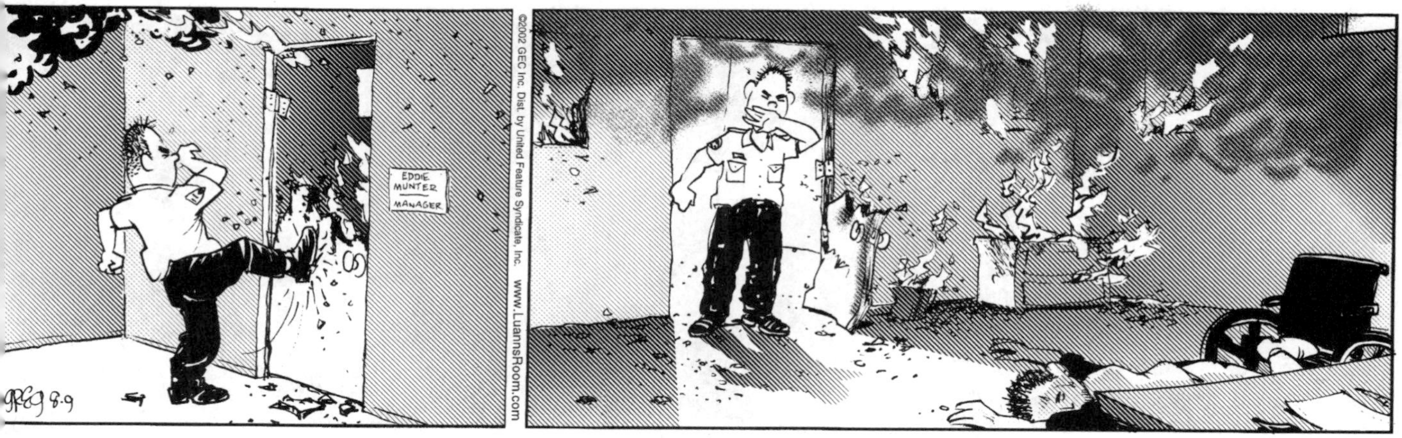
EDDIE MUNTER MANAGER
GREG 8-9
©2002 GEC Inc. Dist. by United Feature Syndicate, Inc. www.LuannsRoom.com

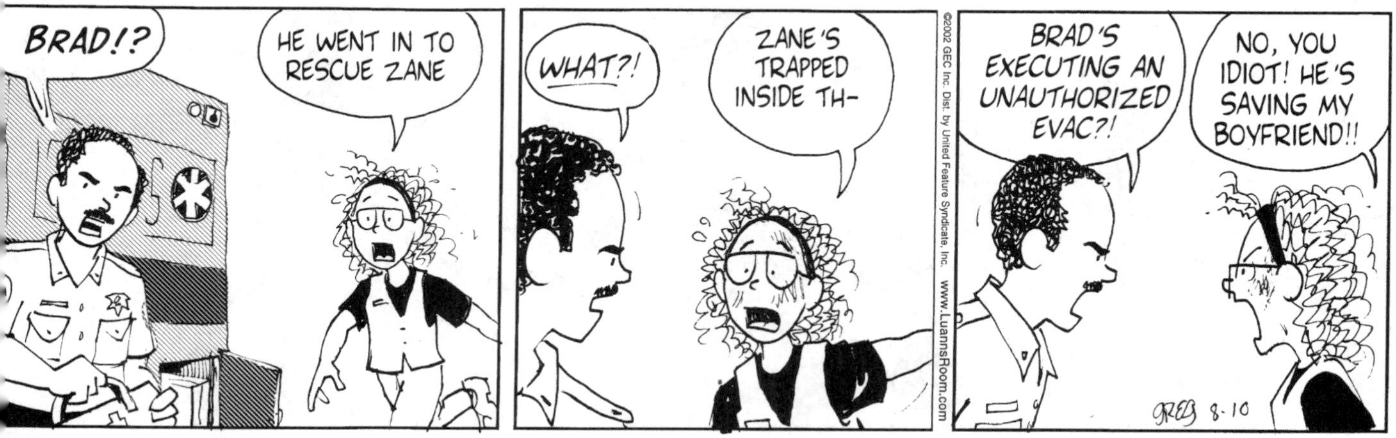
BRAD!?
HE WENT IN TO RESCUE ZANE
WHAT?!
ZANE'S TRAPPED INSIDE TH-
©2002 GEC Inc. Dist. by United Feature Syndicate, Inc. www.LuannsRoom.com
BRAD'S EXECUTING AN UNAUTHORIZED EVAC?!
NO, YOU IDIOT! HE'S SAVING MY BOYFRIEND!!
GREG 8-10

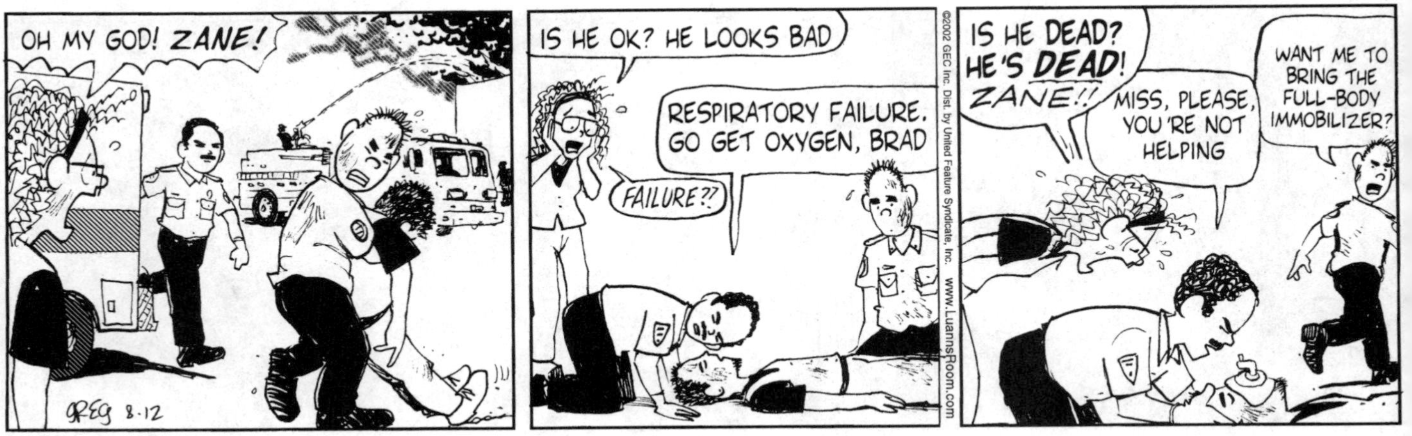
OH MY GOD! ZANE!
GREG 8-12
IS HE OK? HE LOOKS BAD
RESPIRATORY FAILURE. GO GET OXYGEN, BRAD
FAILURE??
©2002 GEC Inc. Dist. by United Feature Syndicate, Inc. www.LuannsRoom.com
IS HE DEAD? HE'S DEAD! ZANE!!
MISS, PLEASE, YOU'RE NOT HELPING
WANT ME TO BRING THE FULL-BODY IMMOBILIZER?

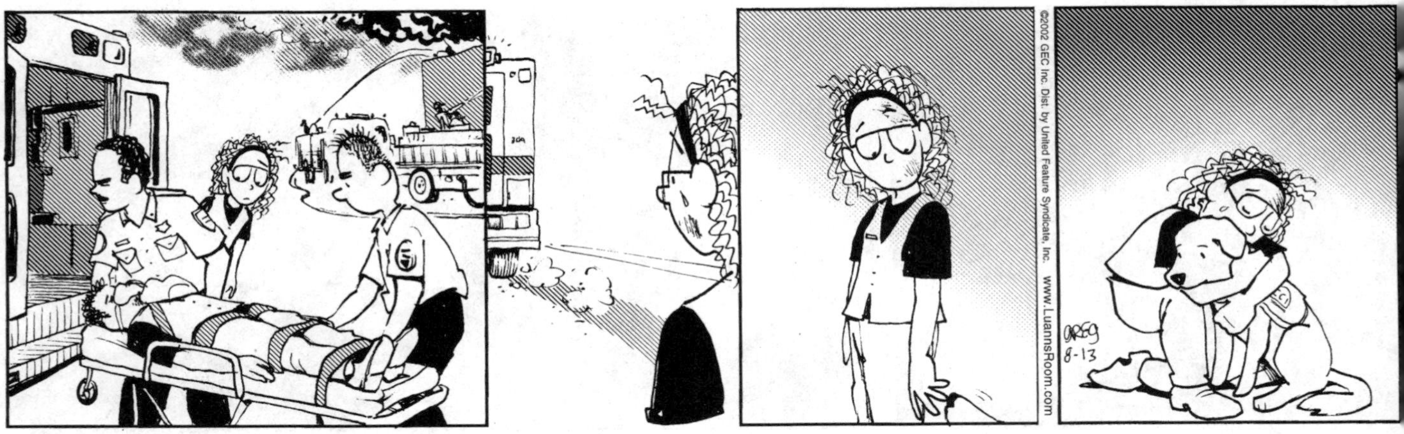
©2002 GEC Inc. Dist. by United Feature Syndicate, Inc. www.LuannsRoom.com
GREG 8-13

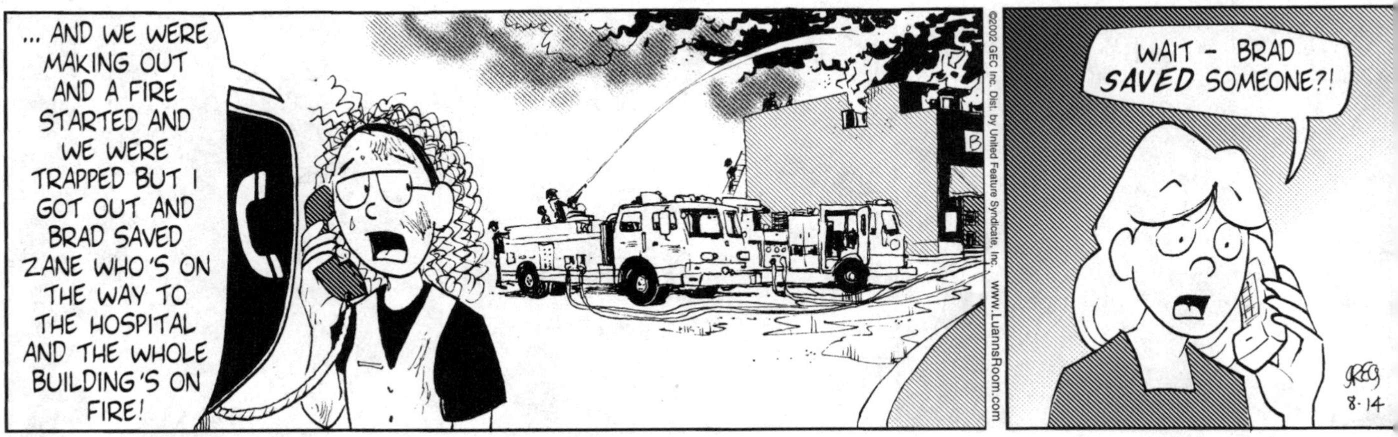
... AND WE WERE MAKING OUT AND A FIRE STARTED AND WE WERE TRAPPED BUT I GOT OUT AND BRAD SAVED ZANE WHO'S ON THE WAY TO THE HOSPITAL AND THE WHOLE BUILDING'S ON FIRE!
©2002 GEC Inc. Dist. by United Feature Syndicate, Inc. www.LuannsRoom.com
WAIT - BRAD SAVED SOMEONE?!
GREG 8-14

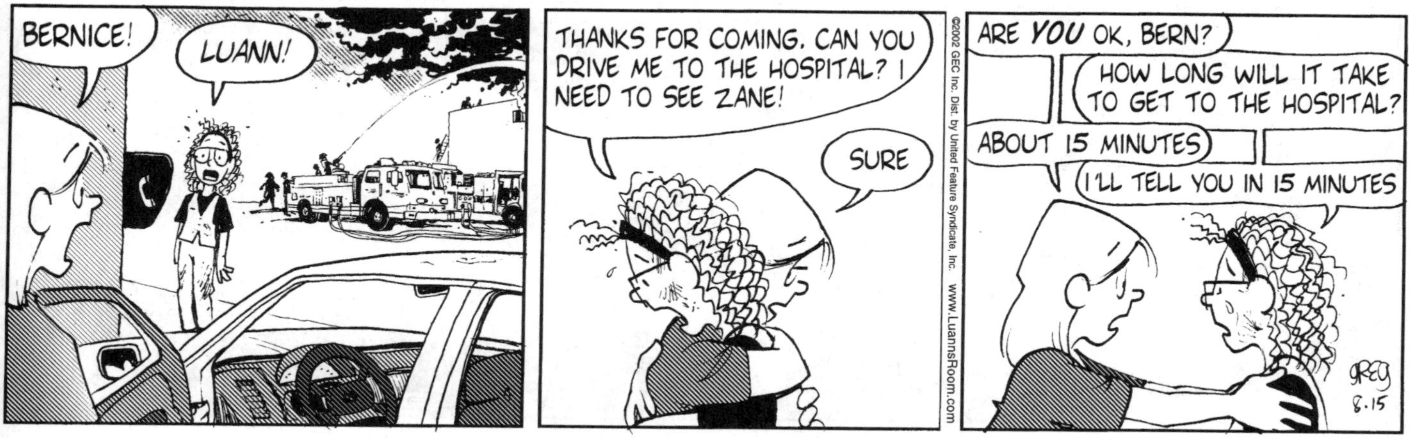
BERNICE!
LUANN!
THANKS FOR COMING. CAN YOU DRIVE ME TO THE HOSPITAL? I NEED TO SEE ZANE!
SURE
©2002 GEC Inc. Dist. by United Feature Syndicate, Inc. www.LuannsRoom.com
ARE YOU OK, BERN?
HOW LONG WILL IT TAKE TO GET TO THE HOSPITAL?
ABOUT 15 MINUTES
I'LL TELL YOU IN 15 MINUTES
GREG 8.15

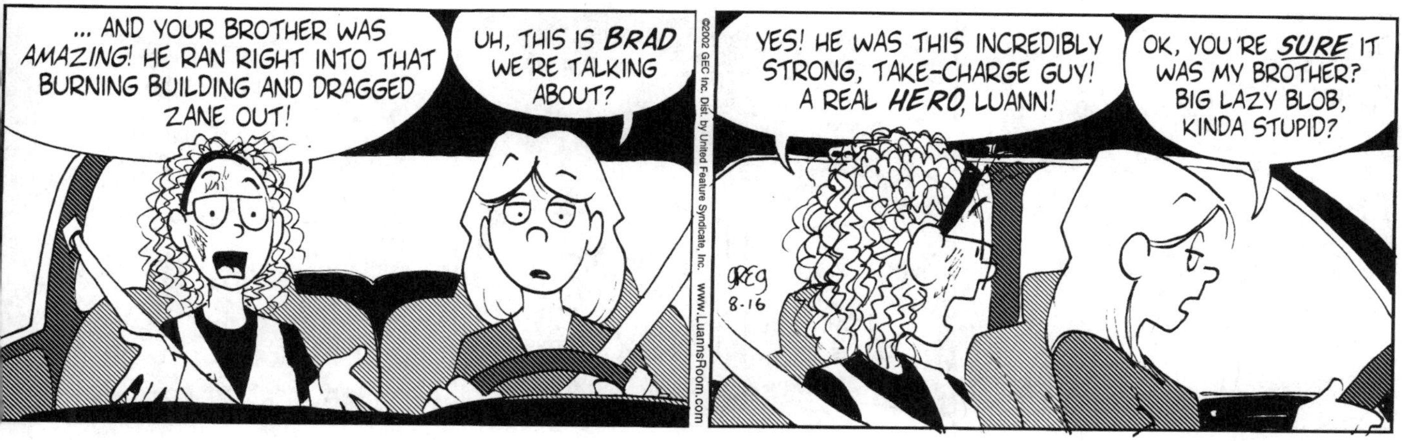
... AND YOUR BROTHER WAS AMAZING! HE RAN RIGHT INTO THAT BURNING BUILDING AND DRAGGED ZANE OUT!
UH, THIS IS BRAD WE'RE TALKING ABOUT?
©2002 GEC Inc. Dist. by United Feature Syndicate, Inc. www.LuannsRoom.com
YES! HE WAS THIS INCREDIBLY STRONG, TAKE-CHARGE GUY! A REAL HERO, LUANN!
OK, YOU'RE SURE IT WAS MY BROTHER? BIG LAZY BLOB, KINDA STUPID?
GREG 8-16

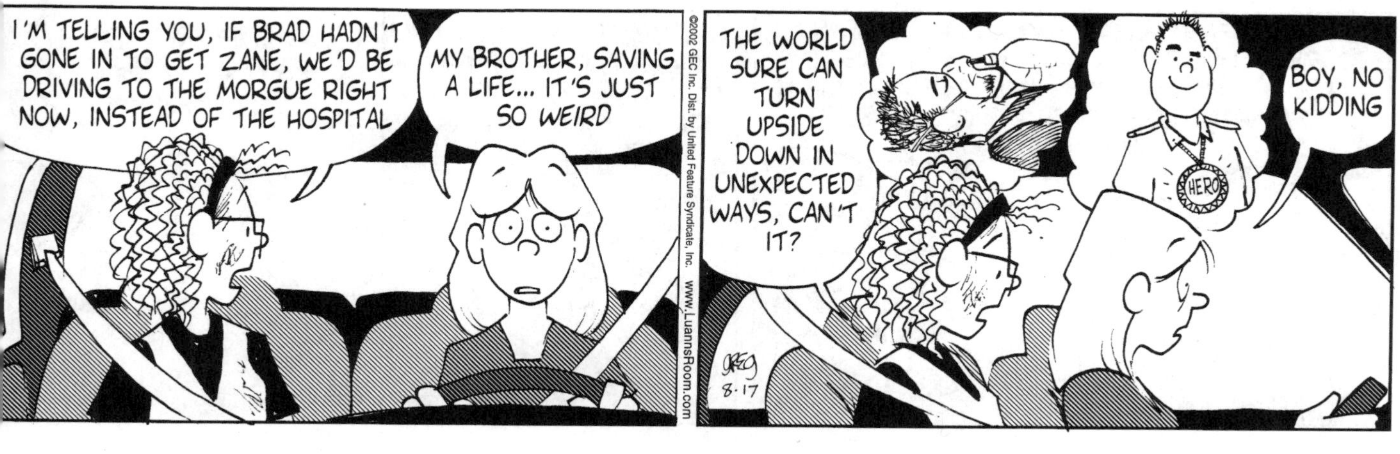
I'M TELLING YOU, IF BRAD HADN'T GONE IN TO GET ZANE, WE'D BE DRIVING TO THE MORGUE RIGHT NOW, INSTEAD OF THE HOSPITAL
MY BROTHER, SAVING A LIFE... IT'S JUST SO WEIRD
©2002 GEC Inc. Dist. by United Feature Syndicate, Inc. www.LuannsRoom.com
THE WORLD SURE CAN TURN UPSIDE DOWN IN UNEXPECTED WAYS, CAN'T IT?
HERO
BOY, NO KIDDING
GREG 8-17

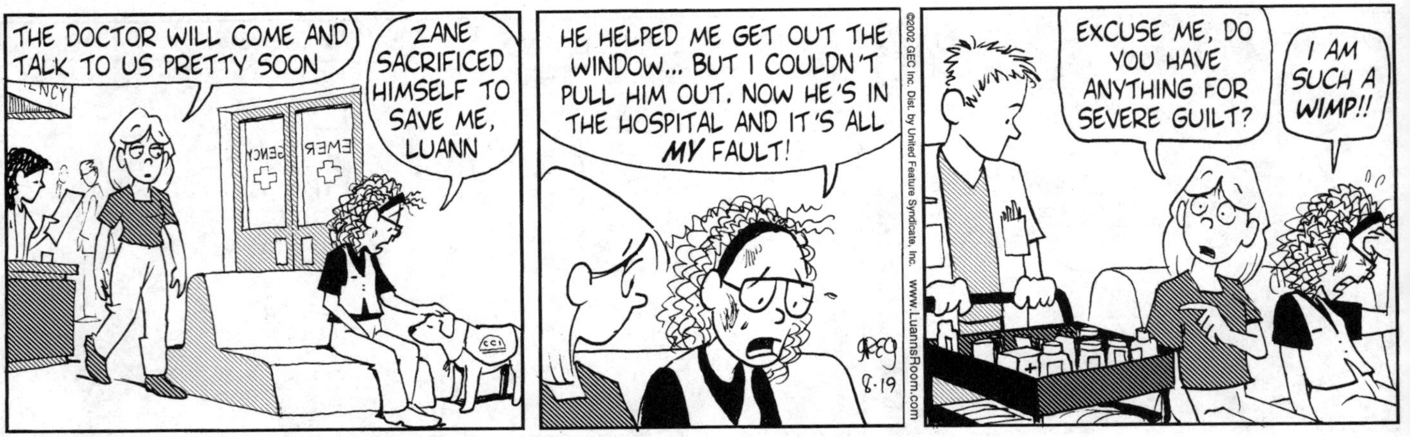
THE DOCTOR WILL COME AND TALK TO US PRETTY SOON
ZANE SACRIFICED HIMSELF TO SAVE ME, LUANN
HE HELPED ME GET OUT THE WINDOW... BUT I COULDN'T PULL HIM OUT. NOW HE'S IN THE HOSPITAL AND IT'S ALL *MY* FAULT!
©2002 GEC Inc. Dist. by United Feature Syndicate, Inc. www.LuannsRoom.com
EXCUSE ME, DO YOU HAVE ANYTHING FOR SEVERE GUILT?
I AM SUCH A *WIMP!!*
GREG 8·19

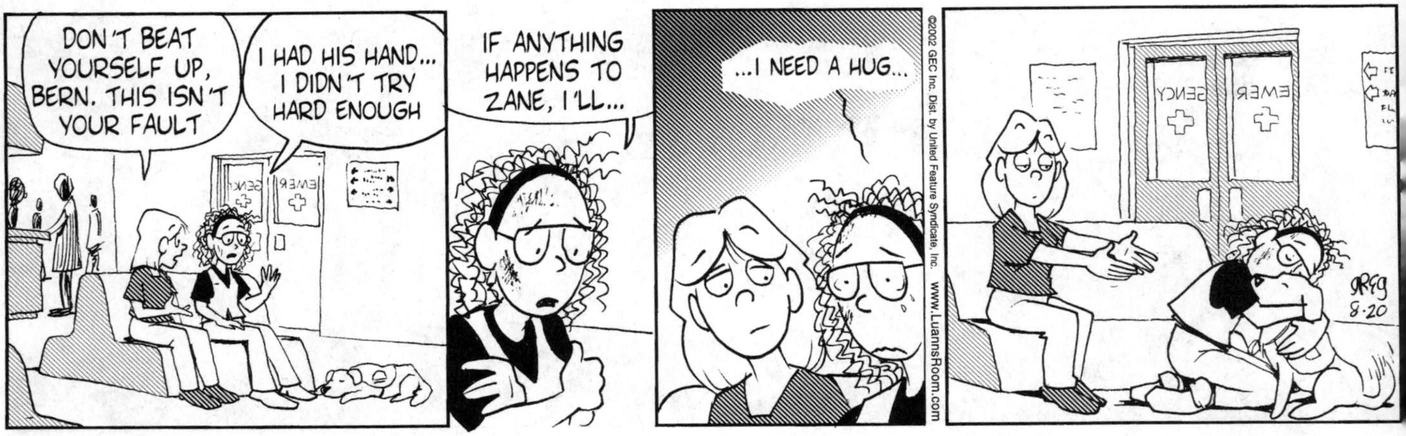
DON'T BEAT YOURSELF UP, BERN. THIS ISN'T YOUR FAULT
I HAD HIS HAND... I DIDN'T TRY HARD ENOUGH
IF ANYTHING HAPPENS TO ZANE, I'LL...
...I NEED A HUG...
©2002 GEC Inc. Dist. by United Feature Syndicate, Inc. www.LuannsRoom.com
GREG 8·20

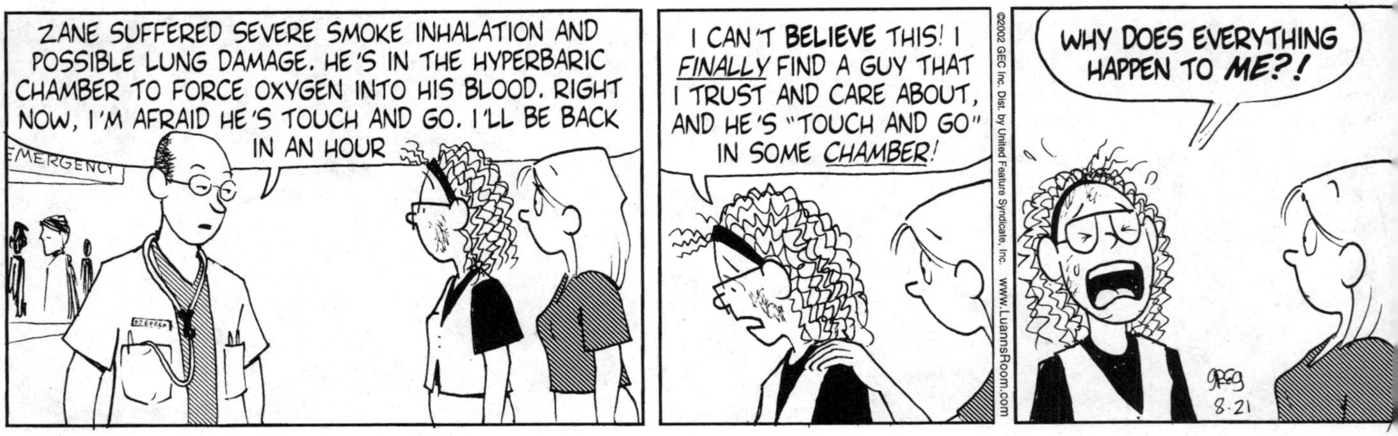
ZANE SUFFERED SEVERE SMOKE INHALATION AND POSSIBLE LUNG DAMAGE. HE'S IN THE HYPERBARIC CHAMBER TO FORCE OXYGEN INTO HIS BLOOD. RIGHT NOW, I'M AFRAID HE'S TOUCH AND GO. I'LL BE BACK IN AN HOUR
I CAN'T **BELIEVE** THIS! I *FINALLY* FIND A GUY THAT I TRUST AND CARE ABOUT, AND HE'S "TOUCH AND GO" IN SOME *CHAMBER*!
©2002 GEC Inc. Dist. by United Feature Syndicate, Inc. www.LuannsRoom.com
WHY DOES EVERYTHING HAPPEN TO *ME?!*
GREG 8·21

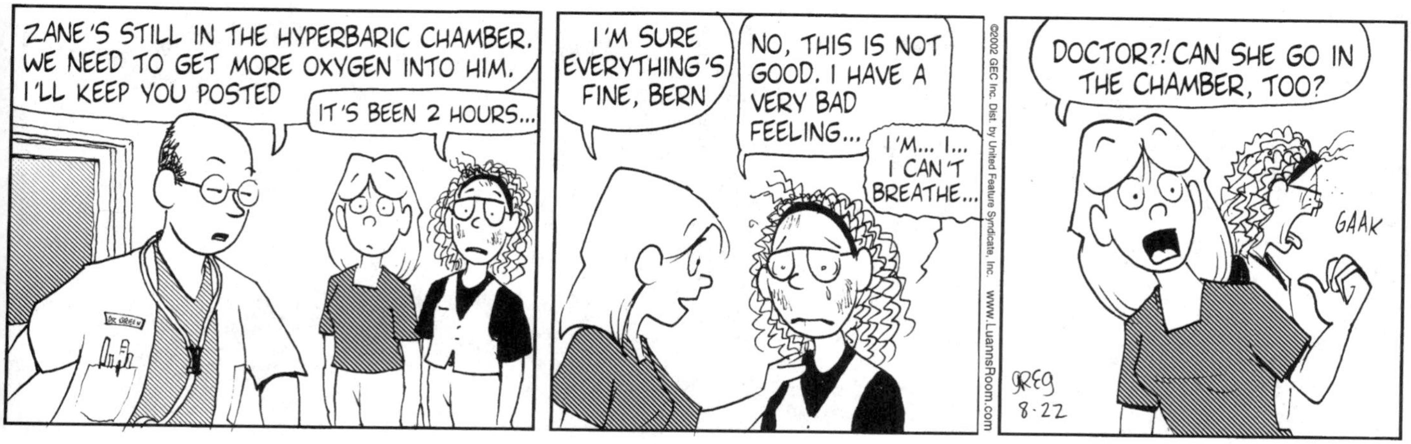
ZANE'S STILL IN THE HYPERBARIC CHAMBER. WE NEED TO GET MORE OXYGEN INTO HIM. I'LL KEEP YOU POSTED
IT'S BEEN 2 HOURS...
I'M SURE EVERYTHING'S FINE, BERN
NO, THIS IS NOT GOOD. I HAVE A VERY BAD FEELING...
I'M... I... I CAN'T BREATHE...
©2002 GEC Inc. Dist. by United Feature Syndicate, Inc.
www.LuannsRoom.com
DOCTOR?! CAN SHE GO IN THE CHAMBER, TOO?
GAAK
GREG 8·22

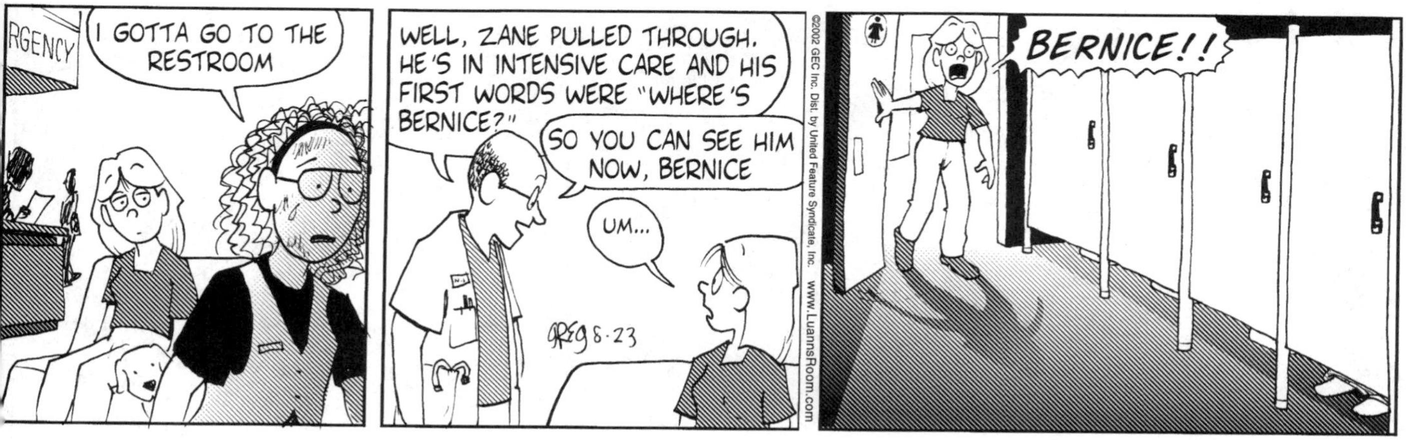
RGENCY
I GOTTA GO TO THE RESTROOM
WELL, ZANE PULLED THROUGH. HE'S IN INTENSIVE CARE AND HIS FIRST WORDS WERE "WHERE'S BERNICE?"
SO YOU CAN SEE HIM NOW, BERNICE
UM...
GREG 8·23
©2002 GEC Inc. Dist. by United Feature Syndicate, Inc.
www.LuannsRoom.com
BERNICE!!

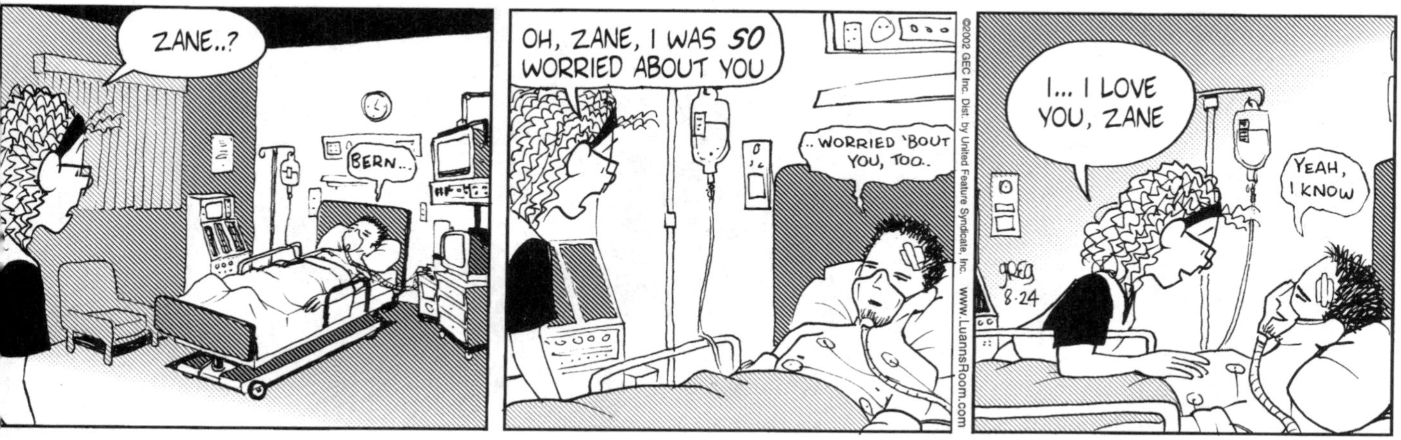
ZANE..?
BERN...
OH, ZANE, I WAS SO WORRIED ABOUT YOU
..WORRIED 'BOUT YOU, TOO..
©2002 GEC Inc. Dist. by United Feature Syndicate, Inc.
www.LuannsRoom.com
I... I LOVE YOU, ZANE
YEAH, I KNOW
GREG 8·24

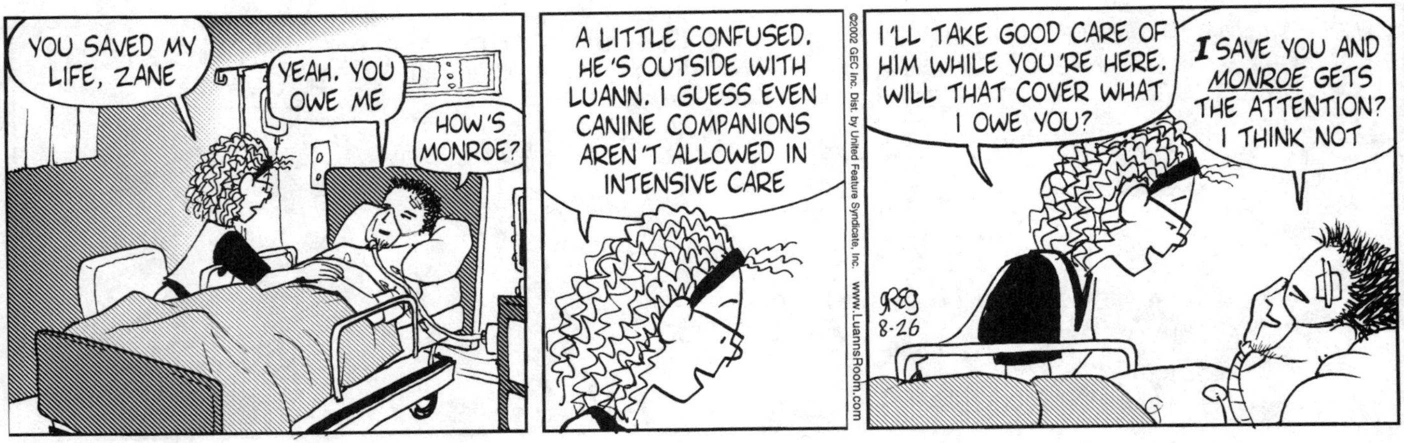
YOU SAVED MY LIFE, ZANE
YEAH. YOU OWE ME
HOW'S MONROE?
A LITTLE CONFUSED. HE'S OUTSIDE WITH LUANN. I GUESS EVEN CANINE COMPANIONS AREN'T ALLOWED IN INTENSIVE CARE
©2002 GEC Inc. Dist. by United Feature Syndicate, Inc.
www.LuannsRoom.com
I'LL TAKE GOOD CARE OF HIM WHILE YOU'RE HERE. WILL THAT COVER WHAT I OWE YOU?
I SAVE YOU AND MONROE GETS THE ATTENTION? I THINK NOT
GREG 8-26

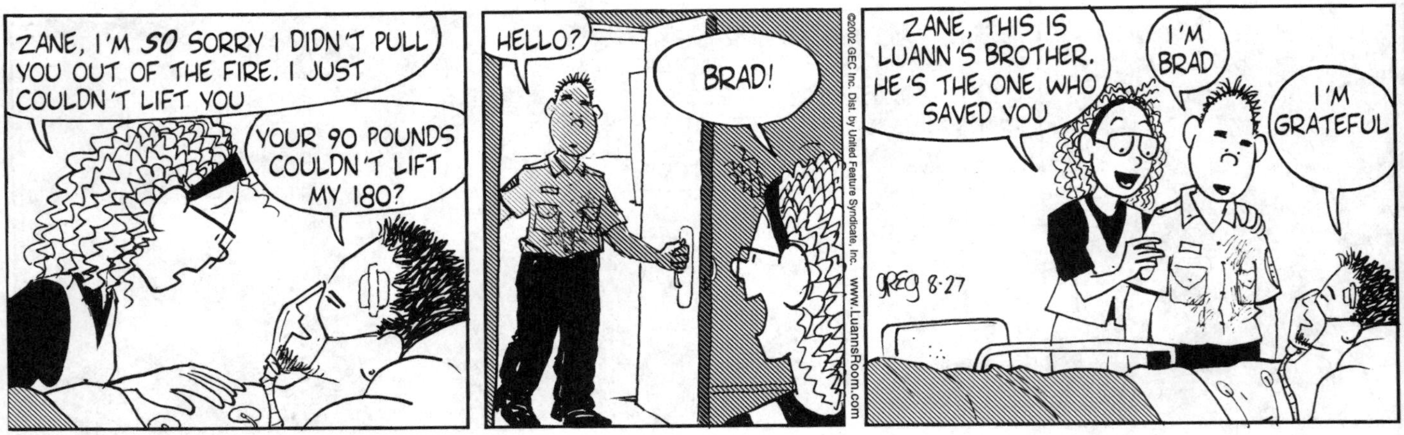
ZANE, I'M SO SORRY I DIDN'T PULL YOU OUT OF THE FIRE. I JUST COULDN'T LIFT YOU
YOUR 90 POUNDS COULDN'T LIFT MY 180?
HELLO?
BRAD!
©2002 GEC Inc. Dist. by United Feature Syndicate, Inc.
www.LuannsRoom.com
ZANE, THIS IS LUANN'S BROTHER. HE'S THE ONE WHO SAVED YOU
I'M BRAD
I'M GRATEFUL
GREG 8-27

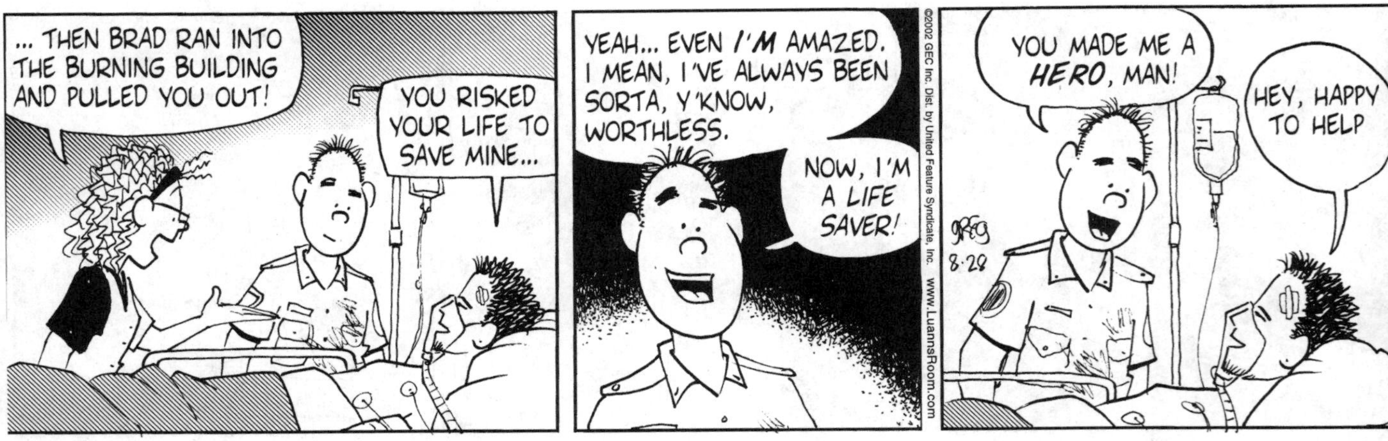
... THEN BRAD RAN INTO THE BURNING BUILDING AND PULLED YOU OUT!
YOU RISKED YOUR LIFE TO SAVE MINE...
YEAH... EVEN I'M AMAZED. I MEAN, I'VE ALWAYS BEEN SORTA, Y'KNOW, WORTHLESS.
NOW, I'M A LIFE SAVER!
©2002 GEC Inc. Dist. by United Feature Syndicate, Inc.
www.LuannsRoom.com
YOU MADE ME A HERO, MAN!
HEY, HAPPY TO HELP
GREG 8-28

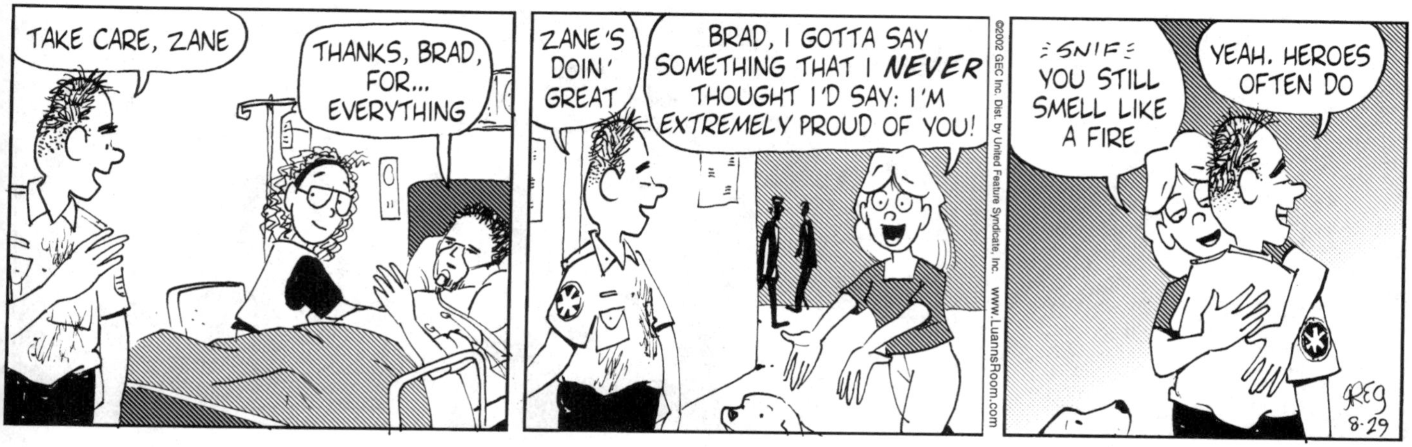
TAKE CARE, ZANE
THANKS, BRAD, FOR... EVERYTHING
ZANE'S DOIN' GREAT
BRAD, I GOTTA SAY SOMETHING THAT I **NEVER** THOUGHT I'D SAY: I'M *EXTREMELY* PROUD OF YOU!
©2002 GEC Inc. Dist. by United Feature Syndicate, Inc. www.LuannsRoom.com
SNIF
YOU STILL SMELL LIKE A FIRE
YEAH. HEROES OFTEN DO
GREG 8-29

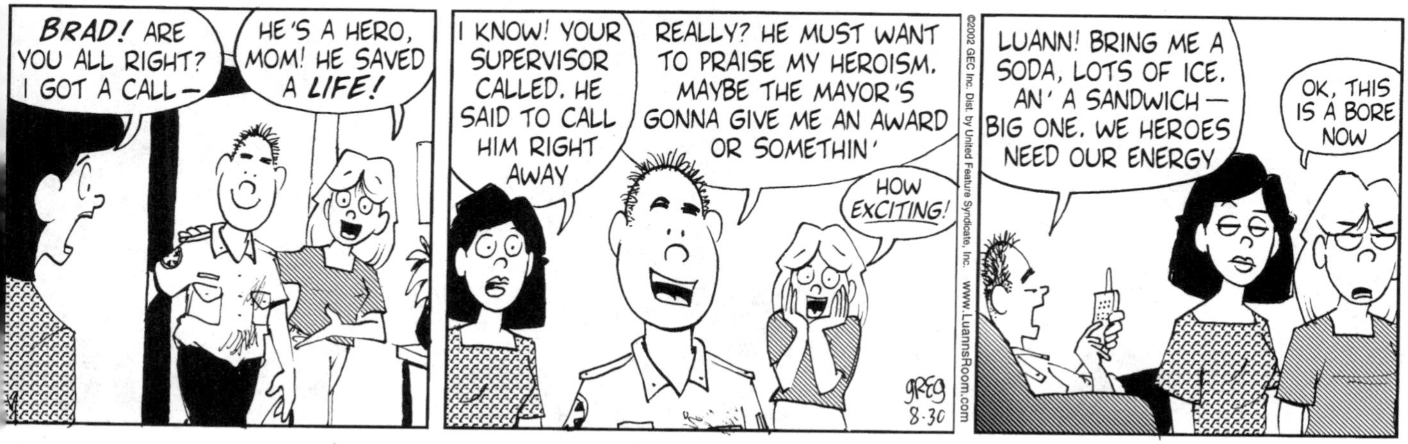
BRAD! ARE YOU ALL RIGHT? I GOT A CALL—
HE'S A HERO, MOM! HE SAVED A ***LIFE!***
I KNOW! YOUR SUPERVISOR CALLED. HE SAID TO CALL HIM RIGHT AWAY
REALLY? HE MUST WANT TO PRAISE MY HEROISM. MAYBE THE MAYOR'S GONNA GIVE ME AN AWARD OR SOMETHIN'
HOW EXCITING!
GREG 8-30
©2002 GEC Inc. Dist. by United Feature Syndicate, Inc. www.LuannsRoom.com
LUANN! BRING ME A SODA, LOTS OF ICE. AN' A SANDWICH— BIG ONE. WE HEROES NEED OUR ENERGY
OK, THIS IS A BORE NOW

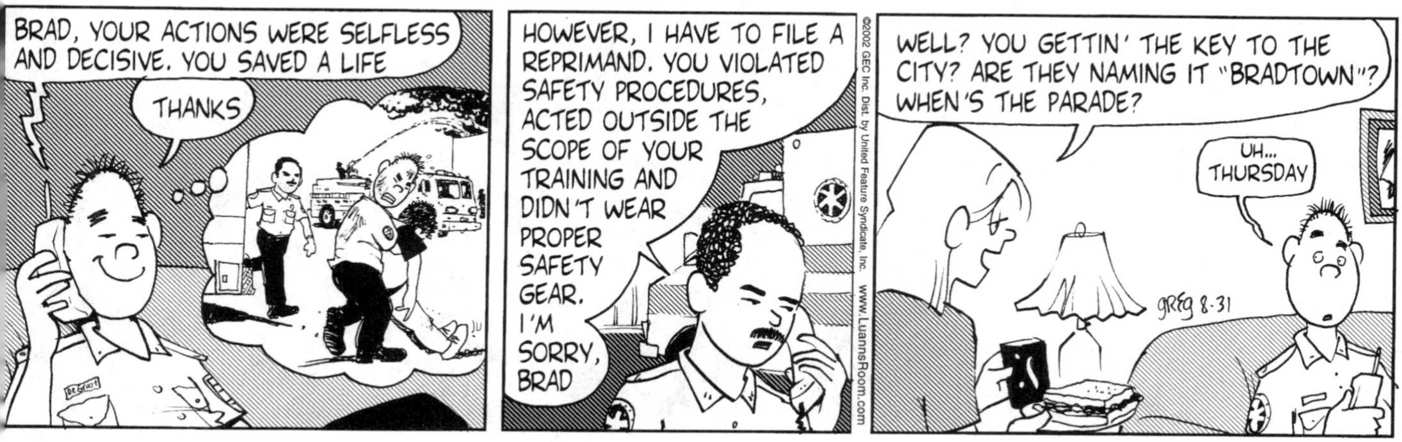
BRAD, YOUR ACTIONS WERE SELFLESS AND DECISIVE. YOU SAVED A LIFE
THANKS
HOWEVER, I HAVE TO FILE A REPRIMAND. YOU VIOLATED SAFETY PROCEDURES, ACTED OUTSIDE THE SCOPE OF YOUR TRAINING AND DIDN'T WEAR PROPER SAFETY GEAR. I'M SORRY, BRAD
©2002 GEC Inc. Dist. by United Feature Syndicate, Inc. www.LuannsRoom.com
WELL? YOU GETTIN' THE KEY TO THE CITY? ARE THEY NAMING IT "BRADTOWN"? WHEN'S THE PARADE?
UH... THURSDAY
GREG 8-31

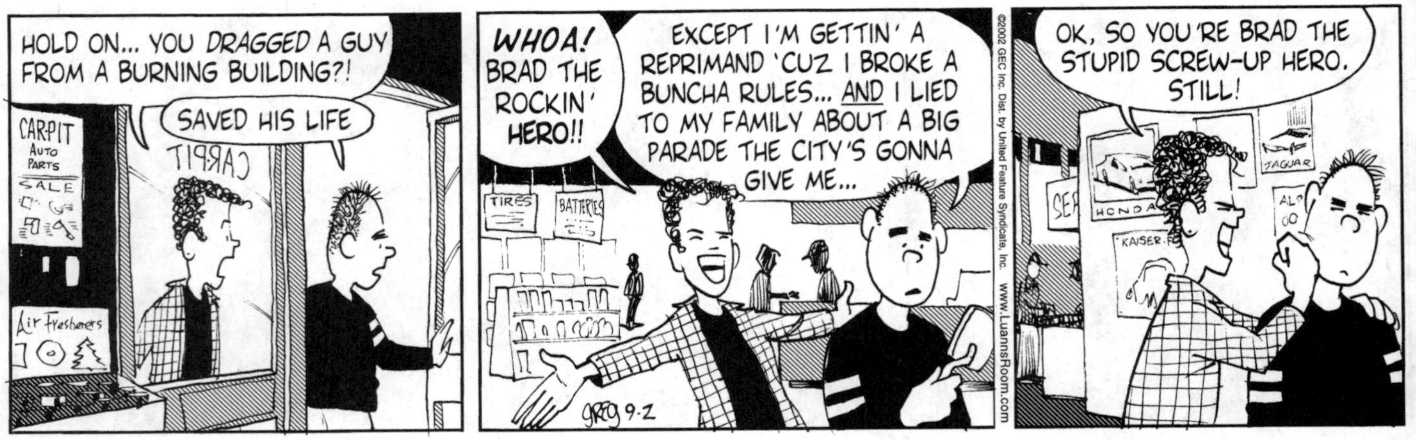
HOLD ON... YOU *DRAGGED* A GUY FROM A BURNING BUILDING?!
SAVED HIS LIFE
CARPIT Auto Parts
SALE
Air Fresheners
WHOA! BRAD THE ROCKIN' **HERO**!!
EXCEPT I'M GETTIN' A REPRIMAND 'CUZ I BROKE A BUNCHA RULES... AND I LIED TO MY FAMILY ABOUT A BIG PARADE THE CITY'S GONNA GIVE ME...
TIRES
BATTERIES
GREG 9-2
©2002 GEC Inc. Dist. by United Feature Syndicate, Inc. www.LuannsRoom.com
OK, SO YOU'RE BRAD THE STUPID SCREW-UP HERO. STILL!
HONDA
KAISER
JAGUAR

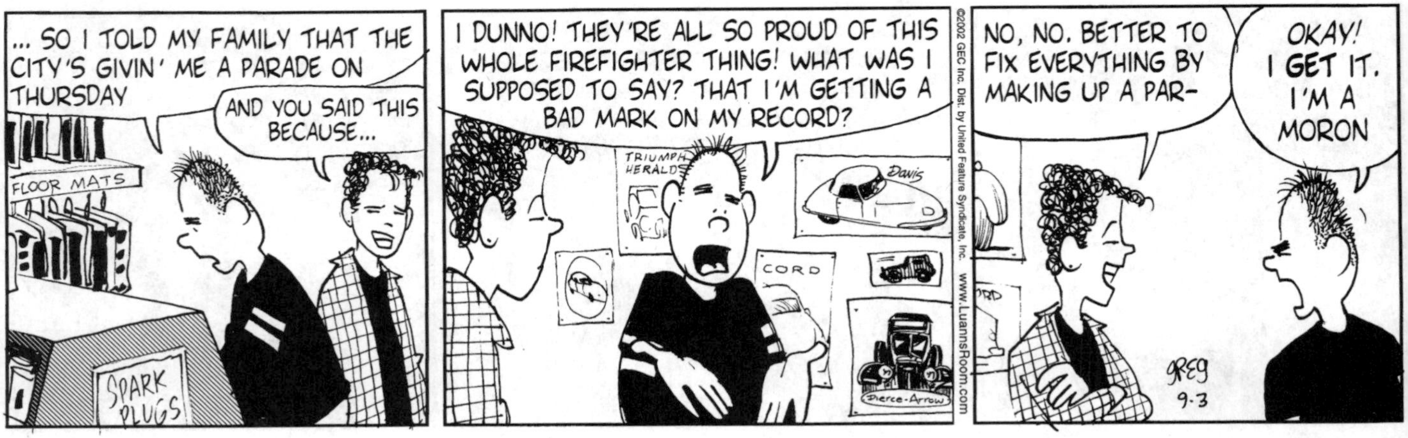
... SO I TOLD MY FAMILY THAT THE CITY'S GIVIN' ME A PARADE ON THURSDAY
AND YOU SAID THIS BECAUSE...
FLOOR MATS
SPARK PLUGS
I DUNNO! THEY'RE ALL SO PROUD OF THIS WHOLE FIREFIGHTER THING! WHAT WAS I SUPPOSED TO SAY? THAT I'M GETTING A BAD MARK ON MY RECORD?
TRIUMPH HERALDS
Davis
CORD
Pierce-Arrow
©2002 GEC Inc. Dist. by United Feature Syndicate, Inc. www.LuannsRoom.com
NO, NO. BETTER TO FIX EVERYTHING BY MAKING UP A PAR-
OKAY! I **GET** IT. I'M A MORON
GREG 9-3

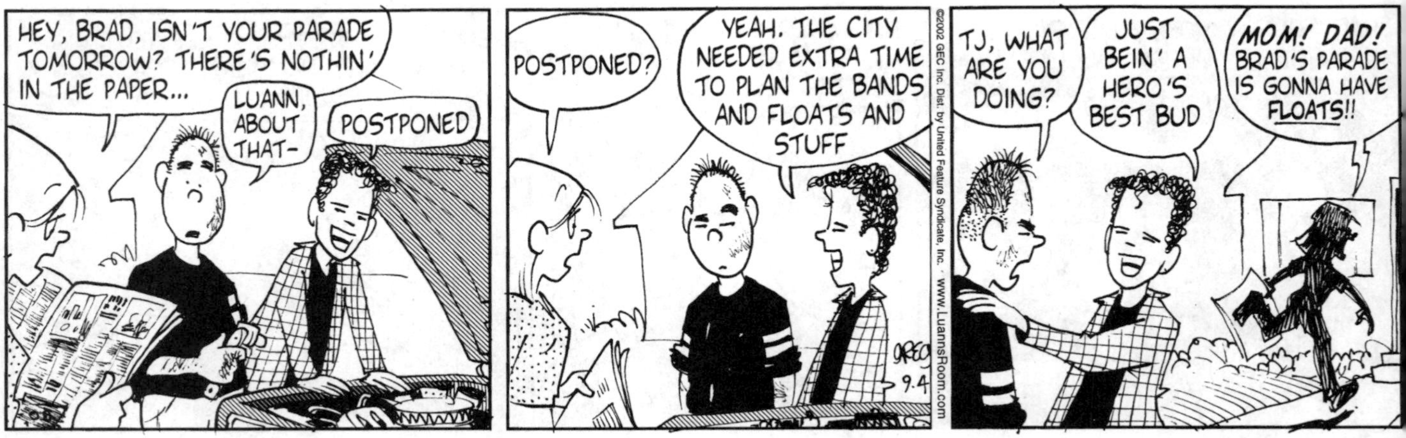
HEY, BRAD, ISN'T YOUR PARADE TOMORROW? THERE'S NOTHIN' IN THE PAPER...
LUANN, ABOUT THAT-
POSTPONED
POSTPONED?
YEAH. THE CITY NEEDED EXTRA TIME TO PLAN THE BANDS AND FLOATS AND STUFF
GREG 9-4
©2002 GEC Inc. Dist. by United Feature Syndicate, Inc. www.LuannsRoom.com
TJ, WHAT ARE YOU DOING?
JUST BEIN' A HERO'S BEST BUD
MOM! DAD! BRAD'S PARADE IS GONNA HAVE FLOATS!!

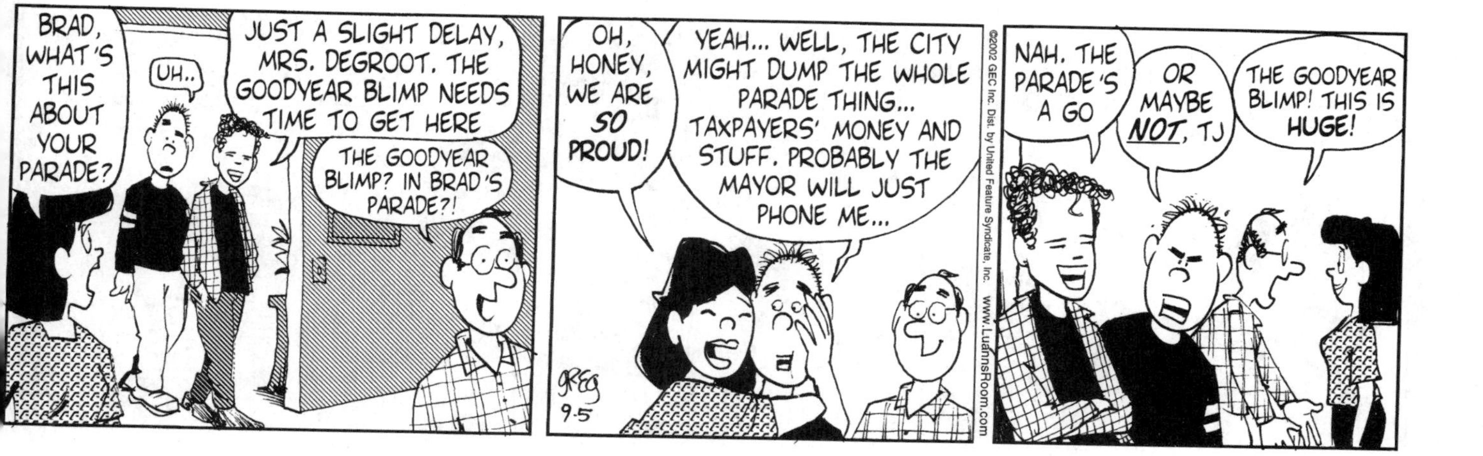
BRAD, WHAT'S THIS ABOUT YOUR PARADE?
UH..
JUST A SLIGHT DELAY, MRS. DEGROOT. THE GOODYEAR BLIMP NEEDS TIME TO GET HERE
THE GOODYEAR BLIMP? IN BRAD'S PARADE?!
GREG 9-5
OH, HONEY, WE ARE SO PROUD!
YEAH... WELL, THE CITY MIGHT DUMP THE WHOLE PARADE THING... TAXPAYERS' MONEY AND STUFF. PROBABLY THE MAYOR WILL JUST PHONE ME...
©2002 GEC Inc. Dist. by United Feature Syndicate, Inc. www.LuannsRoom.com
NAH. THE PARADE'S A GO
OR MAYBE NOT, TJ
THE GOODYEAR BLIMP! THIS IS HUGE!

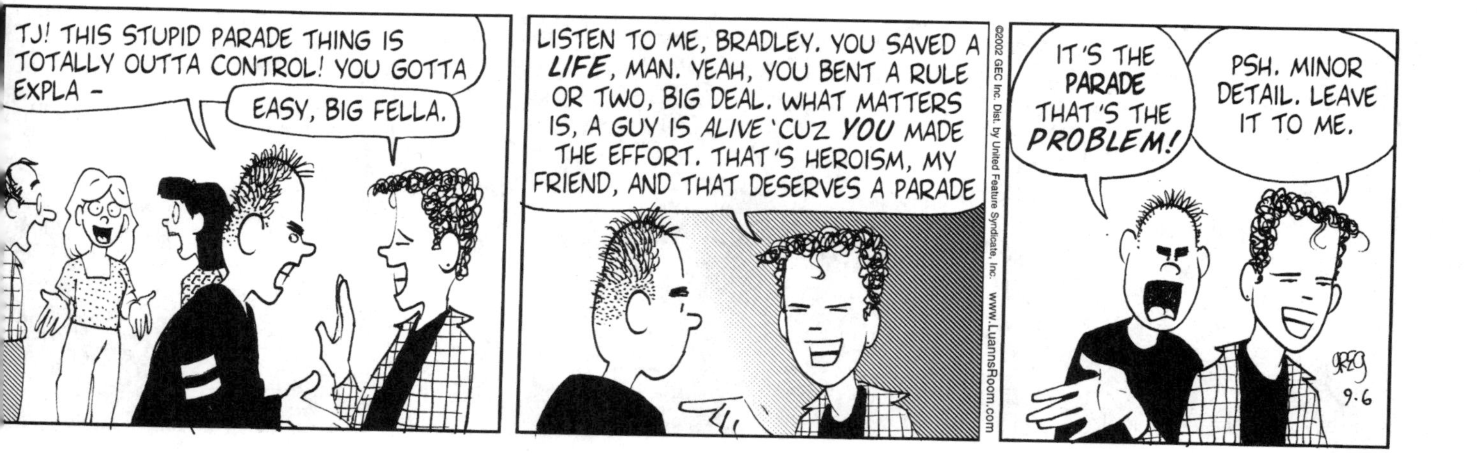
TJ! THIS STUPID PARADE THING IS TOTALLY OUTTA CONTROL! YOU GOTTA EXPLA –
EASY, BIG FELLA.
LISTEN TO ME, BRADLEY. YOU SAVED A LIFE, MAN. YEAH, YOU BENT A RULE OR TWO, BIG DEAL. WHAT MATTERS IS, A GUY IS ALIVE 'CUZ YOU MADE THE EFFORT. THAT'S HEROISM, MY FRIEND, AND THAT DESERVES A PARADE
©2002 GEC Inc. Dist. by United Feature Syndicate, Inc. www.LuannsRoom.com
IT'S THE PARADE THAT'S THE PROBLEM!
PSH. MINOR DETAIL. LEAVE IT TO ME.
GREG 9-6

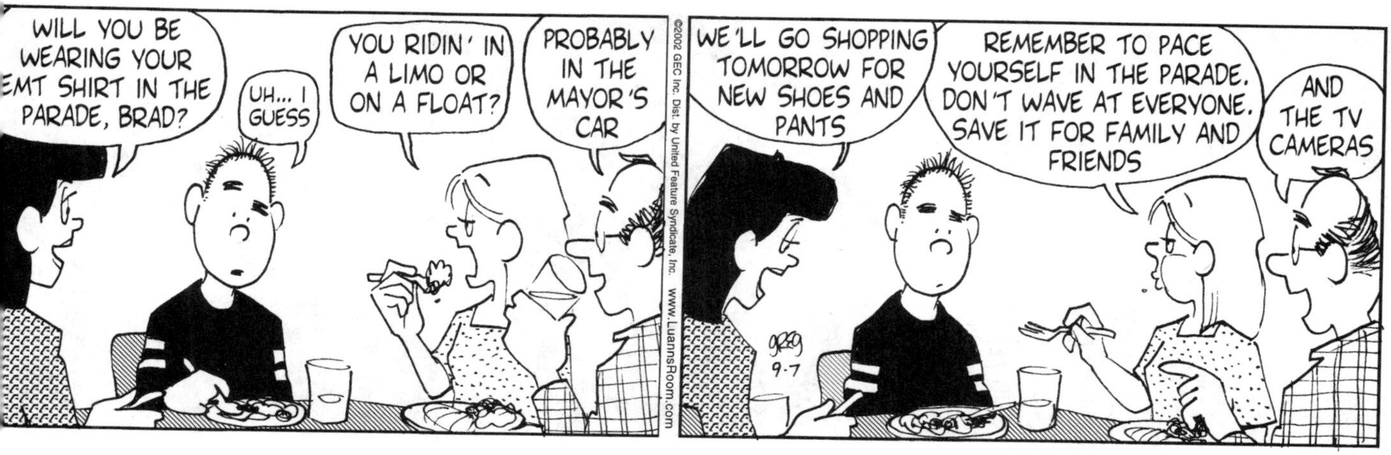
WILL YOU BE WEARING YOUR EMT SHIRT IN THE PARADE, BRAD?
UH... I GUESS
YOU RIDIN' IN A LIMO OR ON A FLOAT?
PROBABLY IN THE MAYOR'S CAR
©2002 GEC Inc. Dist. by United Feature Syndicate, Inc. www.LuannsRoom.com
WE'LL GO SHOPPING TOMORROW FOR NEW SHOES AND PANTS
REMEMBER TO PACE YOURSELF IN THE PARADE. DON'T WAVE AT EVERYONE. SAVE IT FOR FAMILY AND FRIENDS
AND THE TV CAMERAS
GREG 9-7

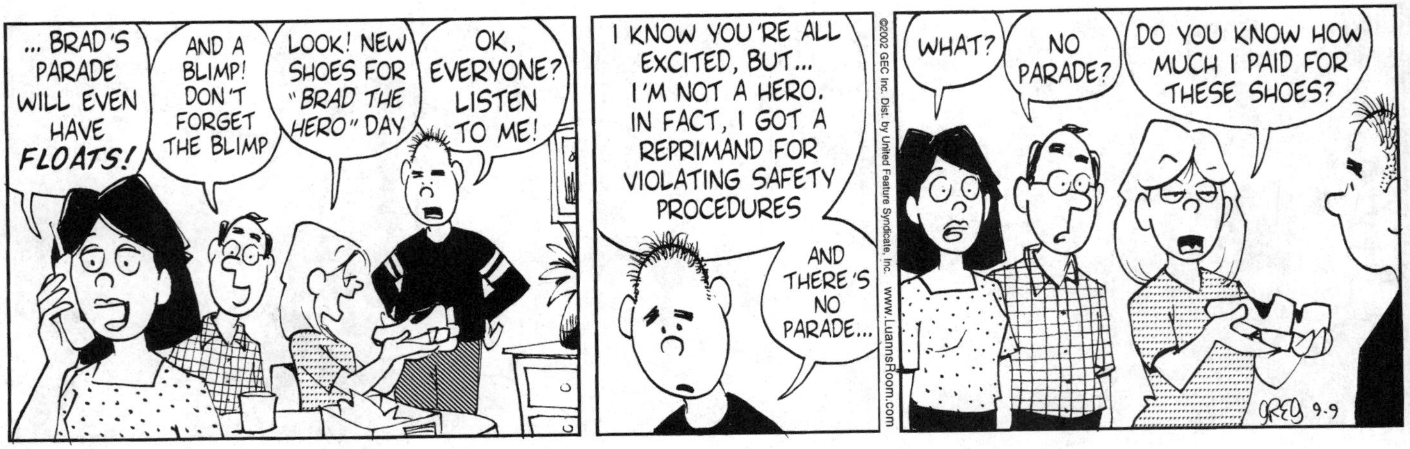
... BRAD'S PARADE WILL EVEN HAVE FLOATS!
AND A BLIMP! DON'T FORGET THE BLIMP
LOOK! NEW SHOES FOR "BRAD THE HERO" DAY
OK, EVERYONE? LISTEN TO ME!
I KNOW YOU'RE ALL EXCITED, BUT... I'M NOT A HERO. IN FACT, I GOT A REPRIMAND FOR VIOLATING SAFETY PROCEDURES
AND THERE'S NO PARADE...
©2002 GEC Inc. Dist. by United Feature Syndicate, Inc. www.LuannsRoom.com
WHAT?
NO PARADE?
DO YOU KNOW HOW MUCH I PAID FOR THESE SHOES?
GREG 9-9

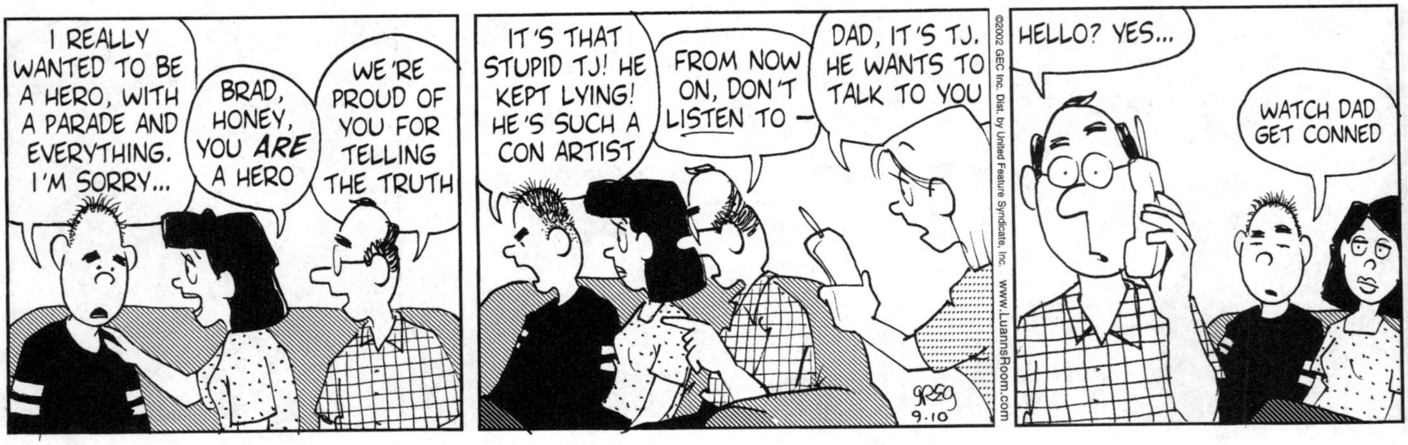
I REALLY WANTED TO BE A HERO, WITH A PARADE AND EVERYTHING. I'M SORRY...
BRAD, HONEY, YOU ARE A HERO
WE'RE PROUD OF YOU FOR TELLING THE TRUTH
IT'S THAT STUPID TJ! HE KEPT LYING! HE'S SUCH A CON ARTIST
FROM NOW ON, DON'T LISTEN TO –
DAD, IT'S TJ. HE WANTS TO TALK TO YOU
GREG 9-10
©2002 GEC Inc. Dist. by United Feature Syndicate, Inc. www.LuannsRoom.com
HELLO? YES...
WATCH DAD GET CONNED

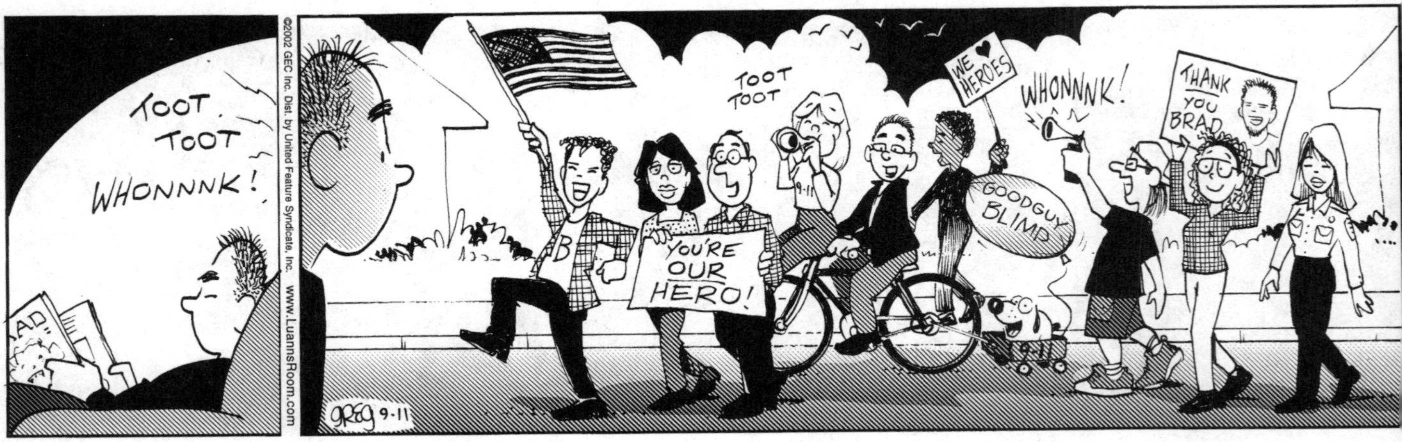
TOOT TOOT
WHONNNK!
©2002 GEC Inc. Dist. by United Feature Syndicate, Inc. www.LuannsRoom.com
TOOT TOOT
WE ♥ HEROES
WHONNNK!
THANK YOU BRAD
YOU'RE OUR HERO!
GOODGUY BLIMP
GREG 9-11

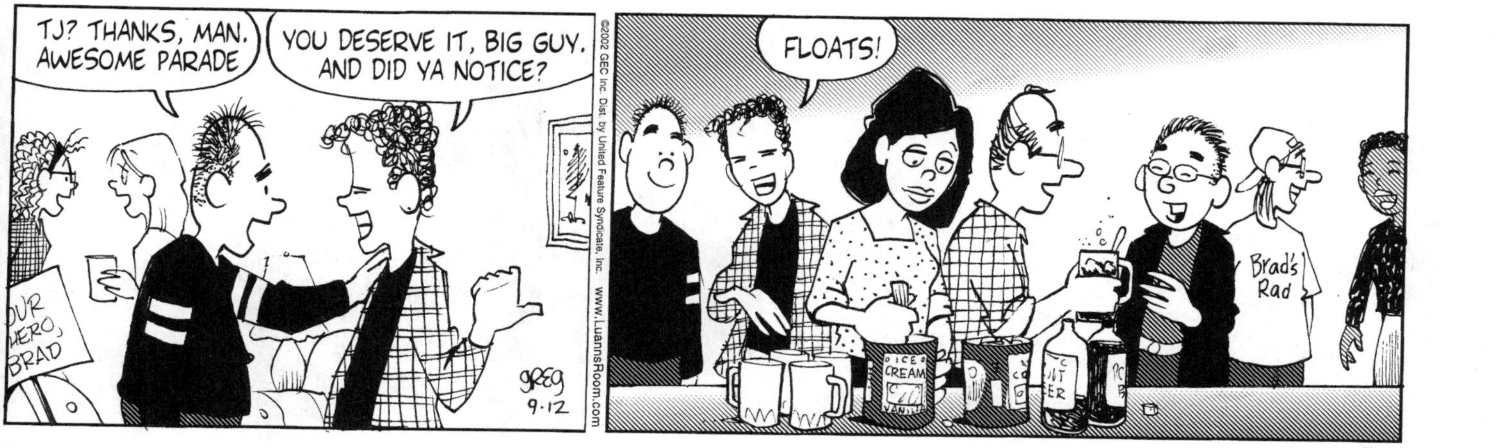
TJ? THANKS, MAN. AWESOME PARADE
YOU DESERVE IT, BIG GUY. AND DID YA NOTICE?
UR HERO, BRAD
GREG 9·12
©2002 GEC Inc. Dist. by United Feature Syndicate, Inc. www.LuannsRoom.com
FLOATS!
ICE CREAM
Brad's Rad

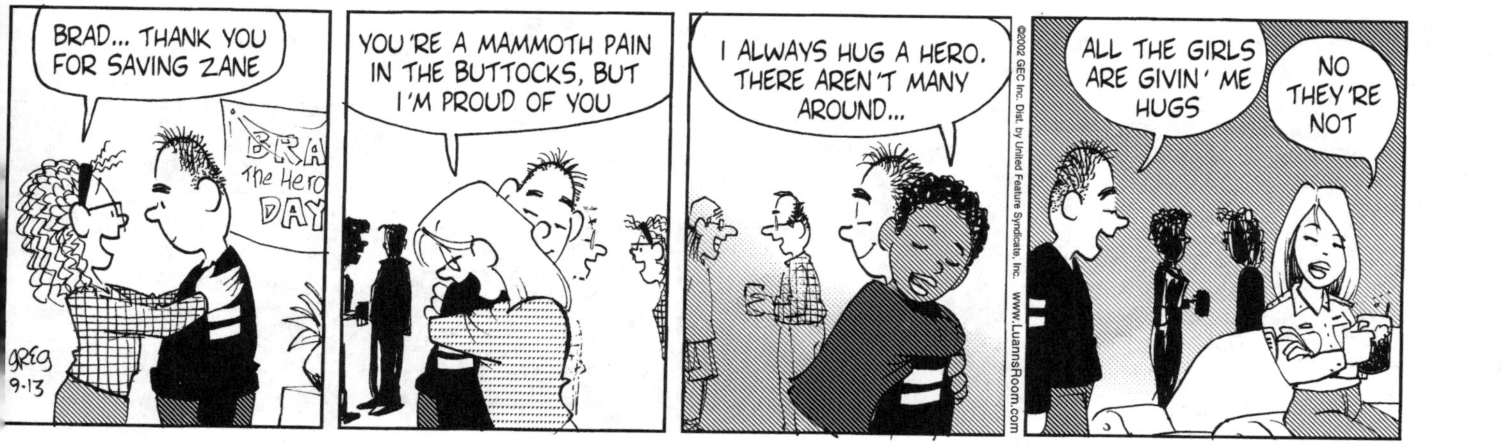
BRAD... THANK YOU FOR SAVING ZANE
GREG 9·13
YOU'RE A MAMMOTH PAIN IN THE BUTTOCKS, BUT I'M PROUD OF YOU
I ALWAYS HUG A HERO. THERE AREN'T MANY AROUND...
©2002 GEC Inc. Dist. by United Feature Syndicate, Inc. www.LuannsRoom.com
ALL THE GIRLS ARE GIVIN' ME HUGS
NO THEY'RE NOT

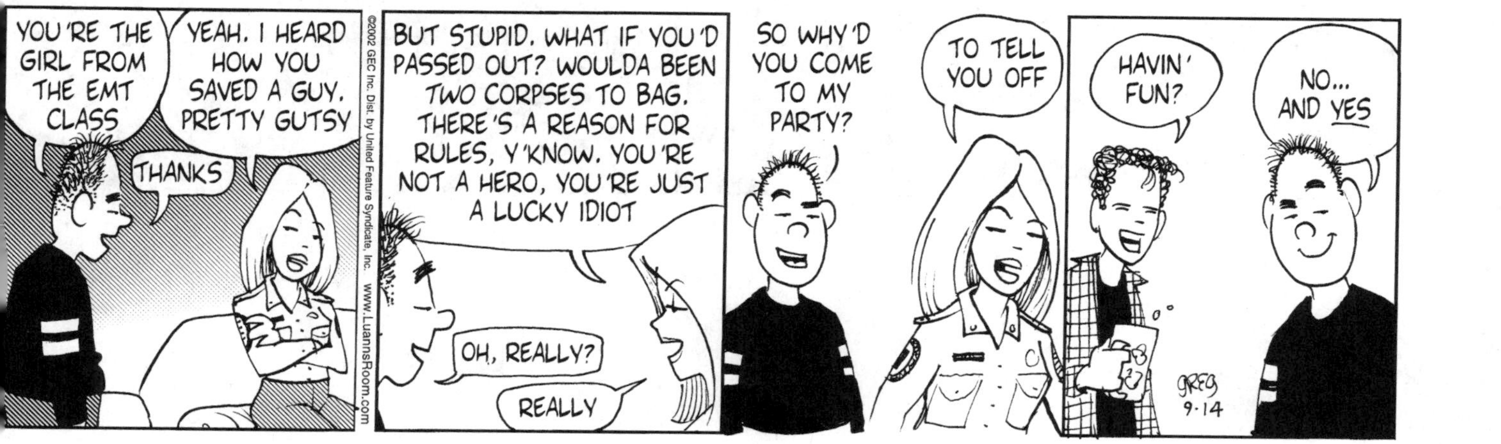
YOU'RE THE GIRL FROM THE EMT CLASS
YEAH. I HEARD HOW YOU SAVED A GUY. PRETTY GUTSY
THANKS
©2002 GEC Inc. Dist. by United Feature Syndicate, Inc. www.LuannsRoom.com
BUT STUPID. WHAT IF YOU'D PASSED OUT? WOULDA BEEN TWO CORPSES TO BAG. THERE'S A REASON FOR RULES, Y'KNOW. YOU'RE NOT A HERO, YOU'RE JUST A LUCKY IDIOT
OH, REALLY?
REALLY
SO WHY'D YOU COME TO MY PARTY?
TO TELL YOU OFF
HAVIN' FUN?
NO... AND YES
GREG 9·14

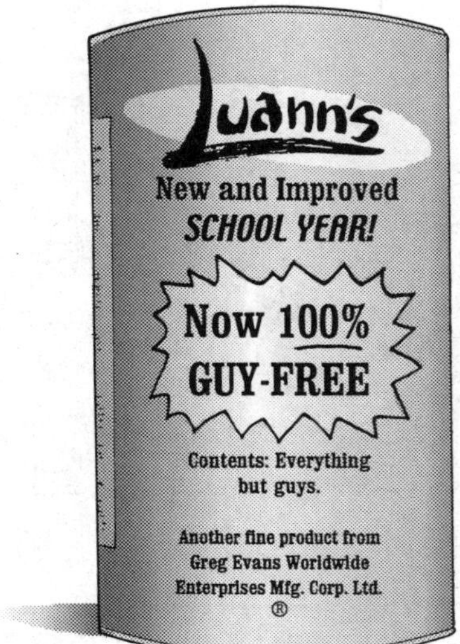
Luann's
New and Improved
SCHOOL YEAR!
Now 100%
GUY-FREE
Contents: Everything but guys.
Another fine product from
Greg Evans Worldwide
Enterprises Mfg. Corp. Ltd.
®

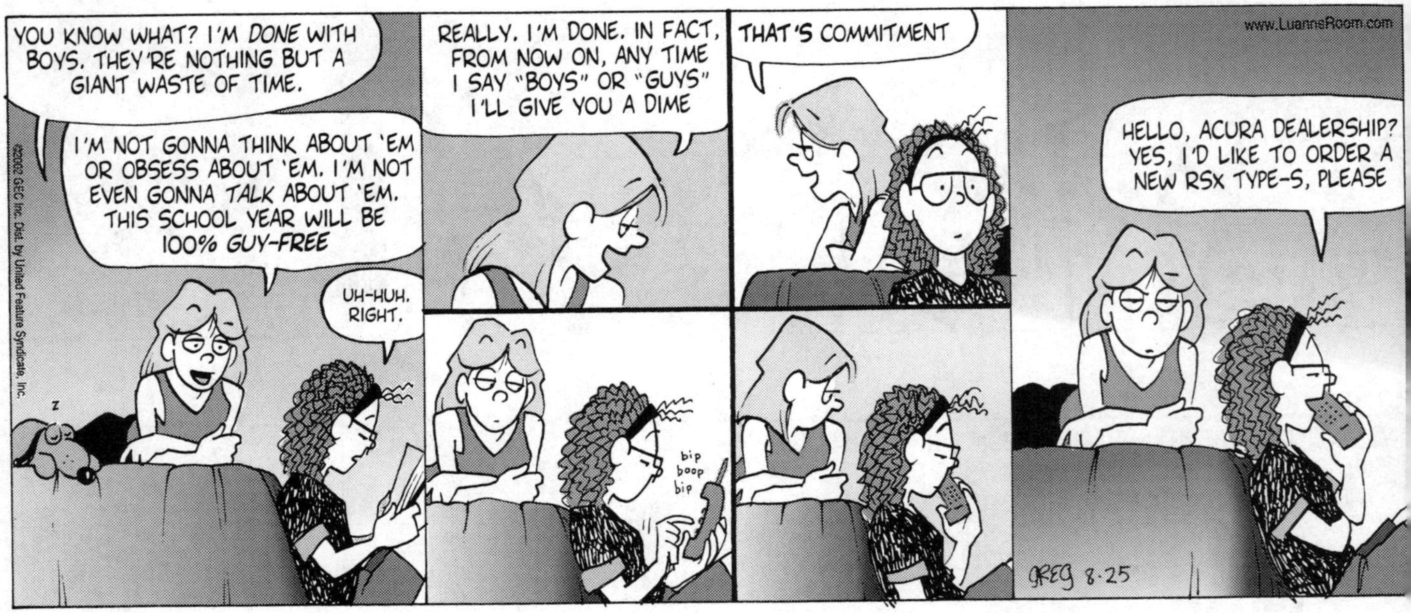
YOU KNOW WHAT? I'M *DONE* WITH BOYS. THEY'RE NOTHING BUT A GIANT WASTE OF TIME.
I'M NOT GONNA THINK ABOUT 'EM OR OBSESS ABOUT 'EM. I'M NOT EVEN GONNA *TALK* ABOUT 'EM. THIS SCHOOL YEAR WILL BE 100% *GUY-FREE*
UH-HUH. RIGHT.
Z
©2002 GEC Inc. Dist. by United Feature Syndicate, Inc.
REALLY. I'M DONE. IN FACT, FROM NOW ON, ANY TIME I SAY "BOYS" OR "GUYS" I'LL GIVE YOU A DIME
bip boop bip
THAT'S COMMITMENT
www.LuannsRoom.com
HELLO, ACURA DEALERSHIP? YES, I'D LIKE TO ORDER A NEW RSX TYPE-S, PLEASE
GREG 8·25

LUANN, I'VE MADE A LIST OF THINGS I DON'T WANT TO HEAR YOU SAY ANYMORE:

"BUT EVERYONE'S DOING IT! I'LL FINISH MY HOMEWORK LATER, I PROMISE. WHY ARE YOU SO OLD-FASHIONED? IF YOU LOVED ME, YOU'D TRUST ME. YOU NEVER LET ME DO ANYTHING. THIS ISN'T FAIR! YUK, WHAT'S THIS STUFF? CAN WE ORDER A PIZZA? YOU'RE WEARING THAT?!"

INTERESTING. I HAPPEN TO HAVE A LIST OF THINGS I DON'T WANT TO HEAR YOU SAY ANYMORE:

"OH, AND IF EVERYONE JUMPED OFF A BRIDGE, YOU WOULD TOO? WHEN I WAS YOUR AGE... YOU DON'T KNOW HOW GOOD YOU HAVE IT. I'M NOT MADE OF MONEY, YOU KNOW. DON'T BE SMART. DON'T BE STUPID. BECAUSE I SAID SO, THAT'S WHY. YOU'RE WEARING THAT?!"

...I'LL RIP UP MINE IF YOU RIP UP YOURS

DONE.

riiip

GREG 9.1

©2002 GEC Inc Dist. by United Feature Syndicate, Inc. WWW.LuannsRoom.com

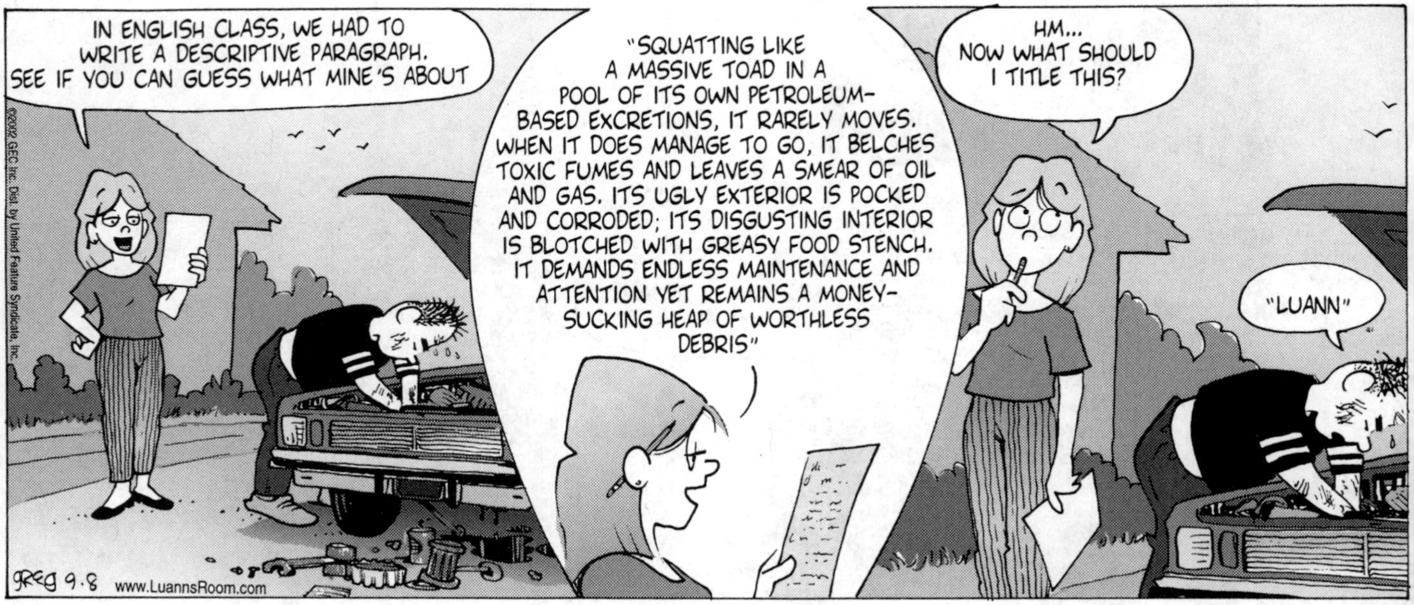
IN ENGLISH CLASS, WE HAD TO WRITE A DESCRIPTIVE PARAGRAPH. SEE IF YOU CAN GUESS WHAT MINE'S ABOUT
"SQUATTING LIKE A MASSIVE TOAD IN A POOL OF ITS OWN PETROLEUM-BASED EXCRETIONS, IT RARELY MOVES. WHEN IT DOES MANAGE TO GO, IT BELCHES TOXIC FUMES AND LEAVES A SMEAR OF OIL AND GAS. ITS UGLY EXTERIOR IS POCKED AND CORRODED; ITS DISGUSTING INTERIOR IS BLOTCHED WITH GREASY FOOD STENCH. IT DEMANDS ENDLESS MAINTENANCE AND ATTENTION YET REMAINS A MONEY-SUCKING HEAP OF WORTHLESS DEBRIS"
HM... NOW WHAT SHOULD I TITLE THIS?
"LUANN"
©2002 GEC Inc. Dist. by United Feature Syndicate, Inc.
GREG 9.8 www.LuannsRoom.com

©2002 GEC Inc. Dist. by United Feature Syndicate, Inc.
THIS SAYS THAT TODAY'S TEENS HAVE A SMALLER VOCABULARY THAN THAT OF PREVIOUS GENERATIONS
WeenieWorld
I DON'T AGREE. WE USE A *DIFFERENT* VOCABULARY, YES. BUT THE QUANTITY IS EQUAL, IF NOT GREATER
NO IT ISN'T. OUR GENERATION EXCELS IN THE REDUNDANT USE OF MONOSYLLABIC GRUNTS AND LAZY CATCH-PHRASES
WHAT DO YOU THINK, LUANN?
UM... I DUNNO. I GUESS I'M LIKE, Y'KNOW. WHATEVER
WOW! *NICELY* PUT! THAT SURE PROVES ***ME*** WRONG!
GREG 9-15
www.LuannsRoom.com

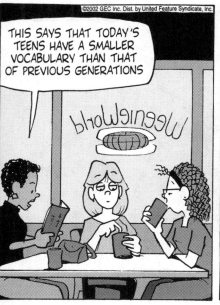

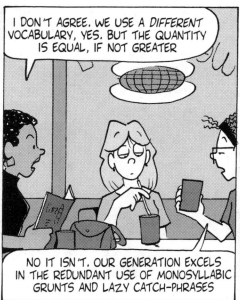

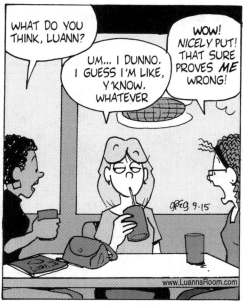

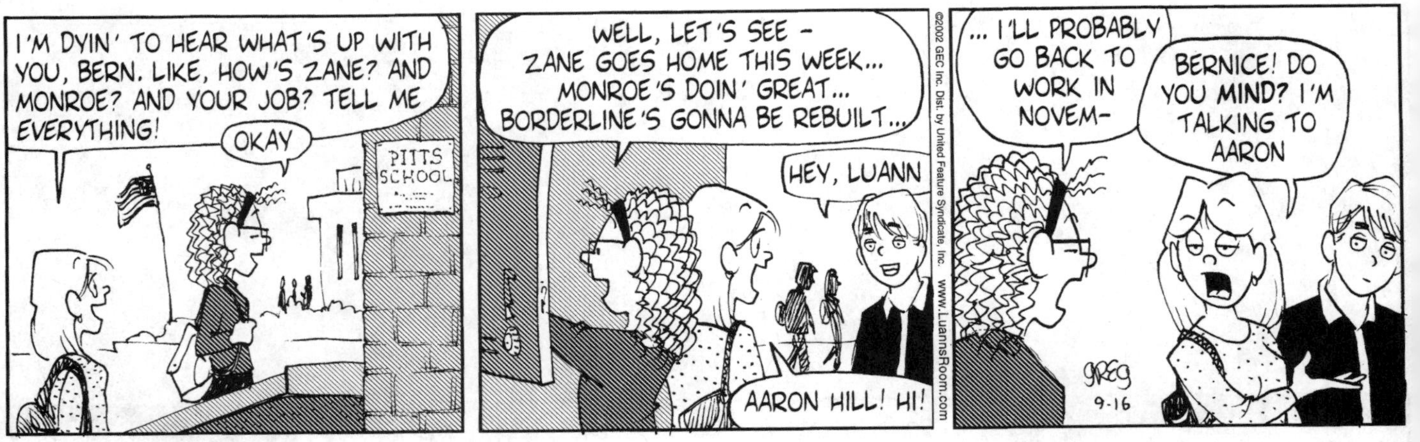
I'M DYIN' TO HEAR WHAT'S UP WITH YOU, BERN. LIKE, HOW'S ZANE? AND MONROE? AND YOUR JOB? TELL ME EVERYTHING!
OKAY
PITTS SCHOOL
WELL, LET'S SEE - ZANE GOES HOME THIS WEEK... MONROE'S DOIN' GREAT... BORDERLINE'S GONNA BE REBUILT...
HEY, LUANN
AARON HILL! HI!
©2002 GEC Inc. Dist. by United Feature Syndicate, Inc. www.LuannsRoom.com
... I'LL PROBABLY GO BACK TO WORK IN NOVEM-
BERNICE! DO YOU **MIND?** I'M TALKING TO AARON
GREG 9-16

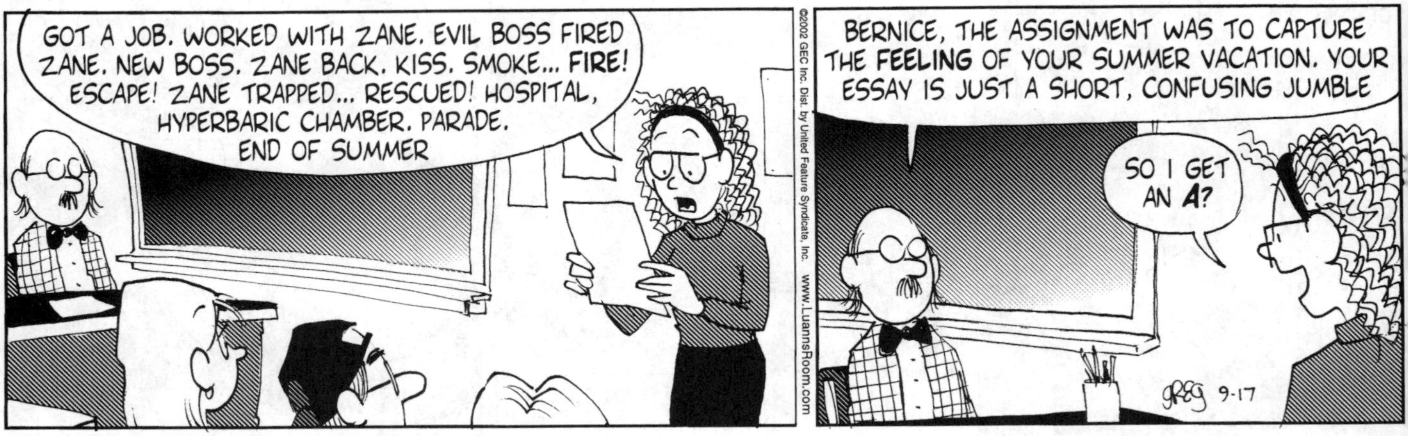
GOT A JOB. WORKED WITH ZANE. EVIL BOSS FIRED ZANE. NEW BOSS. ZANE BACK. KISS. SMOKE... **FIRE!** ESCAPE! ZANE TRAPPED... RESCUED! HOSPITAL, HYPERBARIC CHAMBER. PARADE. END OF SUMMER
©2002 GEC Inc. Dist. by United Feature Syndicate, Inc. www.LuannsRoom.com
BERNICE, THE ASSIGNMENT WAS TO CAPTURE THE **FEELING** OF YOUR SUMMER VACATION. YOUR ESSAY IS JUST A SHORT, CONFUSING JUMBLE
SO I GET AN ***A***?
GREG 9-17

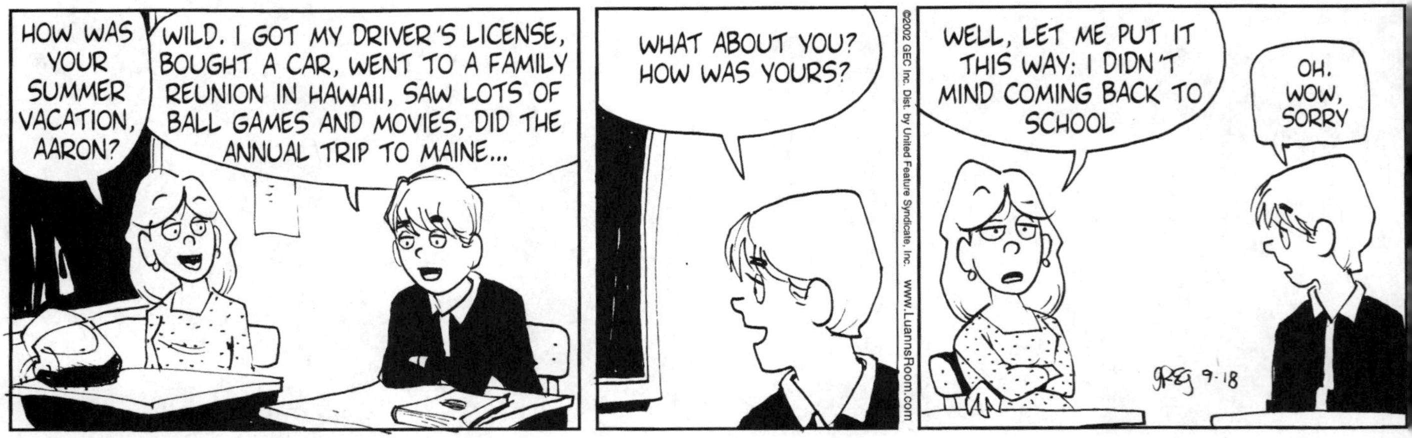
HOW WAS YOUR SUMMER VACATION, AARON?
WILD. I GOT MY DRIVER'S LICENSE, BOUGHT A CAR, WENT TO A FAMILY REUNION IN HAWAII, SAW LOTS OF BALL GAMES AND MOVIES, DID THE ANNUAL TRIP TO MAINE...
WHAT ABOUT YOU? HOW WAS YOURS?
©2002 GEC Inc. Dist. by United Feature Syndicate, Inc. www.LuannsRoom.com
WELL, LET ME PUT IT THIS WAY: I DIDN'T MIND COMING BACK TO SCHOOL
OH. WOW, SORRY
GREG 9-18

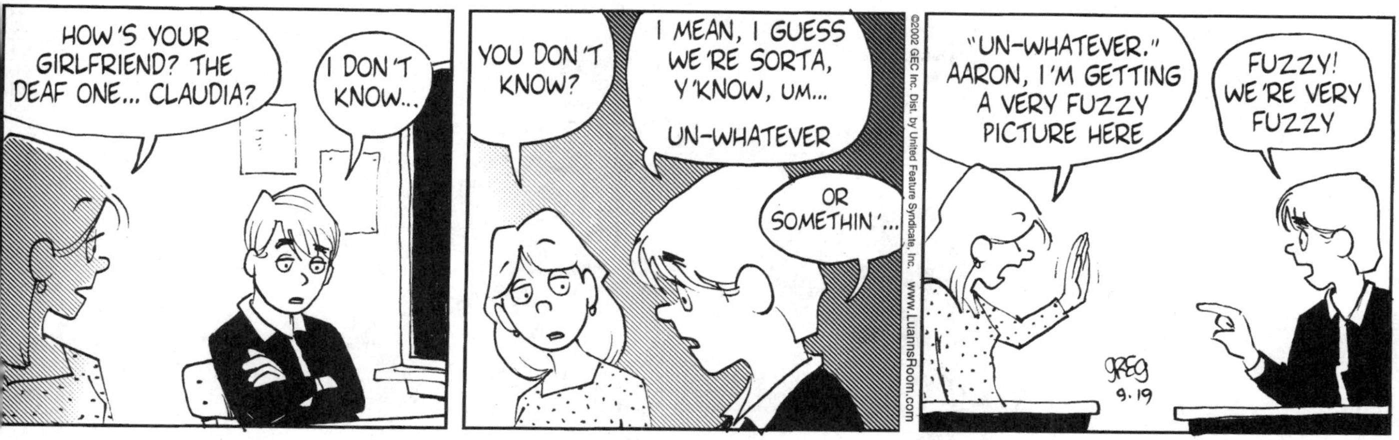
HOW'S YOUR GIRLFRIEND? THE DEAF ONE... CLAUDIA?
I DON'T KNOW...
YOU DON'T KNOW?
I MEAN, I GUESS WE'RE SORTA, Y'KNOW, UM...
UN-WHATEVER
OR SOMETHIN'...
©2002 GEC Inc. Dist. by United Feature Syndicate, Inc. www.LuannsRoom.com
"UN-WHATEVER." AARON, I'M GETTING A VERY FUZZY PICTURE HERE
FUZZY! WE'RE VERY FUZZY
GREG
9.19

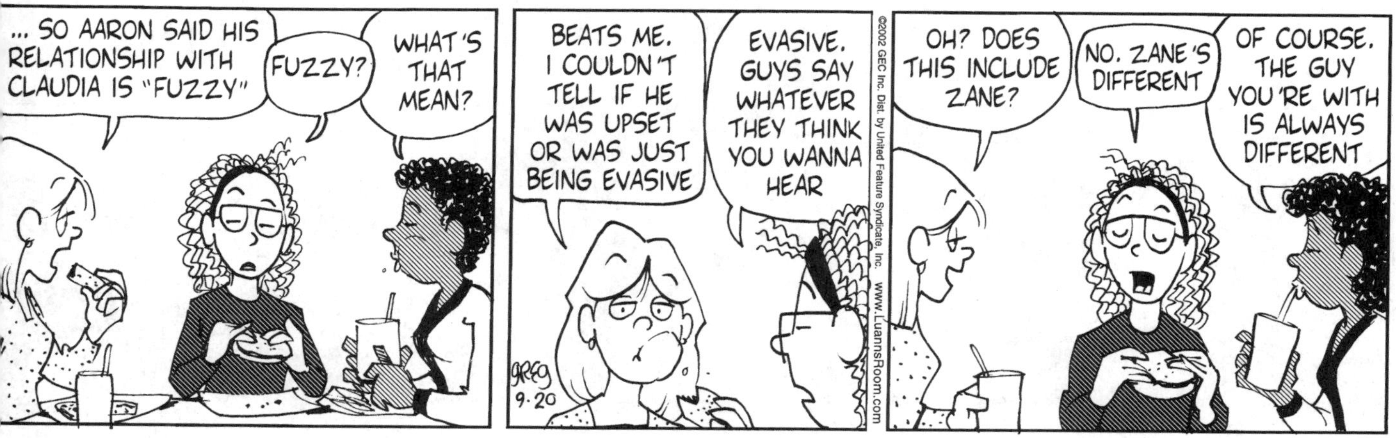
... SO AARON SAID HIS RELATIONSHIP WITH CLAUDIA IS "FUZZY"
FUZZY?
WHAT'S THAT MEAN?
BEATS ME. I COULDN'T TELL IF HE WAS UPSET OR WAS JUST BEING EVASIVE
EVASIVE. GUYS SAY WHATEVER THEY THINK YOU WANNA HEAR
GREG
9.20
©2002 GEC Inc. Dist. by United Feature Syndicate, Inc. www.LuannsRoom.com
OH? DOES THIS INCLUDE ZANE?
NO. ZANE'S DIFFERENT
OF COURSE. THE GUY YOU'RE WITH IS ALWAYS DIFFERENT

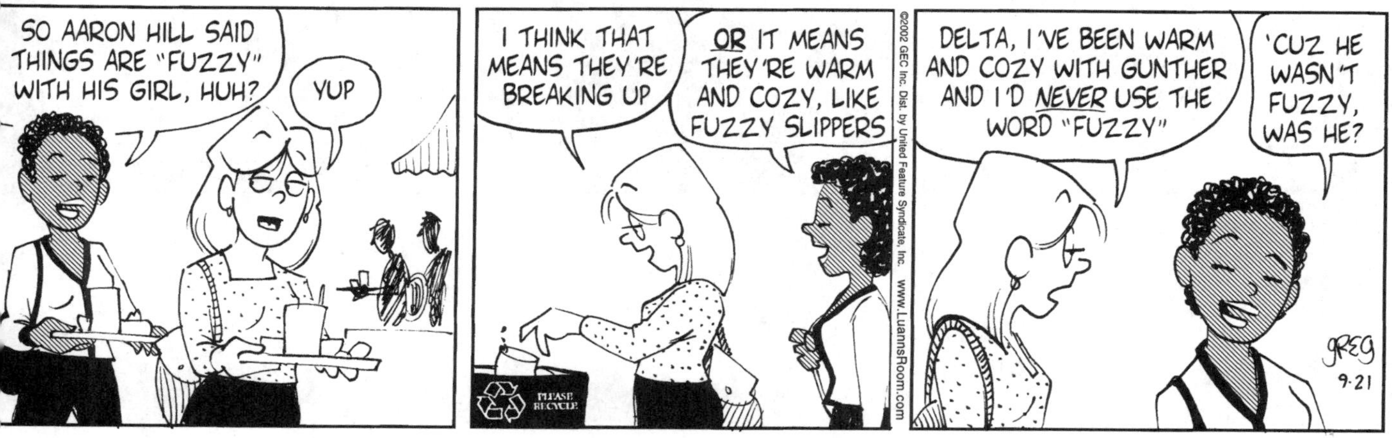
SO AARON HILL SAID THINGS ARE "FUZZY" WITH HIS GIRL, HUH?
YUP
I THINK THAT MEANS THEY'RE BREAKING UP
OR IT MEANS THEY'RE WARM AND COZY, LIKE FUZZY SLIPPERS
PLEASE RECYCLE
©2002 GEC Inc. Dist. by United Feature Syndicate, Inc. www.LuannsRoom.com
DELTA, I'VE BEEN WARM AND COZY WITH GUNTHER AND I'D NEVER USE THE WORD "FUZZY"
'CUZ HE WASN'T FUZZY, WAS HE?
GREG
9.21

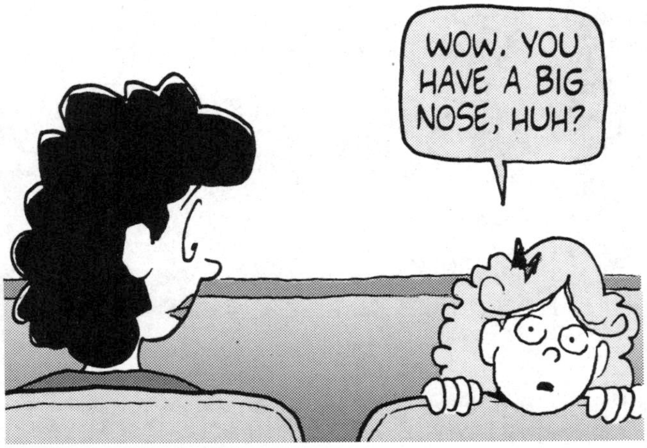
WOW. YOU HAVE A BIG NOSE, HUH?

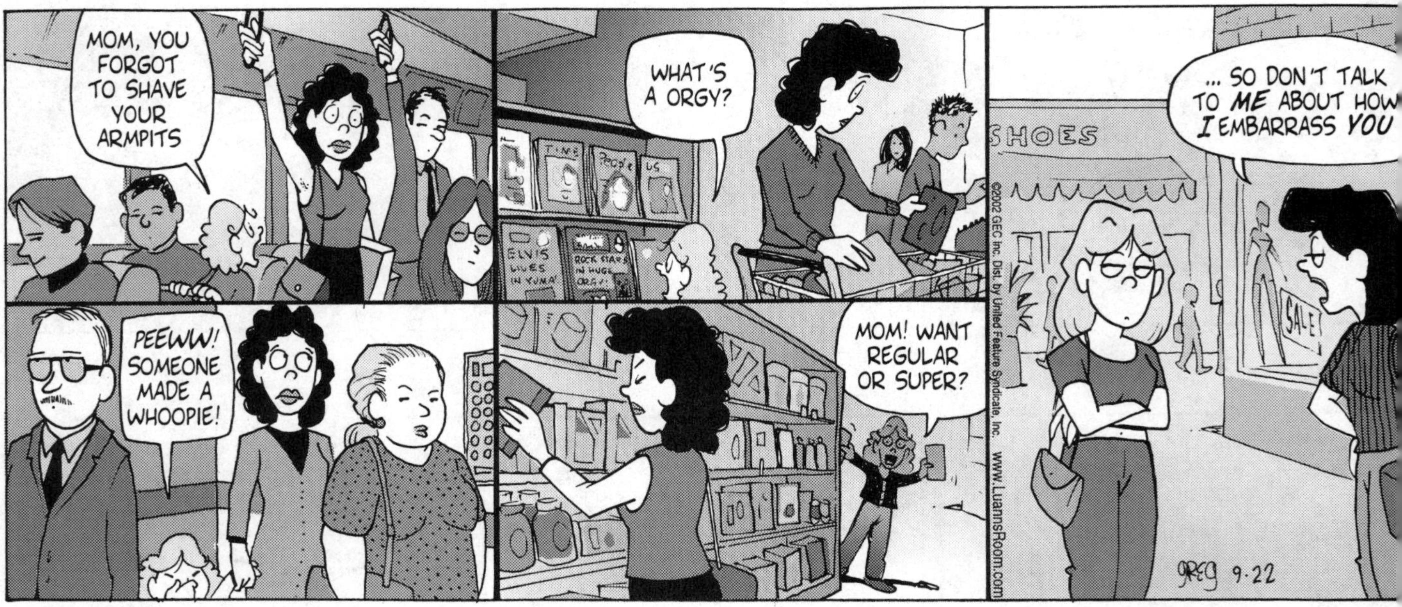
MOM, YOU FORGOT TO SHAVE YOUR ARMPITS
WHAT'S A ORGY?
ELVIS LIVES IN YUMA!
PEEWW! SOMEONE MADE A WHOOPIE!
MOM! WANT REGULAR OR SUPER?
SHOES
... SO DON'T TALK TO *ME* ABOUT HOW *I* EMBARRASS *YOU*
SALE
©2002 GEC Inc. Dist. by United Feature Syndicate, Inc. www.LuannsRoom.com
GREG 9-22

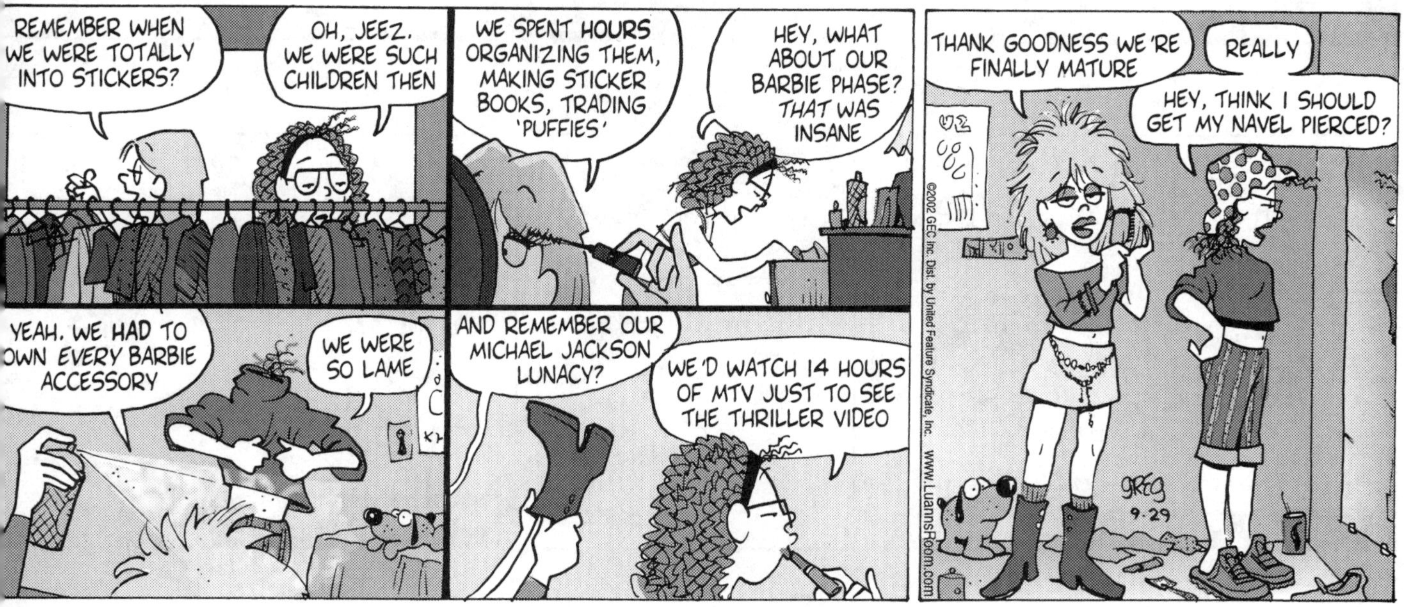
REMEMBER WHEN WE WERE TOTALLY INTO STICKERS?
OH, JEEZ. WE WERE SUCH CHILDREN THEN
WE SPENT **HOURS** ORGANIZING THEM, MAKING STICKER BOOKS, TRADING 'PUFFIES'
HEY, WHAT ABOUT OUR BARBIE PHASE? *THAT* WAS INSANE
YEAH. WE **HAD** TO OWN *EVERY* BARBIE ACCESSORY
WE WERE SO LAME
AND REMEMBER OUR MICHAEL JACKSON LUNACY?
WE'D WATCH 14 HOURS OF MTV JUST TO SEE THE THRILLER VIDEO
THANK GOODNESS WE'RE FINALLY MATURE
REALLY
HEY, THINK I SHOULD GET MY NAVEL PIERCED?
©2002 GEC Inc. Dist. by United Feature Syndicate, Inc.
www.LuannsRoom.com
GREG 9-29

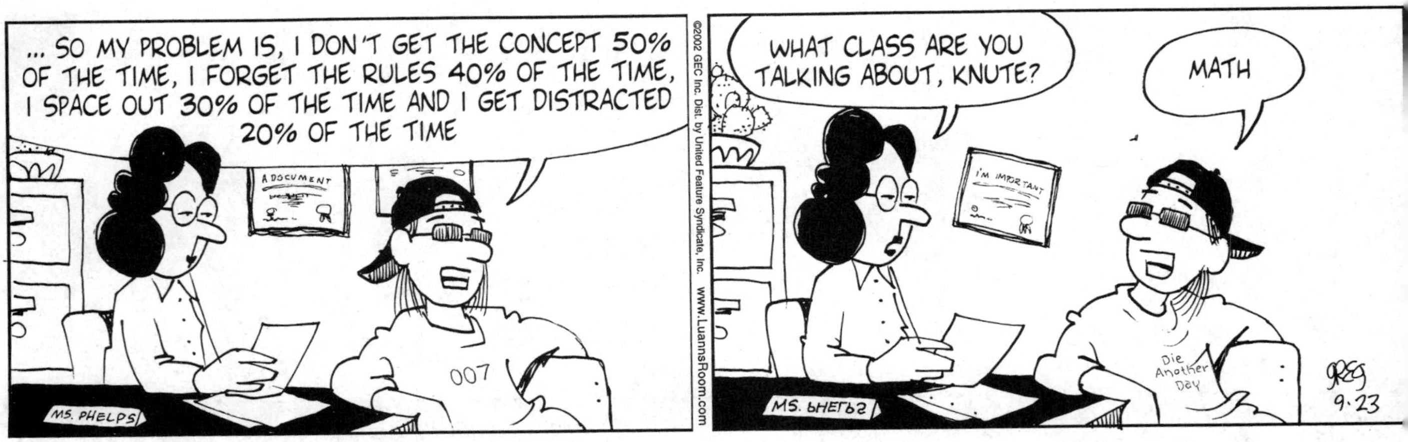
... SO MY PROBLEM IS, I DON'T GET THE CONCEPT 50% OF THE TIME, I FORGET THE RULES 40% OF THE TIME, I SPACE OUT 30% OF THE TIME AND I GET DISTRACTED 20% OF THE TIME
A DOCUMENT
007
MS. PHELPS
©2002 GEC Inc. Dist. by United Feature Syndicate, Inc. www.LuannsRoom.com
WHAT CLASS ARE YOU TALKING ABOUT, KNUTE?
MATH
I'M IMPORTANT
Die Another Day
GREG
9.23

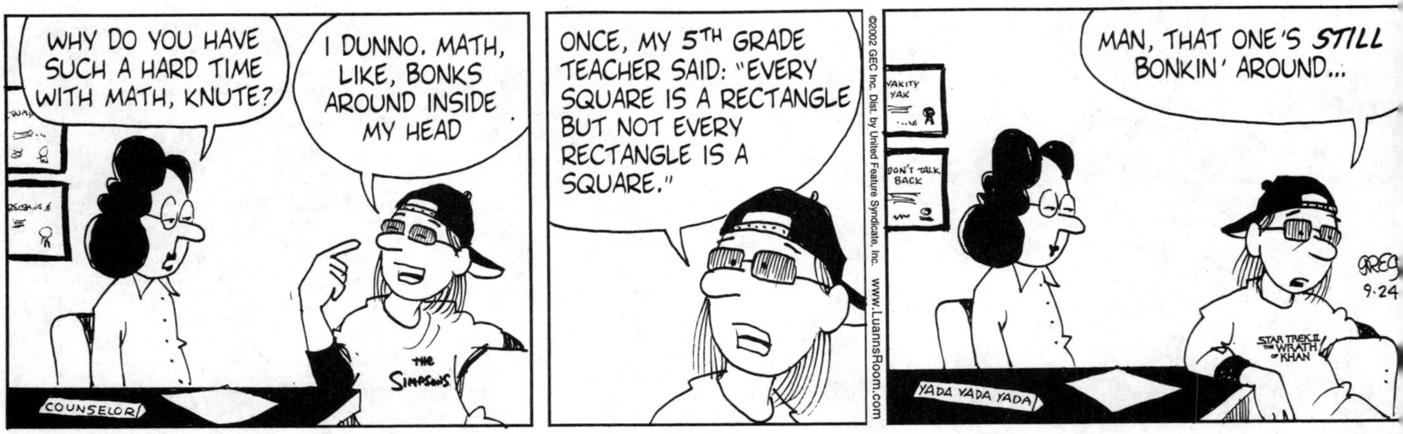
WHY DO YOU HAVE SUCH A HARD TIME WITH MATH, KNUTE?
I DUNNO. MATH, LIKE, BONKS AROUND INSIDE MY HEAD
THE SIMPSONS
COUNSELOR
ONCE, MY 5TH GRADE TEACHER SAID: "EVERY SQUARE IS A RECTANGLE BUT NOT EVERY RECTANGLE IS A SQUARE."
©2002 GEC Inc. Dist. by United Feature Syndicate, Inc. www.LuannsRoom.com
MAN, THAT ONE'S STILL BONKIN' AROUND...
YAKITY YAK
DON'T TALK BACK
GREG
9.24
STAR TREK II THE WRATH OF KHAN
YADA YADA YADA

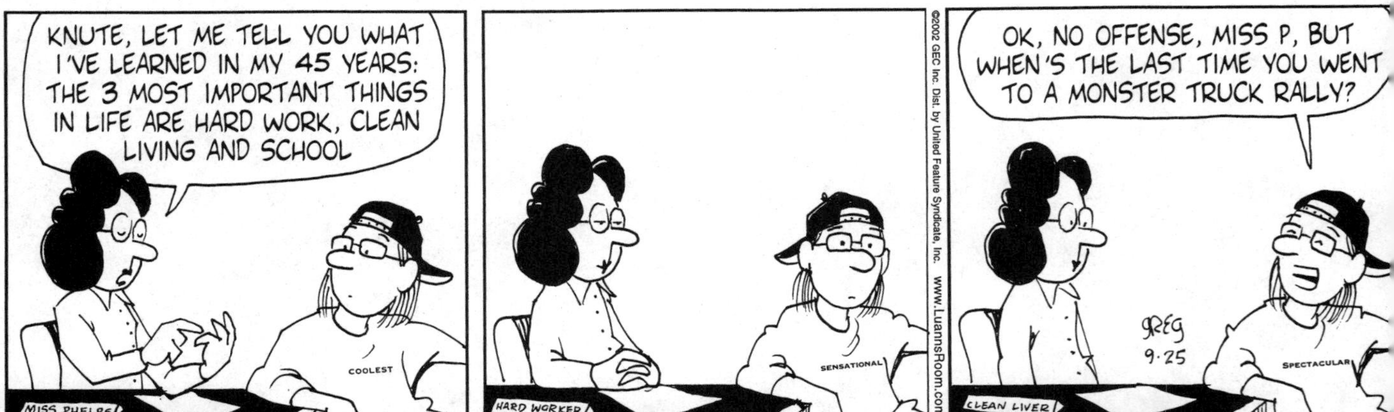
KNUTE, LET ME TELL YOU WHAT I'VE LEARNED IN MY 45 YEARS: THE 3 MOST IMPORTANT THINGS IN LIFE ARE HARD WORK, CLEAN LIVING AND SCHOOL
COOLEST
MISS PHELPS
SENSATIONAL
HARD WORKER
©2002 GEC Inc. Dist. by United Feature Syndicate, Inc. www.LuannsRoom.com
OK, NO OFFENSE, MISS P, BUT WHEN'S THE LAST TIME YOU WENT TO A MONSTER TRUCK RALLY?
GREG
9.25
SPECTACULAR
CLEAN LIVER

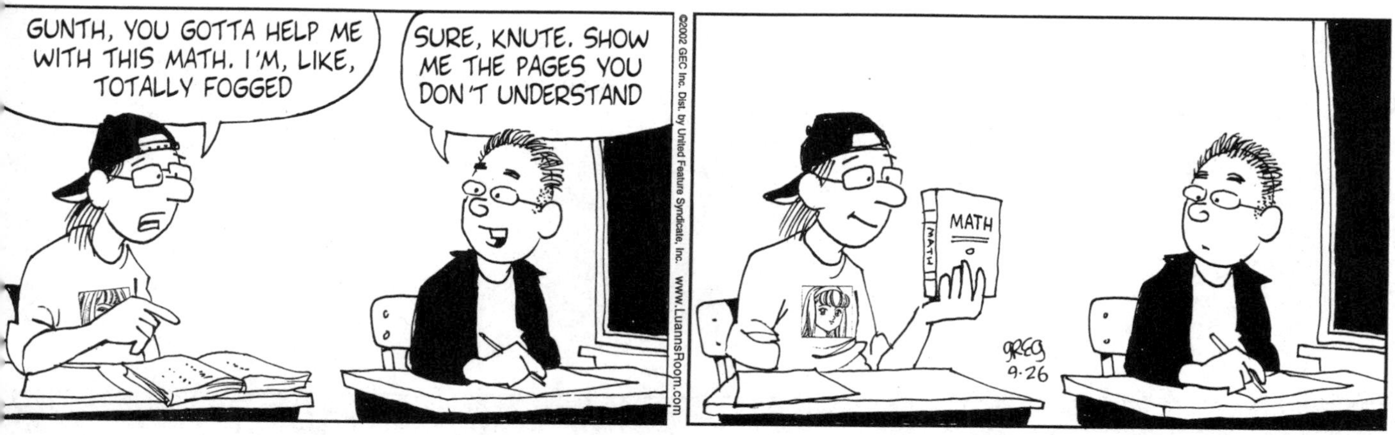
GUNTH, YOU GOTTA HELP ME WITH THIS MATH. I'M, LIKE, TOTALLY FOGGED
SURE, KNUTE. SHOW ME THE PAGES YOU DON'T UNDERSTAND
©2002 GEC Inc. Dist. by United Feature Syndicate, Inc. www.LuannsRoom.com
MATH
GREG 9·26

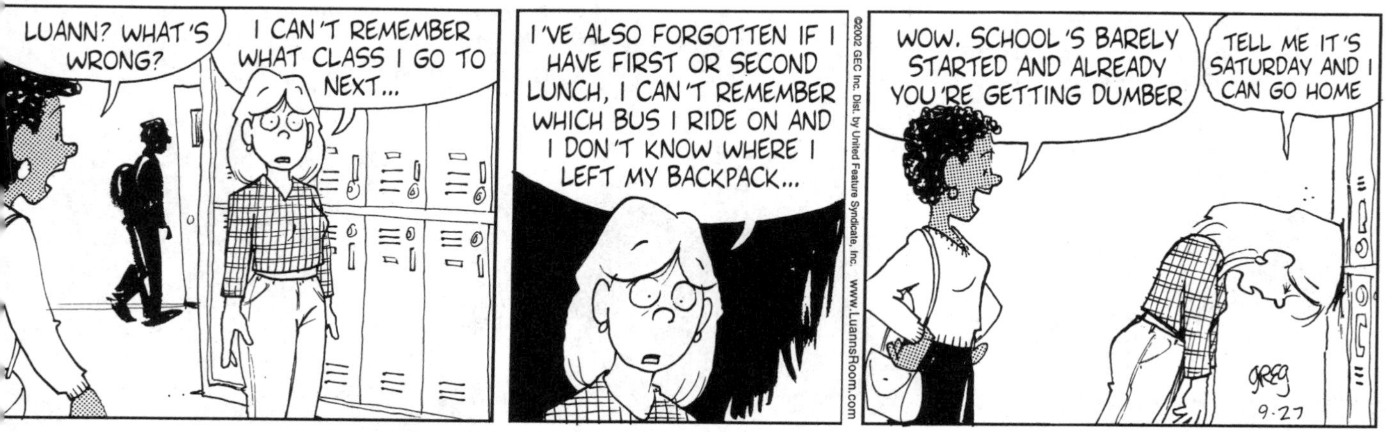
LUANN? WHAT'S WRONG?
I CAN'T REMEMBER WHAT CLASS I GO TO NEXT...
I'VE ALSO FORGOTTEN IF I HAVE FIRST OR SECOND LUNCH, I CAN'T REMEMBER WHICH BUS I RIDE ON AND I DON'T KNOW WHERE I LEFT MY BACKPACK...
©2002 GEC Inc. Dist. by United Feature Syndicate, Inc. www.LuannsRoom.com
WOW. SCHOOL'S BARELY STARTED AND ALREADY YOU'RE GETTING DUMBER
TELL ME IT'S SATURDAY AND I CAN GO HOME
GREG 9·27

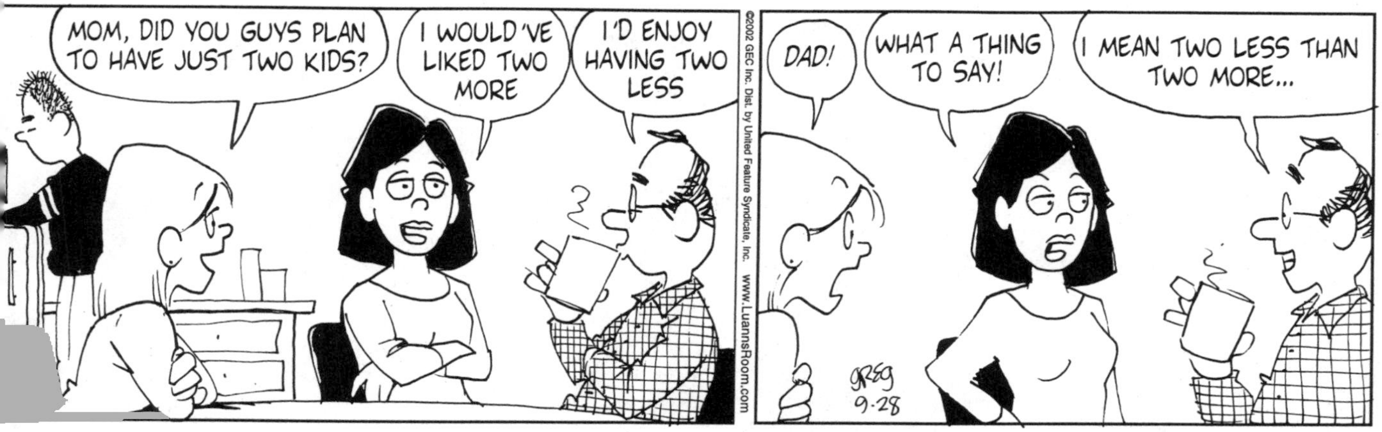
MOM, DID YOU GUYS PLAN TO HAVE JUST TWO KIDS?
I WOULD'VE LIKED TWO MORE
I'D ENJOY HAVING TWO LESS
©2002 GEC Inc. Dist. by United Feature Syndicate, Inc. www.LuannsRoom.com
DAD!
WHAT A THING TO SAY!
I MEAN TWO LESS THAN TWO MORE...
GREG 9·28

A Poem: My Daughter, Age 2
It's one a.m., I lie asleep
And then I hear you cry and weep
You seem to say "It's almost day!
Get up and feed me right away!"
©2002 GEC Inc. Dist. by United Feature Syndicate, Inc.
www.LuannsRoom.com
GREG 10.6
A Poem: My Daughter, Age 16
It's one a.m., I lie asleep
And then I hear you cry and weep
"My science project's due today!
Get up and help me right away!"

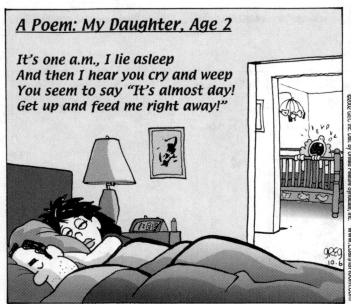

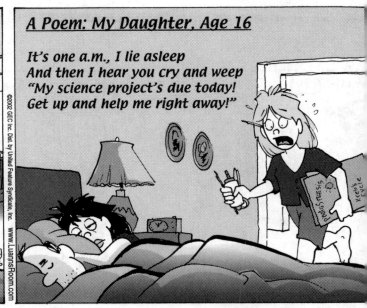

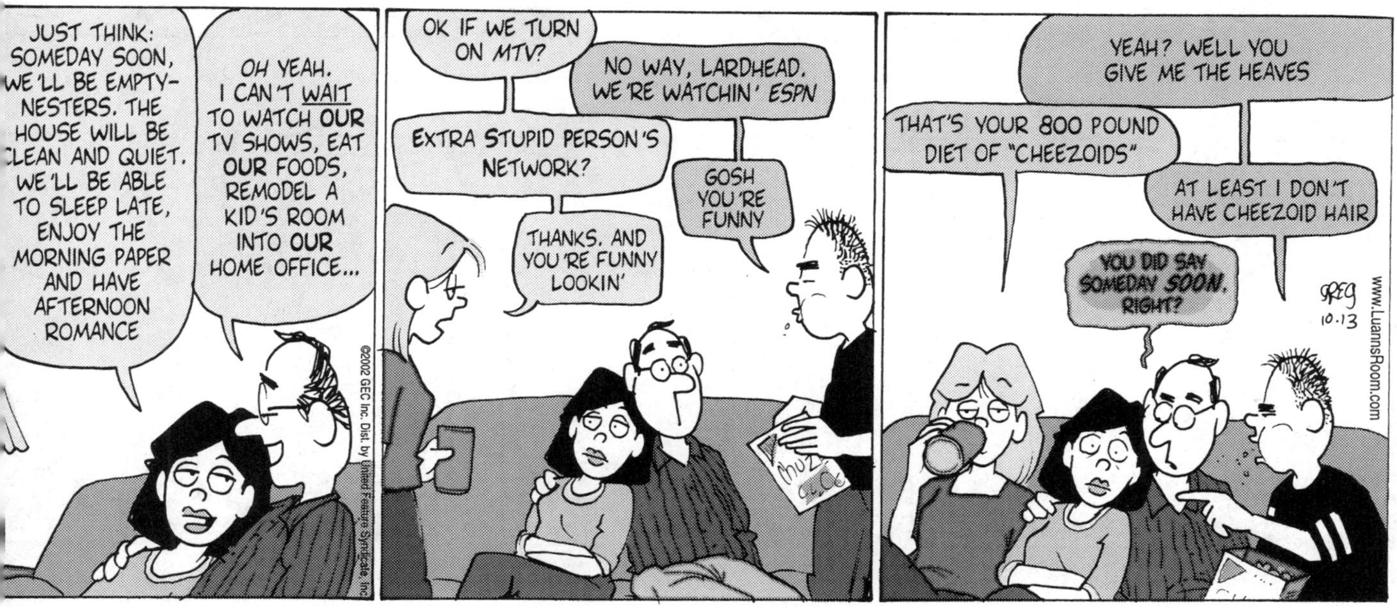
JUST THINK: SOMEDAY SOON, WE'LL BE EMPTY-NESTERS. THE HOUSE WILL BE CLEAN AND QUIET. WE'LL BE ABLE TO SLEEP LATE, ENJOY THE MORNING PAPER AND HAVE AFTERNOON ROMANCE
OH YEAH. I CAN'T WAIT TO WATCH OUR TV SHOWS, EAT OUR FOODS, REMODEL A KID'S ROOM INTO OUR HOME OFFICE...
©2002 GEC Inc. Dist. by United Feature Syndicate, Inc.
OK IF WE TURN ON MTV?
NO WAY, LARDHEAD. WE'RE WATCHIN' ESPN
EXTRA STUPID PERSON'S NETWORK?
GOSH YOU'RE FUNNY
THANKS. AND YOU'RE FUNNY LOOKIN'
YEAH? WELL YOU GIVE ME THE HEAVES
THAT'S YOUR 800 POUND DIET OF "CHEEZOIDS"
AT LEAST I DON'T HAVE CHEEZOID HAIR
YOU DID SAY SOMEDAY SOON, RIGHT?
GREG 10.13
www.LuannsRoom.com

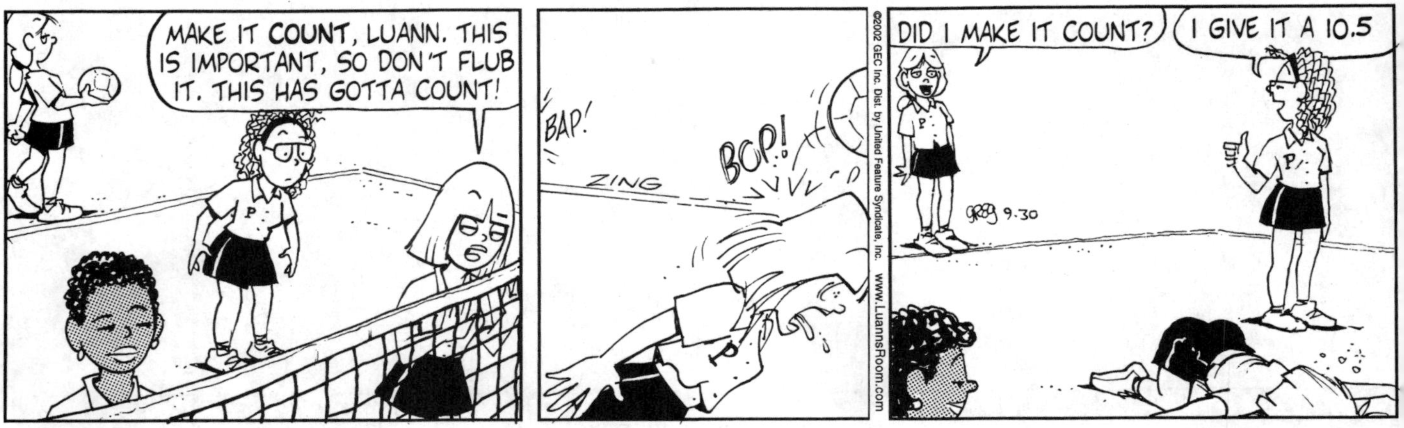
MAKE IT COUNT, LUANN. THIS IS IMPORTANT, SO DON'T FLUB IT. THIS HAS GOTTA COUNT!
BAP!
ZING
BOP!
©2002 GEC Inc. Dist. by United Feature Syndicate, Inc. www.LuannsRoom.com
DID I MAKE IT COUNT?
I GIVE IT A 10.5
GREG 9.30

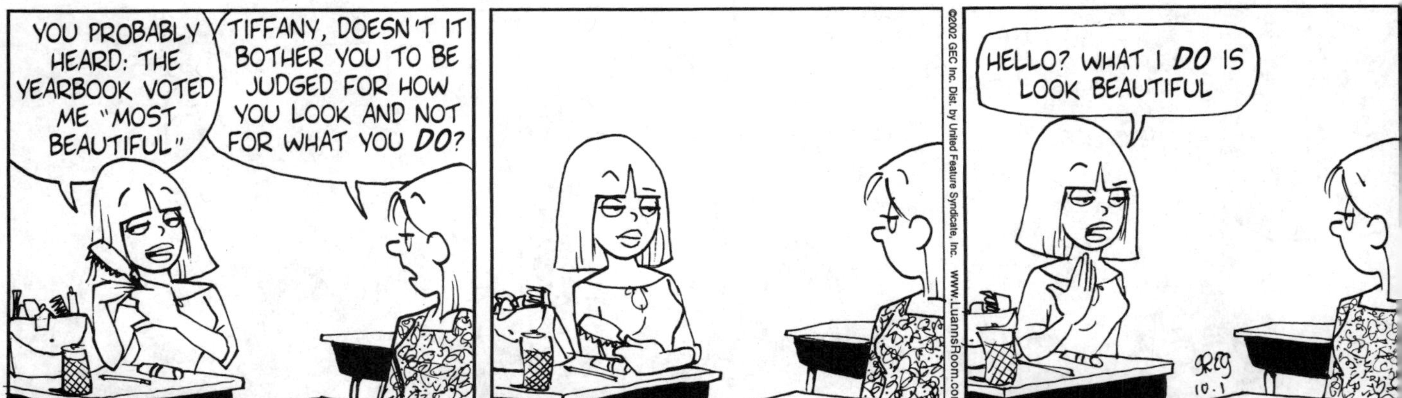
YOU PROBABLY HEARD: THE YEARBOOK VOTED ME "MOST BEAUTIFUL"
TIFFANY, DOESN'T IT BOTHER YOU TO BE JUDGED FOR HOW YOU LOOK AND NOT FOR WHAT YOU DO?
©2002 GEC Inc. Dist. by United Feature Syndicate, Inc. www.LuannsRoom.com
HELLO? WHAT I DO IS LOOK BEAUTIFUL
GREG 10.1

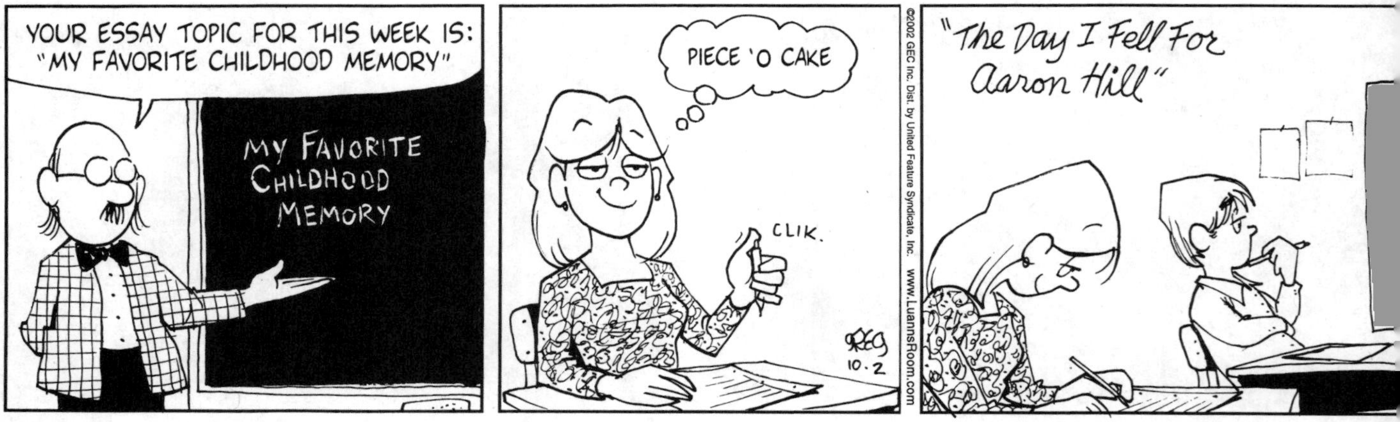
YOUR ESSAY TOPIC FOR THIS WEEK IS: "MY FAVORITE CHILDHOOD MEMORY"
MY FAVORITE CHILDHOOD MEMORY
PIECE 'O CAKE
CLIK.
GREG 10.2
©2002 GEC Inc. Dist. by United Feature Syndicate, Inc. www.LuannsRoom.com
"The Day I Fell For Aaron Hill"

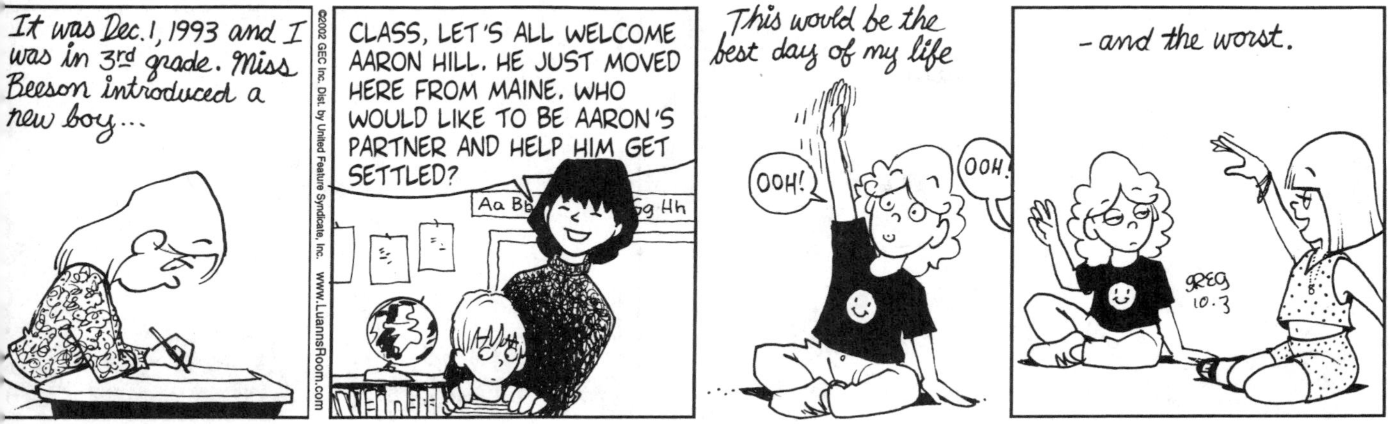

It was Dec. 1, 1993 and I was in 3rd grade. Miss Beeson introduced a new boy...
©2002 GEC Inc. Dist. by United Feature Syndicate, Inc. www.LuannsRoom.com
CLASS, LET'S ALL WELCOME AARON HILL. HE JUST MOVED HERE FROM MAINE. WHO WOULD LIKE TO BE AARON'S PARTNER AND HELP HIM GET SETTLED?
Aa Bb
Gg Hh
This would be the best day of my life
OOH!
OOH!
- and the worst.
GREG 10.3

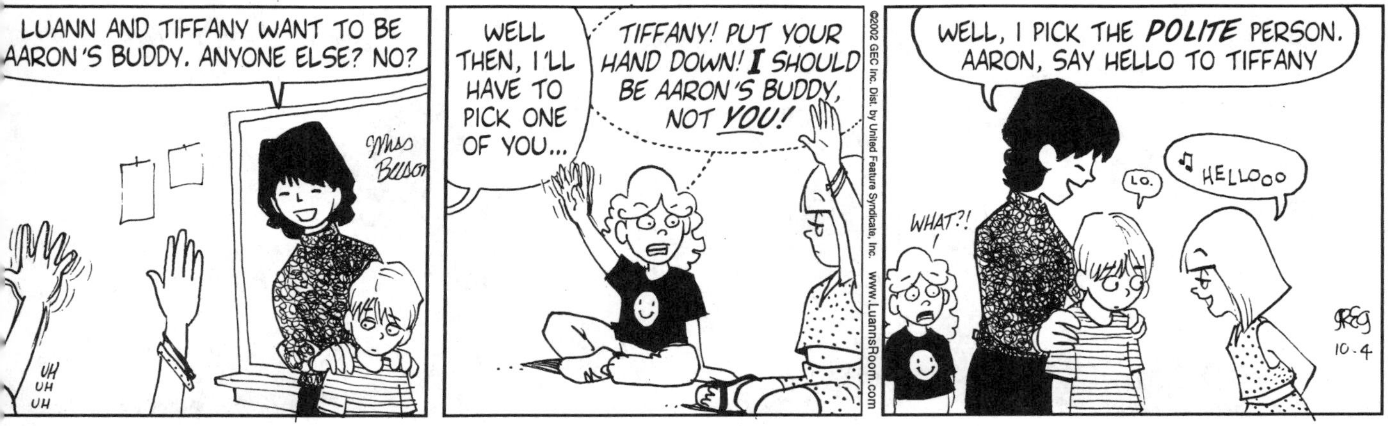

LUANN AND TIFFANY WANT TO BE AARON'S BUDDY. ANYONE ELSE? NO?
Miss Beeson
UH UH UH
WELL THEN, I'LL HAVE TO PICK ONE OF YOU...
TIFFANY! PUT YOUR HAND DOWN! I SHOULD BE AARON'S BUDDY, NOT YOU!
©2002 GEC Inc. Dist. by United Feature Syndicate, Inc. www.LuannsRoom.com
WELL, I PICK THE POLITE PERSON. AARON, SAY HELLO TO TIFFANY
WHAT?!
LO.
HELLOoo
GREG 10.4

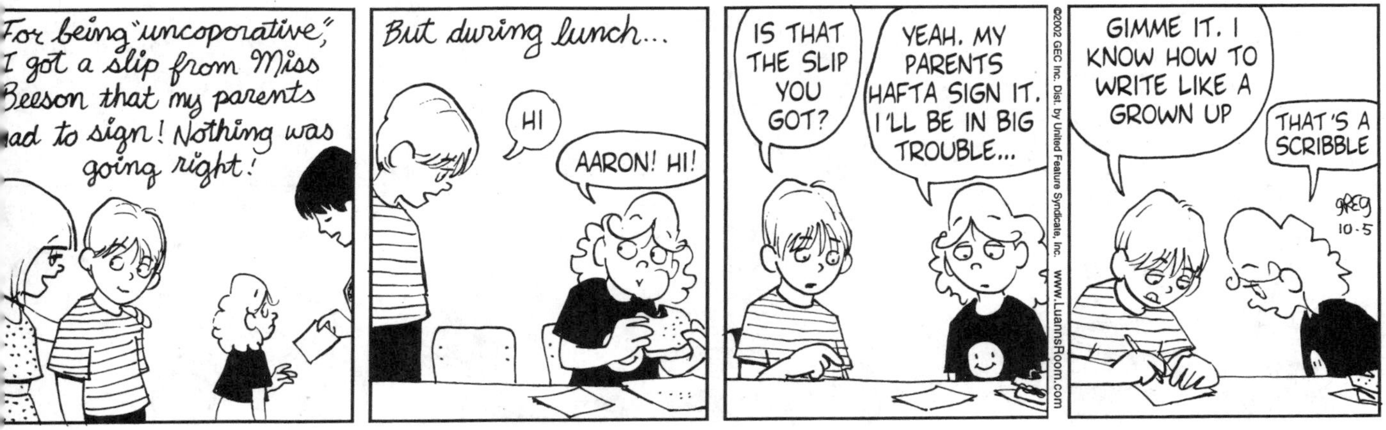

For being "uncoporative", I got a slip from Miss Beeson that my parents had to sign! Nothing was going right!
But during lunch...
HI
AARON! HI!
IS THAT THE SLIP YOU GOT?
YEAH. MY PARENTS HAFTA SIGN IT. I'LL BE IN BIG TROUBLE...
©2002 GEC Inc. Dist. by United Feature Syndicate, Inc. www.LuannsRoom.com
GIMME IT. I KNOW HOW TO WRITE LIKE A GROWN UP
THAT'S A SCRIBBLE
GREG 10.5

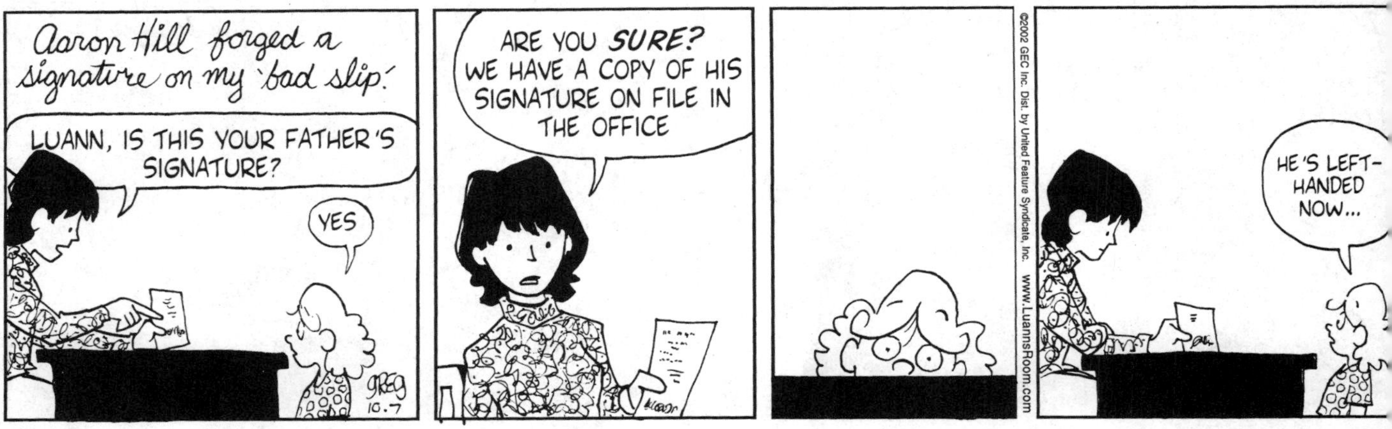
Aaron Hill forged a signature on my 'bad slip.'
LUANN, IS THIS YOUR FATHER'S SIGNATURE?
YES
ARE YOU SURE? WE HAVE A COPY OF HIS SIGNATURE ON FILE IN THE OFFICE
©2002 GEC Inc. Dist. by United Feature Syndicate, Inc. www.LuannsRoom.com
HE'S LEFT-HANDED NOW...

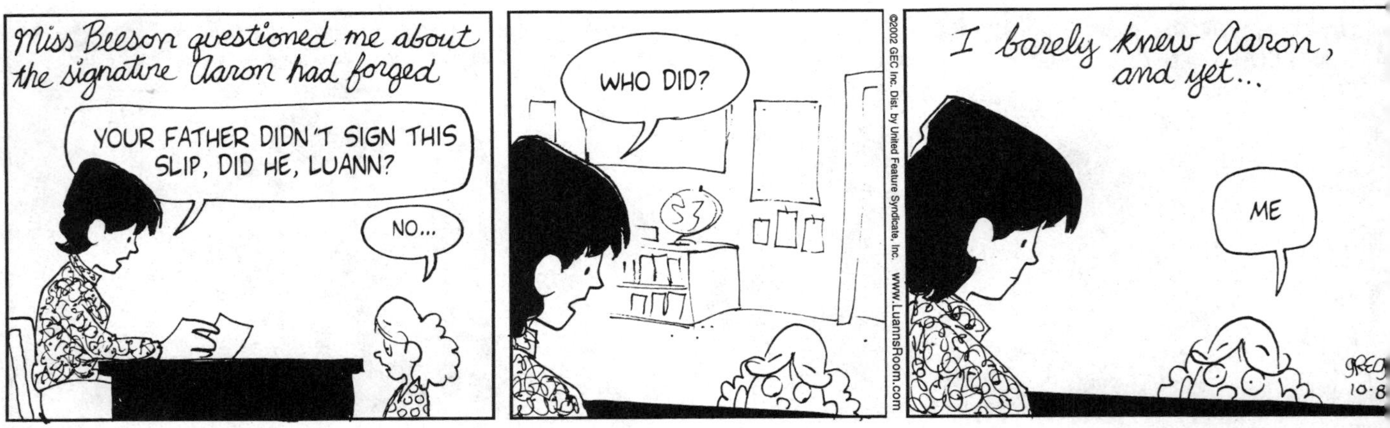
Miss Beeson questioned me about the signature Aaron had forged
YOUR FATHER DIDN'T SIGN THIS SLIP, DID HE, LUANN?
NO...
WHO DID?
©2002 GEC Inc. Dist. by United Feature Syndicate, Inc. www.LuannsRoom.com
I barely knew Aaron, and yet...
ME

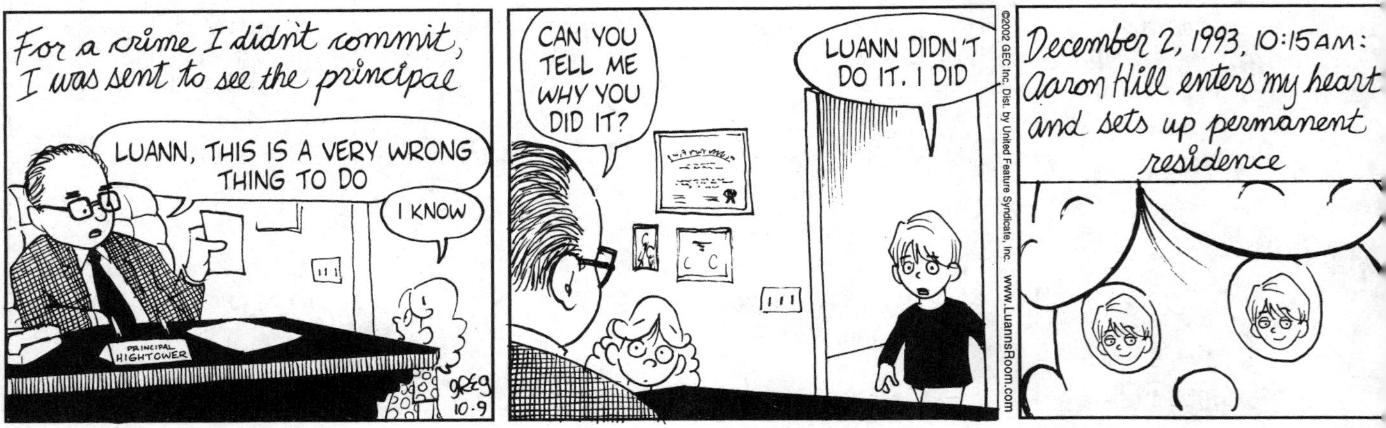
For a crime I didn't commit, I was sent to see the principal
LUANN, THIS IS A VERY WRONG THING TO DO
I KNOW
PRINCIPAL HIGHTOWER
CAN YOU TELL ME WHY YOU DID IT?
LUANN DIDN'T DO IT. I DID
©2002 GEC Inc. Dist. by United Feature Syndicate, Inc. www.LuannsRoom.com
December 2, 1993, 10:15AM: Aaron Hill enters my heart and sets up permanent residence

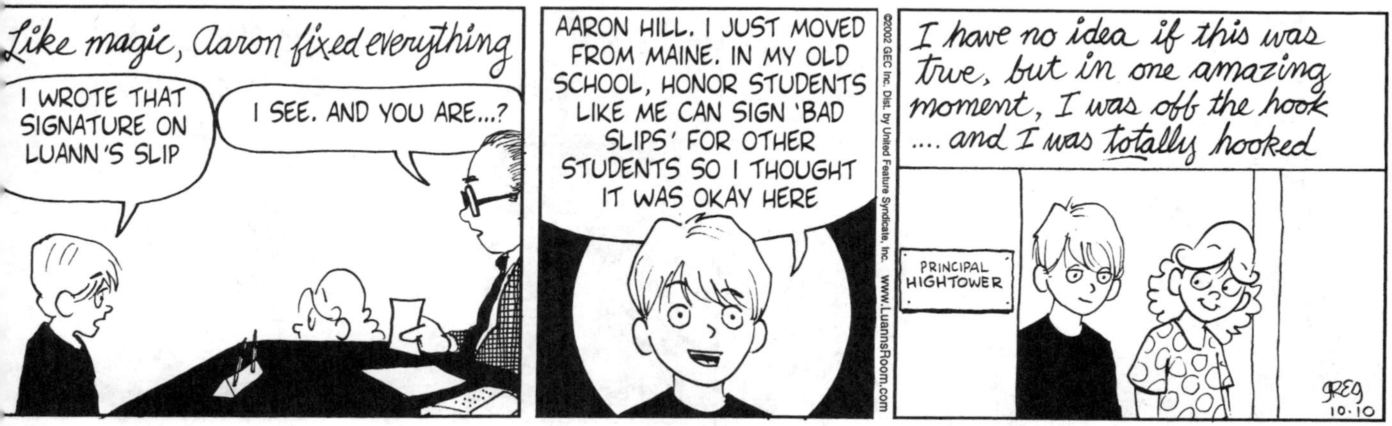
Like magic, Aaron fixed everything
I WROTE THAT SIGNATURE ON LUANN'S SLIP
I SEE. AND YOU ARE...?
AARON HILL. I JUST MOVED FROM MAINE. IN MY OLD SCHOOL, HONOR STUDENTS LIKE ME CAN SIGN 'BAD SLIPS' FOR OTHER STUDENTS SO I THOUGHT IT WAS OKAY HERE
©2002 GEC Inc. Dist. by United Feature Syndicate, Inc. www.LuannsRoom.com
I have no idea if this was true, but in one amazing moment, I was off the hook .... and I was totally hooked
PRINCIPAL HIGHTOWER
GREG 10·10

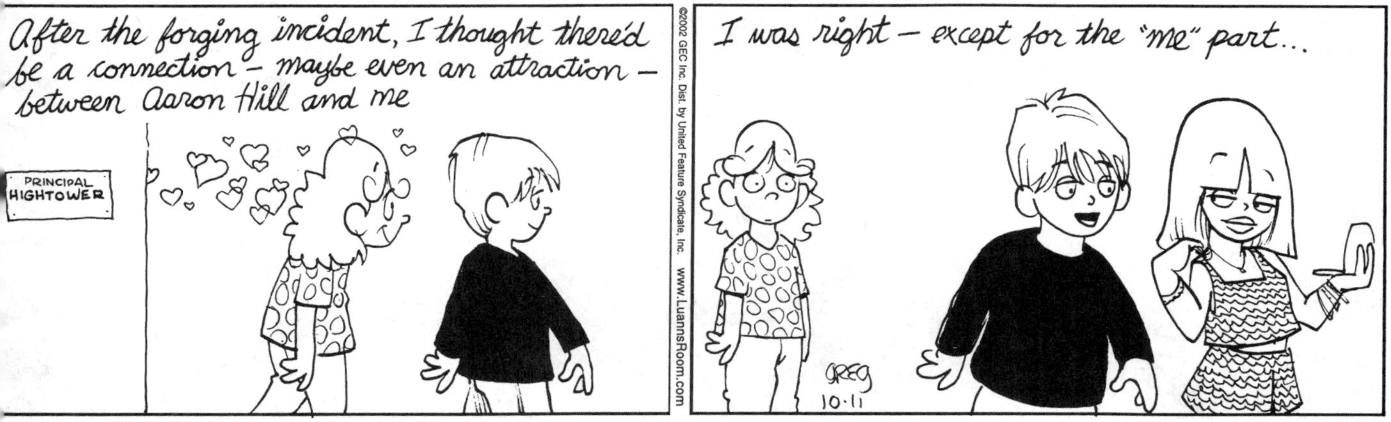
After the forging incident, I thought there'd be a connection – maybe even an attraction – between Aaron Hill and me
PRINCIPAL HIGHTOWER
©2002 GEC Inc. Dist. by United Feature Syndicate, Inc. www.LuannsRoom.com
I was right – except for the "me" part...
GREG 10·11

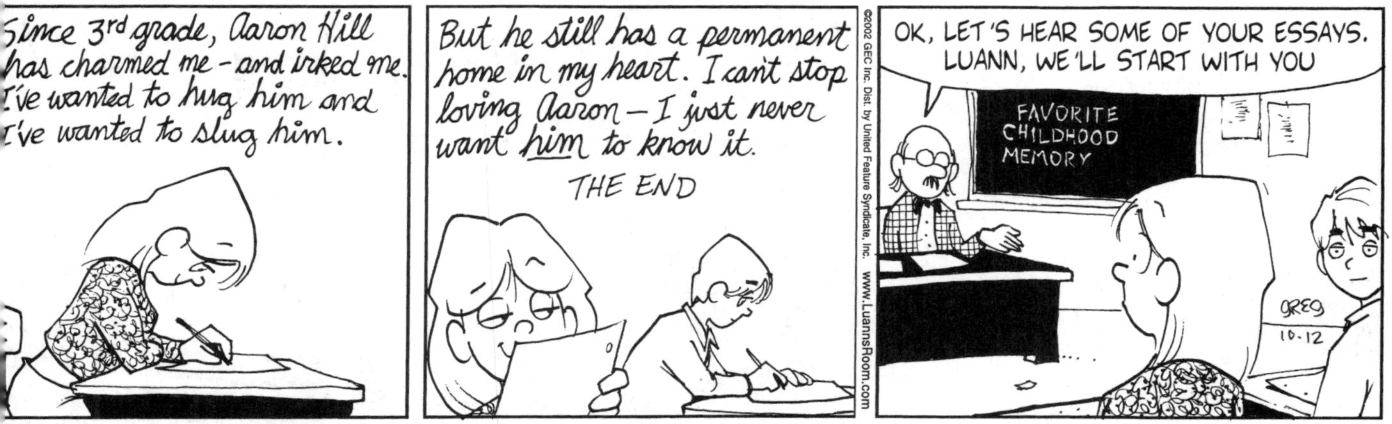
Since 3rd grade, Aaron Hill has charmed me – and irked me. I've wanted to hug him and I've wanted to slug him.
But he still has a permanent home in my heart. I can't stop loving Aaron – I just never want him to know it.
THE END
©2002 GEC Inc. Dist. by United Feature Syndicate, Inc. www.LuannsRoom.com
OK, LET'S HEAR SOME OF YOUR ESSAYS. LUANN, WE'LL START WITH YOU
FAVORITE CHILDHOOD MEMORY
GREG 10·12

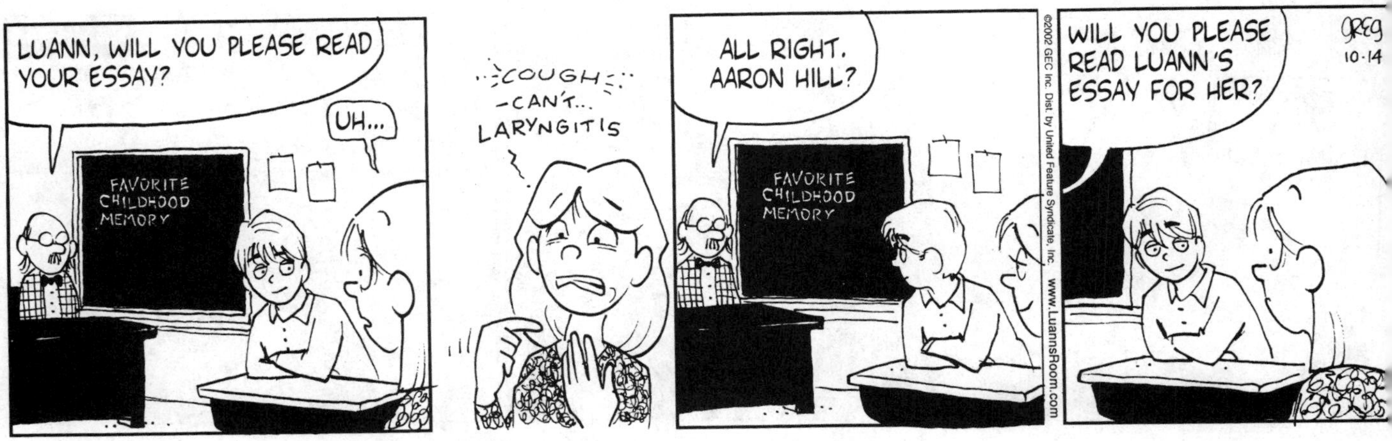
LUANN, WILL YOU PLEASE READ YOUR ESSAY?
UH...
FAVORITE CHILDHOOD MEMORY
COUGH
CAN'T... LARYNGITIS
ALL RIGHT. AARON HILL?
FAVORITE CHILDHOOD MEMORY
©2002 GEC Inc. Dist. by United Feature Syndicate, Inc. www.LuannsRoom.com
WILL YOU PLEASE READ LUANN'S ESSAY FOR HER?
GREG 10·14

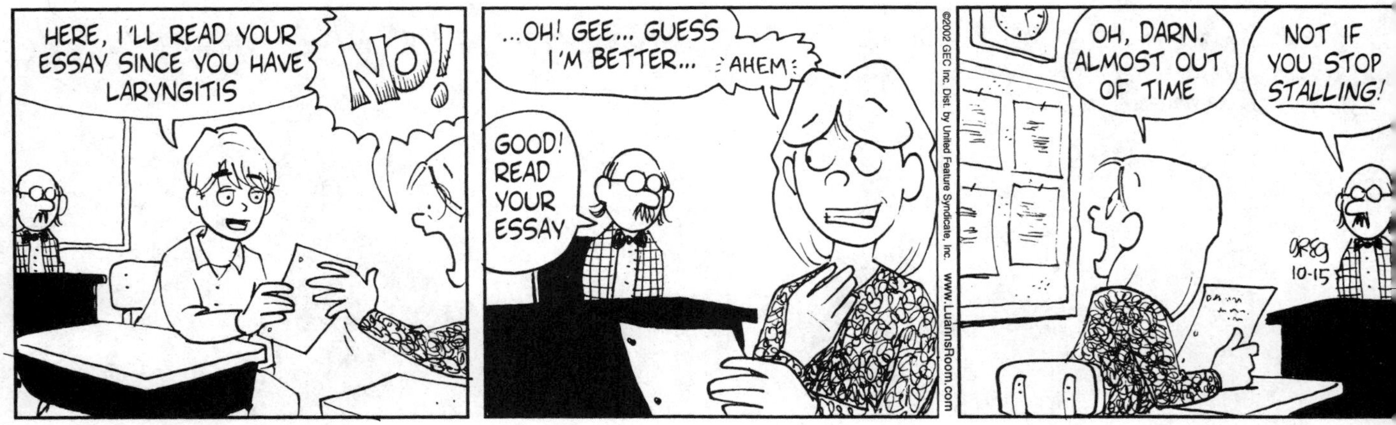
HERE, I'LL READ YOUR ESSAY SINCE YOU HAVE LARYNGITIS
NO!
...OH! GEE... GUESS I'M BETTER...
AHEM
GOOD! READ YOUR ESSAY
©2002 GEC Inc. Dist. by United Feature Syndicate, Inc. www.LuannsRoom.com
OH, DARN. ALMOST OUT OF TIME
NOT IF YOU STOP STALLING!
GREG 10-15

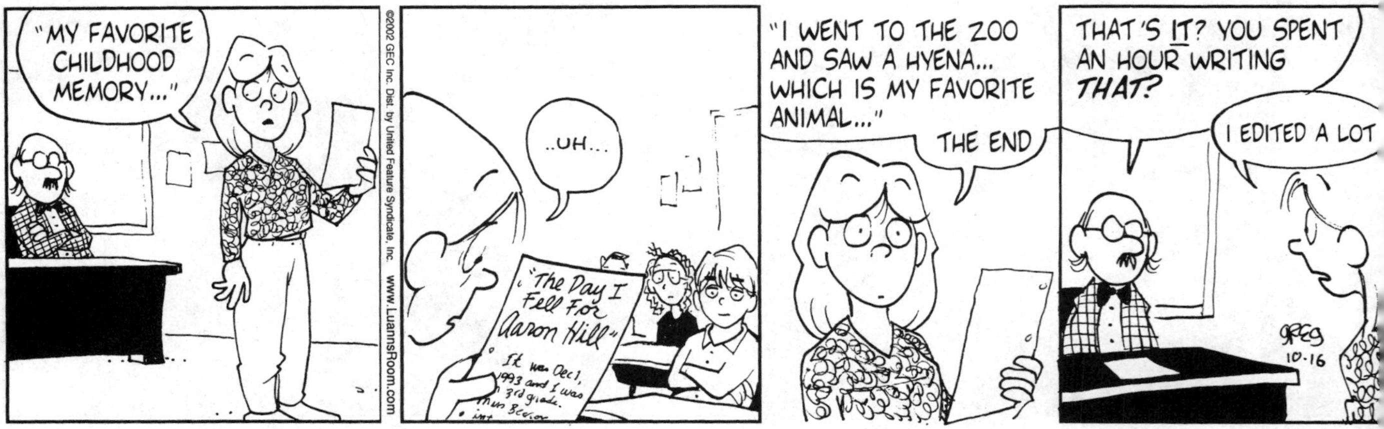
"MY FAVORITE CHILDHOOD MEMORY..."
©2002 GEC Inc. Dist. by United Feature Syndicate, Inc. www.LuannsRoom.com
..UH...
"The Day I Fell For Aaron Hill"
It was Dec 1, 1993 and I was
3rd grade.
"I WENT TO THE ZOO AND SAW A HYENA... WHICH IS MY FAVORITE ANIMAL..."
THE END
THAT'S IT? YOU SPENT AN HOUR WRITING THAT?
I EDITED A LOT
GREG 10-16

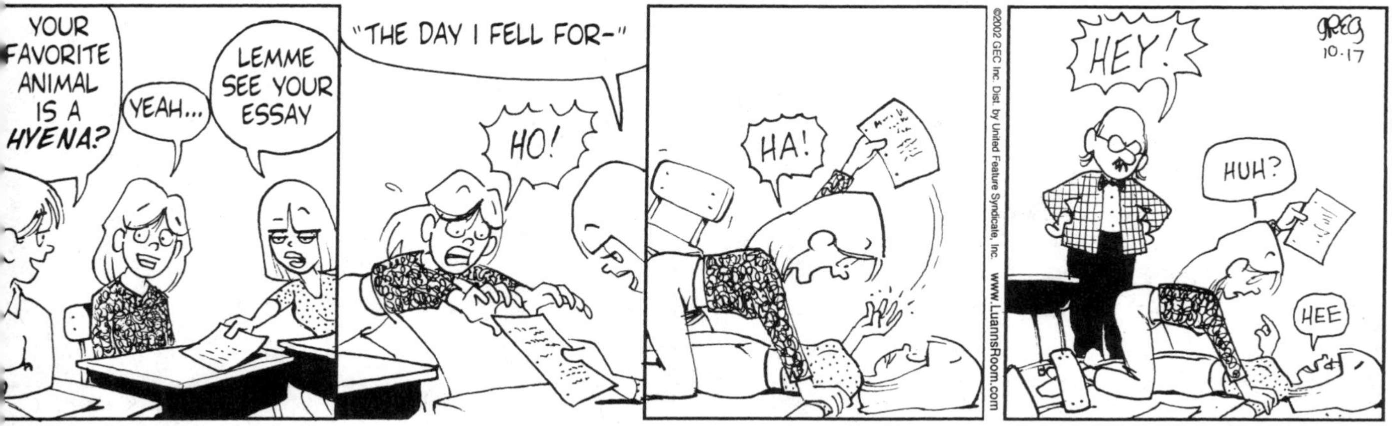
YOUR FAVORITE ANIMAL IS A *HYENA?*
YEAH...
LEMME SEE YOUR ESSAY
"THE DAY I FELL FOR-"
HO!
HA!
©2002 GEC Inc. Dist. by United Feature Syndicate, Inc.
www.LuannsRoom.com
HEY!
GREG 10·17
HUH?
HEE

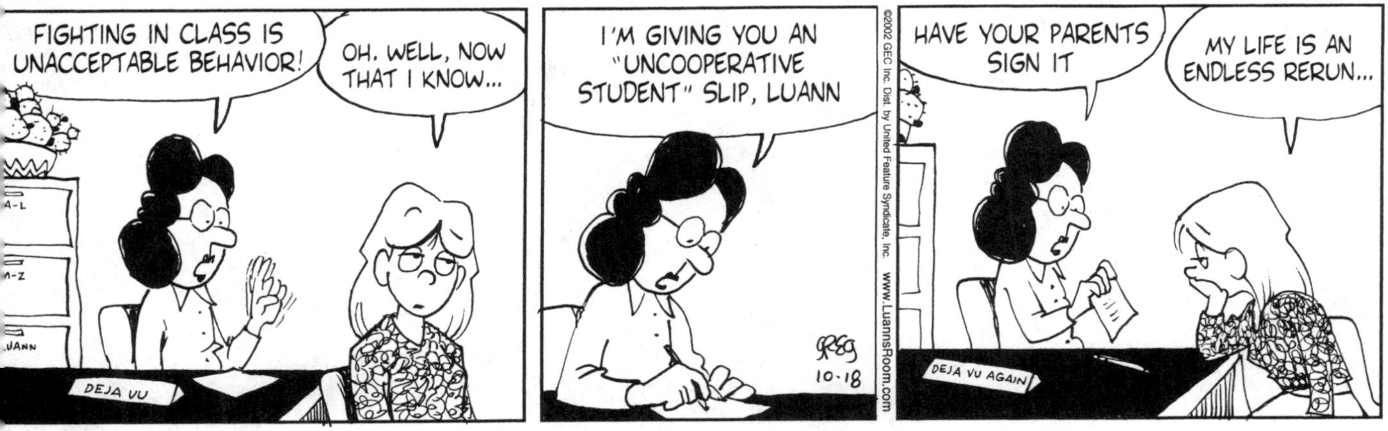
FIGHTING IN CLASS IS UNACCEPTABLE BEHAVIOR!
OH. WELL, NOW THAT I KNOW...
A-L
M-Z
LUANN
DEJA VU
I'M GIVING YOU AN "UNCOOPERATIVE STUDENT" SLIP, LUANN
GREG 10·18
©2002 GEC Inc. Dist. by United Feature Syndicate, Inc.
www.LuannsRoom.com
HAVE YOUR PARENTS SIGN IT
MY LIFE IS AN ENDLESS RERUN...
DEJA VU AGAIN

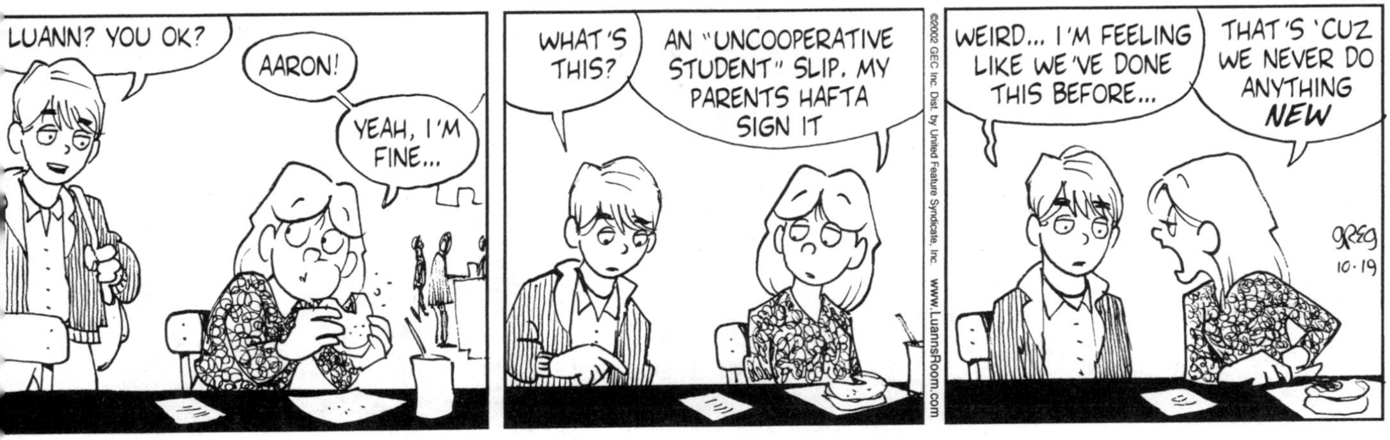
LUANN? YOU OK?
AARON!
YEAH, I'M FINE...
WHAT'S THIS?
AN "UNCOOPERATIVE STUDENT" SLIP. MY PARENTS HAFTA SIGN IT
©2002 GEC Inc. Dist. by United Feature Syndicate, Inc.
www.LuannsRoom.com
WEIRD... I'M FEELING LIKE WE'VE DONE THIS BEFORE...
THAT'S 'CUZ WE NEVER DO ANYTHING ***NEW***
GREG 10·19

"... AND I SPENT HOURS IN THAT SANDBOX, SIFTING THE WARM SAND THROUGH MY LITTLE FINGERS... UNTIL ONE DAY I DISCOVERED THAT THE CAT USED IT FOR A LITTER BOX."
LOVELY, KNUTE. VERY... MOVING
THANKS
©2002 GEC Inc. Dist. by United Feature Syndicate, Inc.
www.LuannsRoom.com
IS THAT WHY YOU'RE SO WEIRD?
NAH. IT'S 'CUZ OF THE TIME I TIED A TOWEL AROUND MY NECK AND FLEW OFF THE ROOF
GREG
10-20

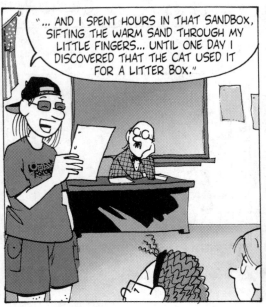

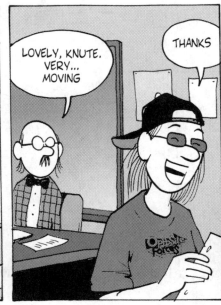

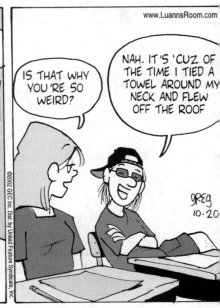

OH, *NICE* HALLOWEEN COSTUME, LUANN. YOU'RE WHAT, A CORPSE?

HEE HEE HEE

©2002 GEC Inc. Dist. by United Feature Syndicate, Inc.   www.LuannsRoom.com

NO! I AM SHE-HULK!!

I DESTROY ALL WHO ANGER ME!

EEP

UH... LUANN?

AM I GETTING GREEN AT ALL?

gReg
10-27

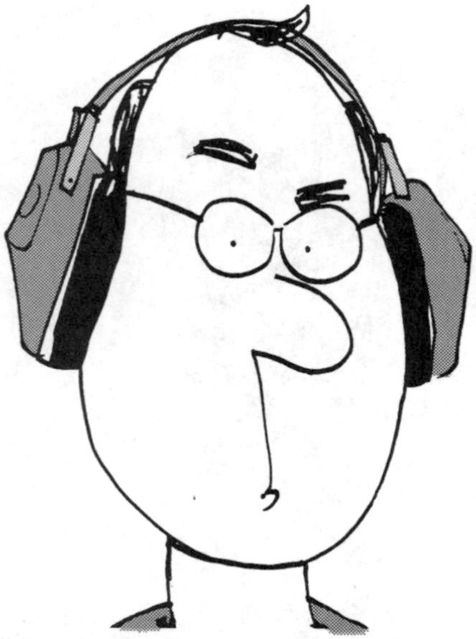

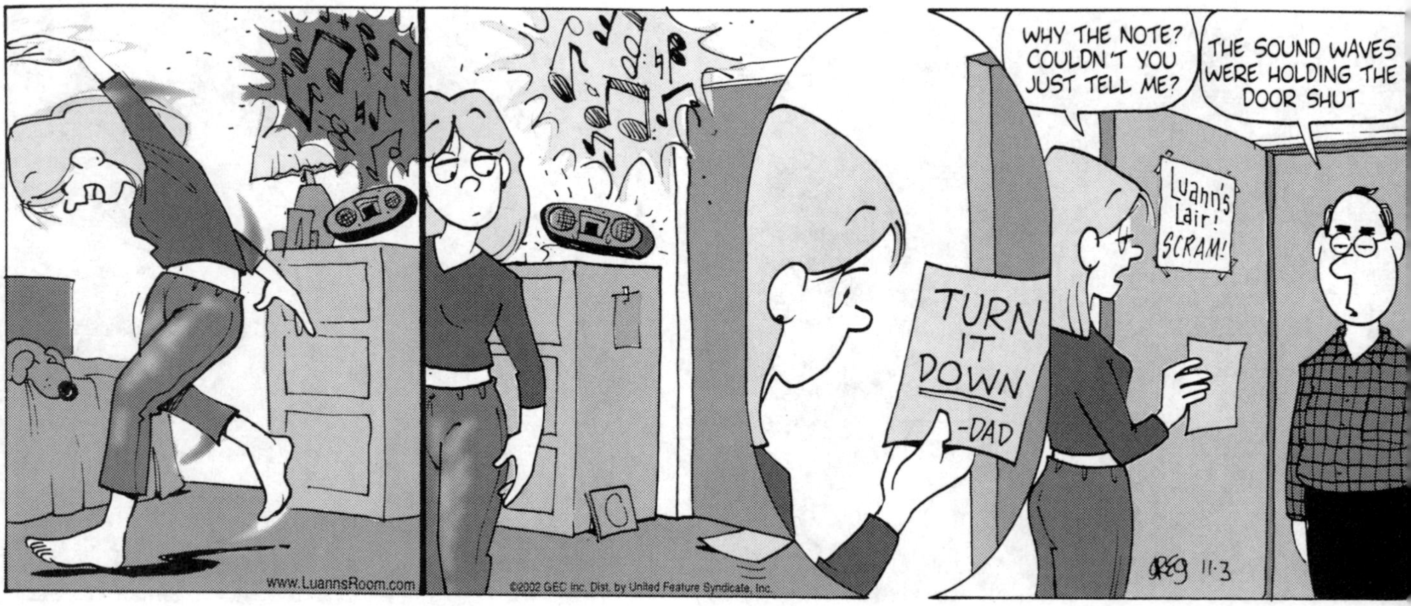
www.LuannsRoom.com
©2002 GEC Inc. Dist. by United Feature Syndicate, Inc.
TURN IT DOWN -DAD
WHY THE NOTE? COULDN'T YOU JUST TELL ME?
THE SOUND WAVES WERE HOLDING THE DOOR SHUT
Luann's Lair! SCRAM!
GREG 11·3

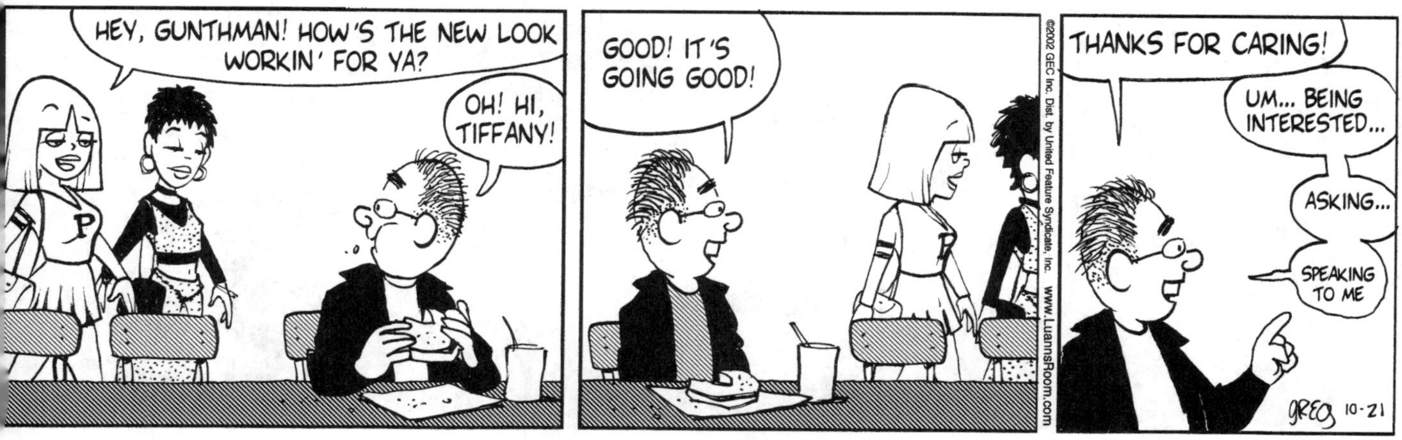
HEY, GUNTHMAN! HOW'S THE NEW LOOK WORKIN' FOR YA?
OH! HI, TIFFANY!
GOOD! IT'S GOING GOOD!
©2002 GEC Inc. Dist. by United Feature Syndicate, Inc. www.LuannsRoom.com
THANKS FOR CARING!
UM... BEING INTERESTED...
ASKING...
SPEAKING TO ME
GREG 10-21

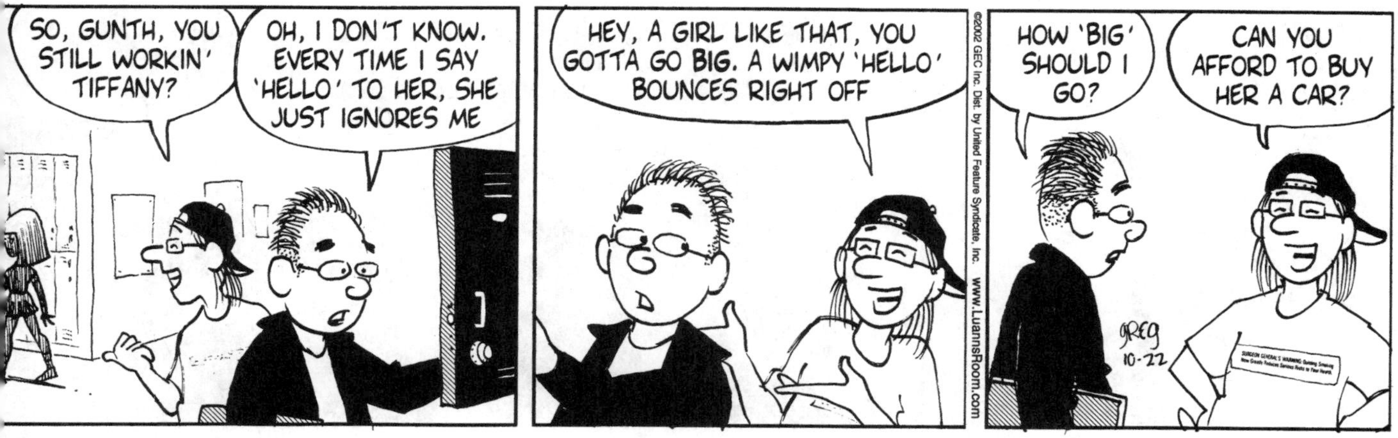
SO, GUNTH, YOU STILL WORKIN' TIFFANY?
OH, I DON'T KNOW. EVERY TIME I SAY 'HELLO' TO HER, SHE JUST IGNORES ME
HEY, A GIRL LIKE THAT, YOU GOTTA GO **BIG**. A WIMPY 'HELLO' BOUNCES RIGHT OFF
©2002 GEC Inc. Dist. by United Feature Syndicate, Inc. www.LuannsRoom.com
HOW 'BIG' SHOULD I GO?
CAN YOU AFFORD TO BUY HER A CAR?
GREG 10-22

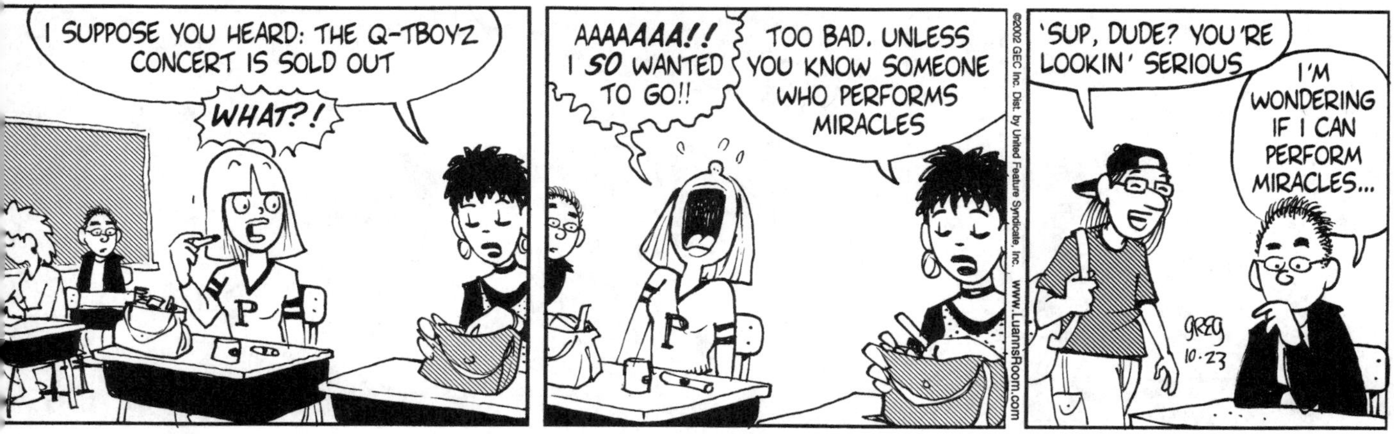
I SUPPOSE YOU HEARD: THE Q-TBOYZ CONCERT IS SOLD OUT
WHAT?!
AAAAAAA!! I ***SO*** WANTED TO GO!!
TOO BAD. UNLESS YOU KNOW SOMEONE WHO PERFORMS MIRACLES
©2002 GEC Inc. Dist. by United Feature Syndicate, Inc. www.LuannsRoom.com
'SUP, DUDE? YOU'RE LOOKIN' SERIOUS
I'M WONDERING IF I CAN PERFORM MIRACLES...
GREG 10-23

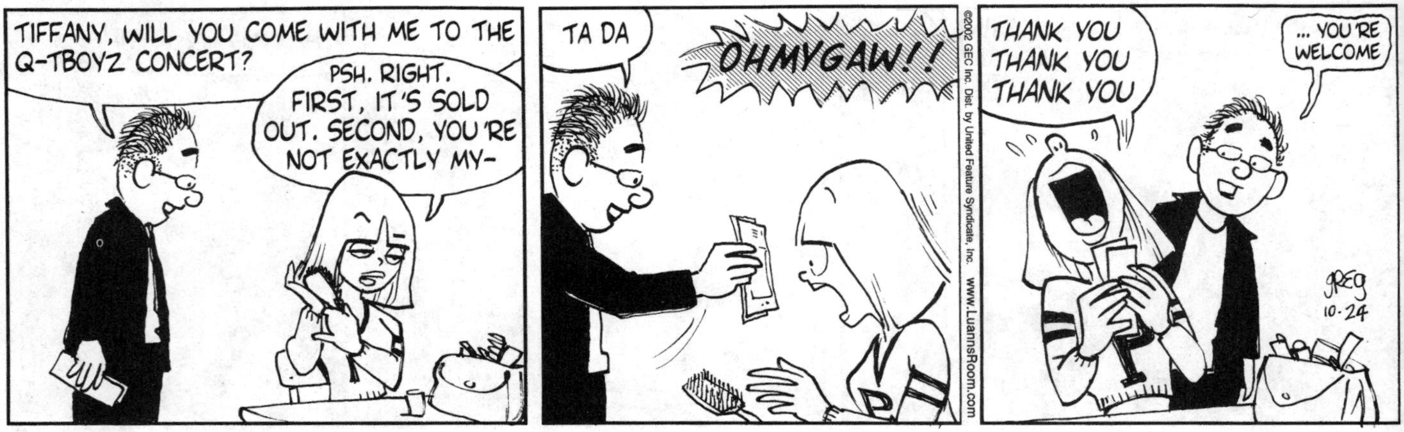
TIFFANY, WILL YOU COME WITH ME TO THE Q-TBOYZ CONCERT?
PSH. RIGHT. FIRST, IT'S SOLD OUT. SECOND, YOU'RE NOT EXACTLY MY-
TA DA
OHMYGAW!!
©2002 GEC Inc. Dist. by United Feature Syndicate, Inc. www.LuannsRoom.com
THANK YOU THANK YOU THANK YOU
... YOU'RE WELCOME
GREG 10-24

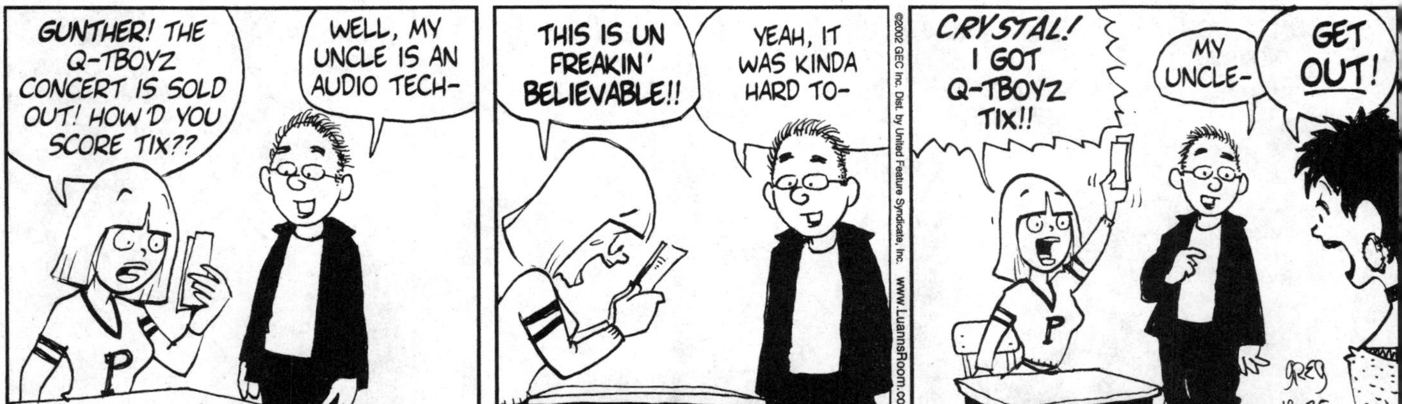
GUNTHER! THE Q-TBOYZ CONCERT IS SOLD OUT! HOW'D YOU SCORE TIX??
WELL, MY UNCLE IS AN AUDIO TECH-
THIS IS UN FREAKIN' BELIEVABLE!!
YEAH, IT WAS KINDA HARD TO-
©2002 GEC Inc. Dist. by United Feature Syndicate, Inc. www.LuannsRoom.com
CRYSTAL! I GOT Q-TBOYZ TIX!!
MY UNCLE-
GET OUT!
GREG 10-25

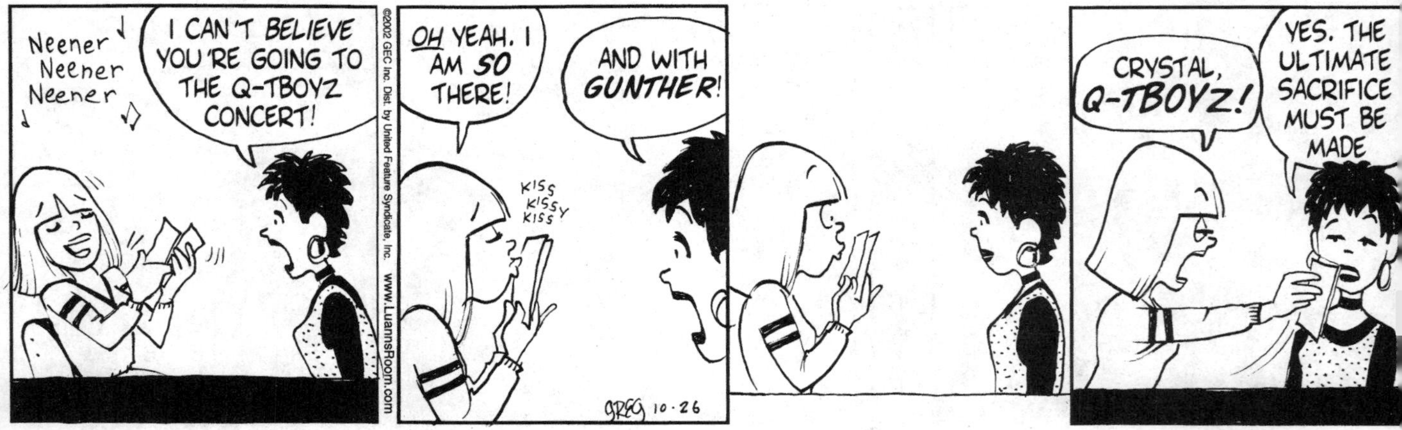
Neener Neener Neener
I CAN'T BELIEVE YOU'RE GOING TO THE Q-TBOYZ CONCERT!
©2002 GEC Inc. Dist. by United Feature Syndicate, Inc. www.LuannsRoom.com
OH YEAH. I AM SO THERE!
AND WITH GUNTHER!
KISS KISSY KISS
GREG 10-26
CRYSTAL, Q-TBOYZ!
YES. THE ULTIMATE SACRIFICE MUST BE MADE

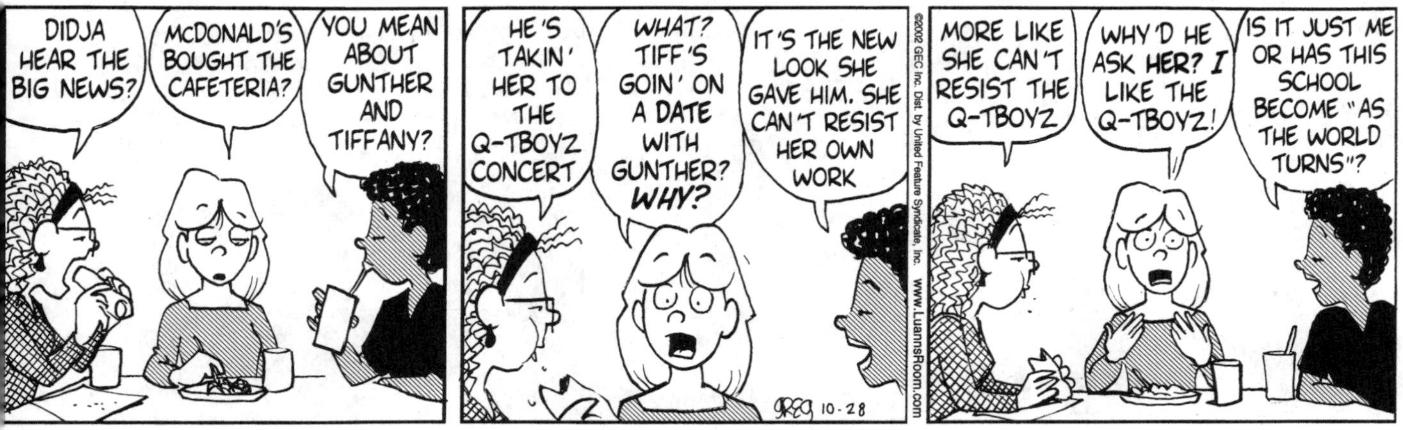
DIDJA HEAR THE BIG NEWS?
McDONALD'S BOUGHT THE CAFETERIA?
YOU MEAN ABOUT GUNTHER AND TIFFANY?
HE'S TAKIN' HER TO THE Q-TBOYZ CONCERT
WHAT? TIFF'S GOIN' ON A DATE WITH GUNTHER? WHY?
IT'S THE NEW LOOK SHE GAVE HIM. SHE CAN'T RESIST HER OWN WORK
GREG 10-28
©2002 GEC Inc. Dist. by United Feature Syndicate, Inc. www.LuannsRoom.com
MORE LIKE SHE CAN'T RESIST THE Q-TBOYZ
WHY'D HE ASK HER? I LIKE THE Q-TBOYZ!
IS IT JUST ME OR HAS THIS SCHOOL BECOME "AS THE WORLD TURNS"?

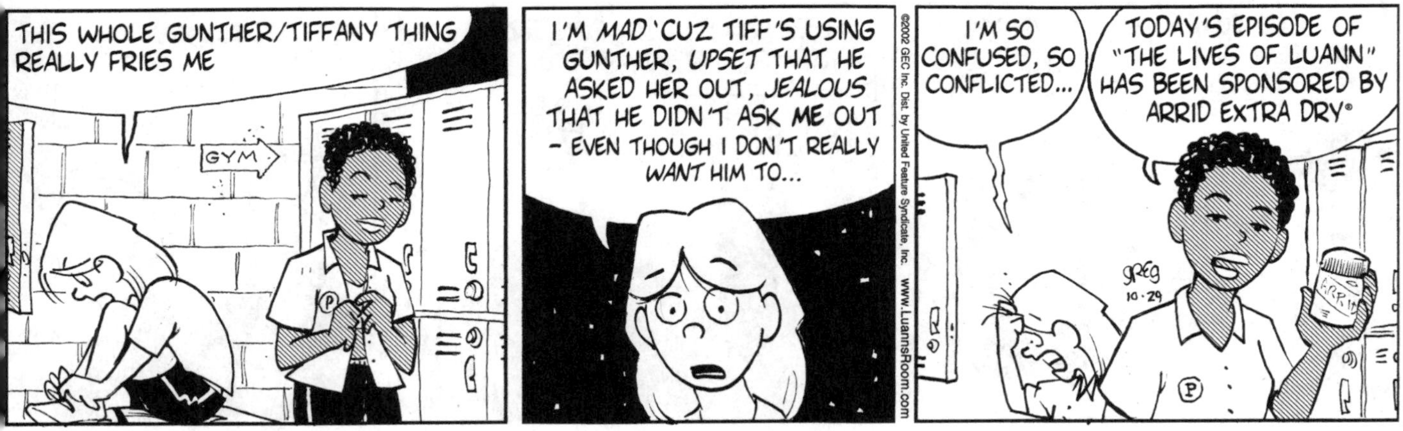
THIS WHOLE GUNTHER/TIFFANY THING REALLY FRIES ME
GYM
I'M MAD 'CUZ TIFF'S USING GUNTHER, UPSET THAT HE ASKED HER OUT, JEALOUS THAT HE DIDN'T ASK ME OUT - EVEN THOUGH I DON'T REALLY WANT HIM TO...
©2002 GEC Inc. Dist. by United Feature Syndicate, Inc. www.LuannsRoom.com
I'M SO CONFUSED, SO CONFLICTED...
TODAY'S EPISODE OF "THE LIVES OF LUANN" HAS BEEN SPONSORED BY ARRID EXTRA DRY®
GREG 10-29

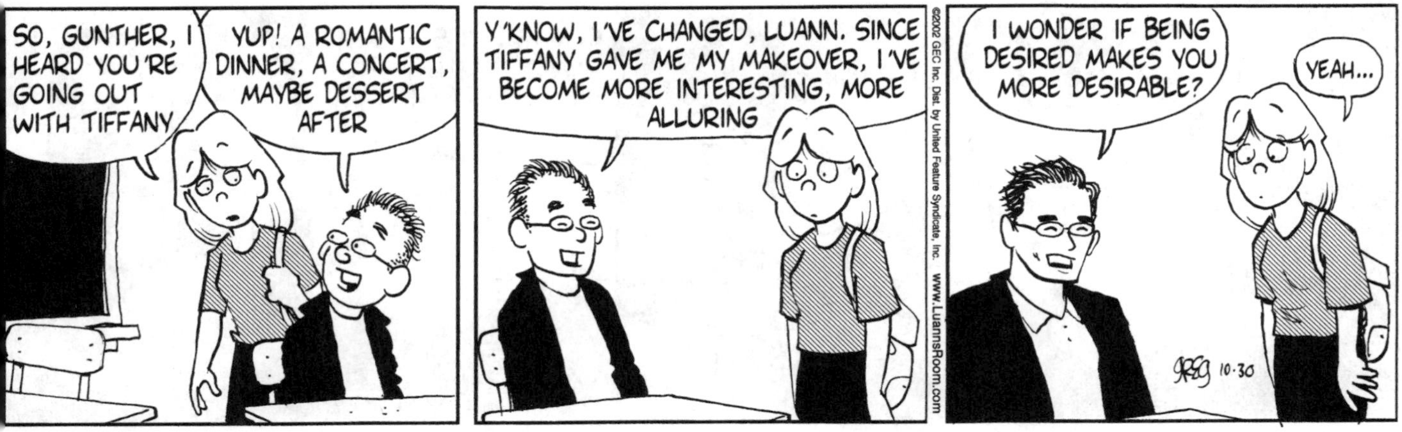
SO, GUNTHER, I HEARD YOU'RE GOING OUT WITH TIFFANY
YUP! A ROMANTIC DINNER, A CONCERT, MAYBE DESSERT AFTER
Y'KNOW, I'VE CHANGED, LUANN. SINCE TIFFANY GAVE ME MY MAKEOVER, I'VE BECOME MORE INTERESTING, MORE ALLURING
©2002 GEC Inc. Dist. by United Feature Syndicate, Inc. www.LuannsRoom.com
I WONDER IF BEING DESIRED MAKES YOU MORE DESIRABLE?
YEAH...
GREG 10-30

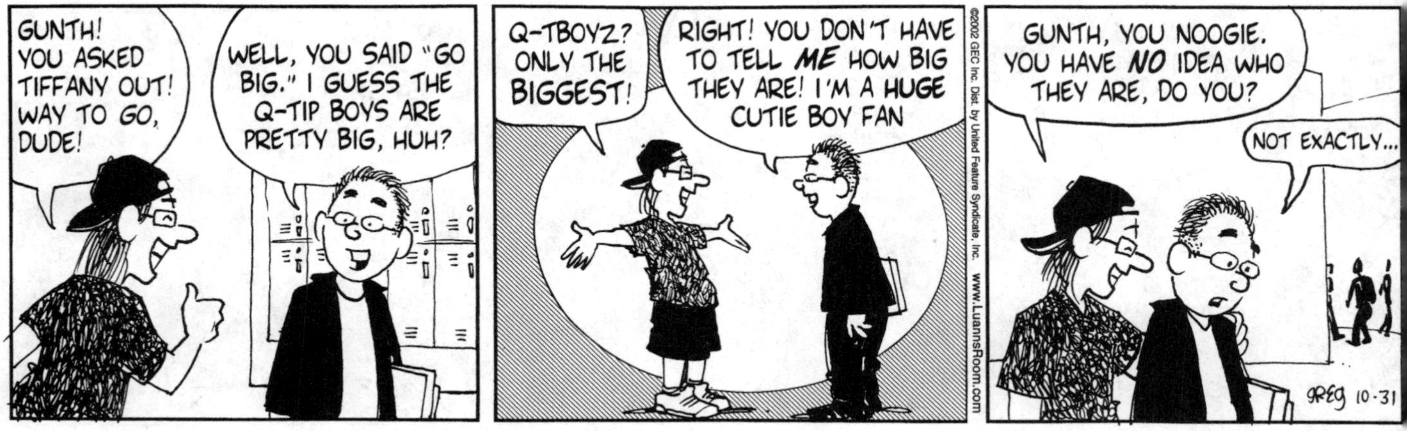
GUNTH! YOU ASKED TIFFANY OUT! WAY TO GO, DUDE!
WELL, YOU SAID "GO BIG." I GUESS THE Q-TIP BOYS ARE PRETTY BIG, HUH?
Q-TBOYZ? ONLY THE BIGGEST!
RIGHT! YOU DON'T HAVE TO TELL ME HOW BIG THEY ARE! I'M A HUGE CUTIE BOY FAN
©2002 GEC Inc. Dist. by United Feature Syndicate, Inc.
www.LuannsRoom.com
GUNTH, YOU NOOGIE. YOU HAVE NO IDEA WHO THEY ARE, DO YOU?
NOT EXACTLY...
GREG 10-31

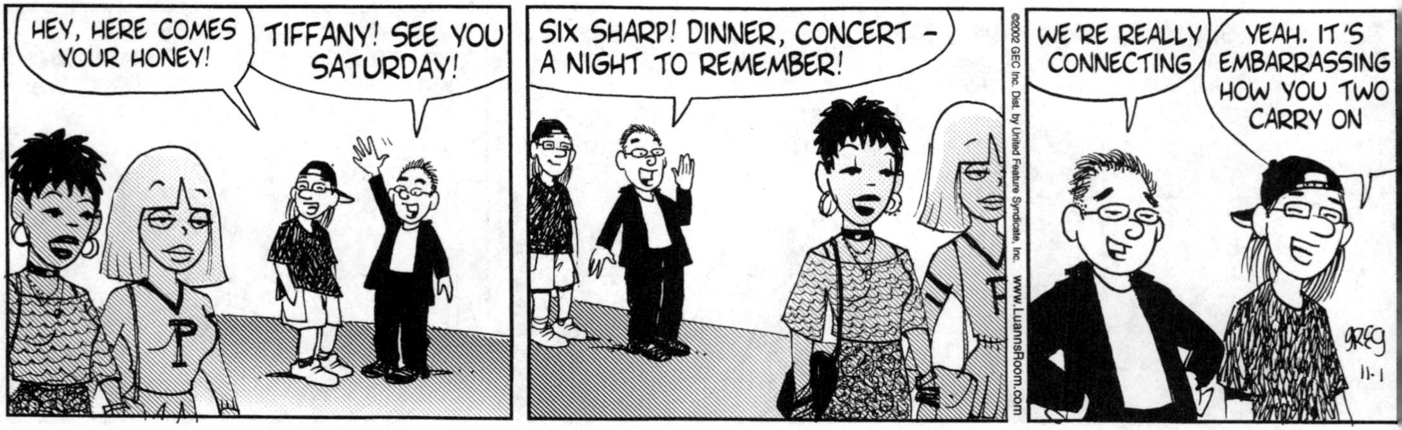
HEY, HERE COMES YOUR HONEY!
TIFFANY! SEE YOU SATURDAY!
SIX SHARP! DINNER, CONCERT - A NIGHT TO REMEMBER!
©2002 GEC Inc. Dist. by United Feature Syndicate, Inc.
www.LuannsRoom.com
WE'RE REALLY CONNECTING
YEAH. IT'S EMBARRASSING HOW YOU TWO CARRY ON
GREG 11-1

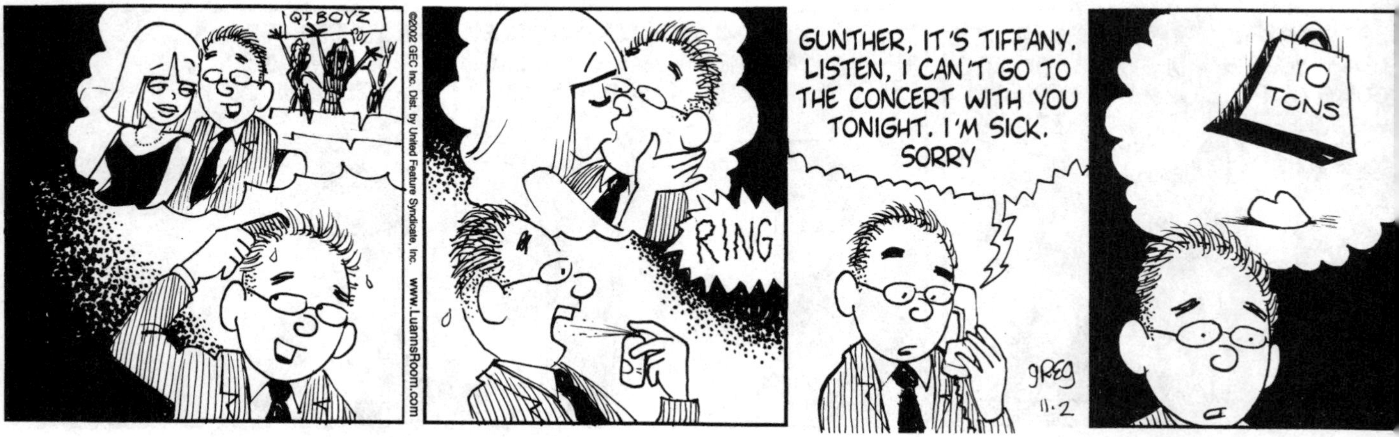
QT BOYZ
©2002 GEC Inc. Dist. by United Feature Syndicate, Inc.
www.LuannsRoom.com
RING
GUNTHER, IT'S TIFFANY. LISTEN, I CAN'T GO TO THE CONCERT WITH YOU TONIGHT. I'M SICK. SORRY
GREG 11-2
10 TONS

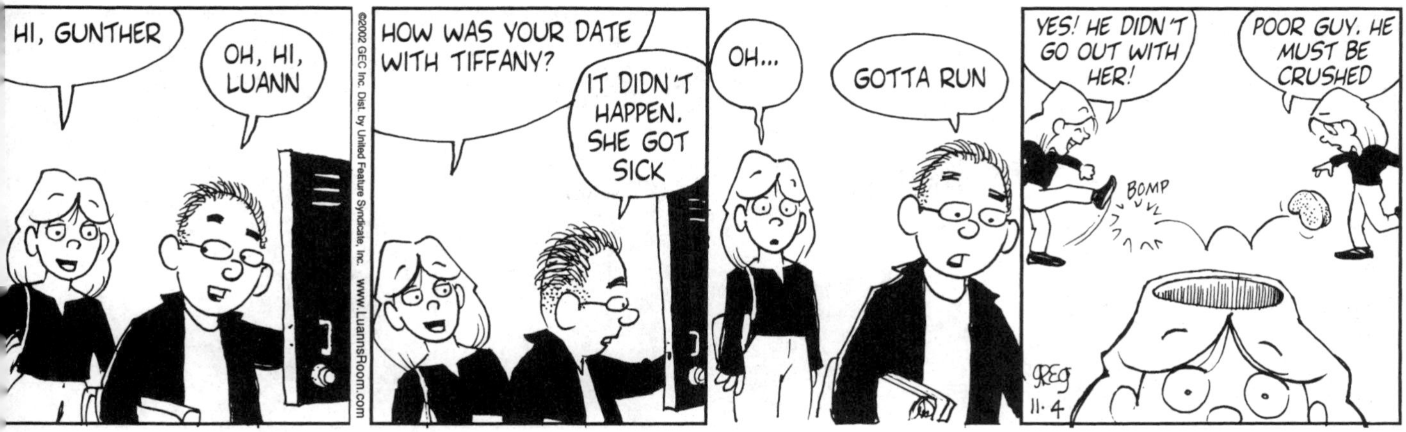

HI, GUNTHER
OH, HI, LUANN
©2002 GEC Inc. Dist. by United Feature Syndicate, Inc. www.LuannsRoom.com
HOW WAS YOUR DATE WITH TIFFANY?
IT DIDN'T HAPPEN. SHE GOT SICK
OH...
GOTTA RUN
YES! HE DIDN'T GO OUT WITH HER!
POOR GUY. HE MUST BE CRUSHED
BOMP
GREG 11·4

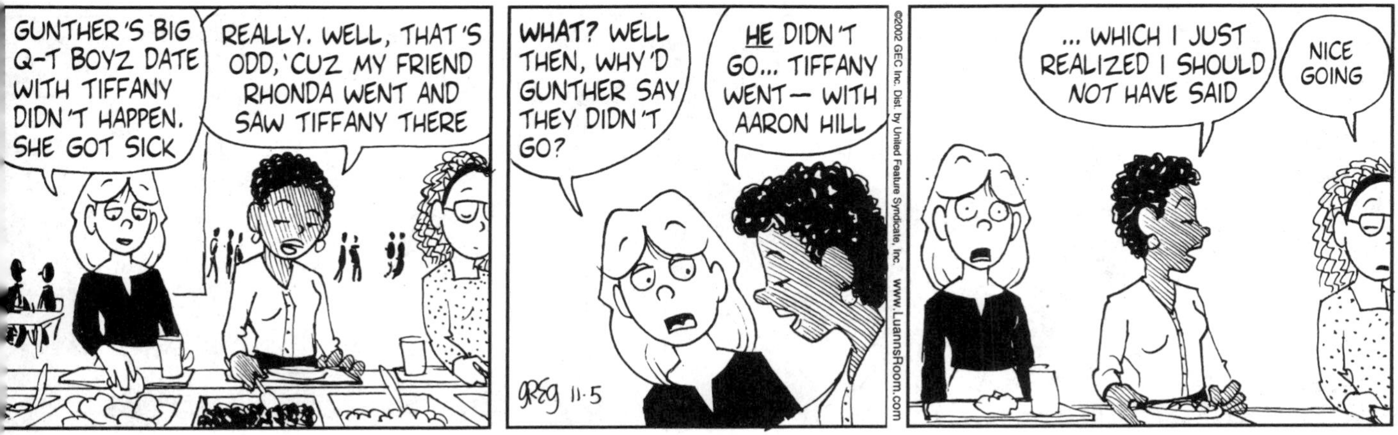

GUNTHER'S BIG Q-T BOYZ DATE WITH TIFFANY DIDN'T HAPPEN. SHE GOT SICK
REALLY. WELL, THAT'S ODD, 'CUZ MY FRIEND RHONDA WENT AND SAW TIFFANY THERE
WHAT? WELL THEN, WHY'D GUNTHER SAY THEY DIDN'T GO?
HE DIDN'T GO... TIFFANY WENT— WITH AARON HILL
GREG 11·5
©2002 GEC Inc. Dist. by United Feature Syndicate, Inc. www.LuannsRoom.com
... WHICH I JUST REALIZED I SHOULD NOT HAVE SAID
NICE GOING

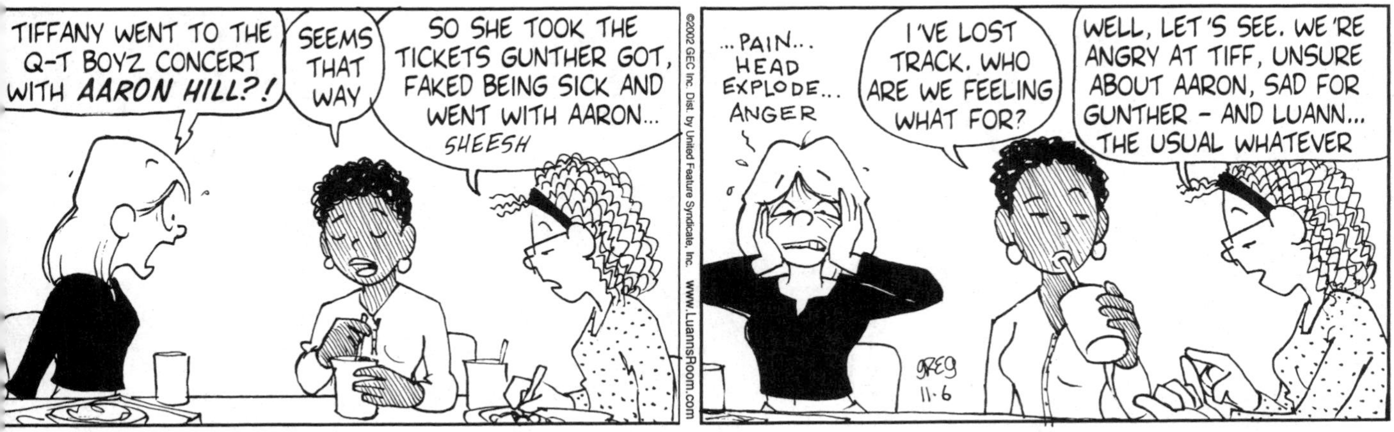

TIFFANY WENT TO THE Q-T BOYZ CONCERT WITH AARON HILL?!
SEEMS THAT WAY
SO SHE TOOK THE TICKETS GUNTHER GOT, FAKED BEING SICK AND WENT WITH AARON...
SHEESH
©2002 GEC Inc. Dist. by United Feature Syndicate, Inc. www.LuannsRoom.com
...PAIN... HEAD EXPLODE... ANGER
I'VE LOST TRACK. WHO ARE WE FEELING WHAT FOR?
WELL, LET'S SEE. WE'RE ANGRY AT TIFF, UNSURE ABOUT AARON, SAD FOR GUNTHER – AND LUANN... THE USUAL WHATEVER
GREG 11·6

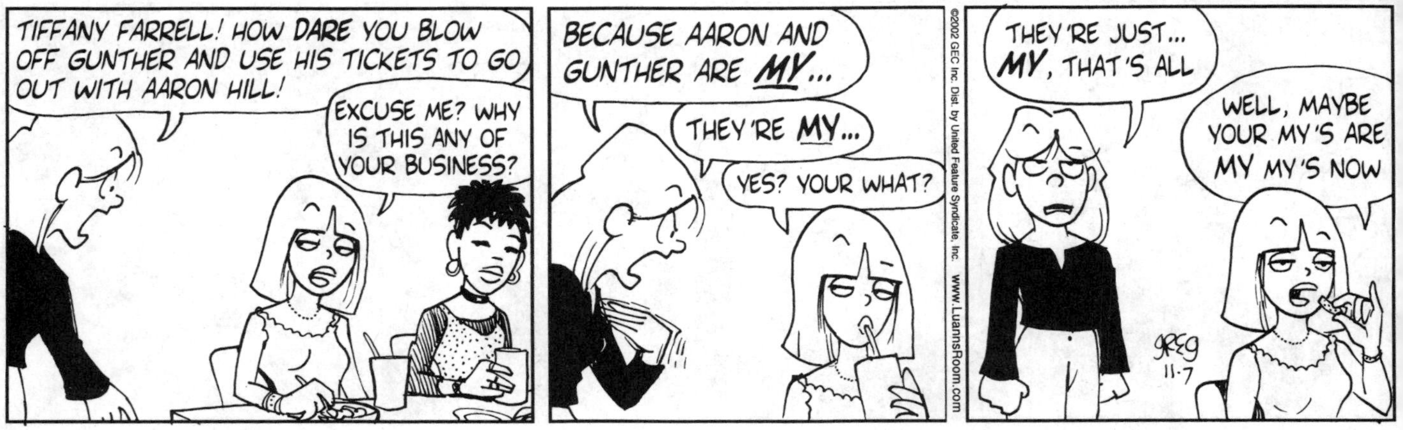
TIFFANY FARRELL! HOW DARE YOU BLOW OFF GUNTHER AND USE HIS TICKETS TO GO OUT WITH AARON HILL!
EXCUSE ME? WHY IS THIS ANY OF YOUR BUSINESS?
BECAUSE AARON AND GUNTHER ARE MY...
THEY'RE MY...
YES? YOUR WHAT?
©2002 GEC Inc. Dist. by United Feature Syndicate, Inc. www.LuannsRoom.com
THEY'RE JUST... MY, THAT'S ALL
WELL, MAYBE YOUR MY'S ARE MY MY'S NOW
GREG 11-7

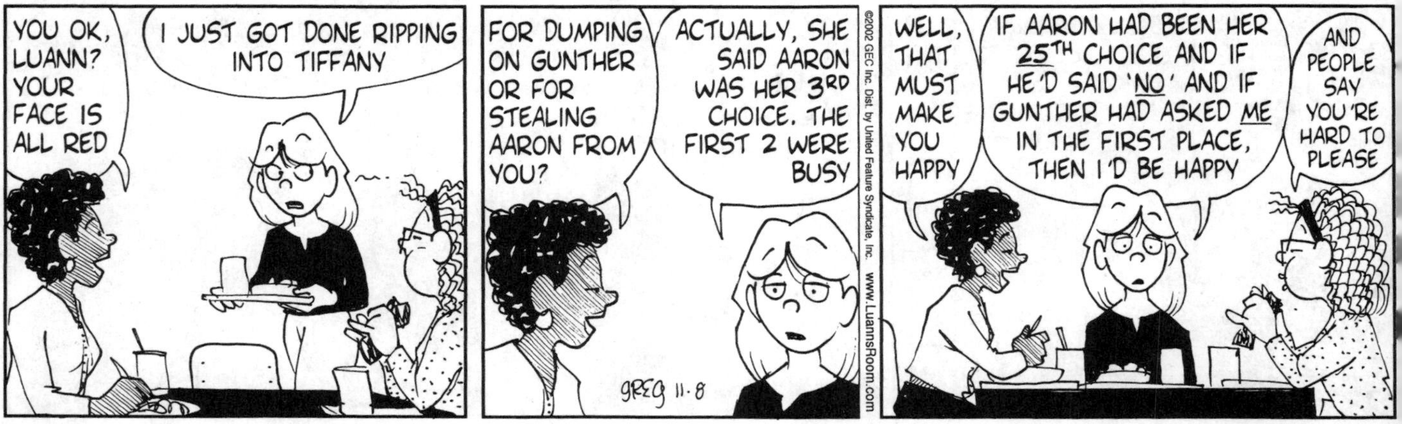
YOU OK, LUANN? YOUR FACE IS ALL RED
I JUST GOT DONE RIPPING INTO TIFFANY
FOR DUMPING ON GUNTHER OR FOR STEALING AARON FROM YOU?
ACTUALLY, SHE SAID AARON WAS HER 3RD CHOICE. THE FIRST 2 WERE BUSY
GREG 11-8
©2002 GEC Inc. Dist. by United Feature Syndicate, Inc. www.LuannsRoom.com
WELL, THAT MUST MAKE YOU HAPPY
IF AARON HAD BEEN HER 25TH CHOICE AND IF HE'D SAID 'NO' AND IF GUNTHER HAD ASKED ME IN THE FIRST PLACE, THEN I'D BE HAPPY
AND PEOPLE SAY YOU'RE HARD TO PLEASE

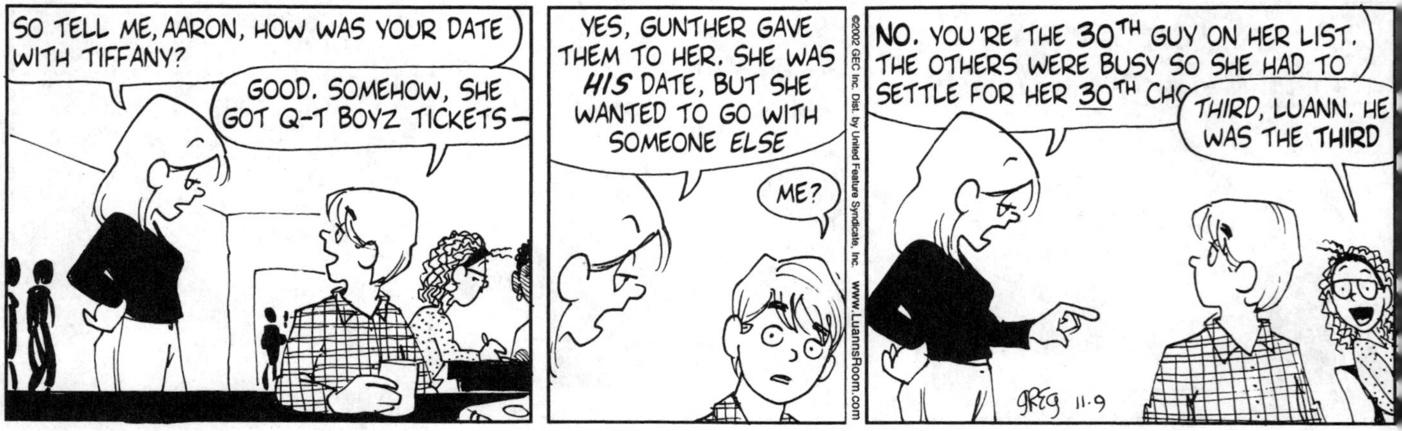
SO TELL ME, AARON, HOW WAS YOUR DATE WITH TIFFANY?
GOOD. SOMEHOW, SHE GOT Q-T BOYZ TICKETS—
YES, GUNTHER GAVE THEM TO HER. SHE WAS HIS DATE, BUT SHE WANTED TO GO WITH SOMEONE ELSE
ME?
©2002 GEC Inc. Dist. by United Feature Syndicate, Inc. www.LuannsRoom.com
NO. YOU'RE THE 30TH GUY ON HER LIST. THE OTHERS WERE BUSY SO SHE HAD TO SETTLE FOR HER 30TH CHO
THIRD, LUANN. HE WAS THE THIRD
GREG 11-9

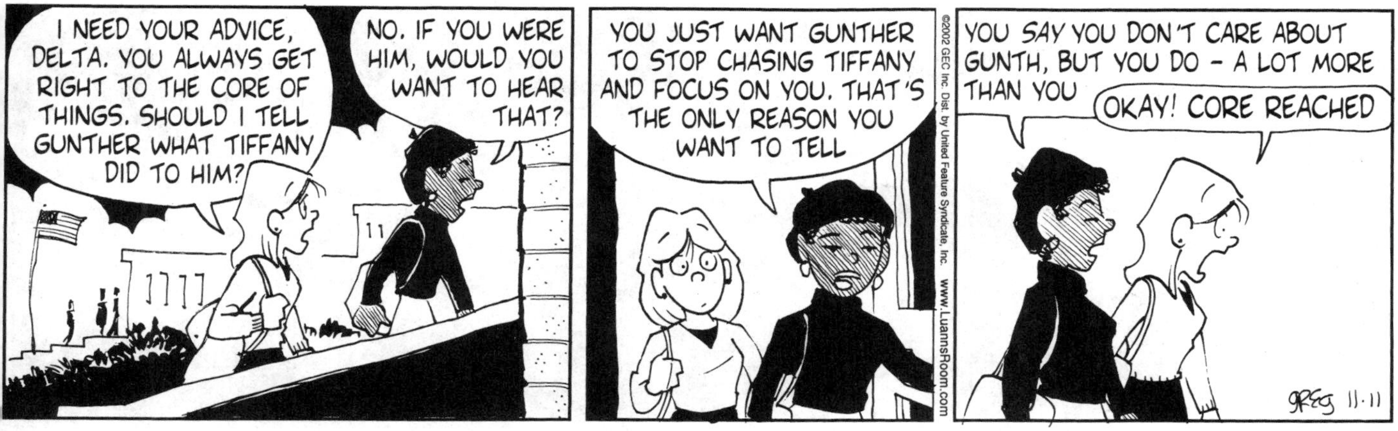
I NEED YOUR ADVICE, DELTA. YOU ALWAYS GET RIGHT TO THE CORE OF THINGS. SHOULD I TELL GUNTHER WHAT TIFFANY DID TO HIM?
NO. IF YOU WERE HIM, WOULD YOU WANT TO HEAR THAT?
©2002 GEC Inc. Dist. by United Feature Syndicate, Inc. www.LuannsRoom.com
YOU JUST WANT GUNTHER TO STOP CHASING TIFFANY AND FOCUS ON YOU. THAT'S THE ONLY REASON YOU WANT TO TELL
YOU *SAY* YOU DON'T CARE ABOUT GUNTH, BUT YOU DO – A LOT MORE THAN YOU
OKAY! CORE REACHED
GREG 11·11

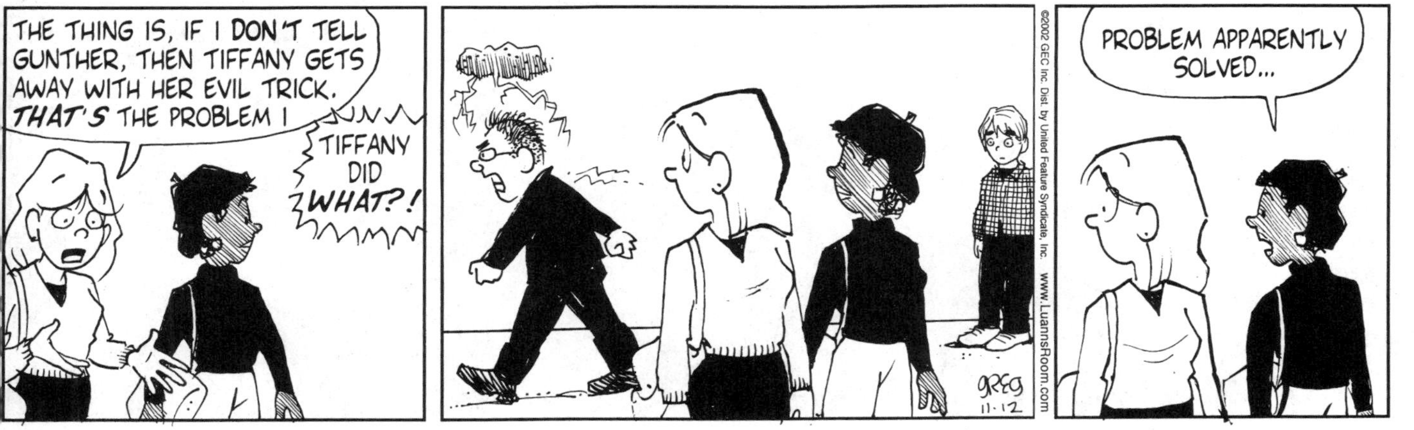
THE THING IS, IF I **DON'T** TELL GUNTHER, THEN TIFFANY GETS AWAY WITH HER EVIL TRICK. ***THAT'S*** THE PROBLEM I
TIFFANY DID ***WHAT?!***
©2002 GEC Inc. Dist. by United Feature Syndicate, Inc. www.LuannsRoom.com
GREG 11·12
PROBLEM APPARENTLY SOLVED...

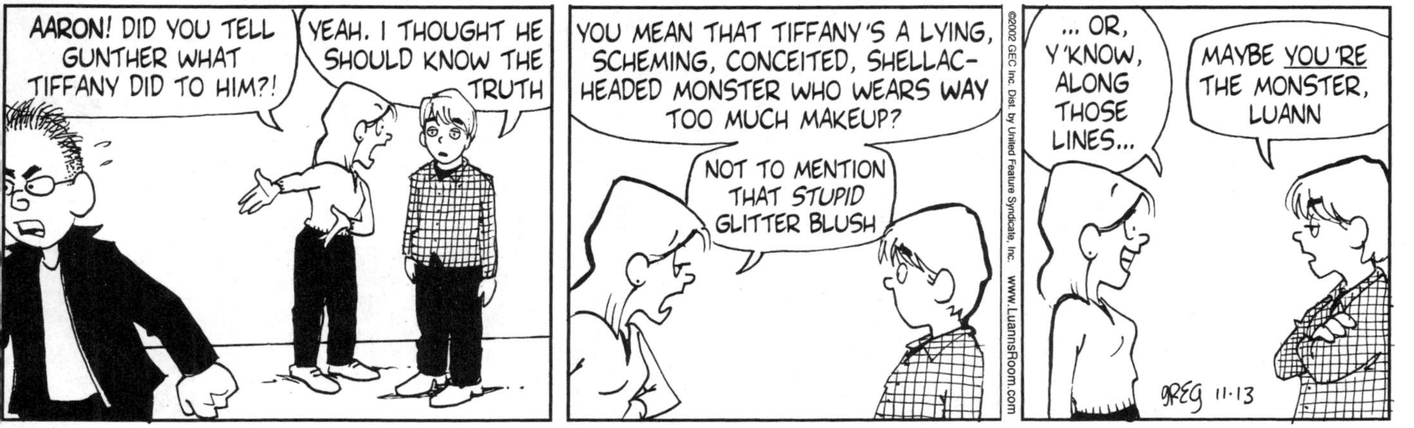
AARON! DID YOU TELL GUNTHER WHAT TIFFANY DID TO HIM?!
YEAH. I THOUGHT HE SHOULD KNOW THE TRUTH
©2002 GEC Inc. Dist. by United Feature Syndicate, Inc. www.LuannsRoom.com
YOU MEAN THAT TIFFANY'S A LYING, SCHEMING, CONCEITED, SHELLAC-HEADED MONSTER WHO WEARS WAY TOO MUCH MAKEUP?
NOT TO MENTION THAT *STUPID* GLITTER BLUSH
... OR, Y'KNOW, ALONG THOSE LINES...
MAYBE YOU'RE THE MONSTER, LUANN
GREG 11·13

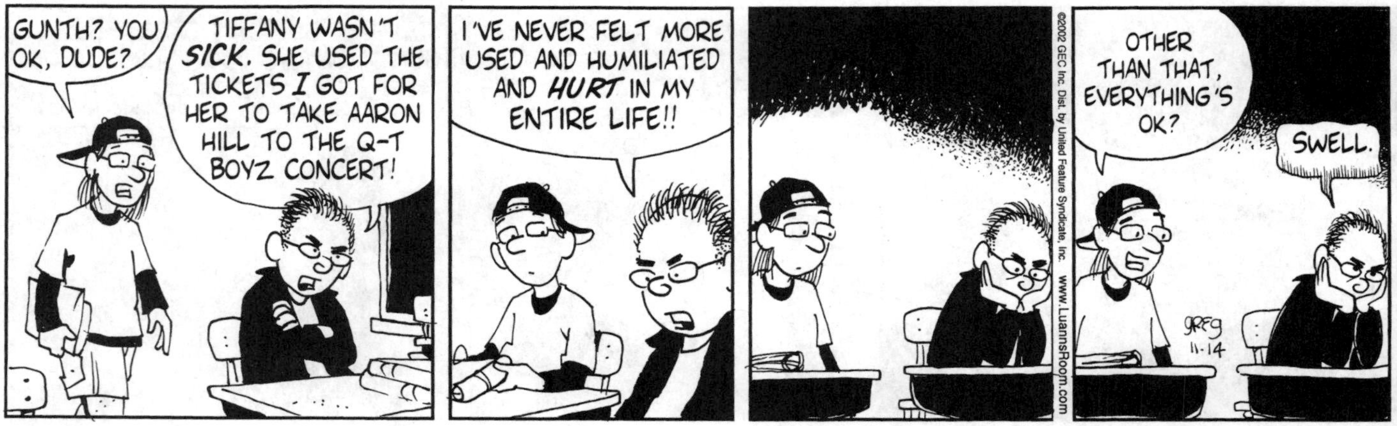
GUNTH? YOU OK, DUDE?
TIFFANY WASN'T SICK. SHE USED THE TICKETS I GOT FOR HER TO TAKE AARON HILL TO THE Q-T BOYZ CONCERT!
I'VE NEVER FELT MORE USED AND HUMILIATED AND HURT IN MY ENTIRE LIFE!!
©2002 GEC Inc. Dist. by United Feature Syndicate, Inc. www.LuannsRoom.com
OTHER THAN THAT, EVERYTHING'S OK?
SWELL.
GREG 11·14

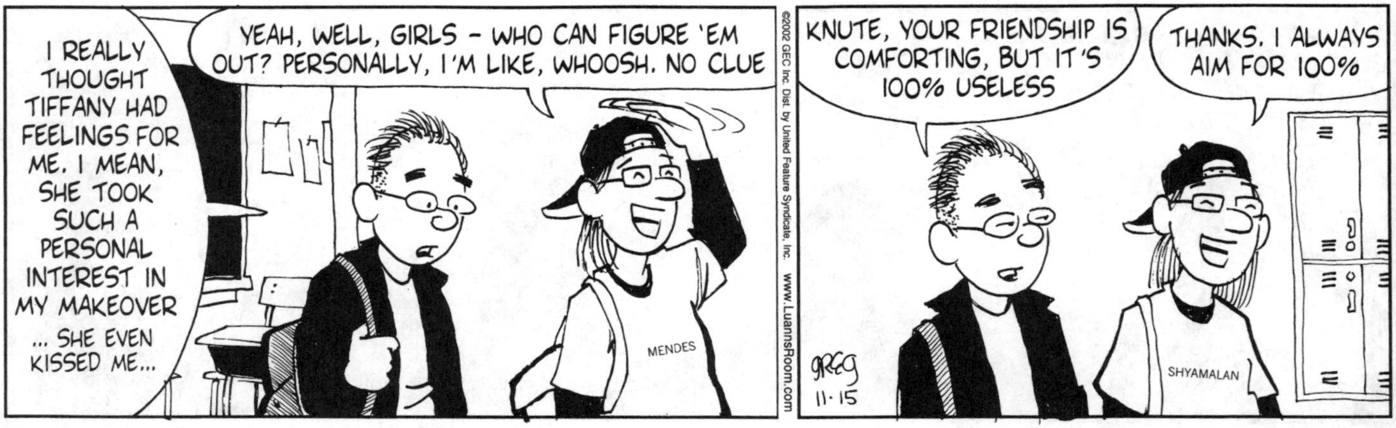
I REALLY THOUGHT TIFFANY HAD FEELINGS FOR ME. I MEAN, SHE TOOK SUCH A PERSONAL INTEREST IN MY MAKEOVER ... SHE EVEN KISSED ME...
YEAH, WELL, GIRLS - WHO CAN FIGURE 'EM OUT? PERSONALLY, I'M LIKE, WHOOSH. NO CLUE
MENDES
GREG 11·15
©2002 GEC Inc. Dist. by United Feature Syndicate, Inc. www.LuannsRoom.com
KNUTE, YOUR FRIENDSHIP IS COMFORTING, BUT IT'S 100% USELESS
THANKS. I ALWAYS AIM FOR 100%
SHYAMALAN

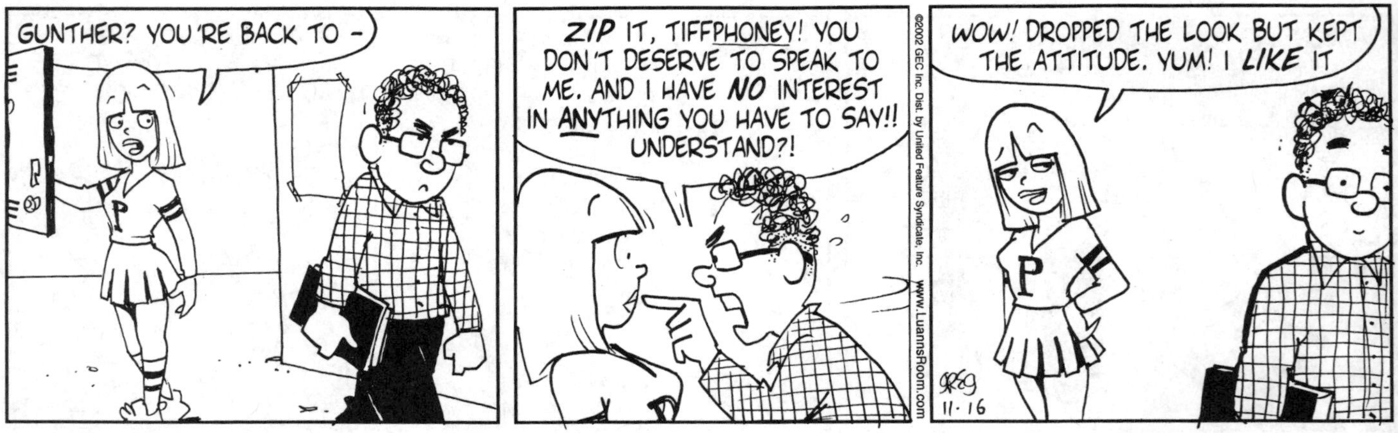
GUNTHER? YOU'RE BACK TO -
ZIP IT, TIFFPHONEY! YOU DON'T DESERVE TO SPEAK TO ME. AND I HAVE NO INTEREST IN ANYTHING YOU HAVE TO SAY!! UNDERSTAND?!
©2002 GEC Inc. Dist. by United Feature Syndicate, Inc. www.LuannsRoom.com
WOW! DROPPED THE LOOK BUT KEPT THE ATTITUDE. YUM! I LIKE IT
GREG 11·16

pedipalpi
eyes
pedicel
cephalothorax
coxa
trochanter
femur
patella
abdomen
tibia
metatarsus
tarsus
claws
scopula
spinnerets

DAD, COULD I MOVE INTO THE ATTIC? Y'KNOW, TURN IT INTO A COZY, PRIVATE BEDROOM?
©2002 GEC Inc. Dist. by United Feature Syndicate, Inc.
www.LuannsRoom.com
LUANN, WE DON'T HAVE AN ATTIC. ALL WE HAVE IS A DARK, DUSTY, STUFFY CRAWL SPACE FULL OF INSULATION AND WIRES AND SPIDER WEBS
SOUNDS PERFECT FOR YOU. C'MON, I'LL HELP YOU MOVE
GREG
11-10

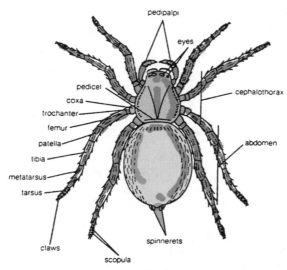

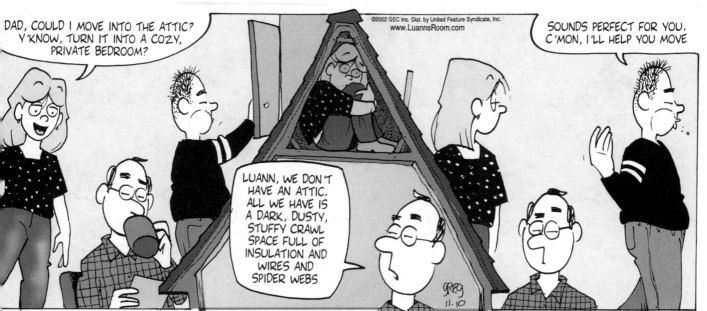

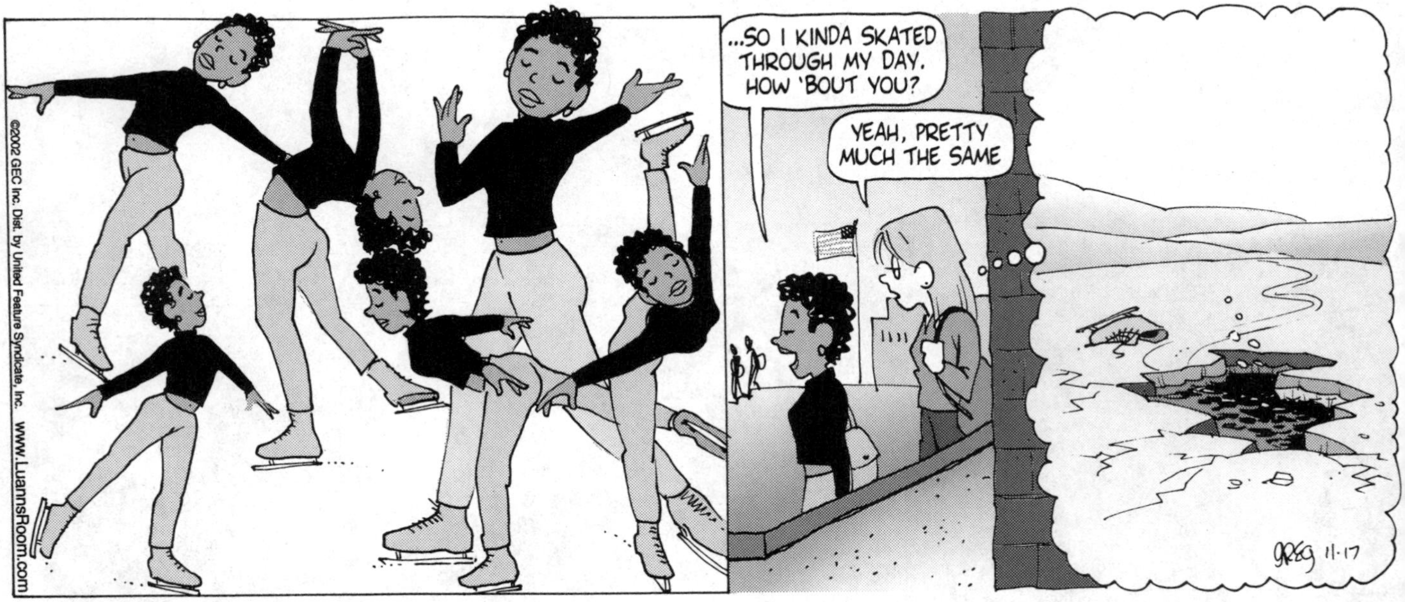
©2002 GEC Inc. Dist. by United Feature Syndicate, Inc. www.LuannsRoom.com
...SO I KINDA SKATED THROUGH MY DAY. HOW 'BOUT YOU?
YEAH, PRETTY MUCH THE SAME
GREG 11-17

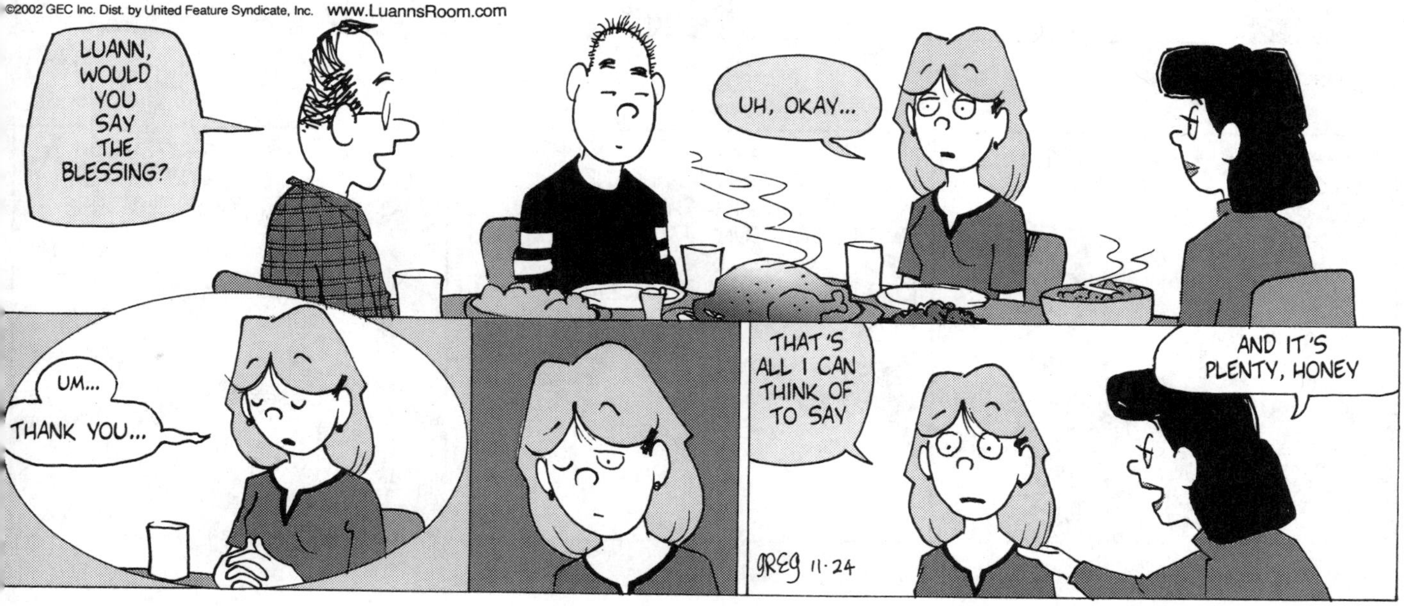
LUANN, WOULD YOU SAY THE BLESSING?
UH, OKAY...
UM...
THANK YOU...
THAT'S ALL I CAN THINK OF TO SAY
AND IT'S PLENTY, HONEY
GREG 11·24

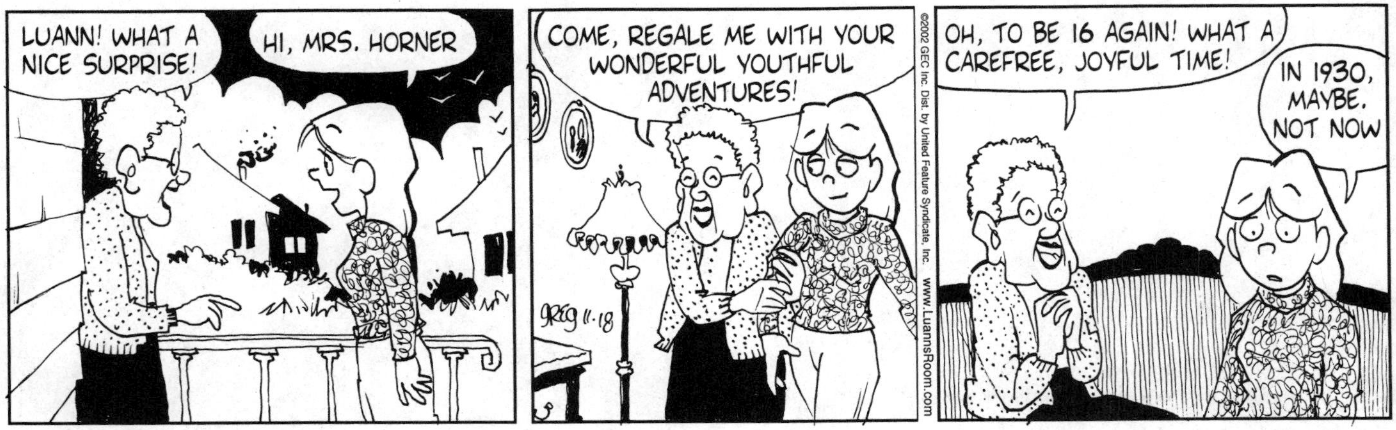
LUANN! WHAT A NICE SURPRISE!
HI, MRS. HORNER
COME, REGALE ME WITH YOUR WONDERFUL YOUTHFUL ADVENTURES!
GREG 11-18
©2002 GEC Inc. Dist. by United Feature Syndicate, Inc. www.LuannsRoom.com
OH, TO BE 16 AGAIN! WHAT A CAREFREE, JOYFUL TIME!
IN 1930, MAYBE. NOT NOW

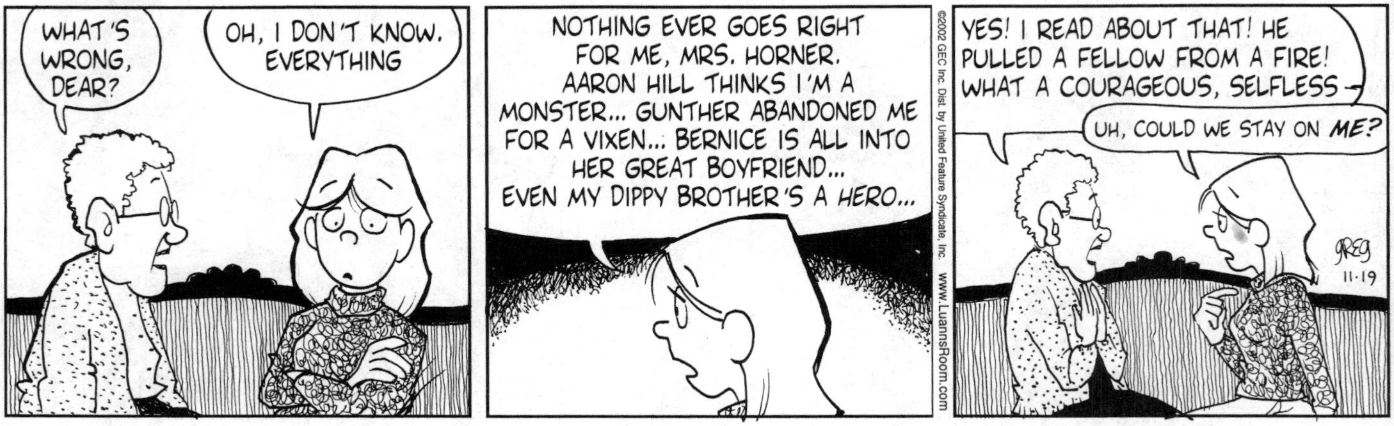
WHAT'S WRONG, DEAR?
OH, I DON'T KNOW. EVERYTHING
NOTHING EVER GOES RIGHT FOR ME, MRS. HORNER. AARON HILL THINKS I'M A MONSTER... GUNTHER ABANDONED ME FOR A VIXEN... BERNICE IS ALL INTO HER GREAT BOYFRIEND... EVEN MY DIPPY BROTHER'S A *HERO*...
©2002 GEC Inc. Dist. by United Feature Syndicate, Inc. www.LuannsRoom.com
YES! I READ ABOUT THAT! HE PULLED A FELLOW FROM A FIRE! WHAT A COURAGEOUS, SELFLESS –
UH, COULD WE STAY ON ***ME?***
GREG 11-19

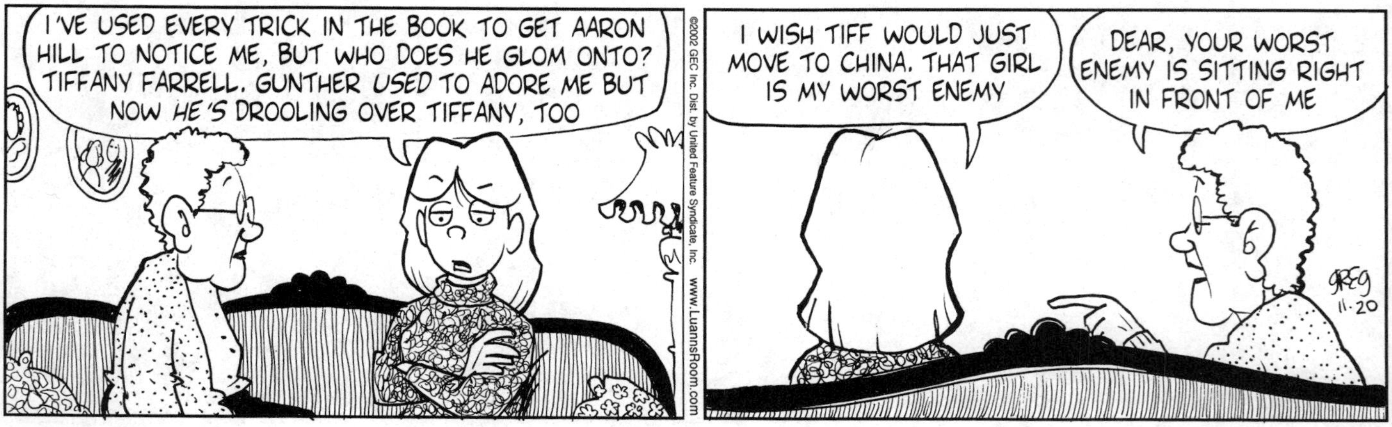
I'VE USED EVERY TRICK IN THE BOOK TO GET AARON HILL TO NOTICE ME, BUT WHO DOES HE GLOM ONTO? TIFFANY FARRELL. GUNTHER *USED* TO ADORE ME BUT NOW *HE'S* DROOLING OVER TIFFANY, TOO
©2002 GEC Inc. Dist. by United Feature Syndicate, Inc. www.LuannsRoom.com
I WISH TIFF WOULD JUST MOVE TO CHINA. THAT GIRL IS MY WORST ENEMY
DEAR, YOUR WORST ENEMY IS SITTING RIGHT IN FRONT OF ME
GREG 11-20

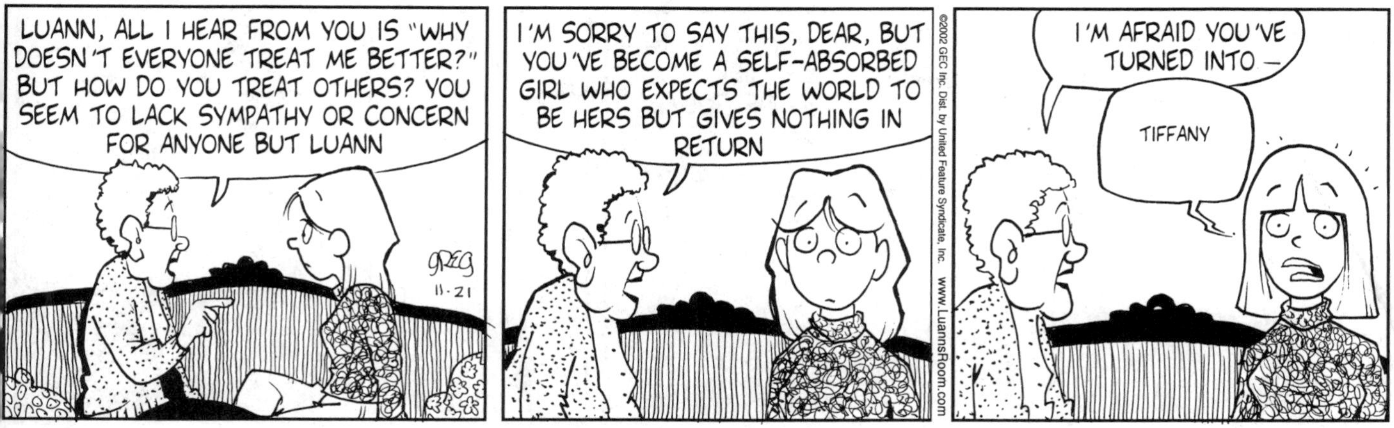
LUANN, ALL I HEAR FROM YOU IS "WHY DOESN'T EVERYONE TREAT ME BETTER?" BUT HOW DO YOU TREAT OTHERS? YOU SEEM TO LACK SYMPATHY OR CONCERN FOR ANYONE BUT LUANN
GREG 11-21
I'M SORRY TO SAY THIS, DEAR, BUT YOU'VE BECOME A SELF-ABSORBED GIRL WHO EXPECTS THE WORLD TO BE HERS BUT GIVES NOTHING IN RETURN
©2002 GEC Inc. Dist. by United Feature Syndicate, Inc. www.LuannsRoom.com
I'M AFRAID YOU'VE TURNED INTO –
TIFFANY

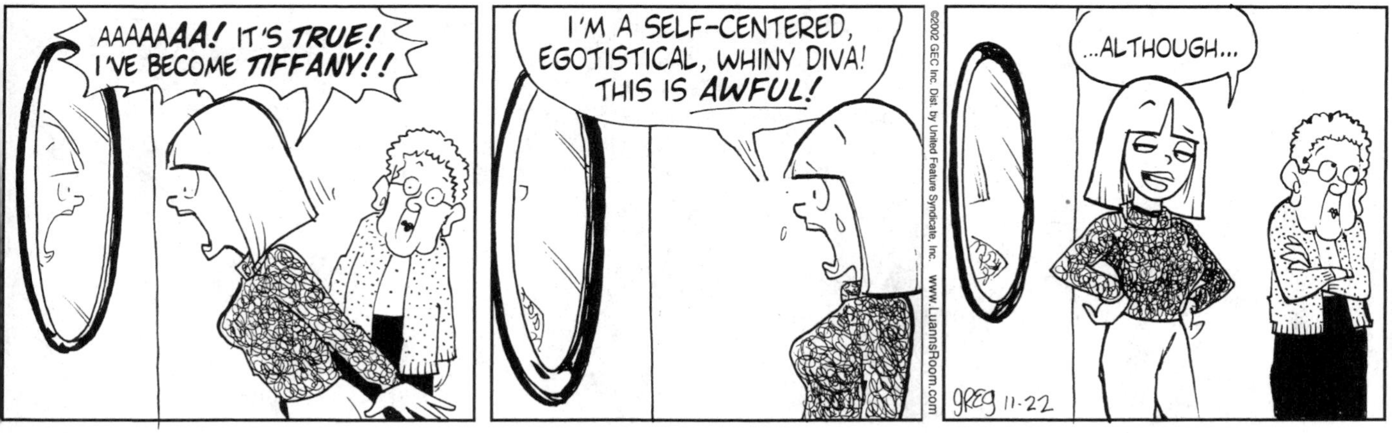
AAAAAAA! IT'S TRUE! I'VE BECOME TIFFANY!!
I'M A SELF-CENTERED, EGOTISTICAL, WHINY DIVA! THIS IS AWFUL!
©2002 GEC Inc. Dist. by United Feature Syndicate, Inc. www.LuannsRoom.com
...ALTHOUGH...
GREG 11-22

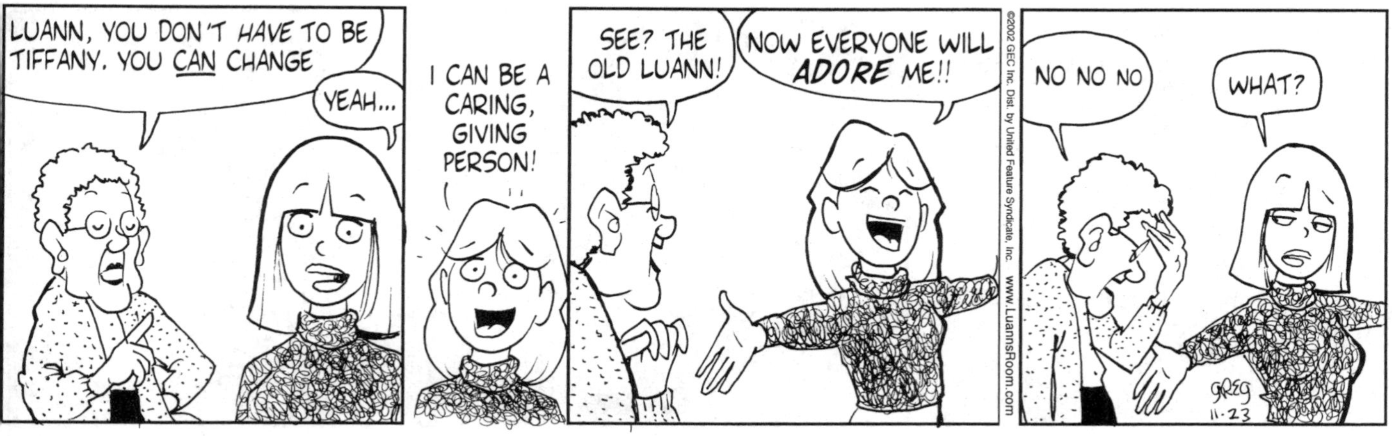
LUANN, YOU DON'T HAVE TO BE TIFFANY. YOU CAN CHANGE
YEAH...
I CAN BE A CARING, GIVING PERSON!
SEE? THE OLD LUANN!
NOW EVERYONE WILL ADORE ME!!
©2002 GEC Inc. Dist. by United Feature Syndicate, Inc. www.LuannsRoom.com
NO NO NO
WHAT?
GREG 11-23

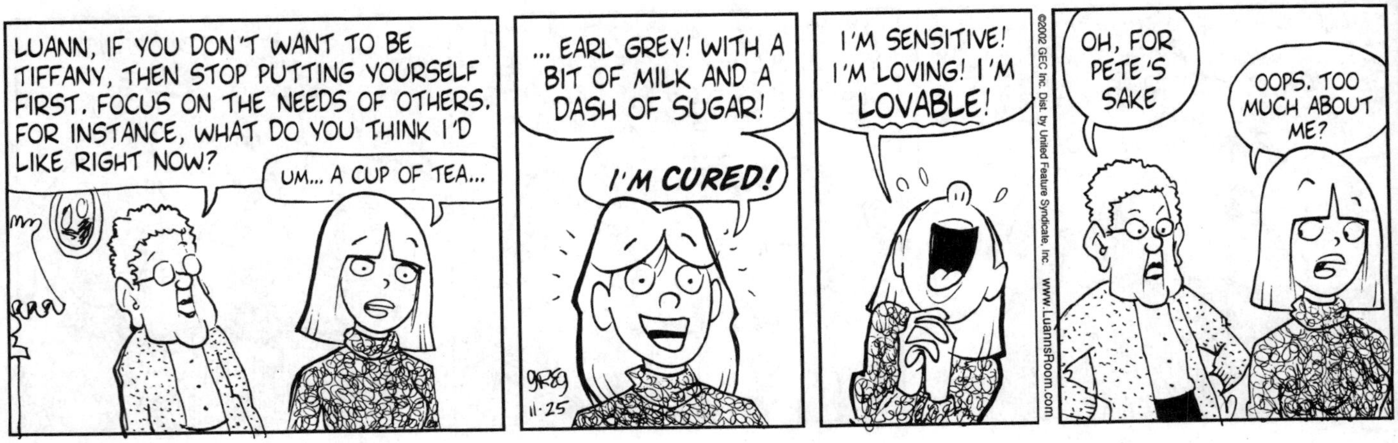
LUANN, IF YOU DON'T WANT TO BE TIFFANY, THEN STOP PUTTING YOURSELF FIRST. FOCUS ON THE NEEDS OF OTHERS. FOR INSTANCE, WHAT DO YOU THINK I'D LIKE RIGHT NOW?
UM... A CUP OF TEA...
... EARL GREY! WITH A BIT OF MILK AND A DASH OF SUGAR!
I'M CURED!
GREG 11-25
I'M SENSITIVE! I'M LOVING! I'M LOVABLE!
©2002 GEC Inc. Dist. by United Feature Syndicate, Inc. www.LuannsRoom.com
OH, FOR PETE'S SAKE
OOPS. TOO MUCH ABOUT ME?

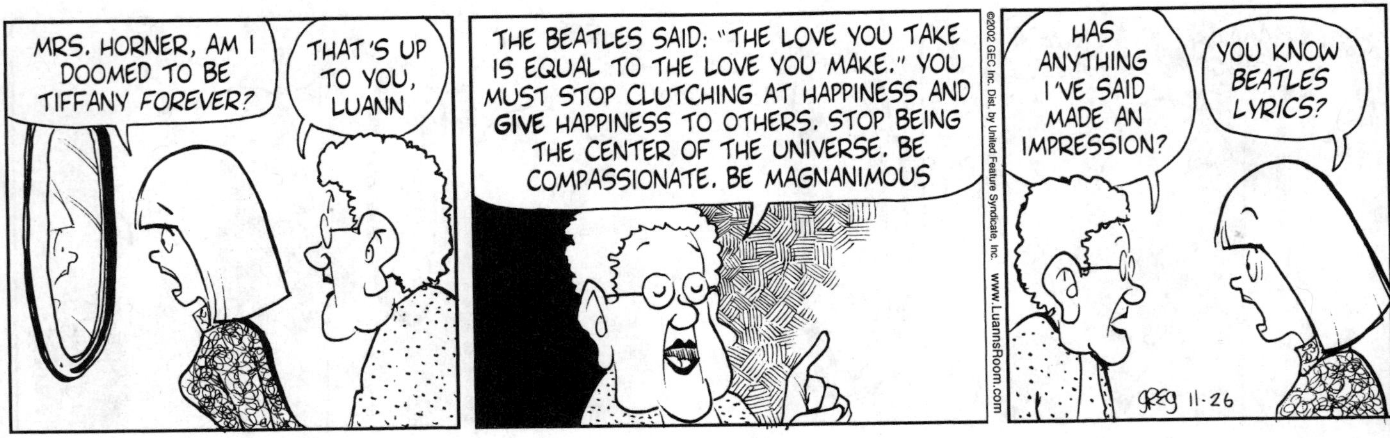
MRS. HORNER, AM I DOOMED TO BE TIFFANY FOREVER?
THAT'S UP TO YOU, LUANN
THE BEATLES SAID: "THE LOVE YOU TAKE IS EQUAL TO THE LOVE YOU MAKE." YOU MUST STOP CLUTCHING AT HAPPINESS AND GIVE HAPPINESS TO OTHERS. STOP BEING THE CENTER OF THE UNIVERSE. BE COMPASSIONATE. BE MAGNANIMOUS
©2002 GEC Inc. Dist. by United Feature Syndicate, Inc. www.LuannsRoom.com
HAS ANYTHING I'VE SAID MADE AN IMPRESSION?
YOU KNOW BEATLES LYRICS?
GREG 11-26

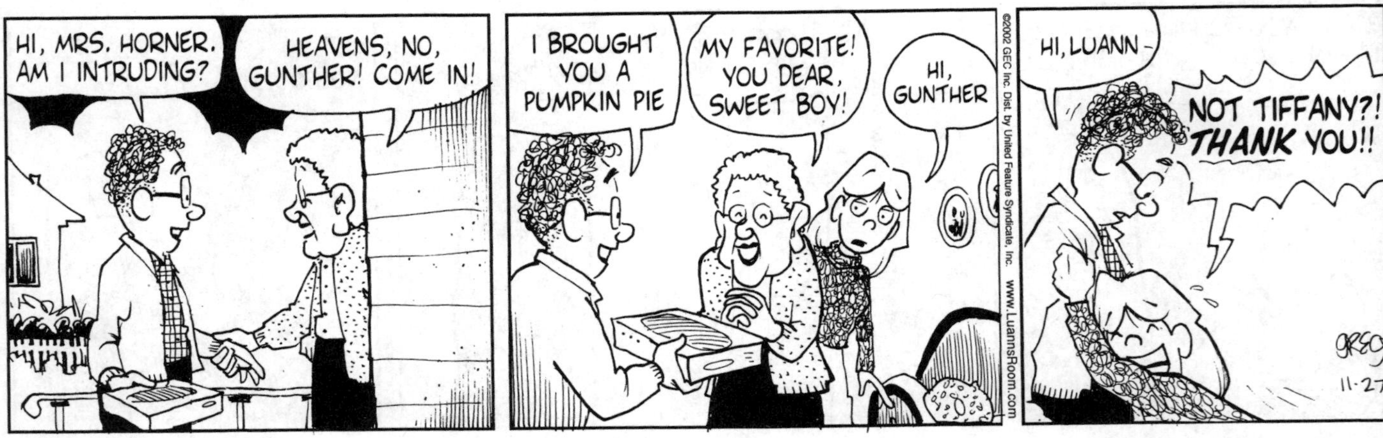
HI, MRS. HORNER. AM I INTRUDING?
HEAVENS, NO, GUNTHER! COME IN!
I BROUGHT YOU A PUMPKIN PIE
MY FAVORITE! YOU DEAR, SWEET BOY!
HI, GUNTHER
©2002 GEC Inc. Dist. by United Feature Syndicate, Inc. www.LuannsRoom.com
HI, LUANN
NOT TIFFANY?! THANK YOU!!

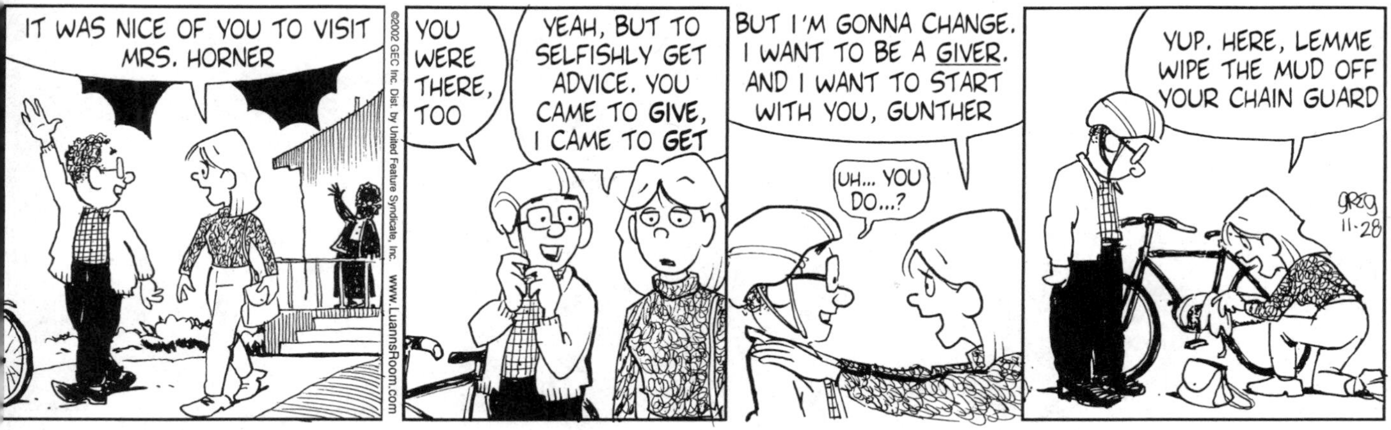
IT WAS NICE OF YOU TO VISIT MRS. HORNER
©2002 GEC Inc. Dist. by United Feature Syndicate, Inc. www.LuannsRoom.com
YOU WERE THERE, TOO
YEAH, BUT TO SELFISHLY GET ADVICE. YOU CAME TO GIVE, I CAME TO GET
BUT I'M GONNA CHANGE. I WANT TO BE A GIVER. AND I WANT TO START WITH YOU, GUNTHER
UH... YOU DO...?
YUP. HERE, LEMME WIPE THE MUD OFF YOUR CHAIN GUARD
GREG 11-28

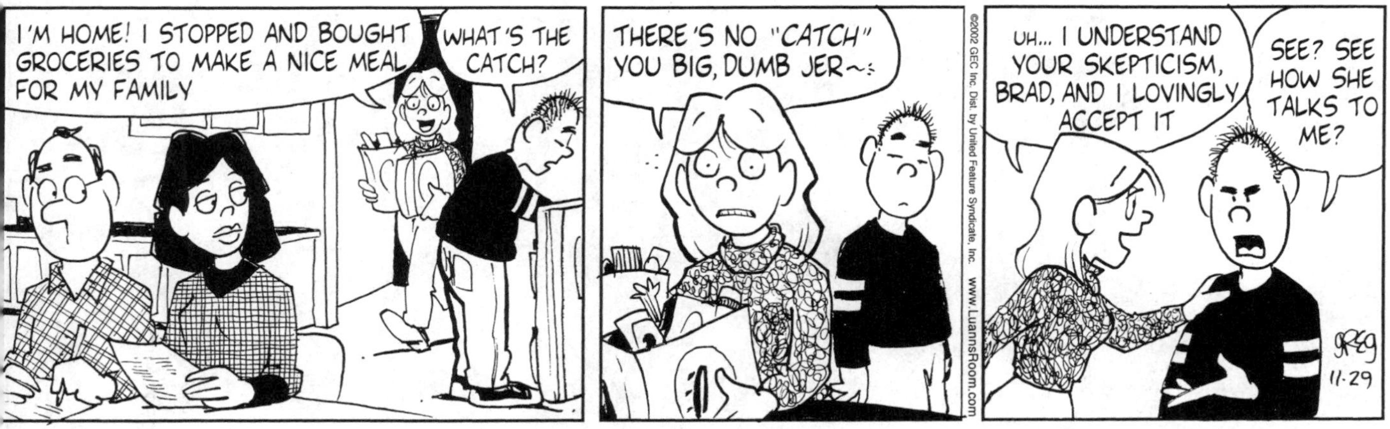
I'M HOME! I STOPPED AND BOUGHT GROCERIES TO MAKE A NICE MEAL FOR MY FAMILY
WHAT'S THE CATCH?
THERE'S NO "CATCH" YOU BIG, DUMB JER~
©2002 GEC Inc. Dist. by United Feature Syndicate, Inc. www.LuannsRoom.com
UH... I UNDERSTAND YOUR SKEPTICISM, BRAD, AND I LOVINGLY ACCEPT IT
SEE? SEE HOW SHE TALKS TO ME?
GREG 11-29

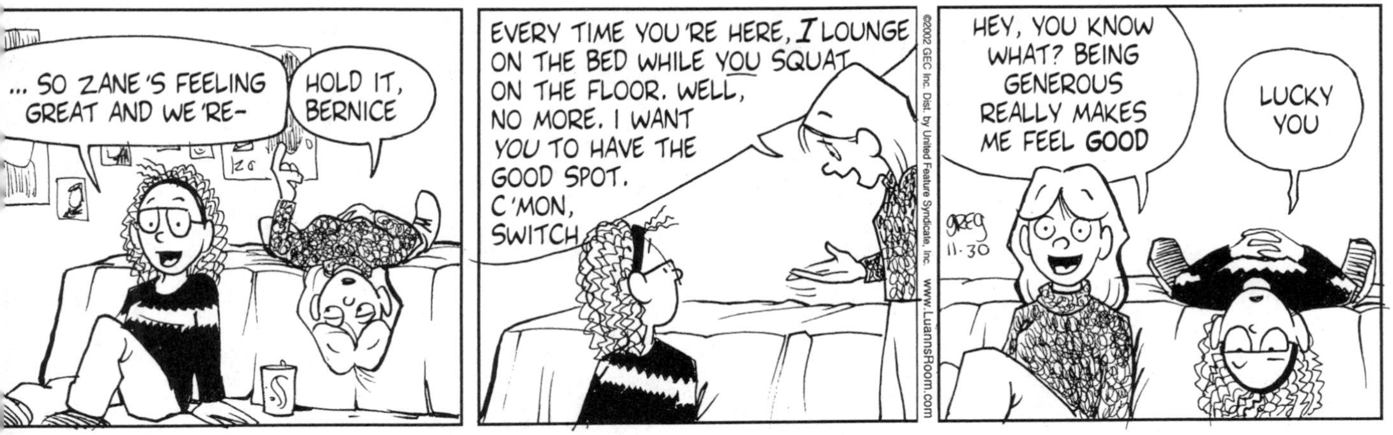
... SO ZANE'S FEELING GREAT AND WE'RE-
HOLD IT, BERNICE
EVERY TIME YOU'RE HERE, I LOUNGE ON THE BED WHILE YOU SQUAT ON THE FLOOR. WELL, NO MORE. I WANT YOU TO HAVE THE GOOD SPOT. C'MON, SWITCH
©2002 GEC Inc. Dist. by United Feature Syndicate, Inc. www.LuannsRoom.com
GREG 11-30
HEY, YOU KNOW WHAT? BEING GENEROUS REALLY MAKES ME FEEL GOOD
LUCKY YOU

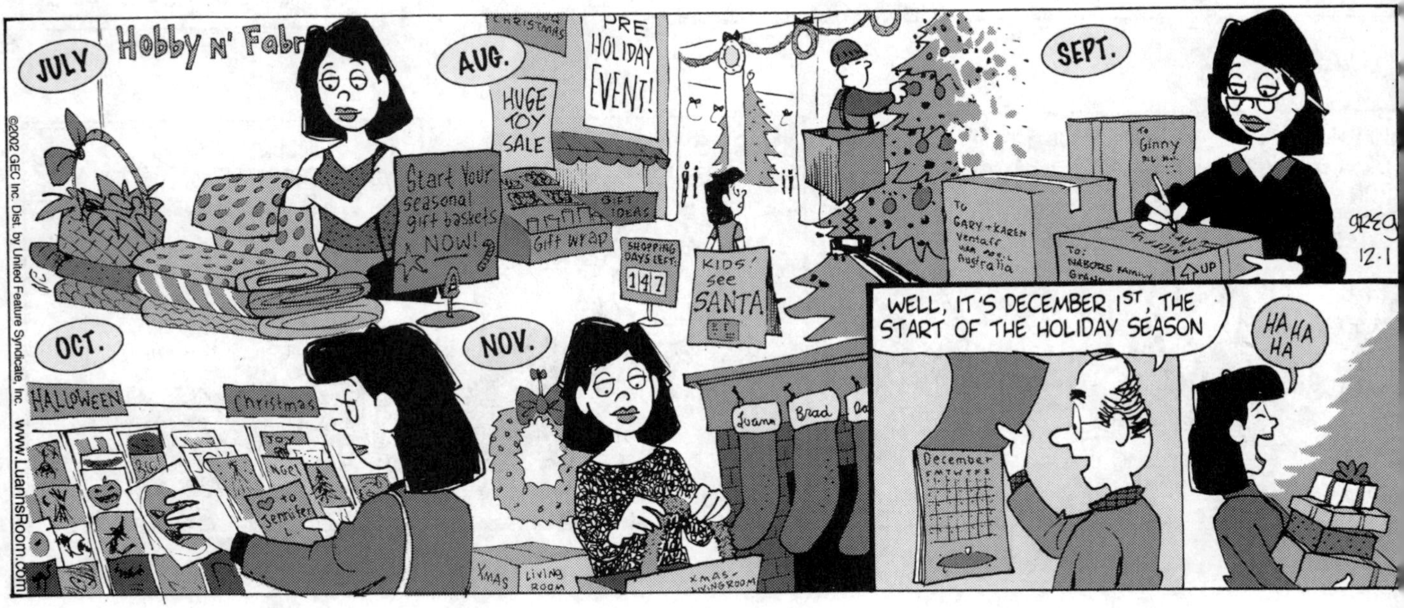
JULY
Hobby N' Fabr
Start Your seasonal gift baskets NOW!
AUG.
HUGE TOY SALE
PRE HOLIDAY EVENT!
Gift Wrap
GIFT IDEAS
SHOPPING DAYS LEFT
147
KIDS! see SANTA
SEPT.
To GARY + KAREN
Ginny
UP
GREG
12·1
OCT.
HALLOWEEN
Christmas
NOEL
to Jennifer
NOV.
Luann
Brad
XMAS
LIVING ROOM
XMAS-LIVING ROOM
WELL, IT'S DECEMBER 1ST, THE START OF THE HOLIDAY SEASON
HA HA HA
December
©2002 GEC Inc. Dist. by United Feature Syndicate, Inc.
www.LuannsRoom.com

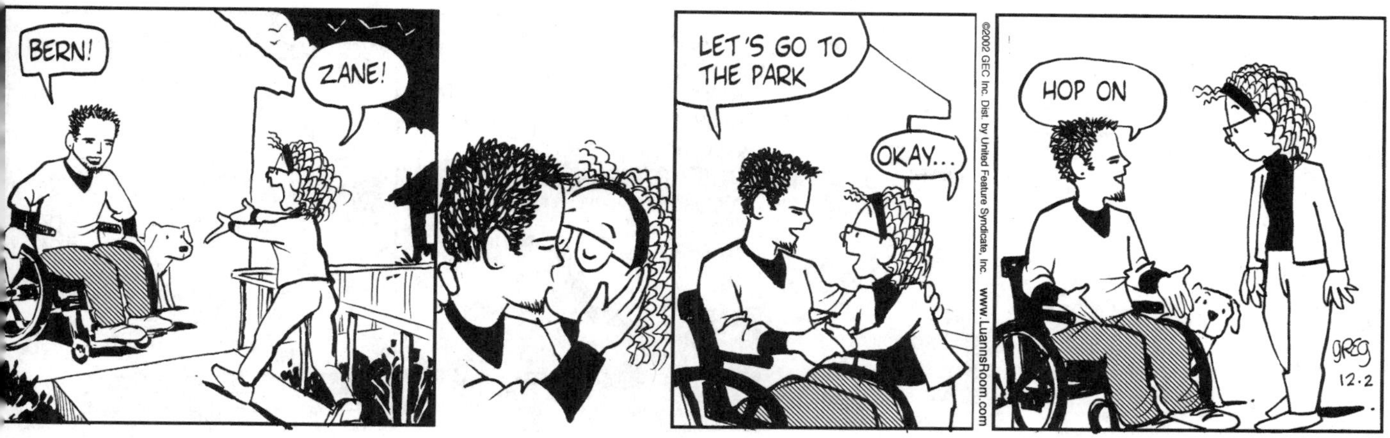
BERN!
ZANE!
LET'S GO TO THE PARK
OKAY...
©2002 GEC Inc. Dist. by United Feature Syndicate, Inc.
www.LuannsRoom.com
HOP ON
GREG 12.2

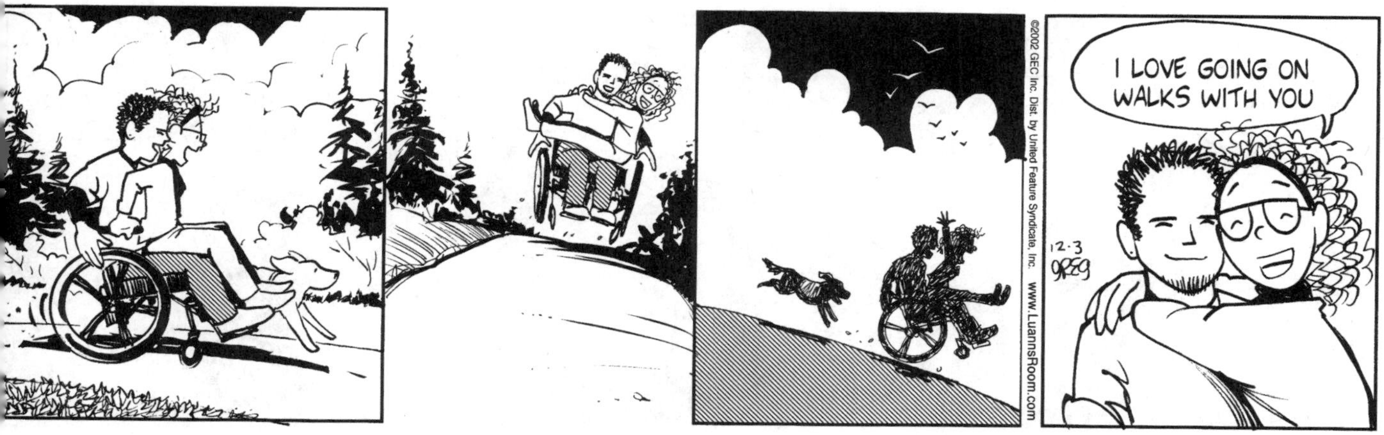
©2002 GEC Inc. Dist. by United Feature Syndicate, Inc.
www.LuannsRoom.com
12.3 GREG
I LOVE GOING ON WALKS WITH YOU

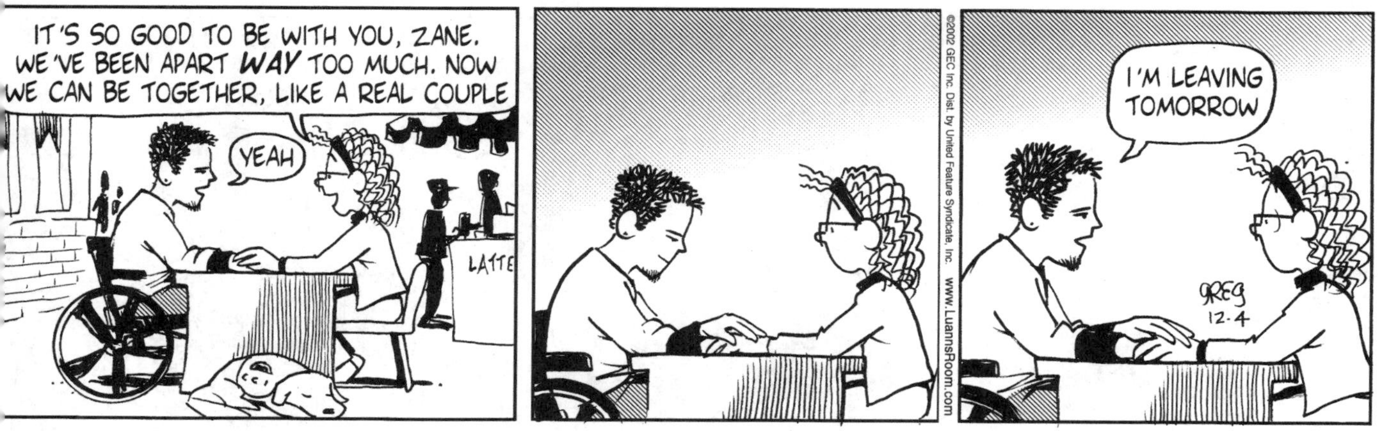
IT'S SO GOOD TO BE WITH YOU, ZANE. WE'VE BEEN APART ***WAY*** TOO MUCH. NOW WE CAN BE TOGETHER, LIKE A REAL COUPLE
YEAH
LATTE
©2002 GEC Inc. Dist. by United Feature Syndicate, Inc.
www.LuannsRoom.com
I'M LEAVING TOMORROW
GREG 12.4

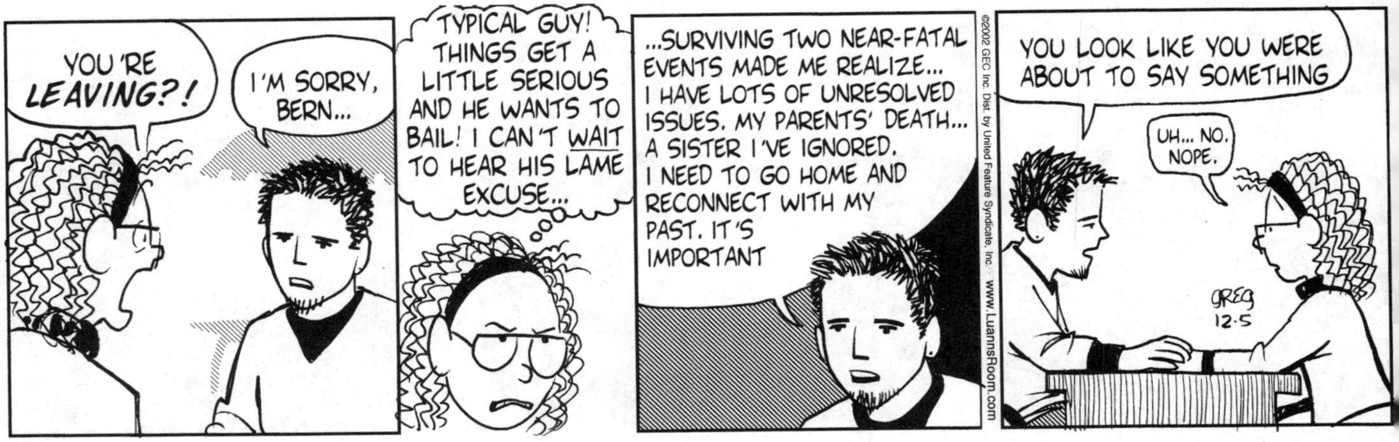
YOU'RE *LEAVING?!*
I'M SORRY, BERN...
TYPICAL GUY! THINGS GET A LITTLE SERIOUS AND HE WANTS TO BAIL! I CAN'T WAIT TO HEAR HIS LAME EXCUSE...
...SURVIVING TWO NEAR-FATAL EVENTS MADE ME REALIZE... I HAVE LOTS OF UNRESOLVED ISSUES. MY PARENTS' DEATH... A SISTER I'VE IGNORED. I NEED TO GO HOME AND RECONNECT WITH MY PAST. IT'S IMPORTANT
©2002 GEC Inc. Dist. by United Feature Syndicate, Inc. www.LuannsRoom.com
YOU LOOK LIKE YOU WERE ABOUT TO SAY SOMETHING
UH... NO. NOPE.
GREG 12·5

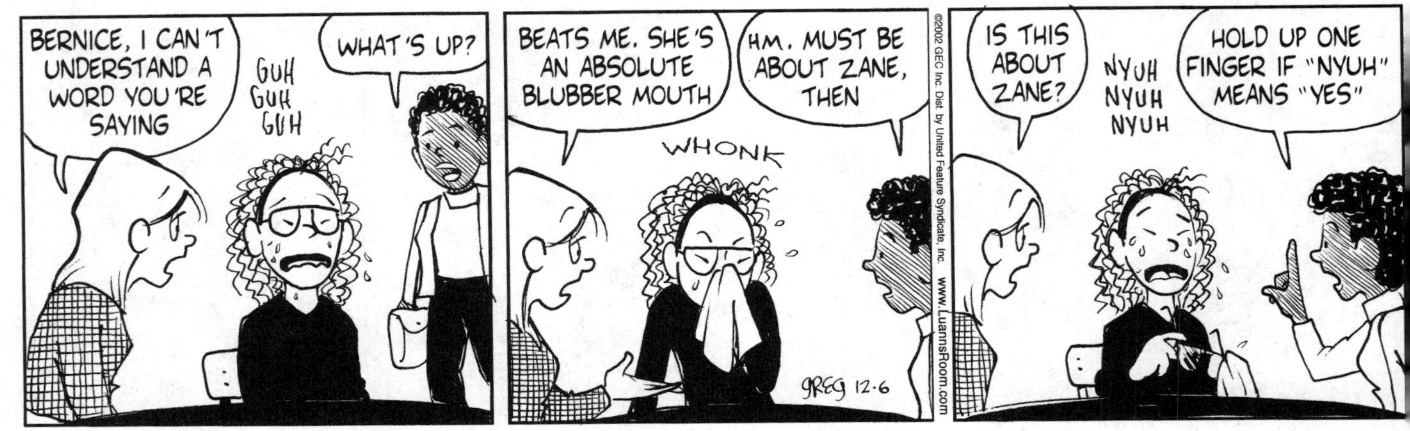
BERNICE, I CAN'T UNDERSTAND A WORD YOU'RE SAYING
GUH GUH GUH
WHAT'S UP?
BEATS ME. SHE'S AN ABSOLUTE BLUBBER MOUTH
HM. MUST BE ABOUT ZANE, THEN
WHONK
GREG 12·6
©2002 GEC Inc. Dist. by United Feature Syndicate, Inc. www.LuannsRoom.com
IS THIS ABOUT ZANE?
NYUH NYUH NYUH
HOLD UP ONE FINGER IF "NYUH" MEANS "YES"

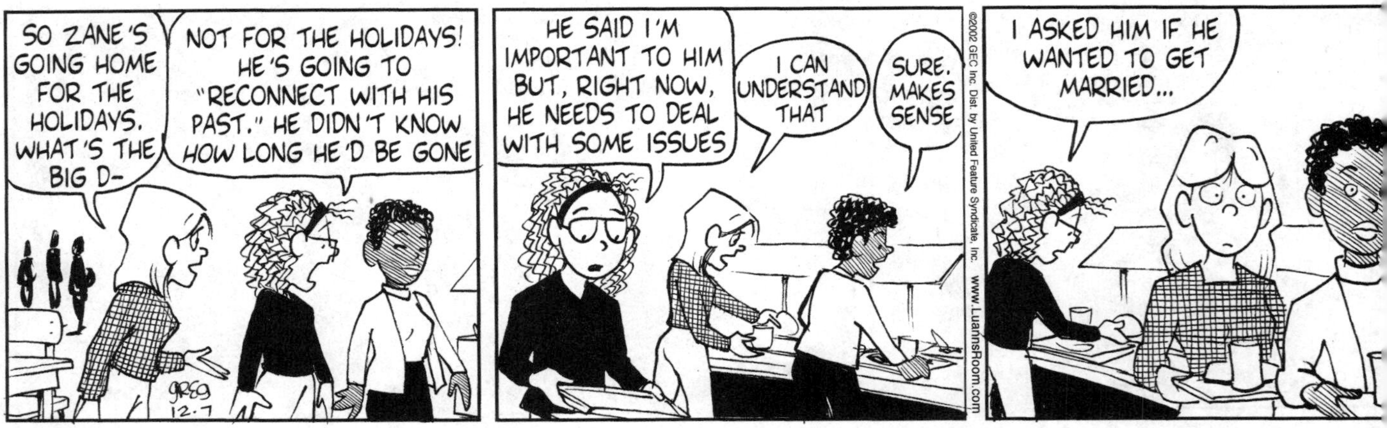
SO ZANE'S GOING HOME FOR THE HOLIDAYS. WHAT'S THE BIG D–
NOT FOR THE HOLIDAYS! HE'S GOING TO "RECONNECT WITH HIS PAST." HE DIDN'T KNOW HOW LONG HE'D BE GONE
GREG 12·7
HE SAID I'M IMPORTANT TO HIM BUT, RIGHT NOW, HE NEEDS TO DEAL WITH SOME ISSUES
I CAN UNDERSTAND THAT
SURE. MAKES SENSE
©2002 GEC Inc. Dist. by United Feature Syndicate, Inc. www.LuannsRoom.com
I ASKED HIM IF HE WANTED TO GET MARRIED...

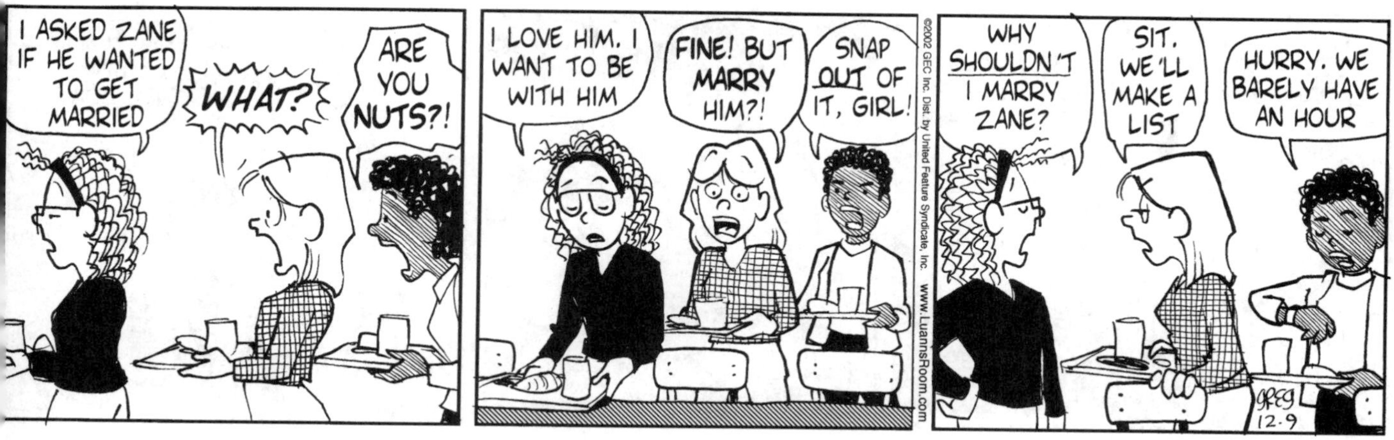
I ASKED ZANE IF HE WANTED TO GET MARRIED
WHAT?
ARE YOU NUTS?!
I LOVE HIM. I WANT TO BE WITH HIM
FINE! BUT MARRY HIM?!
SNAP OUT OF IT, GIRL!
©2002 GEC Inc. Dist. by United Feature Syndicate, Inc. www.LuannsRoom.com
WHY SHOULDN'T I MARRY ZANE?
SIT. WE'LL MAKE A LIST
HURRY. WE BARELY HAVE AN HOUR
GREG 12-9

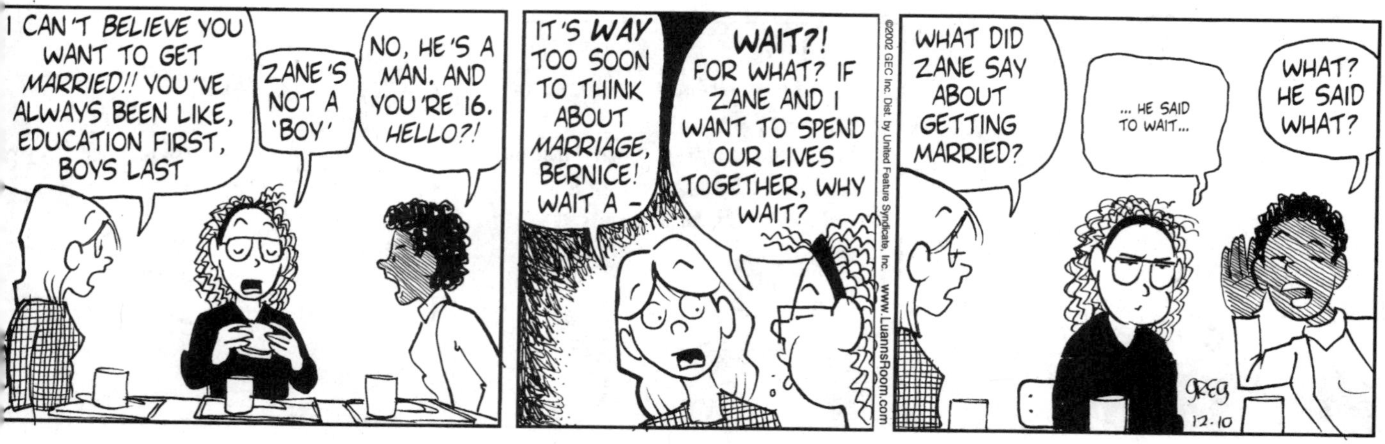
I CAN'T BELIEVE YOU WANT TO GET MARRIED!! YOU'VE ALWAYS BEEN LIKE, EDUCATION FIRST, BOYS LAST
ZANE'S NOT A 'BOY'
NO, HE'S A MAN. AND YOU'RE 16. HELLO?!
IT'S WAY TOO SOON TO THINK ABOUT MARRIAGE, BERNICE! WAIT A –
WAIT?! FOR WHAT? IF ZANE AND I WANT TO SPEND OUR LIVES TOGETHER, WHY WAIT?
©2002 GEC Inc. Dist. by United Feature Syndicate, Inc. www.LuannsRoom.com
WHAT DID ZANE SAY ABOUT GETTING MARRIED?
... HE SAID TO WAIT...
WHAT? HE SAID WHAT?
GREG 12-10

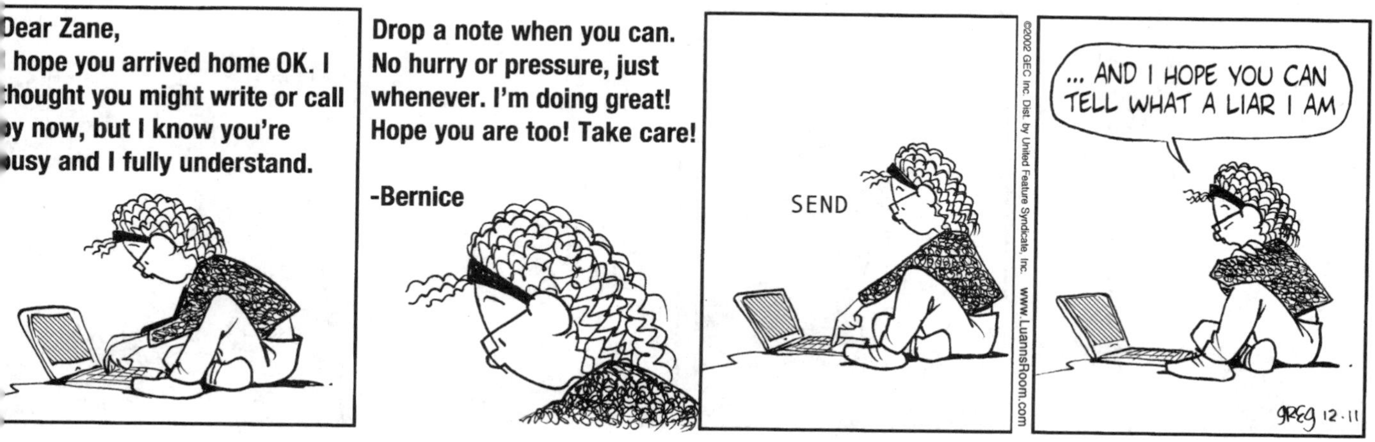
Dear Zane,
I hope you arrived home OK. I thought you might write or call by now, but I know you're busy and I fully understand.
Drop a note when you can. No hurry or pressure, just whenever. I'm doing great! Hope you are too! Take care!
-Bernice
SEND
©2002 GEC Inc. Dist. by United Feature Syndicate, Inc. www.LuannsRoom.com
... AND I HOPE YOU CAN TELL WHAT A LIAR I AM
GREG 12-11

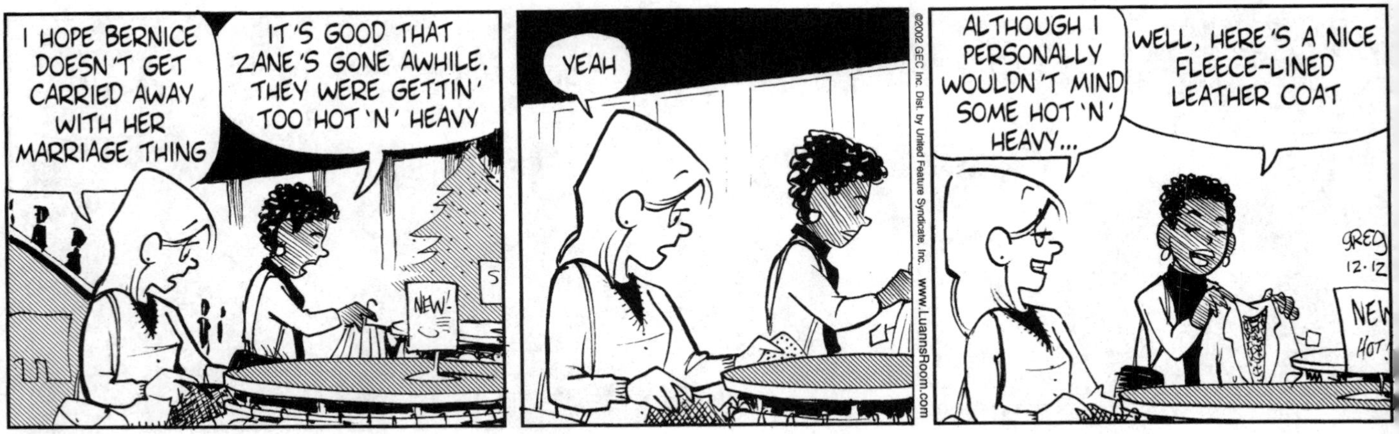
I HOPE BERNICE DOESN'T GET CARRIED AWAY WITH HER MARRIAGE THING
IT'S GOOD THAT ZANE'S GONE AWHILE. THEY WERE GETTIN' TOO HOT 'N' HEAVY
NEW!
YEAH
©2002 GEC Inc. Dist. by United Feature Syndicate, Inc. www.LuannsRoom.com
ALTHOUGH I PERSONALLY WOULDN'T MIND SOME HOT 'N' HEAVY...
WELL, HERE'S A NICE FLEECE-LINED LEATHER COAT
GREG 12·12

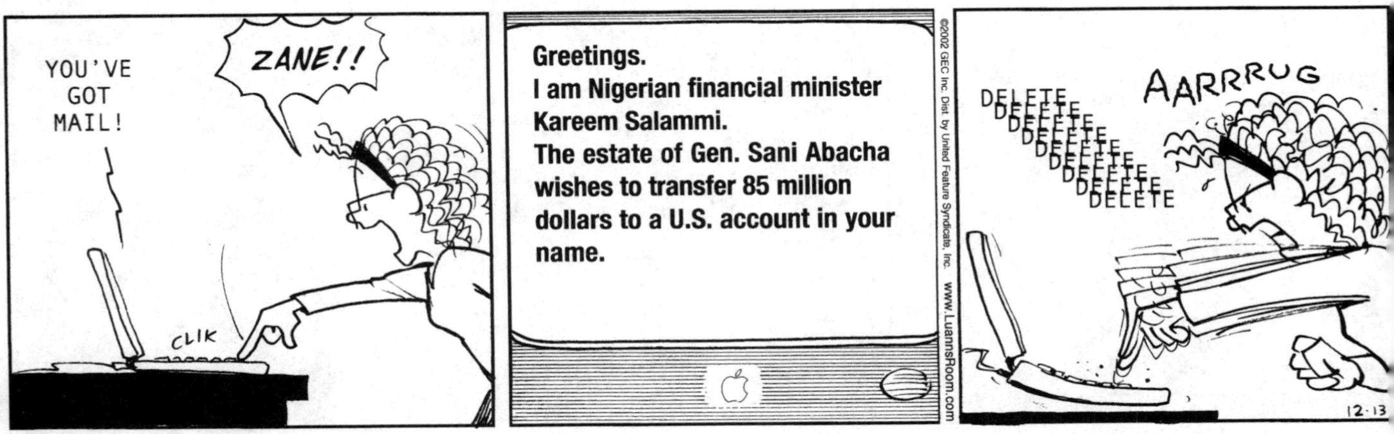
YOU'VE GOT MAIL!
ZANE!!
CLIK
Greetings.
I am Nigerian financial minister Kareem Salammi.
The estate of Gen. Sani Abacha wishes to transfer 85 million dollars to a U.S. account in your name.
©2002 GEC Inc. Dist. by United Feature Syndicate, Inc. www.LuannsRoom.com
AARRRUG
DELETE DELETE DELETE DELETE DELETE DELETE DELETE DELETE DELETE
12·13

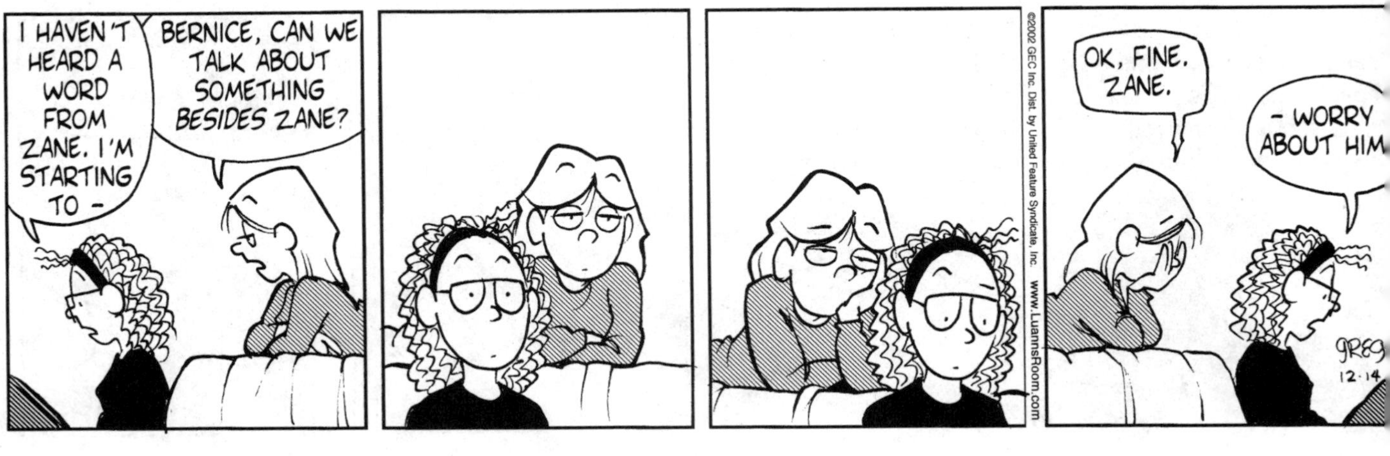
I HAVEN'T HEARD A WORD FROM ZANE. I'M STARTING TO -
BERNICE, CAN WE TALK ABOUT SOMETHING BESIDES ZANE?
©2002 GEC Inc. Dist. by United Feature Syndicate, Inc. www.LuannsRoom.com
OK, FINE. ZANE.
- WORRY ABOUT HIM
GREG 12·14

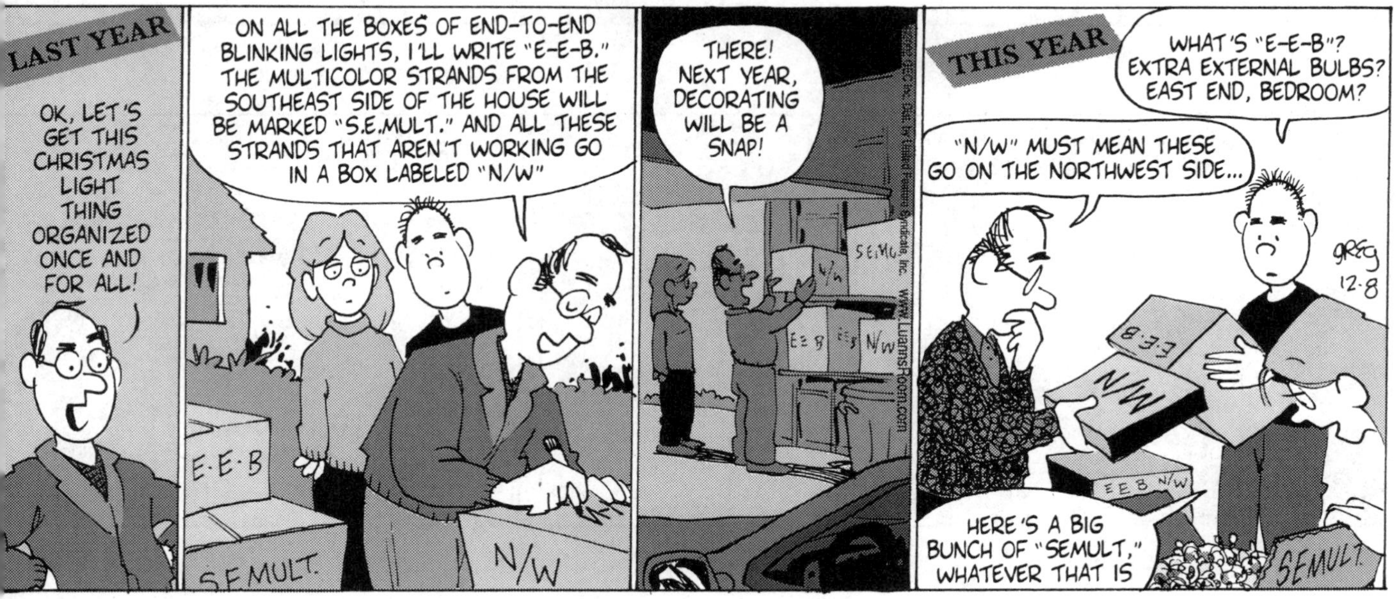
LAST YEAR
OK, LET'S GET THIS CHRISTMAS LIGHT THING ORGANIZED ONCE AND FOR ALL!
E·E·B
S.E.MULT.
ON ALL THE BOXES OF END-TO-END BLINKING LIGHTS, I'LL WRITE "E-E-B." THE MULTICOLOR STRANDS FROM THE SOUTHEAST SIDE OF THE HOUSE WILL BE MARKED "S.E.MULT." AND ALL THESE STRANDS THAT AREN'T WORKING GO IN A BOX LABELED "N/W"
N/W
THERE! NEXT YEAR, DECORATING WILL BE A SNAP!
THIS YEAR
WHAT'S "E-E-B"? EXTRA EXTERNAL BULBS? EAST END, BEDROOM?
"N/W" MUST MEAN THESE GO ON THE NORTHWEST SIDE...
HERE'S A BIG BUNCH OF "SEMULT," WHATEVER THAT IS
SEMULT.
GREG 12·8

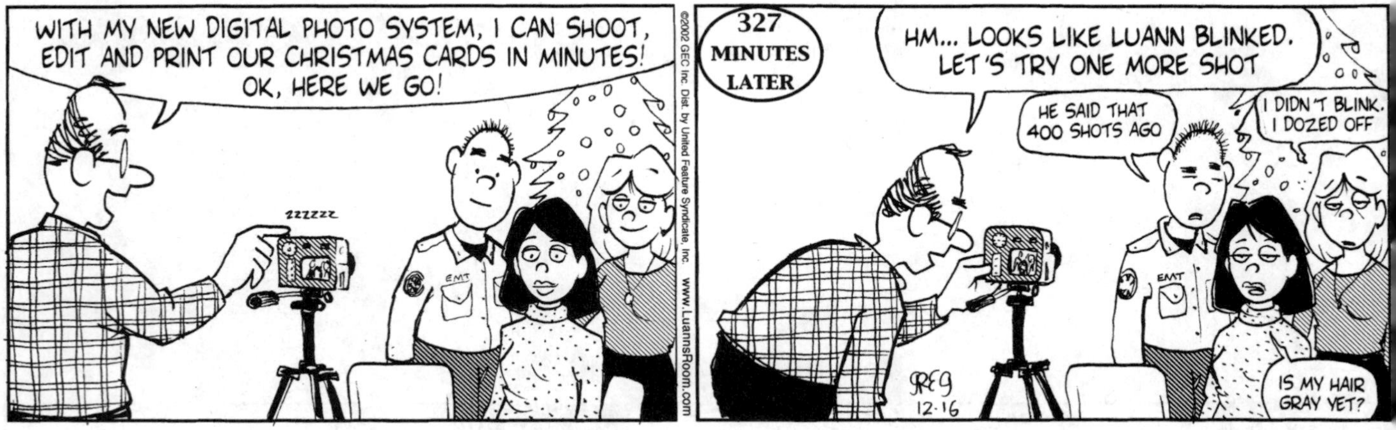
WITH MY NEW DIGITAL PHOTO SYSTEM, I CAN SHOOT, EDIT AND PRINT OUR CHRISTMAS CARDS IN MINUTES! OK, HERE WE GO!
ZZZZZZ
©2002 GEC Inc. Dist. by United Feature Syndicate, Inc. www.LuannsRoom.com
327 MINUTES LATER
HM... LOOKS LIKE LUANN BLINKED. LET'S TRY ONE MORE SHOT
HE SAID THAT 400 SHOTS AGO
I DIDN'T BLINK. I DOZED OFF
IS MY HAIR GRAY YET?
GREG 12·16

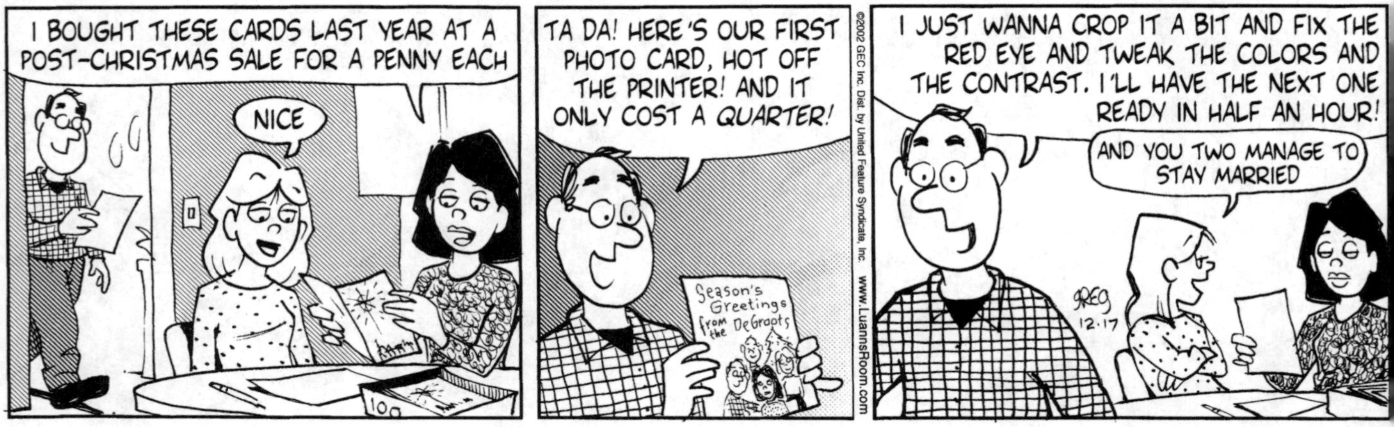
I BOUGHT THESE CARDS LAST YEAR AT A POST-CHRISTMAS SALE FOR A PENNY EACH
NICE
TA DA! HERE'S OUR FIRST PHOTO CARD, HOT OFF THE PRINTER! AND IT ONLY COST A QUARTER!
Season's Greetings from the DeGroots
©2002 GEC Inc. Dist. by United Feature Syndicate, Inc. www.LuannsRoom.com
I JUST WANNA CROP IT A BIT AND FIX THE RED EYE AND TWEAK THE COLORS AND THE CONTRAST. I'LL HAVE THE NEXT ONE READY IN HALF AN HOUR!
AND YOU TWO MANAGE TO STAY MARRIED
GREG 12·17

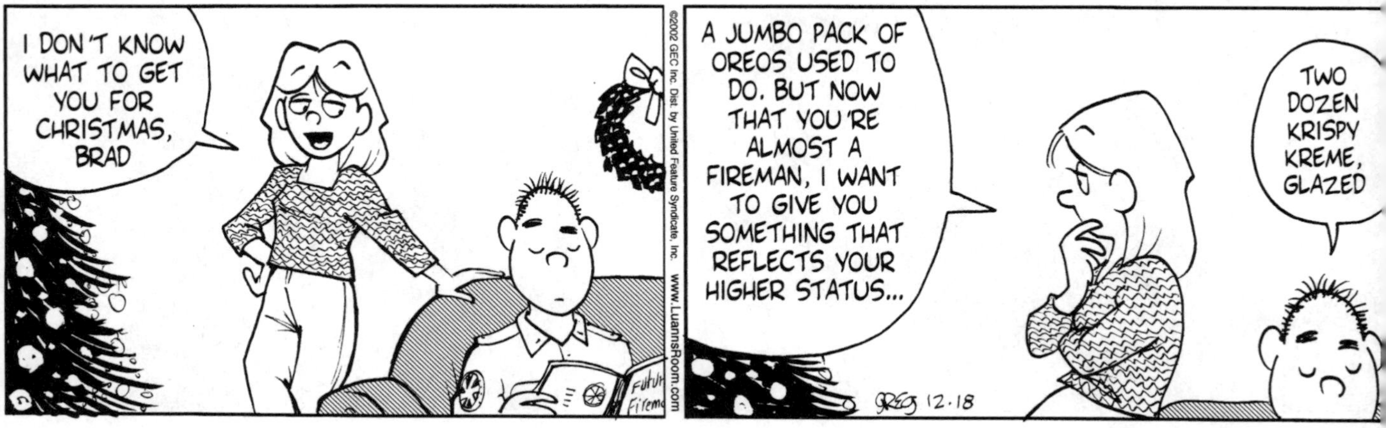
I DON'T KNOW WHAT TO GET YOU FOR CHRISTMAS, BRAD
©2002 GEC Inc. Dist. by United Feature Syndicate, Inc. www.LuannsRoom.com
A JUMBO PACK OF OREOS USED TO DO. BUT NOW THAT YOU'RE ALMOST A FIREMAN, I WANT TO GIVE YOU SOMETHING THAT REFLECTS YOUR HIGHER STATUS...
TWO DOZEN KRISPY KREME, GLAZED
GREG 12·18

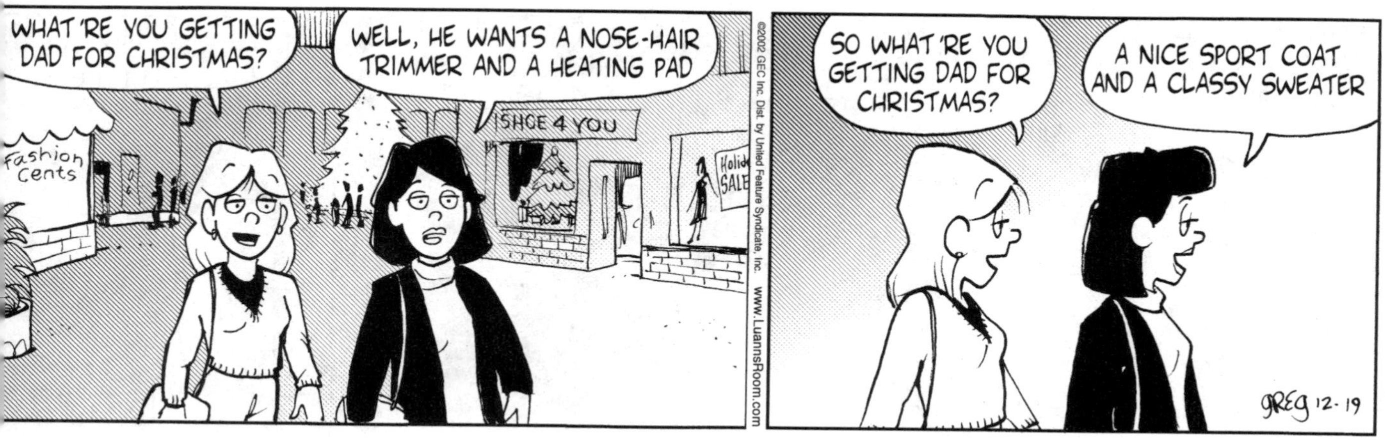
WHAT'RE YOU GETTING DAD FOR CHRISTMAS?
WELL, HE WANTS A NOSE-HAIR TRIMMER AND A HEATING PAD
Fashion Cents
SHOE 4 YOU
©2002 GEC Inc. Dist. by United Feature Syndicate, Inc. www.LuannsRoom.com
SO WHAT'RE YOU GETTING DAD FOR CHRISTMAS?
A NICE SPORT COAT AND A CLASSY SWEATER
GREG 12-19

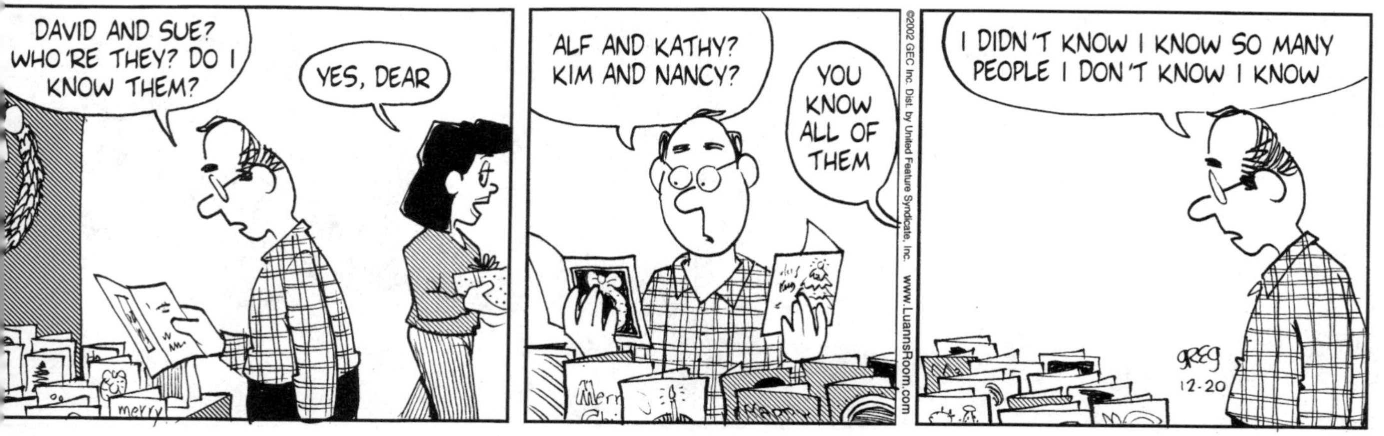
DAVID AND SUE? WHO'RE THEY? DO I KNOW THEM?
YES, DEAR
ALF AND KATHY? KIM AND NANCY?
YOU KNOW ALL OF THEM
©2002 GEC Inc. Dist. by United Feature Syndicate, Inc. www.LuannsRoom.com
I DIDN'T KNOW I KNOW SO MANY PEOPLE I DON'T KNOW I KNOW
GREG 12-20

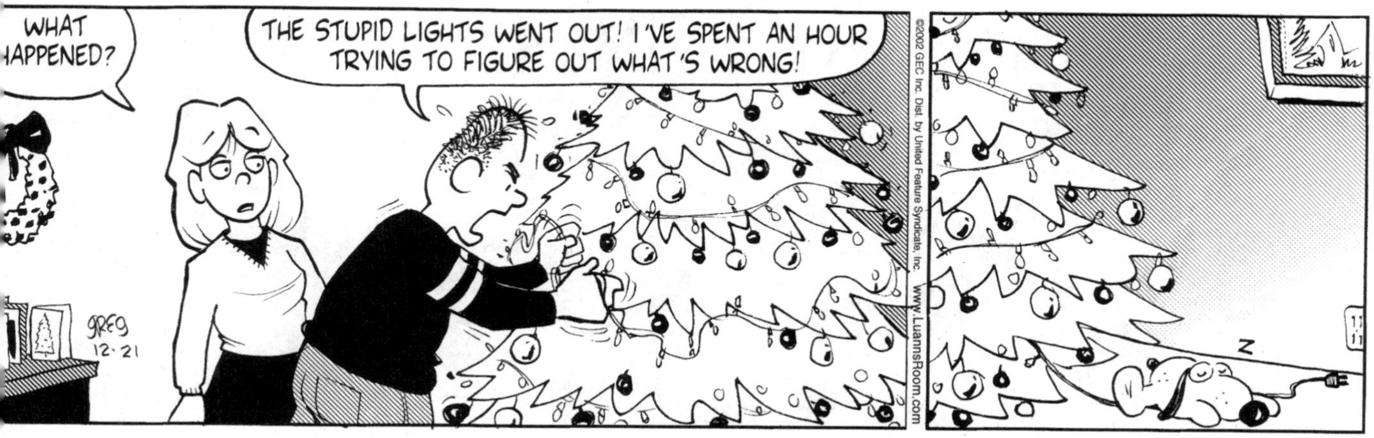
WHAT HAPPENED?
THE STUPID LIGHTS WENT OUT! I'VE SPENT AN HOUR TRYING TO FIGURE OUT WHAT'S WRONG!
GREG 12-21
©2002 GEC Inc. Dist. by United Feature Syndicate, Inc. www.LuannsRoom.com
Z

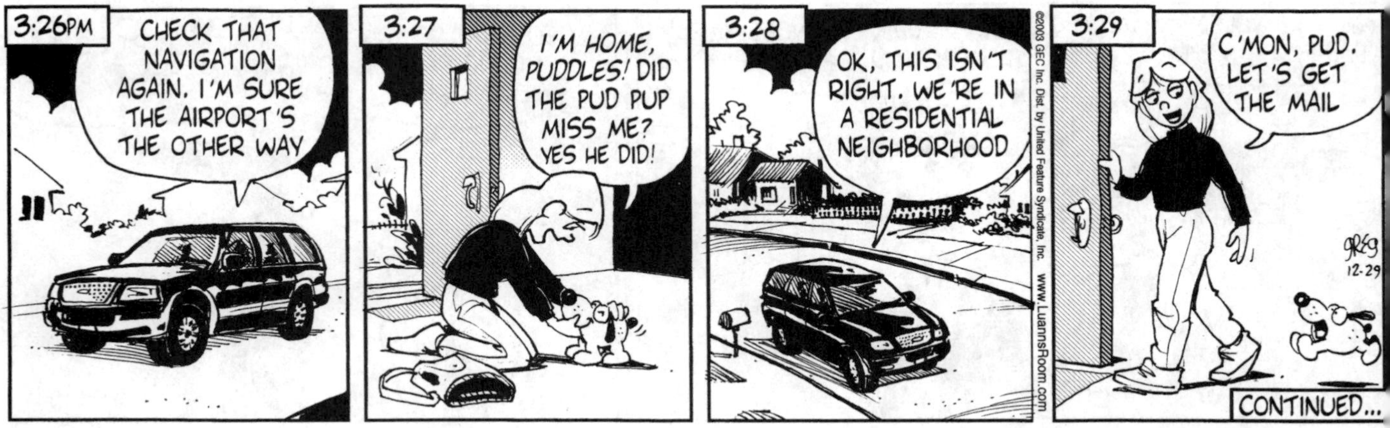
3:26PM
CHECK THAT NAVIGATION AGAIN. I'M SURE THE AIRPORT'S THE OTHER WAY
3:27
I'M HOME, PUDDLES! DID THE PUD PUP MISS ME? YES HE DID!
3:28
OK, THIS ISN'T RIGHT. WE'RE IN A RESIDENTIAL NEIGHBORHOOD
©2003 GEC Inc. Dist. by United Feature Syndicate, Inc. www.LuannsRoom.com
3:29
C'MON, PUD. LET'S GET THE MAIL
GREG 12-29
CONTINUED...

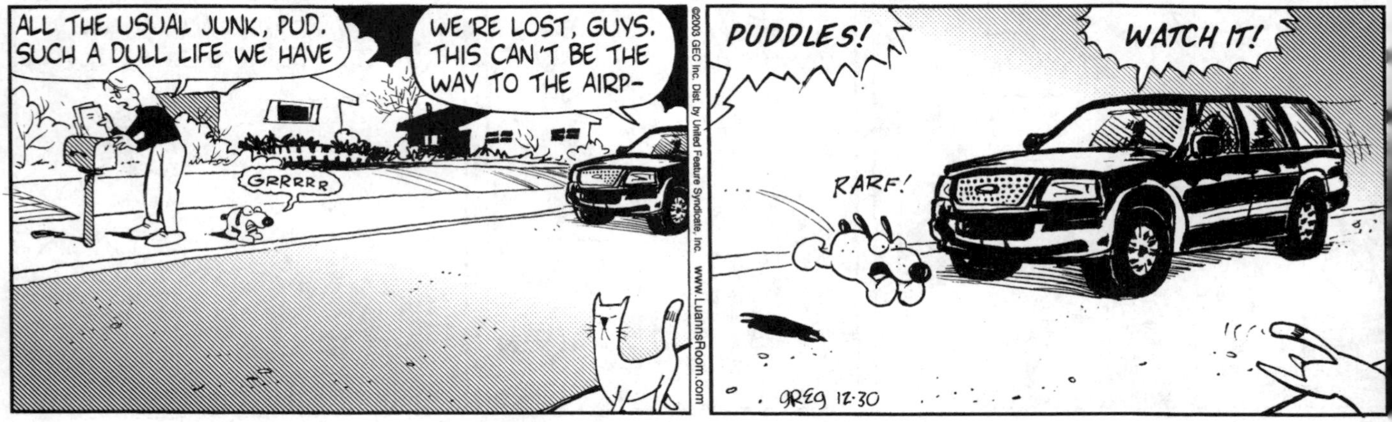
ALL THE USUAL JUNK, PUD. SUCH A DULL LIFE WE HAVE
GRRRRR
WE'RE LOST, GUYS. THIS CAN'T BE THE WAY TO THE AIRP-
©2003 GEC Inc. Dist. by United Feature Syndicate, Inc. www.LuannsRoom.com
PUDDLES!
WATCH IT!
RARF!
GREG 12-30

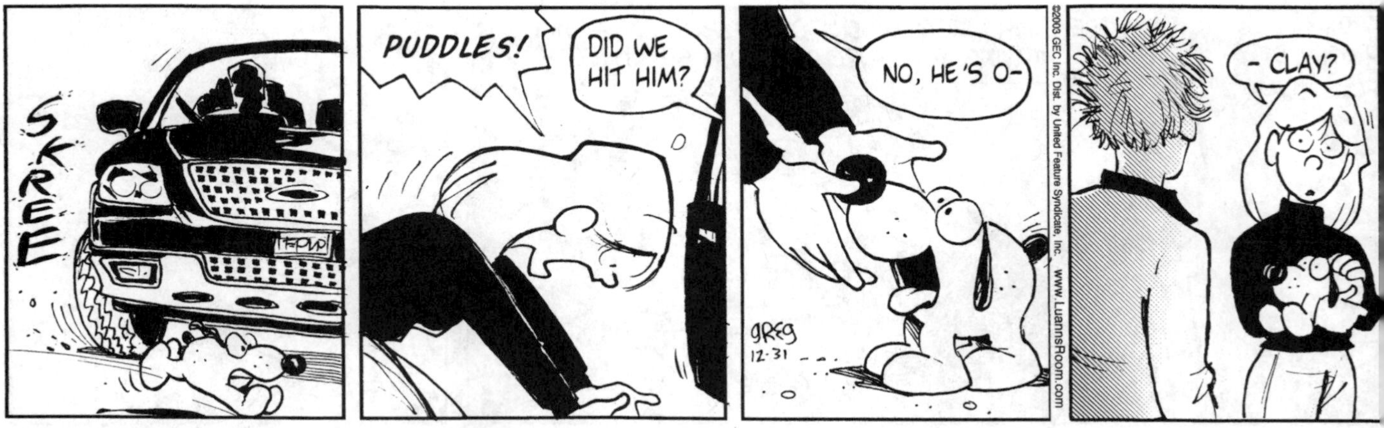
SKREE
PUDDLES!
DID WE HIT HIM?
NO, HE'S O-
GREG 12-31
©2003 GEC Inc. Dist. by United Feature Syndicate, Inc. www.LuannsRoom.com
- CLAY?

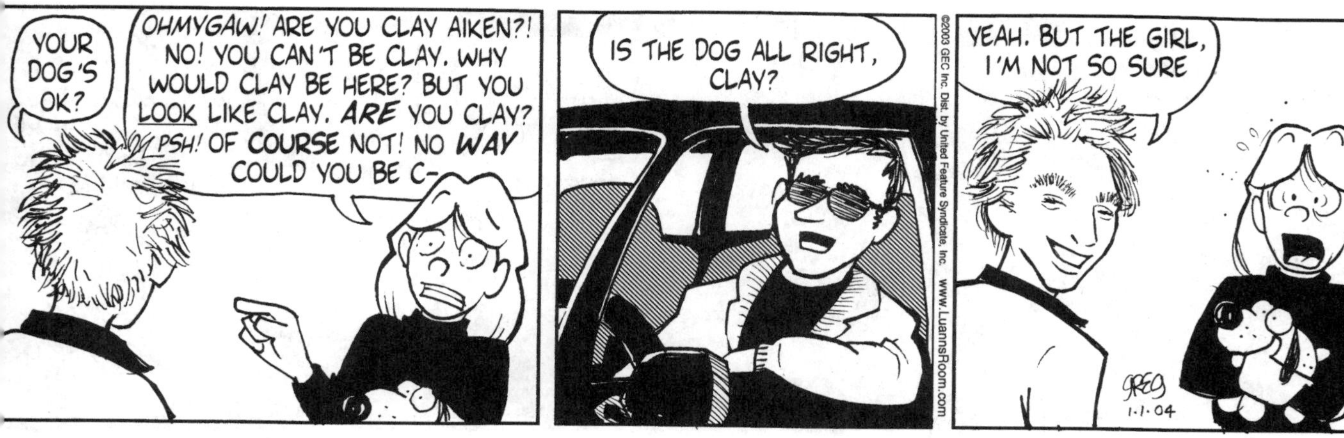
YOUR DOG'S OK?
OHMYGAW! ARE YOU CLAY AIKEN?! NO! YOU CAN'T BE CLAY. WHY WOULD CLAY BE HERE? BUT YOU LOOK LIKE CLAY. ARE YOU CLAY? PSH! OF COURSE NOT! NO WAY COULD YOU BE C–
IS THE DOG ALL RIGHT, CLAY?
©2003 GEC Inc. Dist. by United Feature Syndicate, Inc. www.LuannsRoom.com
YEAH. BUT THE GIRL, I'M NOT SO SURE
GREG 1·1·04

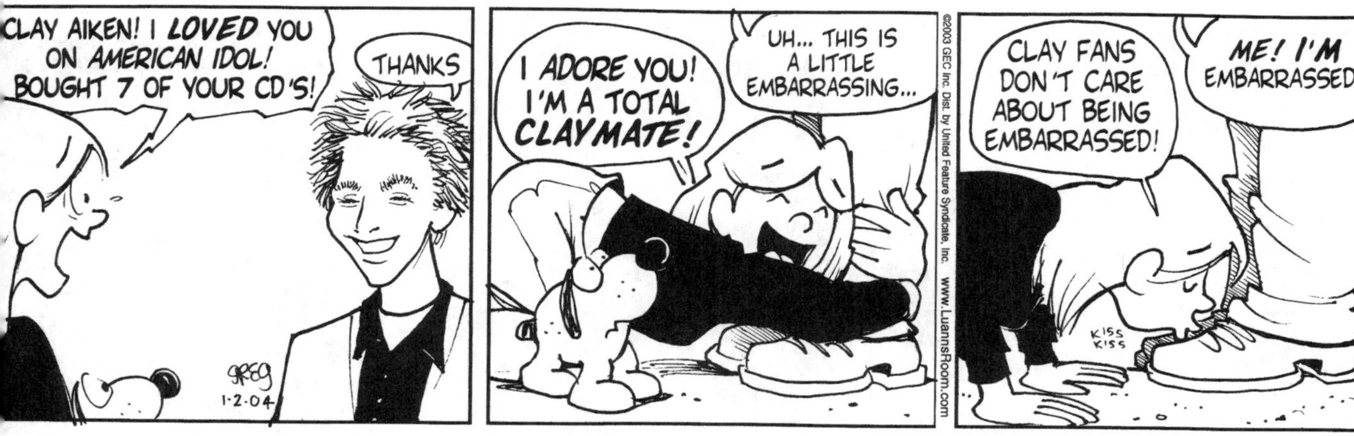
CLAY AIKEN! I LOVED YOU ON AMERICAN IDOL! BOUGHT 7 OF YOUR CD'S!
THANKS
GREG 1·2·04
I ADORE YOU! I'M A TOTAL CLAYMATE!
UH... THIS IS A LITTLE EMBARRASSING...
©2003 GEC Inc. Dist. by United Feature Syndicate, Inc. www.LuannsRoom.com
CLAY FANS DON'T CARE ABOUT BEING EMBARRASSED!
ME! I'M EMBARRASSED!
KISS KISS

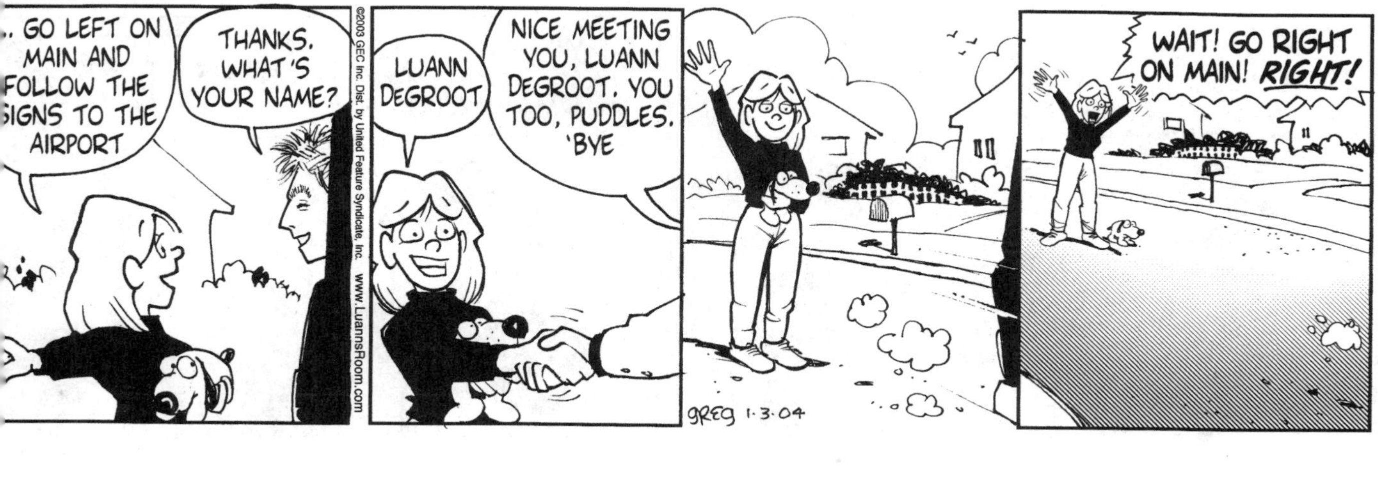
. GO LEFT ON MAIN AND FOLLOW THE SIGNS TO THE AIRPORT
THANKS. WHAT'S YOUR NAME?
©2003 GEC Inc. Dist. by United Feature Syndicate, Inc. www.LuannsRoom.com
LUANN DEGROOT
NICE MEETING YOU, LUANN DEGROOT. YOU TOO, PUDDLES. 'BYE
GREG 1·3·04
WAIT! GO RIGHT ON MAIN! RIGHT!

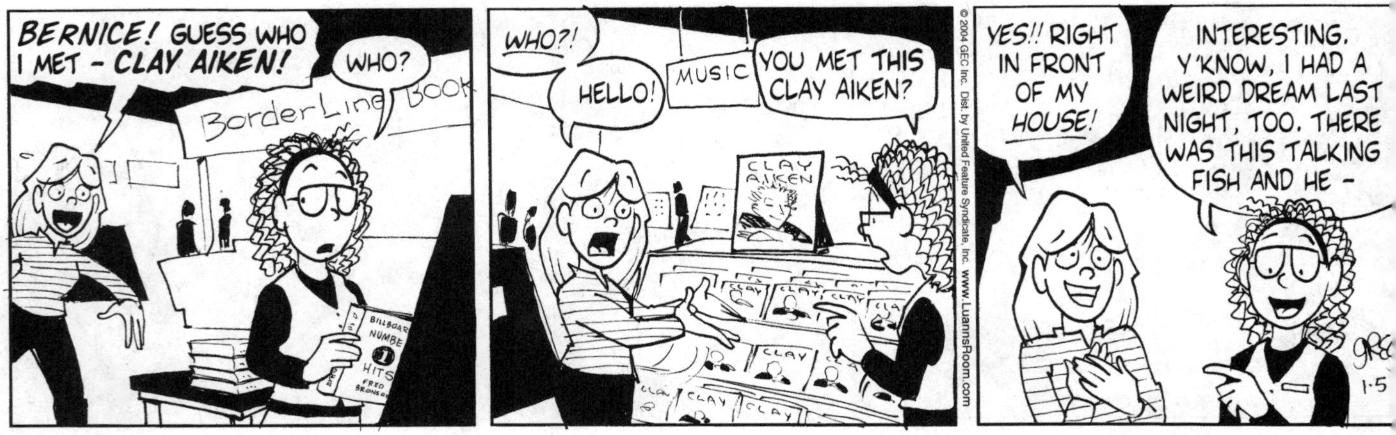
BERNICE! GUESS WHO I MET – CLAY AIKEN!
WHO?
WHO?!
HELLO!
MUSIC
YOU MET THIS CLAY AIKEN?
CLAY AIKEN
© 2004 GEC Inc. Dist. by United Feature Syndicate, Inc. www.LuannsRoom.com
YES!! RIGHT IN FRONT OF MY HOUSE!
INTERESTING. Y'KNOW, I HAD A WEIRD DREAM LAST NIGHT, TOO. THERE WAS THIS TALKING FISH AND HE –
GREG
1·5

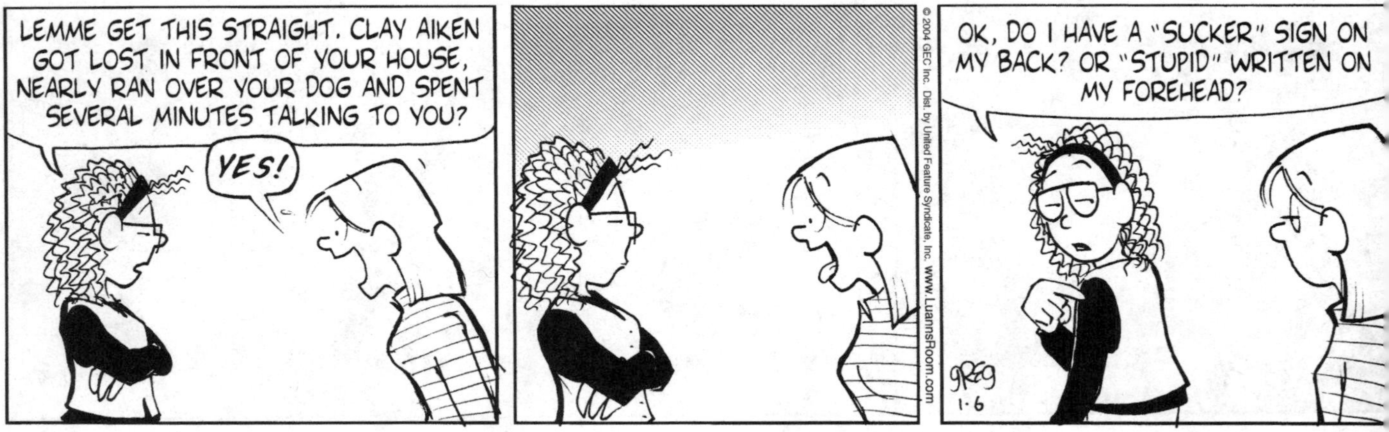
LEMME GET THIS STRAIGHT. CLAY AIKEN GOT LOST IN FRONT OF YOUR HOUSE, NEARLY RAN OVER YOUR DOG AND SPENT SEVERAL MINUTES TALKING TO YOU?
YES!
© 2004 GEC Inc. Dist. by United Feature Syndicate, Inc. www.LuannsRoom.com
GREG
1·6
OK, DO I HAVE A "SUCKER" SIGN ON MY BACK? OR "STUPID" WRITTEN ON MY FOREHEAD?

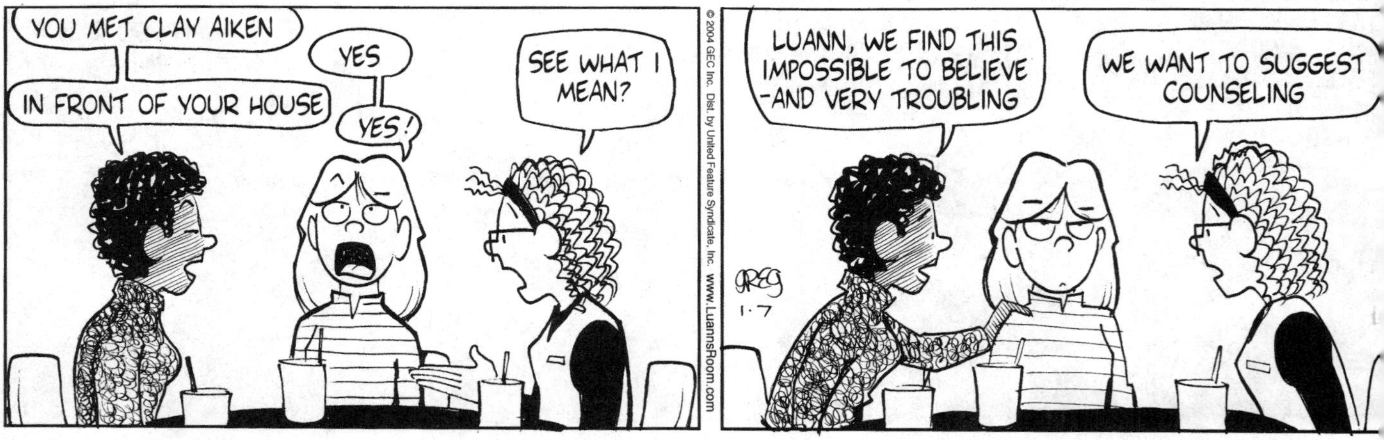
YOU MET CLAY AIKEN
YES
IN FRONT OF YOUR HOUSE
YES!
SEE WHAT I MEAN?
© 2004 GEC Inc. Dist. by United Feature Syndicate, Inc. www.LuannsRoom.com
GREG
1·7
LUANN, WE FIND THIS IMPOSSIBLE TO BELIEVE –AND VERY TROUBLING
WE WANT TO SUGGEST COUNSELING

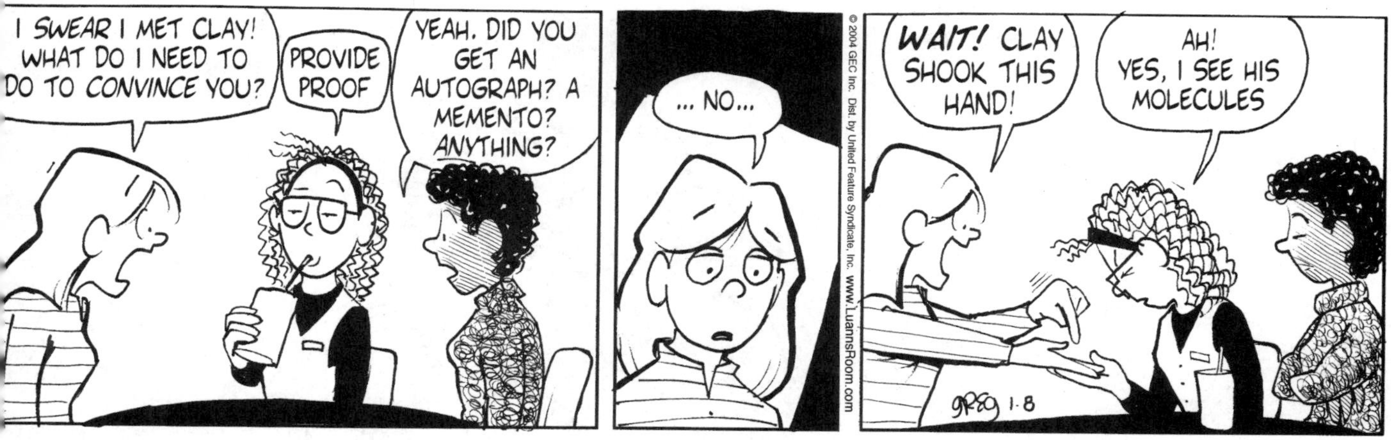
I SWEAR I MET CLAY! WHAT DO I NEED TO DO TO CONVINCE YOU?
PROVIDE PROOF
YEAH. DID YOU GET AN AUTOGRAPH? A MEMENTO? ANYTHING?
... NO...
© 2004 GEC Inc. Dist. by United Feature Syndicate, Inc. www.LuannsRoom.com
WAIT! CLAY SHOOK THIS HAND!
AH! YES, I SEE HIS MOLECULES
GREG 1.8

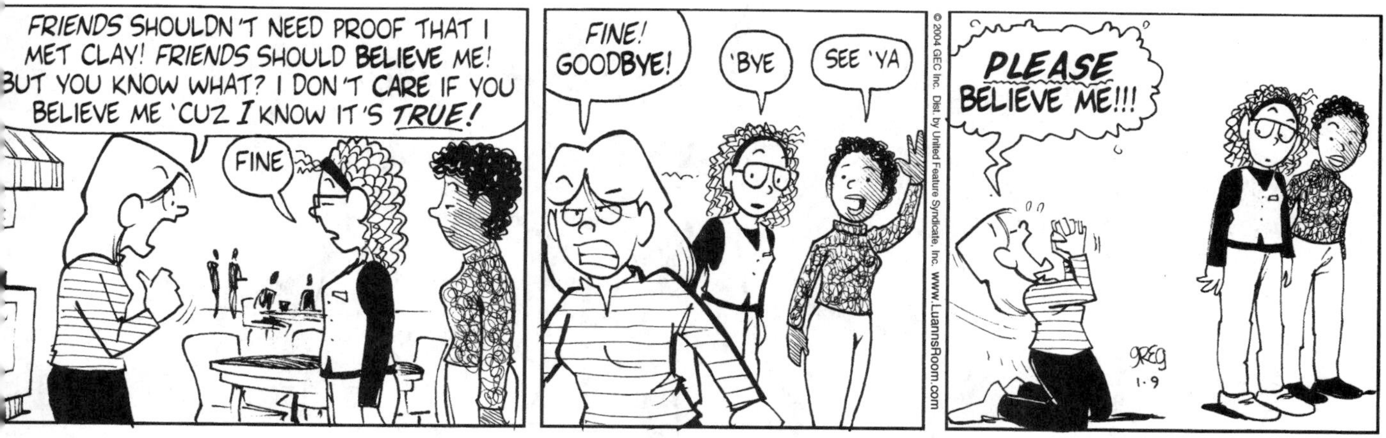
FRIENDS SHOULDN'T NEED PROOF THAT I MET CLAY! FRIENDS SHOULD BELIEVE ME! BUT YOU KNOW WHAT? I DON'T CARE IF YOU BELIEVE ME 'CUZ I KNOW IT'S TRUE!
FINE
FINE! GOODBYE!
'BYE
SEE 'YA
© 2004 GEC Inc. Dist. by United Feature Syndicate, Inc. www.LuannsRoom.com
PLEASE BELIEVE ME!!!
GREG 1.9

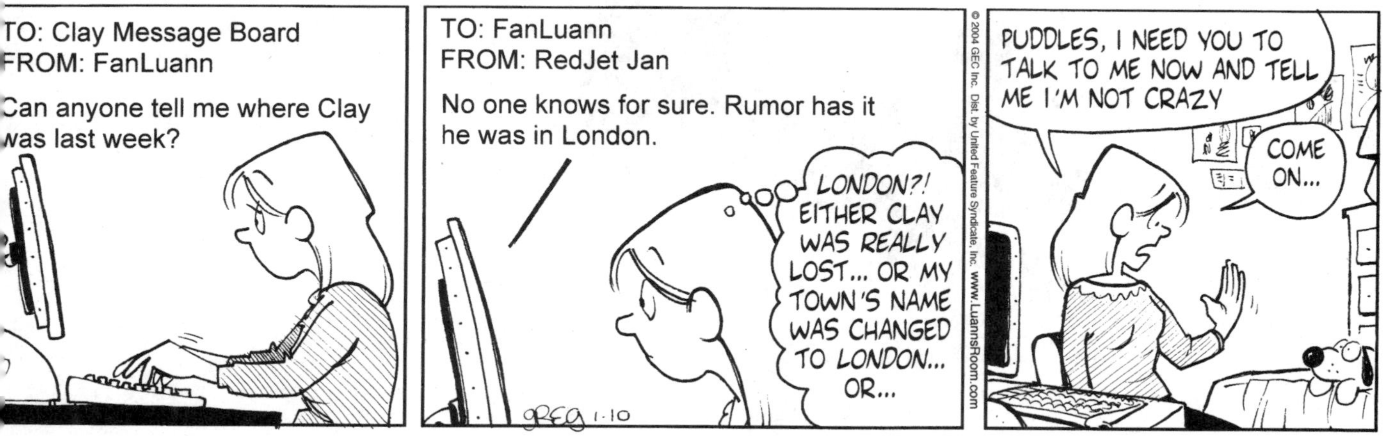
TO: Clay Message Board
FROM: FanLuann
Can anyone tell me where Clay was last week?
TO: FanLuann
FROM: RedJet Jan
No one knows for sure. Rumor has it he was in London.
LONDON?! EITHER CLAY WAS REALLY LOST... OR MY TOWN'S NAME WAS CHANGED TO LONDON... OR...
GREG 1.10
© 2004 GEC Inc. Dist. by United Feature Syndicate, Inc. www.LuannsRoom.com
PUDDLES, I NEED YOU TO TALK TO ME NOW AND TELL ME I'M NOT CRAZY
COME ON...